Volume 19 / Issue 2 / SEPTEMBER 2022

THEORY AND MODERN CHINESE LITERATURE

The Worlds of Southeast Asian Chinese Literature
CHEOW THIA CHAN and CARLOS ROJAS,
Special issue editors

Acknowledgments

To curate content for the special issue, two workshops, under the title "Between Mobility and Place-Making: The Worlds of Southeast Asia in Modern Chinese Literature" 在流動與地方創生之間：現代華文與華人文學裏的東南亞世界, were co-organized in the first quarter of 2021 by the Faculty of Arts and Social Sciences Research Division, National University of Singapore (NUS) and the Department of Asian and Middle Eastern Studies, Duke University. We extend our appreciation and gratitude to all participants and contributors, as well as the following institutions for their sponsorship of the fruitful and dynamic conversations: the Lee Kong Chian NUS-Stanford Distinguished Fellowship on Southeast Asia, Duke University's Department of Asian and Middle Eastern Studies, and the Chiang Ching-kuo Foundation Inter-University Center for Sinological Studies. The NUS-Stanford Fellowship offered further assistance that made the translation of the two Chinese language articles possible.

CARLOS ROJAS

Introduction
Worlds Built of Sand

ABSTRACT Opening with a discussion of Singaporean artist Charles Lim Yi Yong's multiyear art project SEASTATE (2005–), this introduction uses Singapore's recent land reclamation efforts to reflect on more general processes of world building in Sinophone Southeast Asia. More specifically, the essay considers how multiple waves of migration from China to Southeast Asia have resulted in a wide array of Chinese communities throughout the region, and how modern literature may be used as a prism through which to examine some of the sociocultural formations that have been generated by these waves of migration from China throughout Southeast Asia. The essay considers how literature reflects the region's diverse array of Sinitic communities, or "worlds," and how literary production may be viewed as a process of world making in its own right. Although this special issue covers considerable territory (both literally and metaphorically), our objective is not to offer a comprehensive survey of all modern literary production from the entire region. Instead, we seek to showcase a set of novel approaches that may be used to examine the region's eclectic body of literary production, including approaches grounded in concepts of mesology, postloyalism, inter-imperiality, oceanic epistemologies, off-center articulations, and the condition of being "semi-wild."

KEYWORDS Charles Lim Yi Yong, world building, land reclamation, Southeast Asia, Chinese literature

This special issue on the worlds of Southeast Asian Chinese literature examines processes of world making found in Chinese literature from throughout Southeast Asia or the "South Seas" (Nanyang 南洋) region. This introduction begins, however, by looking at how Singapore, Southeast Asia's smallest and most ethnically Chinese nation-state, has been actively pursuing a miniature process of world making as it transforms its own territory in a way that has wide-ranging implications, not only for the city-state itself but also for many of its neighbors.

With a total area of under 750 square kilometers, Singapore is one of the world's smallest sovereign states.[1] At the same time, however, with a population of nearly six million and a per capita GDP (adjusted for purchasing power parity) of nearly US$100,000, it also has the second-highest population density and the third-highest per capita GDP of any sovereign state[2]—meaning that it has both the means and the motivation to pursue expensive land-reclamation projects to expand its existing territory. In fact, since gaining independence from the United

PRISM: THEORY AND MODERN CHINESE LITERATURE • 19:2 • SEPTEMBER 2022
DOI 10.1215/25783491-9966637 • © 2022 LINGNAN UNIVERSITY

Kingdom in 1963, Singapore has used land reclamation to expand its territory by approximately 25 percent. Given that sand is a crucial resource for land reclamation processes, it is not surprising that a 2014 United Nations Environment Programme (UNEP) report found that "having imported a reported 517 million tonnes of sand over the last 20 years, Singapore is by far the largest importer of sand worldwide."[3]

In fact, for 2014, the year the UNEP issued the report cited above, the Observatory of Economic Complexity (OEC) calculated that Singapore was responsible for 10.5 percent of the world's $2.1 billion in total sand imports, making the tiny nation the largest single sand importer that year.[4] The official import figures cited by the OEC, moreover, are just the tip of the iceberg, given that Singapore's official sand imports are dwarfed by the nation's reliance on a vast black market in sand trade. This is because, responding to concerns about the environmental impact of sand mining, all four of Singapore's primary sources of sand have passed regulations limiting or banning sand exports in recent years. For instance, in 1997 Malaysia officially banned sand exports to Singapore (though this appears to have had minimal impact on actual exports), and although it officially lifted the ban in 2017, it promptly imposed a more specific ban on sea sand exports to Singapore the following year. Similarly, in 2003, Indonesia prohibited all sea sand exports, and in 2007 it expanded the ban to include all sand exports. Cambodia similarly barred all sand exports in 2017, the same year Vietnam blocked the export of white silica sand (though it lifted this ban three years later). Despite these official bans, however, sand exports to Singapore have continued mostly unabated, with a significant portion of the nation's sand imports being conducted over the black market.[5]

Singapore's territorial expansion over the past half century is particularly notable given that the nation is also at risk of losing territory due to rising sea levels. With an average elevation of only fifteen meters, Singapore is one of the lowest-lying countries in the world,[6] meaning that significant portions of its territory are vulnerable to flooding and inundation as a result of global warming.[7] Moreover, the nation's delicate dance between territorial loss and expansion is mirrored by the contrast between its growing coastline, on one hand, and the environmental devastation that sand excavation has been wreaking on the riverways and coastlines of its neighbors, on the other. A particularly dramatic illustration of this contrast between Singapore's territorial expansion and the environmental devastation it is causing can be seen in a set of 2010 reports stating that Singapore's voracious appetite for sand for land reclamation projects had contributed to the disappearance of at least twenty-four Indonesian islands off the coast of Aceh, North Sumatra, Papua, and Riau since 2005.[8]

Coincidentally, it was also in 2005—which is to say, the beginning of the five-year period cited in the reports on the disappearing Indonesia islands—that Singaporean artist Charles Lim Yi Yong 林育荣 launched an ambitious multiyear art project titled SEASTATE.[9] Already a champion sailor before he began working as a professional artist (he won silver and bronze medals in the men's 470 event at the 1994 and 1998 Asian Games, and he represented Singapore at the 1996 Olympics), Lim describes SEASTATE as an attempt to use the sea as a prism through which to reexamine the nation of Singapore itself:

> [SEASTATE] initiates a dialogue on Singapore's relationship with the sea. It also meditates upon land reclamation as a constant and ongoing activity in Singapore. Singapore continues to grow through this process. It could be said, SEASTATE opens up newer ways of engaging with water and its other—land; from mutating landscapes and islands that have been consumed and generated in this constant need making more space to the imaginary boundaries of a future landmass. SEASTATE negotiates the concerns of Singapore through situating the debates surrounding land reclamation, resource use, and territorial sovereignty in global, transnational terms.[10]

As an archipelago consisting of one major island and over sixty islets, Singapore spans both land and sea. Although the nation is generally viewed as a landmass surrounded by water, Lim's SEASTATE project instead takes as its starting point the sea itself. As art critic Pauline Yao observes, SEASTATE is a "multichaptered, manifold constellation of videos, photographs, found objects, audio recordings, nautical maps, and digital prints [that] casts the sea as the lead character in the unfolding drama of Singapore's maritime existence."[11] At the same time, however, as cultural studies scholar Elizabeth Wijaya observes, a crucial theme that runs through the project is its focus on "the slow violence wrought by the state on the land/sea/people triad due to its justification for expansion beyond the limits of the earth's surface."[12]

Each work in SEASTATE has the same main title, followed by a single numeral and one or more subtitles. The numerals refer not to the order in which the works were produced but rather to the World Meteorological Organization's code for the surface conditions of a large body of water, which ranges from a low of 0, designating "calm (glassy)" conditions, to a high of 9, designating "phenomenal" conditions. In some cases, the numeral in the title roughly matches the conditions of the sea as visible in the work itself, such as in the project's inaugural work, *SEASTATE 1: inside/outside* (2005), which features a collection of paired photographs of marker buoys floating in calm ocean waters near Singapore's nautical port limits (fig. 1). Each buoy was photographed both inside and outside the invisible maritime boundary, thereby revealing, as Pauline Yao notes, not only "the arbitrary nature of nautical boundaries but their sheer porosity," as well as "the ways in which such borders are always representations—appearing as lines on maps, as fences in the ground, and now, as buoys floating in the water."[13] The

FIGURE 1. Charles Lim Yi Yong, *SEASTATE 1: inside/outside*, 2005. Image courtesy of Charles Lim Yi Yong.

sea's apparent calmness in these images, accordingly, belies the dynamic interaction between artificial maritime borders and the sea's fluid surface.

Other works in Lim's project span a variety of different media and formats, and their relationship to the sea conditions alluded to in their titles is often considerably more abstract. For instance, *SEASTATE 0: All the Lines Flow Out* (2011) is a short film exploring Singapore's drainage system, *SEASTATE 4: Line in the Chart* (2008) features a photograph of a sea wall that Lim found on Singapore's northeast border, and *SEASTATE 8: The Grid* (2014) consists of a 2014 nautical chart that has been divided into one portion featuring the original landmass and another featuring reclaimed land and the surrounding sea. *SEASTATE 6: Capsize* (2016) is a short film on Singapore's Jurong Rock Caverns, a vast underground cavern for oil and fuel storage located beneath Banyan Basin on Jurong Island; *SEASTATE 9: Proclamation (drag), (drop), (pour)* (2018) is a three-part work featuring drone video footage of three different methods used for land reclamation; and the similarly titled *SEASTATE 9: Proclamation Garden* (2019) is a "living

FIGURE 2. Charles Lim Yi Yong, *SEASTATE 9: Proclamation Garden*, 2019. Image courtesy of National Gallery Singapore.

art exhibition" installed in the roof garden of Singapore's National Gallery, featuring thirty lesser-known plant species found on Singapore's reclaimed land (fig. 2). In each work, the focus is less on the sea itself than on the unstable interface between (rising) sea and (reclaimed) land.

The term *proclamation* in the titles of the preceding two works derives from Singapore's Foreshores Act (originally passed in 1972 and revised in the 1980s), which decreed that "the President may, by proclamation published in the Gazette, declare any lands formed by the reclamation of any part of the foreshore of Singapore, or any areas of land reclaimed from the sea to be State land." This proclamation process is one of the central concerns of *SEASTATE 9: the sandpapers* (2020), which consists of a box set of thirteen books with sandpaper covers. The books contain a set of public government documents and presidential proclamations of land reclamation dating from 1965 to 2017. Similarly, this proclamation process also occupies an absent presence in two more recent works in the project: *SEASTATE 7: sand print (400,000 sqm, 2015, Tuas)* and *SEASTATE 7: negative print*, both of which debuted in 2021 (figs. 3 and 4). The former features a sand print molded in the form of an area of reclaimed land located at Tuas, an industrial site in southwestern Singapore, while the latter features the plastic mold that was used to create the sand print. The work's tacit commentary on the contingent and artificial nature of Singapore's land reclamation process is reinforced by the fact that, as art critic Vivyan Yeo observes, "this area of Tuas has not undergone proclamation by the Singapore president, [meaning that] the land is still officially part of the sea; it hence exists in a comical and absurd in-between state."[14] Just as Lim's sand print alludes to the material role that sand plays in the land

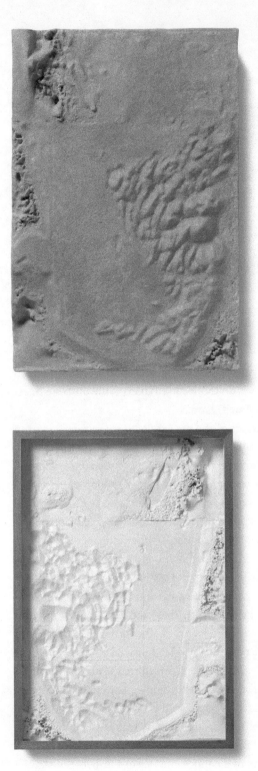

FIGURE 3. Charles Lim Yi Yong, *SEASTATE 7: sand print (400,000 sqm, 2015, Tuas)*, 2021. Sand on STPI casted paper, 88×65×11.7 cm. © Charles Lim Yi Yong/STPI. Image courtesy of Charles Lim Yi Yong and STPI.

FIGURE 4. Charles Lim Yi Yong, *SEASTATE 7: negative print*, 2021. 3D-printed PLA plastic, 93.6×66×13 cm. © Charles Lim Yi Yong/STPI. Image courtesy of Charles Lim Yi Yong and STPI.

reclamation process, the corresponding "negative print" points to the legal and political abstractions on which this process necessarily relies.

Like the dozens of islands and islets that make up Singapore itself, the works that compose SEASTATE appear in constantly shifting configurations, alternatively presented either as independent works or as parts of larger assemblages. For instance, the film *SEASTATE 0: All the Lines Flow Out* premiered in May 2011 as a stand-alone work at the 2011 Singapore Biennale and was rescreened in August at the 68th Venice Film Festival, where it received a Special Mention, making Lim the first Singaporean director to be recognized at the festival. The film was screened again in 2016 along with several of Lim's other works for a solo exhibition at the NTU Centre for Contemporary Art Singapore, which was the center's first major exhibit by a Singaporean artist. Several components of SEASTATE were also exhibited as part of the Singapore Pavilion at the Venice Biennale in 2015,[15] and although Lim remarked at the time that this marked "a sort of culmination" of the decade-long project,[16] he nevertheless has continued adding to it. Most recently, new iterations of the project debuted at a 2021–2022 exhibition titled *Staggered Observations of a Coast* at the STPI Gallery in Singapore, which featured works from the SEASTATE project alongside others from two of Lim's newer series, titled Staggered Observations and Zone of Convergence (the latter is discussed in Cheow Thia Chan's conclusion to this special issue).

Among the works that debuted at *Staggered Observations of a Coast* was a six-part series titled *SEASTATE 9: Pulau* (fig. 5). Borrowing the Malay word for "island," this series consists of representations of six artificial islands made from laser-cut handmade paper. The surface of each imaginary landmass is etched with an identical grid pattern, beneath which one finds multiple layers of irregularly shaped paper fragments, suggesting that beneath their relatively homogeneous surfaces, each artificial island contains the sedimented remains of countless individual islets that "disappeared" after being subsumed by the new landmasses.

For instance, what is now Jurong Island to the south of Singapore's mainland is an amalgamation of islets originally named Pulau Pesek Kechil, Pulau Ayer Chawan, Pulau Sakra, Pulau Ayer Merbau, Pulau Meskol, Pulau Merlimau, Pulau Seraya, Pulau Pesek, Pulau Mesemut Laut, and Pulau Mesemut Darat. Although many of these latter names still appear on contemporary maps, they no longer designate discrete islets but rather refer to geographically continuous areas within the larger Jurong Island landmass. In *SEASTATE 9: Pulau*, meanwhile, these vestigial islets are represented not only by the multiple layers of paper out of which the new imaginary landmasses are composed, but also by the concatenated names of those earlier islets that appear in the works' amusingly baroque subtitles, such as Satuasviewdamartekongmarinajurongcovebranibaratchangilautekongsajahatsenanghantupunggolsebaraokeastsamalunbukomsento,

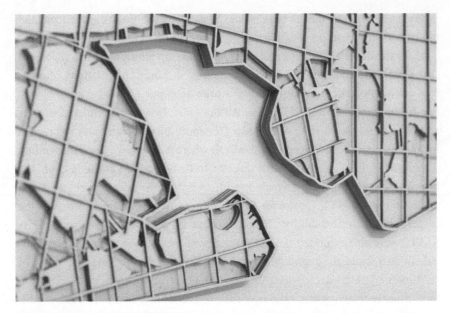

FIGURE 5. Charles Lim Yi Yong, *SEASTATE 9: Pulau Punggolsebaraokeastsamalunbukomsentosatuasviewdamartekongmarinajuron gcovebranibaratchangilautekongsajahatsenanghantu*, 2021. Laser-cut STPI handmade paper, 65.3×86.3×1.02 cm, edition of two. © Charles Lim Yi Yong/STPI. Image courtesy of Charles Lim Yi Yong and STPI.

Punggolsebaraokeastsamalunbukomsentosatuasviewdamartekongmarinaju-rongcovebranibaratchangilautekongsajahatsenanghantu, and Damartekong-marinajurongcovebranibaratchangilautekongsajahatsenanghantupunggolseba-raokeastsamalunbukomsentosatuasview. The exhibition catalog notes that "these satirically named landmasses call attention to the many islands—and thus, the cultures and histories of their people—that were taken over or altogether lost due to being repurposed for the state's use,"[17] underscoring the fact that Singapore's dialectics of land reclamation and destruction has not only geographic implica-tions but also complex sociocultural and ecological ramifications.

Although the subtitles of the works in the *SEASTATE 9: Pulau* series directly reference Singaporean islets that have disappeared because of the nation's land reclamation efforts, the fact that *pulau* means "island" not only in Malay but also in Indonesian suggests that these works may also be seen as an allusion to the nearby Indonesian islands that have been destroyed as a result of illegal sand mining. Similarly, while SEASTATE engages with specific aspects of Singapore's geography and history, the title is polysemic and overdetermined. As Pauline Yao observes, "'SEASTATE' refers to the state of the sea, the sea as (nation-) state, and, more obliquely, the state of SEA (as Southeast Asia is sometimes abbreviated)," suggesting that the project may be viewed as a commentary on issues pertaining not only to Singapore but also to the region as a whole.[18] Accordingly, the local processes of land reclamation that inform the SEASTATE 9: Pulau series and the entire SEASTATE project may also be viewed as an implicit commentary on more general processes of world making that are continually shaping the entire Southeast Asian region, including not only material transformations resulting from land reclamation, construction, and ecological degradation, but also corresponding sociopolitical, demographic, and cultural transformations.

While the focus on sand that runs throughout the SEASTATE project alludes most directly to the role that the resource plays in Singapore's land reclamation efforts, it also resonates with a powerful metaphor in twentieth-century Chinese political thought. In 1905, exactly a century before Lim inaugurated his SEASTATE project, Sun Yat-sen 孫逸仙 (aka Sun Zhongshan 孫中山) first proposed his "Three People's Principles"—nationalism, democracy, and livelihood—in a short statement for the founding of *Minbao* 民報, the journal for Sun's newly established China Alliance Society (*Tongmeng hui* 同盟會).[19] Two decades later, Sun elaborated on this notion in *Three People's Principles* 三民主義, when he famously compared the Chinese to "a sheet of loose sand" 一片散沙. Noting that Western revolutions are often regarded as quests for more freedom, Sun contends that the Chinese revolution should instead be viewed as a quest for more cohesion—as an attempt to enable the Chinese to "become pressed together into an unyielding body like the firm rock which is formed by the addition of cement to sand" 結成很堅固的團體，像把士敏土參加到散沙裡頭，結成一塊堅固石頭一樣.[20]

Building on these connotations of dispersal and agglutination, we may similarly use sand as a metaphor for the multiple waves of migration that have dispersed millions of people from China throughout Southeast Asia. Contrary to Sun's "loose sand" metaphor, however, these migrants have not remained isolated and independent; instead they have aggregated into a variety of different community formations, with some remaining relatively attached to the notion of a Chinese motherland and others becoming more integrated with local communities.

This special issue uses modern literature as a prism through which to examine some of the sociocultural formations that have been generated by these waves of migration from China throughout Southeast Asia. We consider how literature reflects the region's diverse array of Sinitic communities, or "worlds," and how literary production may be viewed as a process of world making in its own right. Although this issue covers considerable territory (both literally and metaphorically), our objective is not to offer a comprehensive survey of all modern literary production from the entire region. Instead, we seek to showcase a set of novel approaches that may be used to examine the region's eclectic body of literary production, including approaches grounded in concepts of mesology, postloyalism, interimperiality, oceanic epistemologies, off-center articulations, and the condition of being "semiwild."

Our project builds on (and shares some contributors with) the 2021 *Prism* special issue on "Chinese Literature across the Borderlands," which editor David Der-wei Wang described as an attempt "to explore the shifting definitions of the borderland as a geopolitical space, a territorial gateway, a contact zone, a liminal terrain, a 'state of exception,' and an imaginary portal."[21] However, whereas that earlier project examined literary formations from a wide array of Chinese borderlands, stretching "from the Northeast to the Southwest, from Inner Mongolia to Tibet, and from Nanyang 南洋 (Southeast Asia) to Nanmei 南美 (Latin America),"[22] ours instead focuses more specifically on Southeast Asia in order to better attend to the network of themes and concerns that run through this region's literary production. Similarly, our special issue also engages with—but is distinct from—a Sinophone approach. We share with the latter an interest in literary production originating from the margins or outside mainland Chinese sovereignty, though our approach is simultaneously narrower and broader than a conventional Sinophone one. On one hand, we focus only on literary production from Southeast Asia (while the Sinophone approach encompasses the entire global Chinese diaspora), but on the other hand, we cover works written in multiple different languages (while the Sinophone approach is generally restricted to Chinese-language texts). In this way, we attempt to probe some of the distinctive qualities of Sinophone literature from Southeast Asia, while at the same time complicating common assumptions about the structural limits of the category of the Sinophone itself.

The thirteen articles in this special issue examine a diverse array of literary formations, ranging from Chinese-language Singaporean flash fiction to English-language Philippine speculative fiction, and from 1920s poems composed in a Batavian-Hokkien creole to midcentury Chinese-language elegies memorializing the deaths of dozens of teachers and students in Penang, in what is now Malaysia. Several articles focus on works from Singapore, where ethnic Chinese make up nearly 80 percent of the population, and from neighboring Malaysia, where nearly seven million Chinese make up over a fifth of the population.[23] Two other articles examine literature from what is now Indonesia, where the total number of individuals of Chinese descent is estimated be even larger than in Malaysia,[24] while one article considers literature by Filipino writers of Chinese descent—a demographic that accounts for less than 2 percent of the nation's total population. At the same time, it is important to remember that each of these modern nations—like the artificial landmasses in *Lim's SEASTATE 9: Pulau* series—is the product of a complex process of historical sedimentation, whereby concatenated processes of migration, trade, imperialism, and local resistance have left their mark not only on each region's distinctive demographics, but also on their ideology, politics, and cultural production.

This special issue opens with four articles that don't map neatly onto South-east Asia's current national configurations, including one article that speaks to issues relevant to the entire region, and three others that straddle two or more contemporary nations. First, David Der-wei Wang's "Of Wind, Soil, and Water: On the Mesology of Sinophone/Xenophone Southeast Asian Literature" proposes that Southeast Asian Sinophone literature may be approached via a paradigm of mesology, or "the study of the mutual relationships between living creatures and their biological, social, and environmental surroundings." More specifically, Wang contends that this mesological approach can be used to probe the vari-ous "sociopolitical, cultural, and environmental entanglements" of the region's assorted Chinese-speaking communities.

Three other articles that similarly straddle contemporary national boundaries are Shuang Shen's "Popular Literature in the Inter-imperial Space of Hong Kong and Singapore/Malaya," Nicholas Y. H. Wong's "Inter-imperial, Ecological Inter-pretations of the 'Five Coolies' Myth in Penang and Medan," and Nicolai Vol-land's "Fluid Horizons: Oceanic Epistemologies and Sinophone Literature." First, Shen uses Laura Doyle's "inter-imperial" paradigm to examine midcentury pop-ular literary production from Hong Kong and parts of what was then still British Malaya. In particular, Shen proposes to use "popular literature as a wedge to pry open some foundational critical discourses that inform existing locality-focused literary histories in order to make way for a regional conceptualization of Sino-phone cultural production." Similarly taking inspiration from Doyle's inter-impe-rial paradigm, Wong examines how two early to mid-twentieth century authors who straddle the categories of Malayan Chinese and Indonesian Chinese both wrote about a "myth" relating to an 1871 incident in which five Chinese coolies on a plantation in East Sumatra were executed on charges of having murdered their Dutch foreman. Wong underscores the degree to which these two works play out against the backdrop of a cross-straits coolie trade between "the two imperial jurisdictions of Penang (Straits Settlements) and Medan (East Sumatra), now part of Malaysia and Indonesia respectively."

Finally, Volland uses the concept of what he calls oceanic epistemologies to examine contemporary works by the Indigenous author Syaman Rapongan and the Malaysian Chinese author Ng Kim Chew. As Volland notes, although Syaman Rapongan, who is a member of Taiwan's Tao ethnic group, is often classified as an Indigenous Taiwanese author, his writings are nevertheless centered around his home island of Lanyu (aka Orchid Island), which is located some forty miles southeast of the main island of Taiwan and whose population is more closely related to Indigenous populations in the Philippines than to Taiwan's other Indig-enous peoples. Similarly, although Ng Kim Chew is now a naturalized Taiwanese citizen, he is originally from Malaysia, and most of his fiction is set in or around that region. Volland suggests that by examining the ways in which Rapongan and

Ng thematize oceans and archipelagoes in their writings, we may better understand "how thinking with and through the ocean shapes patterns of place-making and identity formation," and in this way he attempts to rethink Sinophone literatures "from a maritime perspective."

The next two articles focus on literature from Singapore. First, Cheow Thia Chan's article "Off-Center Articulations: Social Class, Postcolonial Singapore, and Reorienting Southeast Asian Chinese Literary Studies" uses an attention to the sociodemographic category of Chinese-educated Singaporeans to develop a novel approach to modern Chinese-language literature from Singapore. In particular, Chan analyzes Singaporean Chinese author Chia Joo Ming's 2015 novel *Exile or Pursuit* with attention to how this work portrays the differences between early Chinese who migrated to Singapore from China, on the one hand, and contemporary Chinese-educated Singaporeans on the other. In this way he seeks to develop an "off-center" perspective that approaches Singaporean literature through the lens of the local concept of "Chinese-educated" Singaporeans. Second, Brian Bernards's "Iridescent Corners: Sinophone Flash Fiction in Singapore" examines the genre of Sinophone flash fiction that has become increasingly influential in Singapore since the 1970s. Bernards argues that flash fiction is a platform that invites "amateur, informal, collaborative participation" and that it is frequently used to "scope out or test the bounds of the state's OB [out-of-bounds] markers, even while acknowledging such counternarratives are likely to be met with indifference by a larger public."

The following four articles turn to literature from the region that is now Malaysia, and particularly what is commonly referred to as Mahua literature, or literature by Malayan/Malaysian Chinese authors. First, in "Chinese-Language Memories under the Conflagration of War: On the Martyrdom of Chung Ling High School's Teachers and Students," Ko Chia-Cian examines an array of textual records relating to the deaths of several dozen teachers and students from the Chung Ling High School in Penang, Malaya, resulting from a Japanese attack during World War II. In the following article, "Why Does a Failed Revolution Also Need Fiction? On the Mahua Genre of Failed Revolutionary Historical Fiction," Ng Kim Chew uses Chinese communist fiction to reexamine the genre of Malayan communist fiction. Ng notes that unlike Chinese communist fiction, which tends to be defined by its triumphal tone, Malayan communist fiction is instead characterized by its focus on failure, specifically the Malayan Communist Party's ultimate failure to carry out a revolution.

In "Counter-discourse: Strategies of Representing Ethnic Minorities in Sinophone Malaysian Literature," Boon Eng Khor uses a Foucauldian notion of counter-discourse to examine the interplay of valorizing and pejorative connotations that run through many literary descriptions of Malaysia's ethnic minorities in literary works written by Mahua authors. One prominent Mahua author whose works devote considerable attention to Malaysia's Indigenous peoples but who is not covered in detail in Khor's article is Zhang Guixing, and in "Becoming Semi-wild: Colonial Legacies and Interspecies Intimacies in Zhang Guixing's Rainforest Novels" I examine the interplay between a set of interethnic and interspecies relations in two of Zhang's "rainforest" novels set in the multicultural and multiethnic environment of the Malaysian state of Sarawak, in the northern portion of the island of Borneo.

The next two articles focus on literature from the region that is now Indonesia. In "Urban Life in Two 1920s Sino-Malay Poems," Tom G. Hoogervorst examines two early twentieth-century Sino-Malay poems from Batavia, the capital of the former Netherlands Indies (now the Indonesian city of Jakarta). Written by Indies-Chinese authors, these works are composed in a creole derived from the Batavian dialect of Malay and the Hokkien dialect of Chinese. Part of this article's interest involves not only the way that it uses an analysis of these poems to probe some of the sociocultural conditions of Batavia's ethnic Chinese communities, but also the way in which Hoogervorst deciphers the meaning of the poems' rather obscure romanized and creolized Hokkien dialect. Next, in "Ethnic Loyalty versus Spring Fancy: Gender and Southeast Asia in Hei Ying's Fiction," Josh Stenberg examines several 1930s fictional works by the Sumatra-born author Hei Ying. Although Hei Ying is currently best known as a Shanghai-based author associated with the modernist New Perceptionist Movement, he also produced a body of work set in the Dutch East Indies, where he was born and grew up. Stenberg focuses on Hei Ying's treatment of gender and ethnicity in his works, and particularly on how the author's attention to the sensuality of Southeast Asian women yields a "distinctly pseudocolonial aesthetic."

This special issue's final article is Shirley O. Lua's "Recreating the World in Twenty-First Century Philippine-Chinese Speculative Fiction," which examines a collection of speculative fiction by several Filipino-Chinese authors, emphasizing the ways in which the stories use a variety of conceits familiar from speculative fiction (such as zombies) to comment allegorically on contemporary issues in the Philippines (including ethnic tensions). While this special issue's other articles all focus on works written either in some version of Chinese or a Chinese creole, Lua instead examines works written in English; and while most of the other articles examine works that turn to the past, Lua instead considers future-oriented works that project "an array of imagined worlds and alternate universes, pushing the boundaries of the real and transgressing the limits of the possible." In this way, her article captures the way in which this special issue showcases approaches that can be used to examine not only the Southeast Asia's

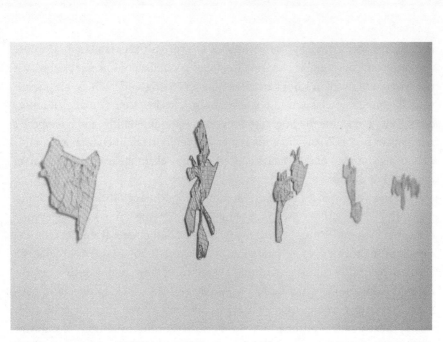

FIGURE 6. Charles Lim Yi Yong, *SEASTATE 9: Pulau* (exhibition photograph, 2021). Image courtesy of Charles Lim Yi Yong and STPI.

histories, but also its contemporary present and its possible futures. Similar reflections on the field's possible future trajectories are then examined through the lens of Charles Lim's recent artwork in Cheow Thia Chan's conclusion to this special issue.

This issue's thirteen contributors include several scholars based in North America (Bernards, Rojas, Shen, Volland, and Wang), Europe (Hoogervorst), and Australia (Stenberg). Three of our contributors (Ng, Ko, and Wong) are based in East Asia (Taiwan or Hong Kong), though each of them is originally from Southeast Asia (Malaysia and/or Singapore). In addition, three others are both originally from and currently based in the Southeast Asian nations of Singapore (Chan), Malaysia (Khor), and the Philippines (Lua). Finally, one of our contributors, Ng Kim Chew, is well recognized not only as a leading scholar of Mahua literature but also as an influential Mahua author in his own right.

The cover image of this special issue is a photograph of Charles Lim's *SEASTATE 9: Pulau* series as displayed at the 2021–2022 *Staggered Observations of a Coast* exhibit (fig. 6). Supplied by the artist's studio, the original photograph was taken with a camera positioned to the left of the horizontal row of wall-mounted works, with a shallow depth of field such that the foreground appears in sharp focus and the midground is increasingly blurry. We have reoriented the image vertically, to appear as though the viewer were gazing at a string

FIGURE 7. Charles Lim Yi Yong, *SEASTATE 8: The Grid, Whatever Whenever Wherever*, 2021. Image courtesy of STPI—Creative Gallery and Workshop, Singapore.

of islands stretching out toward the horizon. The five artificial islands visible in the cover image mirror this special issue's five "artificial" clusters of articles (focusing on Singapore, Malaya/Malaysia, Indonesia, the Philippines, and transregional concerns). Meanwhile, the sixth island positioned just outside the cover's field of vision could be viewed as a symbol of all the regions, genres, methodologies, and perspectives that have been left out of this necessarily finite project.

Similarly positioned just outside the cover photograph's field of vision is another work that was also enjoying its debut at the 2021–2022 *Staggered Observations of a Coast* exhibit. Titled *SEASTATE 8: The Grid, Whatever Whenever Wherever* (2021), the latter work consists of a large magnetic rubber sheet that was printed with the image of a large nautical map and then cut into small pieces that could be affixed to the metallic surface of the gallery's walls and columns, where visitors were invited to move them around and arrange them into different configurations (figs. 7 and 8). One of Lim's most fluid and interactive creations, *SEASTATE 8: The Grid* is not an autonomous, self-contained work, but rather a basic template that visitors can transform as they wish, in much the same way that we, as editors, hope that readers may take some of the novel methodologies proposed here and use them to develop new analyses, approaches, and methodologies.

FIGURE 8. Charles Lim Yi Yong, *SEASTATE 8: The Grid, Whatever Whenever Wherever*, 2021. Screenprint on paper, magnetic rubber sheets, dimensions variable. Exhibition installation image at Singapore Art Museum's *Wikicliki: Collecting Habits on an Earth Filled with Smartphones* (2021), first presented as *SEA STATE 8: the grid*. Artwork © Charles Lim Yi Yong/STPI. Image courtesy of Charles Lim Yi Yong and STPI.

CARLOS ROJAS is professor of Chinese Cultural Studies, Gender, Sexuality, and Feminist Studies (GSF), and Cinematic Arts at Duke University. He is the author, editor, and translator of many volumes, including *Homesickness: Culture, Contagion, and National Transformation in Modern China.*

///////////////////////////////

Notes

1   Singapore ranks twentieth on Statista's list of the smallest sovereign states. See Jaganmohan, "Smallest Countries."

2   See "Countries by Population Density." Per capita GDP figures are as of 2017. See "GDP per Capita."

3   Here and in the following discussion, "sand" often includes both sand and gravel. See Peduzzi, "Sand, Rarer Than One Thinks."

4   "Sand."

5   Banergee, "South Asia's Vanishing Sand Bans."

6   "Singapore."

7   Chua et al., "Saving Singapore's Shores."

8   The statistic about Indonesia's two dozen lost islands was first reported in late 2007, just before a UN climate change conference was scheduled to convene on the Indonesian resort island of Bali. See "Minister Says 24 Indonesian Islands." The statistic resurfaced in 2010, when it was widely reported by international papers like *The Guardian* and the *New York Times*. Although the loss of the islands was attributed to factors that included global warming and a tsunami in the final days of 2004, the reports also cited sand

exports to China, Hong Kong, and Thailand as an important contributing factor. See Parry, "Black Marketeers."

9   The project is sometimes referred to as two words: *SEA STATE*. An overview of the project can be found on the artist's website: https://www.seastate.sg/seastate.

10   Lau, "Exclusive Interview."

11   Yao, "Close Up."

12   Wijaya, "Learning to See," 30.

13   Yao, "Close Up."

14   Yeo, "'Staggered Observations of a Coast.'"

15   The works featured at the Venice Biennale included *SEASTATE 3: inversion* (2015), *SEASTATE 7: sand man* (2015), *SEASTATE 2: as evil disappears (Sajahat Buoy)* (2014), *SEASTATE 7: sandwich* (2015), *SEASTATE 6: capsize* (2015), *SEASTATE 2: as evil disappears (quadrant 0124)* (2012), *SEASTATE 9: Proclamation* (2015), and *SEASTATE 6: phase 1* (2015). See Tan, "SEASTATE."

16   Lau, "Exclusive Interview."

17   "Charles Lim Yi Yong."

18   Yao, "Close Up."

19   Sun Zhongshan, 1905.

20   Sun, "Sanmin zhuyi," 721. English translation taken from Sun, *San Min Chu I*, 210.

21   Wang, "Introduction," 315.

22   Ibid.

23   Textor, "Selected Countries."

24   "Chinese in Indonesia."

References

Banergee, Piyali. "South Asia's Vanishing Sand Bans Are Destroying the Region." *Resilience*, July 21, 2018. http://www.resilience.org/stories/2018-06-21/southeast-asias-vanishing -sand-bans-are-destroying-the-region/.

"Charles Lim Yi Yong: Staggered Observations of a Coast." STPI Creative Workshop & Gallery. Accessed June 19, 2022. http://www.stpi.com.sg/exhibitions/charles-lim-yi-yong -staggered-observations-of-a-coast/.

"Chinese in Indonesia." Facts and Details. Updated June 2015. https://factsanddetails.com /indonesia/Minorities_and_Regions/sub6_3a/entry-3993.html.

Chua, Charlene, et al. "Saving Singapore's Shores." *Straits Times*, 2021. https://www.straitstimes .com/multimedia/graphics/2022/01/singapore-protect-sea-levels-rise/index.html?shell.

"Countries by Population Density | Countries by Density 2022." World Population Review. Accessed June 19, 2022. https://worldpopulationreview.com/country-rankings/countries -by-density.

"GDP per Capita." Worldometer. Accessed June 19, 2022. https://www.worldometers.info /gdp/gdp-per-capita/.

Jaganmohan, Madhumitha. "The Smallest Countries in the World as of 2020, by Land Area (in Square Kilometers)." Statista, January 29, 2021. https://www.statista.com/statistics /1181994/the-worlds-smallest-countries/.

Lau, Yunyi. "Exclusive Interview with the Artist Charles Lim." *The Artling*, April 14, 2016. https://theartling.com/en/artzine/exclusive-interview-artist-charles-lim/.

"Minister Says 24 Indonesian Islands Have Already Disappeared: Report." *Terra Daily*, November 29, 2007. https://www.terradaily.com/reports/Minister_says_24 _Indonesian_islands_disappeared_report_999.html.

Parry, Richard Lloyd. "The Black Marketeers Stealing Indonesia's Islands by the Boat Load."
   The Times, March 23, 2010. https://www.thetimes.co.uk/article/the-black-marketeers
   -stealing-indonesias-islands-by-the-boat-load-3dqmrf9gw7l.

Peduzzi, Pascal. "Sand, Rarer Than One Thinks." UNEP Global Environmental Alert Service.
   March 2014. https://wedocs.unep.org/bitstream/handle/20.500.11822/8665/GEAS
   _Mar2014_Sand_Mining.pdf?sequence=3.

"Sand." Observatory of Economic Complexity. Accessed June 19, 2022. https://oec.world/en
   /profile/hs92/sand?yearSelector1=tradeYear6.

"Singapore." WorldData.info. Accessed June 19, 2022. https://www.worlddata.info/asia
   /singapore/index.php.

Sun Yat-sen. *San Min Chu I—The Three Principles of the People*, translated by Frank W. Price.
   Shanghai: China Committee, Institute of Pacific Relations, 1927.

Sun Zhongshan 孫中山. "Sanmin zhuyi—Minquanzhuyi" 三民主義・民權主義 [Three People's Principles—Democracy]. In *Sun Zhongshan xuanji* 孫中山選集 [Sun Zhongshan
   Collected Works]. Shanghai: Zhonghua shuju, 1984.

Tan, Melvin. "SEASTATE, Singapore Pavilion, Venice Biennale 2015." Accessed June 19,
   2022. https://www.behance.net/gallery/27099533/SEASTATE-Singapore-Pavilion-Venice
   -Biennale-2015.

Textor, C. "Selected Countries with the Largest Number of Overseas Chinese 2020 (in millions)." Statistica. January 25, 2022. https://www.statista.com/statistics/279530/countries
   -with-the-largest-number-of-overseas-chinese/https://www.dosm.gov.my/v1/index.php?
   r=column/cthemeByCat&cat=155&bul_id=OVByWjg5YkQ3MWFZRTN5bDJiaEVhZz0
   9&menu_id=L0pheU43NWJwRWVSZklWdzQ4TlhUUT09.

Wang, David Der-wei. "Introduction: Chinese Literature across the Borderlands." *Prism:
   Theory and Modern Chinese Literature* 18, no. 2 (2021): 315–20.

Wijaya, Elizabeth. "Learning to See, Finally: Charles Lim Yi Yong's *Staggered Observations
   of a Coast*." In *Staggered Observations of a Coast*, by Charles Lim Yi Yong, 20–85.
   Singapore: STPI, 2022.

Yao, Pauline J. "Close Up: Floating World." *Artforum*, April 2015. https://www.artforum.com
   /print/201504/pauline-j-yao-on-charles-lim-s-sea-state-2005-50740.

Yeo, Vivyan. "'Staggered Observations of a Coast' at STPI." *Arts and Market*, January 4, 2022.
   https://www.artandmarket.net/reviews/2022/1/4/staggered-observations-of-a-coast-at-stpi.

DAVID DER-WEI WANG

Of Wind, Soil, and Water
On the Mesology of Sinophone/Xenophone
Southeast Asian Literature

ABSTRACT This essay seeks to reconsider the current paradigm of Sinophone studies, which is largely based on theories from postcolonialism to empire critique. While Sinophone studies derives its critical thrust from confronting China as a hegemonic force, some approaches have taken a path verging on Sinophobia, the reverse of Sinocentrism. Implied in the argument is a dualistic mapping of geopolitics such as assimilation versus diaspora, resistance versus hegemony, theory versus history, and Sinophone relationality versus China.

KEYWORDS Sinophone, mesology, Nanyang, literature, xenophone

There is an elephant in the theoretical room: while theory is purportedly without boundary lines, Sinophone theoreticians have, by and large, been eager to draw inspiration from anywhere but China. I contend that to truly generate the critical force of Sinophone studies, one has to engage China in terms of not merely geopolitical reality but also historical dynamics and discursive ramifications. To that end, I have proposed elsewhere the model of *huayi feng* 華夷風 (hereafter Sinophone/xenophone) that contests the time-honored Chinese discourse of "distinction between *hua* and *yi*" (*huayi zhibian* 華夷之辨).[1] Instead of *bian* 辨, I call attention to its homophonic counterpart, 變, thereby highlighting the factors of alterity and changeability inherent in any dualistic schema between cultural and ethnic selfhood and otherness, indigeneity and foreignness. I bring such an investigation to bear on the multifarious concept of *feng* 風, which etymologically means wind, sound, trend, propensity, and above all, poetic sounding and cultural articulation.[2]

In this essay, I will further my inquiry by critically engaging with the model of mesology 風土論, or the study of the mutual relationships between living creatures and their biological, social, and environmental surroundings. Mesology has had a long tradition in both Western and Asian histories. In China, the concept of *fengtu* 風土 (wind and soil, or milieu) can be traced back as far as the Zhou dynasty (1046–256 BCE). My intervention is derived from its modern incarnations as evinced by Watsuji Tetsurô's 和辻哲郎 (1889–1960) *Fûdo: Ningengakuteki kôsatsu*

PRISM: THEORY AND MODERN CHINESE LITERATURE • 19:2 • SEPTEMBER 2022
DOI 10.1215/25783491-9966647 • © 2022 LINGNAN UNIVERSITY

風土：人間学的考察 (Milieus: A Study of the Human Linkage, 1935), as well as the French environmental philosopher Augustin Berque's (1942–) related studies. Watsuji introduces a founding distinction between the environment (*kankyô* 環境), as abstractly objectified by modern science, and the milieu (*fûdo* 風土), as concretely experienced by a certain society. He contends that the milieu/*fûdo* finds its manifestation in "the structural moment of human existence." For "human existence" (*ningen* 人間), he has in mind not merely individuals as such, but the collective linkages and interstices between people, and between people and phenomena in the ecosystem.

I suggest that Sinophone/xenophone changeability and mesology offer new perspectives from which to assess the sociopolitical, cultural, and environmental entanglements of a Chinese-speaking milieu. With this thesis in mind, I introduce a new project, the *Sinophone Nanyang Reader* (南洋讀本, hereafter *Reader*), which I coedited with Professor Ko Chia-Cian 高嘉謙 of National Taiwan University.[3] I contend that Sinophone studies cannot move forward without a renewed and more expansive engagement with Nanyang or Sinophone Southeast Asia, not only because it boasts the largest Chinese-speaking population outside of mainland China (as many as 34 million as of 2019), but also because it encapsulates almost all issues that concern Sinophone studies. Through five modules—"Winds," "Islands," "Straits," "Peninsulas and Gulfs," and "Oceans"—the *Reader* seeks to navigate the rich ecology of Southeast Asia in which Sinophone settlers and travelers created their own societies while mingling with Indigenous and other settler/colonial cultures.

Sinophone/Xenophone Changeability

Sinophone is arguably the most provocative keyword of Chinese literary studies since the turn of the new millennium. Although the term has been used since the 1990s in select contexts, it was popularized in 2007 when Shu-mei Shih published *Visuality and Identity: Sinophone Articulations across the Pacific*.[4] In her book, Shih invokes the Sinophone as a language-based critical perspective from which to engage linguistic, cultural, ethnic, and political dynamics in China, as well as Chinese-speaking communities worldwide.[5] In opposition to conventional reference to "China" as a homogenized entity, she argues that the dispersal of the Chinese people across the world needs to be reconceptualized in terms of vibrant or vanishing communities of Sinitic-language cultures rather than of ethnicity and nationality.

One discerns in Shih's endeavor a complex of theoretical efforts, from postcolonial criticism to minority studies, from humanist Marxism to multiculturalism. Of these theories, postcolonialism stands out as her main stake. Shih tackles the common wisdom that colonialism is a modern political and economic maneuvering undertaken only by Western imperialist powers. She calls attention to three types of Chinese colonialism: "continental colonialism," "internal colonialism," and "settler colonialism."[6] Her research concludes with the claim that the Sinophone subjectivity is predicated on the disavowal of diaspora. If diaspora studies focuses on issues such as the loss of roots and the yearning for homecoming, Sinophone studies, according to Shih, seeks to pin down the "expiration date" of diaspora. That is, insofar as (im)migration projects the immigrant's eventual assimilation into the culture where he or she relocates, Sinophone subjectivity may very well be gradually minoritized as time passes, and even become de-Sinicized in the end.

Shih has made an enormous contribution to Sinophone studies, but her approach also points to areas where additional critical efforts are desired. Whereas Shih's distinction between (socialist) China and the Sinophone world unwittingly duplicates the polarized agenda of the Cold War era, *colonialism* has been used as a blanket term to describe variegated forms of conquest, oppression, and hegemony in such a way as to lose its historical specificity and critical rigor. For one thing, in view of the fact that the Qing is an empire established by the Manchus, who by Shih's definition should have been labeled a minority, how do we construe the paradox that the ethnically Han-centered China under the Manchu rule is already a colonized polity while exerting its colonial power over other ethnicities? Shih's critique of settler colonialism brings into view the predatory side of the narrative of Chinese diaspora, but it may at the same time downplay the existential circumstance that, for good or ill, underlies overseas Chinese's need for linguistic and ethnic solidarity. Moreover, although her concept of *anti-diaspora* projects a desired horizon of multicultural assimilation, the history of global migration, as illustrated by the Hakka and the Jewish people, belies the wisdom of any sanguine belief in the immigrant subjectivity's unilateral "plasticity" in joining a new society.[7]

In my view, for a Sinophone project to exert its critical potential, one must not engage merely with the domain of conventional overseas Chinese cultures plus ethnic minorities in mainland China. In light of transcultural dynamics on the global scale as well as the intricate ethnic histories of premodern China, one needs to reimagine the cartography of the Chinese center versus the periphery so as to enact a new linguistic and literary arena of contestations. To challenge the nation-state discourse of contemporary China, one should no longer consider it apart from the Sinophone system in oppositional terms. Beyond polarized ethnic and geopolitical mapping as proposed by Shih, one should observe mainland China as part of the global Sinophone circuit. One should even venture to tease out variegated soundings—from gender to class, age, region, and belief—*within* the Han-centered nation-state of China so as to foreground the heteroglossia inherent in the unison of standardized Chinese mandated by the authorities.

Moreover, in an effort to understand China as not merely a modern polity but also a historical flux of multiple Sinophone civilizations, I call for a critical—and creative—inquiry into the genealogical implications of Sinophone discourse.[8] I have tackled elsewhere the premodern discourse of *huayi zhibian* 華夷之辨 (distinction between *hua* and *yi*) and translated it as a "Sinophone/xenophone distinction."[9] This is an ancient discourse traceable to the Zhou dynasty, which originated from the ancient cartographic mapping of central China in the Yellow River valley vis-à-vis neighboring tribal cultures such as the *rong* 戎, *yi* 夷, *yue* 越, and *di* 狄. As time passed, it developed into a geopolitical terminology underlined by ethnic, cultural, and even moral stratifications. The character *yi* thus takes on multiple meanings, ranging from "outsider," "barbarian," "alien," "foreigner," and "the other," to what is to be explained in the following, "xenophone."[10]

Historians have observed that the valence of the distinction between *hua* and *yi* fluctuated in relation to the vicissitudes of Han and non-Han powers throughout medieval China. Whereas the Six Dynasties saw the first major migration of Han Chinese to the south as the north was occupied by barbarians, the Tang dynasty thrived on its multicultural vitality and ethnic hybridity. It was in the Song dynasty that the distinction between *hua* and *yi* gained an increased political thrust, partially because of the barbarian threat from the north, which prompted an ethnic and territorial awareness suggestive of the incipient mode of nationhood,[11] and partially because of the holistic view of Confucian state craftmanship. The fall of the northern Song to the Jurchens and the fall of the southern Song to the Mongols gave rise to a discourse of loyalty, martyrdom, and consequently loyalism (*yimin* 遺民) on behalf of authentic Han Chinese civilization.[12]

The debate over *hua* versus *yi* culminated in the seventeenth century. In the midst of dynastic cataclysm, Ming loyalists such as Gu Yanwu 顧炎武 (1613–1682) and Huang Zongxi 黃宗羲 (1610–1695) engaged with political and philosophical treatises to stress the lasting authenticity of the Han-centered Chinese civilization despite dynastic turnovers.[13] Meanwhile, the Manchu regime sought to solidify its legitimacy by both oppressing and co-opting ethnic Han intellectuals.[14] In 1728, after uncovering an anti-Manchu conspiracy plot by the intellectual Zeng Jing 曾靜 (1679–1735) in Hunan, the Yongzheng 雍正 emperor issued a response throughout the empire arguing against the rationale of Zeng's plot, which was based on the distinction between the Han Chinese and the barbarian, and stating that when it comes to the mandate of heaven, there is really no difference between ethnicities: ancient Chinese sages and kings were all from barbarian regions. What really matters is the ruler's capacity to demonstrate his virtue in line with the quintessence of Confucian heritage.

The distinction between *hua* and *yi* took a more intriguing twist when the Japanese commercial translators–cum–Confucian scholars Hayashi Gahō 林春勝 (1618–1680) and Hayashi Hōkō 林信篤 (1644–1732) came up with *Kai hentai* 華夷變態 (The alerted state of China and the barbarian), a compilation of records describing the changes of Han Chinese culture in China in the aftermath of the Manchu conquest. The Japanese scholars conclude by stating that Japan, not China, turned out to be the civilization that carries on Chinese legacies at its most authentic. In a similar logic, the eighteenth-century Korean envoy Kim Chonghu 金鐘厚 (1721–1780) famously stated, "There is no China after the fall of the Ming" (明朝後無中國).[15]

All three discourses introduced above, though each is addressed from the Manchu, the Japanese, or the Korean perspective, share an acute awareness that time changes, and the meanings of history and civilization as such are subject to renegotiation. For all their political and ethnic divergences, these discourses subtly converge on one point: the factor that valorizes the "Chineseness" of Chinese civilization has less to do with consanguinity or ethnic origin than with the degree of acculturation. As a result of the fall of Ming China, not only the Manchus but also the Japanese and Koreans could boast their acquired heritage so as to represent—and even become—China. To be sure, the concepts of *culture* and *virtue* under discussion are rooted in Sinocentrism and require further scrutiny. But what concerns us more is the connotation of contingency, transformation, and hybridization implied in *bian* 變. Just as a foreigner endowed with Chinese cultural bearings can become *hua*, so a Han Chinese deprived of Chinese cultural bearings can become *yi*.

If the conventional discourse of *hua* versus *yi* stresses *bian* 辨 (distinction)—which is oriented more to a spatial verification of inside, center, and orthodoxy in opposition to outside, margin, and heterogeneity—the late Ming and early Qing cases suggest the possibility of *bian* 變, which foregrounds the change and changeability of *hua* versus *yi* over time. This is only the beginning of more changes in subsequent centuries. When Wei Yuan 魏源 (1794–1857) advocated that one "master the barbarians' skill in order to control the barbarians" 師夷長 技以制夷 in the aftermath of the Opium War, he introduced a new figure of barbarians—namely, Westerners equipped with formidable military, economic, and epistemological forces—to the conventional *hua/yi* discourse. He tipped the delicate *hua/yi* balance again, this time by insinuating the supremacy of *yi* over *hua* in cultural as well as political terms. Wei Yuan and his followers, from Guo Songtao 郭嵩燾 (1818–1891) to Huang Zunxian 黃遵憲 (1848–1905) and Tan Sitong 譚 嗣同 (1865–1898), thus paved the way for the rise of a modern paradigm of *hua* and *yi*, which is still inciting debates.

I argue that the changeability of *hua* versus *yi* emerged in late imperial China to signal the epistemological shakeup of the relationships between China and the world in multiple terms. If the distinction between *hua* and *yi* helps define the world of China as a self-contained polity that oversees the taxonomy of Han Chinese versus barbarians, "changeability between *hua* versus *yi*" informs a China entering the world with expanding horizons, ethnically and otherwise, beyond the purview of the old civilization. It may not be a coincidence that *yi* takes on bifurcated connotations at this juncture. Whereas the *yi* within the conventional geopolitical mapping of China undertook the new designation in terms of ethnicity, to be contained, assimilated, and eventually naturalized into the Chinese nation, the *yi* from the world outside China represents the agents of modernity, ever ready to be emulated or contested. The national narratives of the Republic of China (Taiwan) and the People's Republic of China, from "there is only one China" 中華民族是一個 to "the homogeneous body of multiple ethnicities" 多元一體格局,[16] testify to the continued entanglement with modern ramifications of *hua* and *yi*.

The rise of Sinophone discourse, accordingly, may be understood as a most recent impulse to renegotiate the definition of China vis-à-vis the changing world. However resistant critics in the vein of Shih may be to China's impact in post–Cold War dynamics, they may actually gain rather than lose critical force if they took a few historical lessons about China in relation to ethnicities and regional cultures in premodern times. This also prods us to rethink the linguistic model of extant Sinophone studies. As Shih indicates, language in regional, dialectical, and spoken terms serves as the least common denominator of Sinophone communities. Such a "Sinophone articulation" is also said to be a barometer by which a Sinophone subject gauges the degree of his or her Chinese identity; and Sinophone articulation is, after all, destined to dissipate in a xenophone community as time passes. While Shih may have empirical grounding in making such an observation, she still betrays a flirtation with phonocentrism, treating vocal articulation as the sole indicator to verify her agenda of being "against diaspora."

To critically supplement such a linguistic model, I offer the model of *wen* 文 (literature/cultural literacy) as one that helps define the dialectic between Sinophone and xenophone. Etymologically, *wen* refers to a wide range of meanings, from the patterns of nature to illustrative ornamentations, from script to *belles lettres*, from individual cultural bearing to civilization in crystalized form. *Wen* has been described as that which has encapsulated Chinese civilization since ancient times, bringing to mind the quote from the *Zuozhuan* 左傳: "China is called Xia because it boasts the magnanimity of ritual, and it is called Hua because of the beauty of cultural ornaments" 中國有禮儀之大，故稱夏；有服章之美，謂之華.[17] Scholars, however, have long noted the mercurial nature of *wen* and bring it to bear on the changeability of *hua* versus *xia*. That is, insofar as cultural edification is something to be acquired and cultivated, *wen*, unlike consanguinity and ethnicity, is always susceptible to transplantation and refashioning in both figurative and bodily terms. In consonance with the late Ming and early Qing cases described above, the late Kyoto School master Miyazaki Ichisada 宮崎市定 (1901–1995) famously contended that "the distinction between *hua* and *yi* hinges on the availability of *wen*, in other words, *wen* exists only in the condition of *hua*; meanwhile, *hua* becomes what it is because of *wen*."[18]

The modern era has witnessed the increasingly reified definition of *wen*, which is often associated with etiquette and literature. Instead, I call for restoring the rich implications of *wen* as a kind of literacy, or a "structure of feeling," that informs the Sinophone subject of its Chinese connection as both vernacular wisdom and refined knowledge, both linguistic competence and everyday life practice. In other words, I find in the Sinophone an intriguing tapestry of *wen* in textual, performative (ritualistic), and imaginary terms. Spoken Chinese is only part of this taxonomy of *wen*.

I hasten to add that by calling for a restoration of the literacy implications of *wen*, I am not promoting the tired notion of cultural China; nor am I projecting a normative conclusion regarding either the persistence or the evaporation of an ideal type of Chinese culture. Rather, by historicizing the question of Sinophone and xenophone through the lens of the *longue durée* of *hua/yi* mutations, a Sinophone scholar will hopefully become less susceptible to either Sinocentric or Sinophobic preconceptions of what *wen* has to be, and more willing to observe the changes and (dis)continuities of its pattern—the primordial meaning of *wen*—in a specific time and space.

I have proposed a critical archaelogy by excavating the discourse of *hua* and *yi* and rethinking its modern relevance in terms of the Sinophone and xenophone. My review is a rough sketch and is merely meant to provide a bird's-eye view of how complex the Sinophone debate could be and how it can help (retroactively) critique the monologic narrative of Chinese history. Whereas the discourse of *hua* and *yi* have mutually implicated each other in making the Chineseness of the past, that of Sinophone and xenophone will hopefully expand the scope of our survey beyond the territorial boundaries of China. Most important, my study has led me to consider that the entanglements of Sinophone and xenophone are not limited to linguistic articulation; they also point to the dynamics of *wen*—a literacy of Chinese cultural bearings that helps gauge the changing circumstances of a Sinophone community. With this historical context in place, I turn to the discourse of Sinophone mesology.

Sinophone Mesology and Mythology

Mesology, a term formerly used to describe the science of ecology, refers to the study of the mutual relationships between living creatures and their biological, social, and environmental surroundings. Rooted in the ancient Greek terms *mésos* (μέσος, "middle") and *logia* (-λογια, "branch of study"),[19] mesology seeks to highlight the contact zones between nature and culture of any given space and investigate the formations arising therefrom. In this study, I venture to highlight the Chinese equivalent to mesology, *fengtu* 風土. *Fengtu* is a compound phrase comprising the two characters *feng* 風 (wind) and *tu* 土 (soil, land, earth), which, when put together, mean the customs and manners characteristic of a place.

As proposed above that the Chinese equivalent of Sinophone/xenophone could be Sino-/xenophone/wind or *huayi feng* 華夷風, now I will explain the rich implications of *feng*/wind/phone. The Chinese character *feng* means "wind" or "air in motion," the quintessential form of meteorology that mobilizes and disseminates a multitude of things. In addition to being a natural phenomenon, *feng* takes on a cosmic dimension as the source of heavenly, earthly, and human sounds. By association, it refers to sonic expressions in ancient times, such as *guofeng* 國風 (folk songs of various regions) of the *Shijing* 詩經 (Classic of Poetry). *Feng* constitutes the essential part of compound expressions ranging from individual upbringing and personality (*fengge* 風格, *fengfan* 風範), to customs and mores (*fengsu* 風俗, *fenghua* 風化), trend (*fengqi* 風氣), landscape (*fengjing* 風景), and culture (*fengjiao* 風教). What remains consistent in these phrases is the connotation of something expressive of and susceptible to change. Based on this understanding, I propose to treat Sinophone/xenophone as the wind/sound/culture that reverberates between the Indigenous and the foreign, a momentum that enacts traffic and communication in both human and transhuman terms.

Tu 土 is regarded by Chinese people as the foundation of the five elements (metal, wood, water, fire, earth) in the making of epistemological and material frameworks. Earth is invoked in close association with agricultural undertakings, seasonal cycles, territorial sovereignty, and above all, cultural nourishment. It is said that the goddess Nüwa molded soil to create the first human, while the Yellow Emperor, the originator of Chinese civilization, is an embodiment of the yellow earth. Whereas wind is that which is changeable and hard to harness, earth represents the principles of stability and productiveness. Earth gives rise to the sense of positionality and thus provides the matrix of topography. While modern scholars from Gaston Bachelard to Martin Heidegger have extracted symbolic and philosophical meanings from their thinking about earth, contemporary scholars Yang Rubin 楊儒賓 and Donna Haraway have offered new interpretations of earth: for Yang, a refurbished ontology of the five elements, and for Haraway, a contemplation of the "Chthulucene," the underworld and the subterranean existence where all life is birthed from.[20]

The phrase *fengtu* appeared as early as *Guoyu* 國語 (attributed to Zuo Qiuming 左丘明 556–451 BCE), in which ethnohistorians and music officers were said to observe the wind/sound of a place so as to gauge popular sentiments. In other words, wind and earth have long been conceived as the constituents of not only an environment but also a habitus. *Fengtu* has since been used to refer to both landscape and local color, both natural variables and cultural manifestations, in genres from gazettes to travelogues and ethnographic accounts. It was not until the early twentieth century that scholars sought to tease out its theoretical potential from a comparative perspective. In 1935, Japanese philosopher Watsuji Tetsurô published *Milieus*, in which he introduces a founding distinction between *kankyô* 環境 (the environment) and *fûdo* 風土 (the milieu). Watsuji was inspired by Heidegger's rumination on being and time, but he took issue with the German master's engagement only with time and proposed to look into space-in-time in terms of *fûdo*, which can be roughly translated into "milieu." For Watsuji, the ontological concept of *fûdosei* 風土性 (the sense and tendency of the relationship of a society with its environment) hinges on "the structural moment of the being-human."[21] His research leads him to observe the *aidagara* 間柄, the linkage inter-twined between people, and through this linkage, between people and things, historically constituting a milieu. Instead of a deterministic conclusion, however, Wastuji contends that *fûdosei* manifests itself as a result of continued negotiation between the land and the humans living on the land.

In *Fûdo*, Wastuji began by engaging Johann Gottfried von Herder's treatise on locality and ethnicity, which are purported to be integral to the formation of national culture. While endorsing Herder's ethnographical approach, Watsuji recommended a more rigorous examination of the land and weather in relation to the human condition. He introduces three types of cultures in correspondence with three distinct environmental factors: the monsoon area (east Asia, South-east Asia, and India), the desert area (central Asia), and the ranch area (eastern Europe and the Mediterranean). He ponders how rainfall, humidity, seasonal change, and soil conditions have profoundly influenced the way in which resi-dents of each area shape their psychological and sensory data, lifestyles, and even morals and manners. Instead of a deterministic conclusion, however, Wastuji contends that *fûdosei* manifests itself as a result of continued negotiation between the land and the humans living on the land.

French scholar Augustin Berque was inspired by Watsuji's study and picked up where Watsuji left off in the late 1960s by looking into the medial condition that shapes human existence in specific contexts. Berque translated Watsuji's *fûdo-sei* as *médiance*, a neologism derived from the Latin *medietas*, which means "half." Echoing Watsuji, Berque regards the human condition as a venue in which natural and cultural variables meet halfway to be molded into a "moment" of existence. In other words, *médiance* points to the eco-techno-symbolic entanglements through which the human makes sense of the milieu. Thus, *fûdo* derives its recognizable pattern of meaning from not only the interaction between biosphere and instru-mental agency but also from the infiltration of sensibilities and imaginaries into every layer of milieu. In an effort to deconstruct the dualistic program that under-pins the discourse of modernity, Berque bases his argument on what he calls the "tetralemma": A (assertion), non-A (negation), neither A nor non-A (binegation), both A and non-A (biassertion). He urges one to reckon with the "trajection" of a milieu, in which "words and things, the things and our existence are co-awaiting, all this producing historically that 'third and other gender' which is nothing else than the *médiance* of our milieu: both the imprint and the matrix of our genesis."[22]

For all Berque's indebtedness to Watsuji, he distinguishes himself by high-lighting the cumulative, porous, and contingent dimensions in the process of *médiance*. Whereas Watsuji's *fûdo* tends to generalize the human condition in such a way as to betray a Hegelian bent of sublation as well as the imperialist sentiment of late 1930s Japan, Berque's engagement with the ternary terms of any case in discussion is aimed at subverting the dualism that he believes plagues the logic of modernity. Most significantly, the bio-techno-symbolic approach to the milieu brings into view the dynamics of semiotic taxonomy.

In the context of this essay, I take Berque's bio-techno-symbolic mesology to bear on the "wind and soil" of Sinophone Southeast Asia. The earliest Chinese-language text about Southeast Asia that uses *fengtu* 風土 or mesology as its theme is *Zhenla fengtu ji* 真臘風土記 (A Record of Cambodia, the Land and its People) by Zhou Daguan 周達觀 (1266?–1350?). A native of Wenzhou in the Yuan dynasty, Zhou was sent by Temür Khan as part of a diplomatic missión to Cambodia in 1296 and spent eleven months in the capital area of Angkor Thom. During his sojourn, Zhou was given access to the royal palace, where he had more chances to observe the religious practices, parades, and ceremonies of festivities, as well as the daily life of the people. He also traveled to the countryside and took note of folk customs and farming practices. Zhou's account was first translated into French by Jean-Pierre Abel-Rémusat in 1819, which purportedly led to the rediscovery of Angkor Wat by European explorers in the mid-nineteenth century.

One who was following the postcolonial discourse could easily suggest that Zhou's imperial mission was an attempt to subjugate the Cambodian kingdom, and his record is couched in the genre of colonial exoticism in modern terms. However, a closer look from a perspective of Sinophone/xenophone mesology reveals more. Although Zhou framed his narrative in the traditional *hua/yi* discourse, his own ethnic and political identity is subject to question. Zhou was a Han Chinese southerner in service of a Mongol court, and his mission took him to the south of China, a new terrain of *yi*/barbarian. In addition, he composed his record in the Han Chinese script, punctuated with dialectical expressions of his home region, and he showed few qualms speaking from a "Chinese" perspective on behalf of the "barbarian" empire of the Yuan. The "distinction" between the Sinophone and the xenophone keeps shifting through his observation of Cambodian customs. Meanwhile, Zhou was keen on how the tropical environment, its heat and humidity, fashioned local agricultural styles and gender customs. Zhou spent eleven months in Cambodia not because his mission was challenging but because the delegation had to wait for the next monsoon season to come, so as to facilitate its homebound voyage. A diplomatic mission presupposed a favorable wind.

We now turn to the modern mesological and mythological inscriptions of the Southeast Asian Sinophone community. Take, for example, beliefs about Tua Pek

Kong (大伯公, Grand Uncle or the God of Prosperity), the most popular deity throughout Malaysia, Singapore, Indonesia, and other Nanyang communities. Research tracing the deity's identity has produced a variety of results. Tua Pek Kong is associated either with the gangster leader Zhang Li 張理 from the Hakka clan, whose Indonesian Sumatra-bound boat was struck by wind and accidentally landed on Penang Island of the Malay peninsula in the early eighteenth century; or with Taibo 太伯, the legendary prince of the Zhou exiled to the south who founded the state of Wu. The renowned Sinophone scholar Hsu Yun Tsiao 許雲樵 (1905–1981) nevertheless concluded that Tua Pek Kong is none other than an overseas reincarnation of the Tutelary God (God of Earth/Land), the most "down to earth" deity worshiped all over China.[23]

All three clues point to the fact that in the settler community of Nanyang, a new mythology system was developed in response to the changed milieu. The Zhang Li story suggests the treacherous natural condition of maritime migration as well as the immigrants' social class and ethnic background; the Taibo story suggests the immigrants' genealogical longing by linking their diasporic experience with the ultimate exile in ancient China. The Tutelary God story moves the guardian of land out of the pantheon of supernatural China and relocates it overseas. When wind and soil change, even the deity steadfastly rooted in the Chinese soil can resettle in a foreign space. Mesology and mythology are intertwined in such a way as to give rise to the "genesis" and "exodus" discourse of the Nanyang community.

In the domain of literature and the humanities, I introduce three cases. Lim Boon Keng 林文慶 (1869–1957) and Koh Hong Beng 辜鴻銘 (1857–1928) were both born to Peranakan families and initially had comparatively little exposure to Chinese cultural influence. Lim received his medical degree at the University of Edinburgh, while Koh acquired his education in England, Germany, and France to become a civil engineer. Both, however, became engaged in Chinese culture at some point in their careers.

In 1921, upon the request of Sun Yat-sen, Lim served as the second president of Xiamen University and became an advocate of Confucianism, a position resulting in his bitter confrontation with Lu Xun during the latter's brief tenure at the university. On the other hand, Koh learned his Chinese only after his sojourn in Europe, yet ended up becoming an ultraconservative Sinophile after seting foot in China. His fetishistic embrace of Chinese canon made him a most notorious figure during the era of May Fourth Enlightenment. As such, Lim and Koh each created a "mythology," à la Roland Barthes's definition, of China.[24] Their Malayan/European experience served as an incentive rather than an impediment to their search for the Chinese dreamland.

In sharp contrast to Lim's and Ko's cases, Jin Zhimang 金枝芒 (1912–1988), a communist from the Jiangsu Province, arrived in Singapore in 1937, and over the following decade he was increasingly involved in local anticolonial activities. In 1947, a vehement debate broke out among Sinophone literati in Malaya about the nature of Chinese Malayan literature. Jin emerged to become the most vociferous proponent of indigenous Sinophone-Malayan realism in opposition to those who proclaimed the cause of overseas Chinese nationalism. What concerned Jin most was not Chinese identity as such but Malayan local color that had transformed Chinese immigrants into a Sinophone community. As he would have it, the wind and soil of Malaya have created a unique ecumene with which Chinese immigrants should identify. Moreover, Jin contended that a true believer in Marxism should embrace revolution on a global scale rather than succumbing merely to nationalism.

Soon after the debate, Jin withdrew into the rainforest of northern Malaya as a guerrilla fighter. Against all odds, he continued to write, and his works such as *Ji'e* 飢餓 (Hunger, 1960), produced in mimeographic and handwritten forms, came across as a testimony to the most horrific environment in which a holy crusade was fought in the name of Karl Marx. The novel's title refers as much to the guerrilla fighters' hopeless condition of surviving the jungle as to their insatiable desire for ideological salvation. The rainforest constitutes the most poignant natural *and* mythical stage, on which the terms of fighting and writing as a revolutionary on the Malay Peninsula during the Cold War era are brought into play. Jin was deported back to China in 1961, and *Hunger* was not allowed to be published in Malaysia until 2008.

Toward a Sinophone Nanyang Reader

Above, I have proposed two discourses as a way to intervene with the extant paradigm of Sinophone Studies. Whereas Sinophone/xenophone changeability points to the effects of the "altered state" of the Sinophone as a result of historical contingencies, Sinphone/xenophone mesology offers a look into the socioecological conditions of a Sinophone milieu. Both are intended to reorient the post–Cold War confrontational narrative toward broader horizons of the human condition and beyond. It is to test the feasibility of these discourses that I have undertaken the *Sinophone Nanyang Reader* project.

The *Reader* has two dimensions. First, it is meant to be a compilation of Sinophone writings since the late nineteenth century in multiple genres, including fiction, memoir, travelogue, gazette jottings, and folk songs, all instantiating the lived and imaginary experiences of Nanyang communities. In the meantime, in the spirit of *fûdo*, the *Reader* pays particular attention to the bio-tech-symbolic junctures that leave imprints on the morals and manners of the Sinophone community. To showcase the conditions of Sinoglossia, the *Reader* will feature writings in both modern and classical Chinese, and more significantly, translations of works from other languages, such as Malay, Indonesian, Burmese, Tamil, and English by heritage and nonheritage writers.

Second, the *Reader* also projects a "virtual" reader in the sense that for each work included in the book, there are many more pieces—in both written and other forms yet to be tangibly realized—evoked in the imagined "book" about Nanyang. In other words, the *Reader* is not a mere sampler but an inexhaustible index of Sinophone Southeast Asia and beyond.

My argument is partially inspired by Emmanuel Levinas's phenomenology of the "book," which is closely related to the doctrine of literature. Levinas contends that in the Talmudic context, *scripture* appears inclusive of all that is yet to be materialized into the form of the secular text,[25] and it can be interpreted not through the exegetic system but via the epiphanic evocation of the other each time the scripture is read. Levinas regards literature at large as the dissemination of "the book," which is "inspired by the infinite and has an infinite potential to inspire."[26] The line between them "emerges as a verse in the flowing of language—no doubt of every language—in order to become text, as proverb, or fable, or poem, or legend, before the stylet or quill imprints it as letters on tablets, parchment or paper."[27]

I try to reinterpret Levinas's invocation of "the book" in a different intellectual vein. Instead of the theologically ridden concept of "the book," I propose *wen* as that which is more ready to reckon with the Sinophone cultures in discussion. It will be recalled that *wen*, as a form of inscription, presupposes the manifestation of traces and patterns in nature. Thus, *renwen* 人文 (patterns of the humanities) is seen as always already implicated in the mutations of cosmos, which give rise to *tianwen* 天文 (patterns of heaven, astronomical configuration) and *diwen* 地文 (patterns of earth, geographic topos).[28] In a way just as suggestive as "the book," *wen* is also "inspired by the infinite and has an infinite potential to inspire."

To repeat, I define *wen* as not only a crystalized form of elite culture or knowledge but also as a vital vernacular conduit through which a Chinese/Sinophone society continues to negotiate its identity in relation with the world. *Wen*, as a pattern or script—*écriture*—writ large, manifests itself in environmental, textual, performative/ritualistic, and imaginary terms. It is the literacy of *wen* that informs the communal sensibilities—encoded in forms from ritualistic protocols to folk beliefs, from ethnic upbringings to kinship values, from dialectical doxa to sartorial and culinary customs—of a Chinese/Sinophone society.

Nanyang, or literally the South Seas, is a Sinophone term for geographical region from the southern coastal regions to the area of Southeast Asia as we understand it today. The naming of Nanyang, to be sure, already signals the inchoate linguistic system available to make sense of the area. Although Chinese settlers appeared in Southeast Asia as early as the Yuan dynasty, large-scale migration to the area started in the seventeenth century, coinciding with the dynastic turmoil from the Ming to the Qing. The naming of Nanyang surfaced at this time. Over the following three centuries, Chinese migrants became a dominant force in helping mobilize trade, plantations, and settlements in regions from the Malay Peninsula to Indonesia, from Myanmar to the Philippines. In the meantime, they had to cope with Western colonizers, Indigenous peoples, and competing powers within the immigrant communities, resulting in a history of exploitations and submissions, resistances and collaborations. To call Chinese immigrants merely "settler colonizers" risks simplifying the entanglements undergirding the making of Sinophone Nanyang.

As previously noted, there are at least 34 million people of Chinese descent living in the Nanyang region, demonstrating various degrees of assimilation to local cultures. Whereas the descendants of Chinese migrants in Thailand have mostly been naturalized into local culture in a peaceful manner, their counter-parts in Indonesia have undergone a series of bloody anti-Chinese riots and mas-sacres since the 1960s to become a silent minority. Singapore boasts over 70 per-cent of its population as having Chinese heritage, even as English has become the dominant language in the island state. Malaysia has the largest Chinese-speaking community in Southeast Asia—totaling 6 million, nearly one-fifth of the national population—with a thriving Sinophone culture. It is no surprise that scholars have paid most attention to the Sinophone phenomenon in Malaysia.

What concerns us here is the highly intricate process of transculturation of the Sinophone, including Indigenous as well as postcolonial communities. Shih declares that Sinoglossia—dialects, topolects, and other soundings of the Sinitic sphere—provides the common denominator that holds overseas Chinese together and sets them apart. She also projects that, as Sinophone speakers are gradually integrated into local societies over time, the influence of Chinese/Sinitic culture will thin out and eventually evaporate. Be that as it may, Shih's observation is underlain by her embrace of the postcolonial method of creolization and her anti-China agenda. Jing Tsu, meanwhile, has offered a counter-discourse of "Sin-ophone governance."[29] That is, insofar as language is an articulation associated less with nativity than with acquisition, Sinophone status need not be a token of ethnicity destined to disappear; rather, it can be a tool of leverage, used on behalf of contested interests. In the wake of the "rise of China," followed by the "One Road, One Belt" project, in the new millennium Mandarin Chinese (*putonghua* 普通話), rather than local dialects, has drawn more and more heritage and non-heritage learners, which speaks to the intricate motivations behind the ebbs and flows of Sinophone culture in Southeast Asia.

All these debates bring back the discourse of Sinophone/xenophone change-ability, discussed above. While the current paradigm of Sinophone studies focuses on the geopolitics of Southeast Asia in relation to China through modern times, it need not always be limited to a symptomatic analysis of topics already on the table. In addition to the language model proposed by Shih, I suggest that one may take up the symbolic *médiance* of *wen* as an alternative option, one that points to the rhizomic web of Chinese cultural legacy—as well as its distortion and disavowal—underneath (or above) geopolitics and linguistic politics.

What an ideal *Reader* will really highlight, however, is Sinophone Nanyang as situated in broad mesological conditions—the peoples, the mountains and islands, and the climate as both weather conditions and the doxa of a society—that have continuously affected Chinese immigrant culture and redefined the identity of Sinophone subjects. The area spans about 4.5 million square kilometers and has a total population of more than 655 million, of which people of Chinese descent account for only 5 percent. The region is culturally and ethnically diverse, with hundreds of languages spoken by more than ninety ethnic groups. Before Chinese appeared in Southeast Asia, Arabians, Indians, Malays, and Austronesians had already formed an active commercial and cultural network in the region. Situated at the junction of four major geological plates (Eurasian, Indian-Australian, Pacific, and Philippine Sea), the region is one of the most tectonically volatile areas on earth, with the volcanic eruption of Mount Tambora in 1815 being the largest in recorded human history. The area is nevertheless blessed with oceanic abundance and meteorological clemency. One of the factors that made Southeast Asia a commercial route is the monsoon, the seasonal reversal of the direction of winds along the shores of the South China Sea, which blows from the southwest for half of the year and from the northeast for the other half. The wind enacts maritime movements, bringing ethnicities, languages, beliefs, and customs into play with each other.

The wind, earth, and water are invoked here not only because they are the natural agents that shape the unique geographical contour of Southeast Asia, but also because they constitute the symbolic repository that gives rise to Sinophone Nanyang. In Chinese, just as *feng* ("wind") refers to both atmospheric phenomenon and literary articulation, *tu* ("soil") similarly encompasses both the mineral association of earth and the ethnographical association of habitus, and *shui* ("water") suggests as much the aquatic zone of the world as it does the fluid force of human disposition. How these notions play out in Sinophone Southeast Asia, as both the matrix and the imprint of a specific moment, points to the mesology of Sinophone studies.

Thus, the *Reader* features works that inscribe but are not confined to major narratives such as colonial and postcolonial adventures, despotic rulers, Cold War battles, and racial and religious confrontations. It also pays more attention to representations of a world enlivened by the fates of multiple ethnic, gendered identities, the aroma of spices, the heat and humidity of rivers and mountains, the monsoon, tropical fauna and flora, chanting from religious sites, melodies from Malay bazaars, Teochew and Fukienese food vendors . . .

As such, the *Reader* seeks to envision a lived and imaged sphere in which environmental and human agents have interacted with each other for thousands of years. The appearance of Chinese people is only one recent factor in the regional dynamics, and the "Sinophone question" has to be asked in relation to the xenophone other, which still remains a lacuna in the field. The discourse of *hua* versus *yi* is invoked only insofar as it casts a historical perspective, one that deconstructs the Sinocentric or Sinophobic stance based on contemporary geopolitics. Finally, if literature, the emblematic expression of *wen*, serves as the mode of our inquiry, it is meant to facilitate the geo-eco-poetics of hospitality: an exercise of dialogue on the fault line of exclusion and inclusion.

DAVID DER-WEI WANG is Edward C. Henderson Professor in Chinse Literature and Comparative Literature at Harvard University. His specialties are modern and contemporary Chinese and Sinophone literature, Late Qing fiction and drama, and comparative literary theory. His recent English publications include *A New Literary History of Modern China* (editor, 2017) and *Why Fiction Matters in Contemporary China* (2020). His most recent Chinese publication is *Nanyang duben: Wenxue, haiyang, daoyu* 南洋讀本：文學，海洋，島嶼 (A Nanyang Reader: Literature, Sea, and Islands, 2022), coedited with Ko Chia-Cian.

///////////////////////////////////

Notes

1 Wang, "Huayi zhibian," 13.
2 Ibid., 18.
3 Wang and Ko, *Nanyang duben*.
4 Shih, *Visuality and Identity*.
5 Ibid.
6 Shih, "Global Literature," "Theory, Asia and the Sinophone," and "The Concept of the Sinophone."
7 For a recent critique, see Shi, "Reconsidering Sinophone Studies."
8 See Wang, *Houyimin xiezuo*.
9 Wang, "Huayi zhibian," 13.
10 I was inspired by the discussion of the xenophone in Chow, *Native Speaker*, chap. 1.
11 Ge, *Zhaizi Zhongguo*.
12 Li, *Ming yimin qunti xintai*, 37.
13 Idema, Li, and Widmer, eds., *Trauma and Transcendence*.
14 See Yang, *Hechu shi Jiangnan*, chap. 6.
15 Wang, "Huayi zhibian."
16 "There is only one China" is a statement made by historian Gu Jiegang 顧頡剛 (1893–1980) on the eve of the Second Sino-Japanese War; China as a "homogeneous body of multiple ethnicities" is a phrase coined by sociologist Fei Xiaotong 費孝通 (1910–2005) in the late 1980s. See my discussion in "Huayi zhibian."
17 Kong, *Chunqiu zuozhuan zhengyi*, 326.
18 Miyazaki, *Gongqi shiding lunwenxuanji xiajuan*, 304.
19 Berque, "Offspring."
20 Yang, *Wuxing yuanlun*, chap. 6; Haraway, "Anthropocene."
21 Quoted in Berque, "Question of Space," 373.
22 Berque, "Mesology (風土論)."

23 Wu, *Chuancheng yu yanxu*.

24 Barthes, *Mythologies*.

25 "My condition—or my un-condition—is my relation to books. It is the very movement-towards-God [*l'a-Dieu*]." Levinas, *Beyond the Verse*, xv.

26 Schonfeld, "Languages of the Universal," 82.

27 Levinas, *Beyond the Verse*, xiv.

28 "This is the pattern of Heaven. It is by means of the enlightenment provided by pattern (i.e., culture) that curbs are set, and this is the pattern of man. One looks to the pattern of Heaven in order to examine the flux of the seasons, and one looks to the pattern of man in order to transform and bring the whole world to perfection." Lynn, trans., *Classic of Changes*, 274–75.

29 Tsu, *Sound and Script*, chap. 1.

References

Barthes, Roland. *Mythologies*, translated by Annette Lavers. New York: Farrar, Straus and Giroux, 1972.

Berque, Augustin. "Mesology (風土論) in the Light of Yamauchi Tokuryû's *Logos and lemma*." In *Philosophizing in Asia*, edited by Tsuyoshi Ishii and Wing-keung Lam, 9–25. Tokyo: University of Tokyo Center for Philosophy, 2013.

Berque, Augustin. "Offspring of Watsuji's Theory of Milieu (*fûdo*)." *GeoJournal* 60, no. 4 (2004): 389–96.

Berque, Augustin. "The Question of Space: From Heidegger to Watsuji." *Ecumene* 3, no. 4 (1996): 373–83.

Chow, Rey. *Not Like a Native Speaker: On Languaging as a Postcolonial Experience*. New York: Columbia University Press, 2014.

Ge Zhaoguang 葛兆光. *Zhaizi Zhongguo: Chongjian youguan Zhongguo de lishi lunshu* 宅茲中國：重建有關中國的歷史論述 (Here Resides China: Reconstructing Discourses about China). Taipei: Linking, 2011.

Haraway, Donna. "Anthropocene, Capitalocene, Chthulucene: Staying with the Trouble." *Environmental Humanities* 6, no. 1 (2015): 159–65.

Idema, Wilt, Wai-yee Li, and Ellen Widmer, eds. *Trauma and Transcendence in Early Qing Literature*. Cambridge, MA: Harvard East Asia Monograph series, 2006.

Kong Yinda 孔穎達. *Chunqiu zuozhuan zhengyi* 春秋左傳正義 [Annotations of *Chunqiu Zuozhuan*]. Taipei: Wunan chuban gongsi, 2001.

Levinas, Emmanuel. *Beyond the Verse: Talmudic Readings and Lectures*, translated by Gary D. Mole. London: Continuum, 2007.

Li Xuan 李瑄. *Ming yimin qunti xintai yu wenxue sixiang yanjiu* 明遺民群體心態與文學思想研究 [Studies on the Group Mentality and Literary Thought of the Ming Loyalists]. Chengdu: Bashu chubanshe, 2009.

Lynn, Richard, trans. *The Classic of Changes*. London: Routledge Curzon, 2002.

Miyazaki, Ichisada 宮崎市定. *Gongqi shiding lunwenxuanji (xiajuan)* 宮崎市定論文選集（下卷) [Essays by Ichisada Miyazaki, Vol. 2], translated and edited by the translation team of the Institute of History, Chinese Academy of Social Sciences. Beijing: Shangwu yinshuguan, 1965.

Schonfeld, Eli. "Languages of the Universal: Levinas's (Scandalous) Doctrine of Literature." In *Levinas and Literature: New Directions*, edited by Michael Fagenblat and Arthur Cools, 77–92. Berlin: De Gruyter, 2020. https://doi.org/10.1515/9783110668926-006.

Shi, Flair Donglai. "Reconsidering Sinophone Studies: The Chinese Cold War, Multiple Sinocentrisms, and Theoretical Generalization." *International Journal of Taiwan Studies* no. 4 (2021): 311–44.

Shih, Shu-mei. "The Concept of the Sinophone." *PMLA* 126, no. 3 (2011): 709–18.

Shih, Shu-mei. "Global Literature and the Technologies of Recognition." *PMLA* 119, no. 1 (2004): 16–30.

Shih, Shu-mei. "Theory, Asia and the Sinophone." *Postcolonial Studies* 13, no. 4 (2010): 465–84.

Shih, Shu-mei. *Visuality and Identity: Sinophone Articulations across the Pacific.* Berkeley: University of California Press, 2007.

Tsu, Jing. *Sound and Script in Chinese Diaspora.* Cambridge, MA: Harvard University Press, 2010.

Wang, David Der-wei 王德威. *Houyimin xiezuo: Shijian yu jiyi de zhengzhixue* 後遺民寫作：時間與記憶的政治學 [Postloyalist Writing: The Politics of Time and Memory]. Taipei: Ryefield, 2007.

Wang, David Der-wei 王德威. "Huayi zhibian: Huayu yuxiyanjiu de xinshijie" 華夷之變：華語語系研究的新視界 [Sinophone/Xenophone Changeability]. *Zhongguo xiandai wenxue* 中國現代文學 [Modern Chinese Literature] no. 34 (2018): 1–27.

Wang, David Der-wei 王德威, and Ko Chia-Cian 高嘉謙, eds. Nanyang duben: Wenxue, haiyang, daoyu 南洋讀本：文學，海洋，島嶼 [A Nanyang Reader: Literature, Sea, and Islands]. Taipei: Ryefield, 2022.

Watsuji Tetsurô 和辻哲郎. *Fengtu* 風土 [Milieus: A Study of Human Linkage], translated by Chen Liwei 陳力衛. Shanghai: Shangwu yinshuguan, 2018.

Wu Shixing 吳詩興. *Chuancheng yu yanxu: Fudezhengshen de chuanshuo yu xinyang yanjiu: yi Malaixiya huaren shehui weili* 傳承與延續：福德正神的傳說與信仰研究——以馬來西亞華人社會為例 [Heritage and Sustenance: A Study of the Legend and Worship of the Tutelary God]. Sibu, Malaysia: Tua Pek Kong Temple, 2014.

Yang Nianqun 楊念群. *Hechu shi Jiangnan: Qingchao zhengtongguan dequeli yushilin jingshende bianyi* 何處是江南：清朝正統觀的確立與士林精神的變異 [Where Is Jiangnan: The Establishment of Qing Orthodoxy and the Spiritual Transformation of the Intelligentsia]. Beijing: Sanlian shudian, 2010.

Yang Rubin 楊儒賓. *Wuxing yuanlun* 五行原論 [An Ontological Study of the Five Elements]. Taipei: Linking, 2018.

SHUANG SHEN

Popular Literature in the Inter-imperial Space of Hong Kong and Singapore/Malaya

ABSTRACT This article addresses the neglect toward popular literary networks with Hong Kong in the Cold War period by influential Mahua scholars. Aiming to make way for a more robust discourse of cultural politics in tandem with a regional conceptualization of Sinophone cultural production, the article proposes to understand popular forms such as romance fiction as arising from and coconstituting a regional Sinosphere that can only be understood, following Laura Doyle's recent study, as inter-imperial. Offering a reading of the Hong Kong writer Liu Yichang's romantic fiction and immigrant stories, I show how the stories signify a geopolitical reckoning with the Cold War patterning of the world. This perspective offers more ways for us to evaluate how the regional literary field intersected with the Cold War beyond the singular defense of its "literariness."

KEYWORDS Mahua, left, inter-imperiality, Liu Yichang, Cold War

First published in the *Story Paper* 小説報 in 1956 or 1957, the novella "Singapore Story" 星加坡故事 by renowned Hong Kong writer Liu Yichang 劉以鬯 has at its center two lines of pursuit in search of answers to a pair of mysteries: one political, the other romantic. The female protagonist, a beautiful singer named Bai Ling, is at the crux of these mysteries. Her instant attraction to—and subsequent flight from—the narrator and protagonist, Zhang Panming, a character roughly modeled on the author himself, sends him on a pursuit from Singapore to Kuala Lumpur and then back to Singapore, as the mystery of Bai Ling's past unravels for the reader. She is the product of her mother's extramarital affair and, as if she were fated to repeat her mother's story, her alluring appearance leads her into another woman's marriage. Regardless of how hard she tries—and even succeeds at one point—to escape from this past, the other mystery is exposed, which makes her run away again. It turns out that Bai Ling had a dishonorable relationship with a certain Hu Ah Shi, a sordid character who somehow gained a fortune during the Japanese occupation of Singapore and "escaped into the jungle" 逃入 '大芭' at the end of the Asia-Pacific War. Is this man a stand-in for the Communist guerrilla fighters against whom the British colonial government in Malaya waged a war from 1948 to 1962? We do not know for sure. But he behaves like a stereotypical terrorist, one just like how

PRISM: THEORY AND MODERN CHINESE LITERATURE • 19:2 • SEPTEMBER 2022
DOI 10.1215/25783491-9966657 • © 2022 LINGNAN UNIVERSITY

colonial propaganda depicted the Communists: he threatens to take Zhang Pan-ming's life if Bai Ling disobeys his order to immediately break off her engagement with Zhang. Bai Ling of course does not dare to disobey him, but she in turn is driven into a downward spiral and ultimately commits suicide.

The *Story Paper* was a tabloid published by the pro-Nationalist publishing house Rainbow Press 虹霓出版社 with funding from the United States Informa-tion Agency (USIA) in Hong Kong. The newspaper started publishing biweekly in June 1955 in Hong Kong, with circulation throughout Southeast Asia. USIA withdrew its support around 1961 citing financial considerations, which might have caused the newspaper to stop publishing soon after that. Taiwan scholar Wang Mei-hsiang 王梅香 informs us that the magazine published three kinds of stories: "1) stories that depict anti-Communist themes; 2) stories that com-bine anti-Communist messages with love stories; 3) popular love stories" 一是反共故事；二是反共與愛情結合的故事；三是通俗的愛情故事. Wang further explains that "to use the language of the USIA, the first two types are 'ideolog-ical stories,' while the third type are 'innocuous stories'" 以香港美新處的術語來說，前兩者是「意識型態故事」(ideological stories), 最後者則是「無害的故事」(innocuous stories).[1]

Whether our reading emphasizes the ideological content of "Singapore Story" or its love plot largely depends on which of the two mysteries we think is the pri-mary secret that the narrative seeks to resolve. Mystery, according to sociologist Luc Boltanski, is not just a narrative fabulation; rather, it has to do with a meta-physical and philosophical approach to reality. Boltanski believes that the power of the state manifests itself by ordering and monitoring reality. He states that "on one side, we have reality as it is actually experienced by individual actors in the diversity of everyday situations; on the other, we have reality as a whole, resting on a framework of formats, rules, procedures, knowledge and tests that purport to be generally applicable, a reality sustained by institutions that determine its shape," and that in the modern era, these institutions are integrated "under the authority of the state."[2] Mystery, which resides at the center of such genres as the detective fiction and the spy fiction, "originates in the possibility of calling into question the *reality* of reality."[3]

The narrator and protagonist, Zhang Panming, is not a detective, in that he does not consistently seek the truth behind Bai Ling's mysteries. But "the *reality* of reality" remains a valid question as we follow Bai Ling's movement and witness how the mysteries surrounding this character unravel. Is Bai Ling's indirect con-nection with the Communists in the jungle the main factor that gets her into an emotional dead end and leads to her suicide? Or is it a number of ancillary factors suggested along the way—Bai Ling's affair with a rubber plantation tycoon, the public defamation of her by the tycoon's wife, her alcoholism, or even Zhang Pan-ming's self-righteous chastisement of her—that contributed to the tragedy of her death? If the story was supposed to serve some propagandistic goal, for instance, the condemnation of the evils of Communism, the narrative trajectory constantly deflects from this objective, offering a variety of distractions along the way that make us ask: what exactly is the reality? Kenny Ng notes that the reader is never told the true identity of Hu Ah Shi: "Hu could well be a triple agent (working for the British, the Japanese and the communists), but his identity is not uncovered after the war, when he continues to fight for the communists in the jungle, plotting armed subversion against the British."[4] Indeed, without solving this mystery, the story nevertheless banks on people's anxiety about the warfare with Communists. When Bai Ling divulges all her secrets in a final letter to Zhang, she writes, "Without question, Hu Ah Shi, who has disappeared for many years, is one of those 'terrorists' in the jungle. You are a journalist. You would of course know all about the conduct of these 'thugs' in Singapore and Malaya. If Hu Ah Shi says he wants to do something, he would have a variety of ways to make it happen" 毫無疑問地，這失蹤多年的胡阿獅現在已經是森林裡的 '恐怖份子' 了。你是一個新聞記者，當然會知道 '暴徒' 在星馬一帶的種種，胡阿獅說要怎麼做，他會有很多辦法可以做到的。[5] Despite its use of the phrase "without question," this passage actually does not confirm that Hu Ah Shi is a Communist, but it addresses people's fear of Communists, which is circulated and fostered by mass media ("You are a journalist. You would of course know . . ."). The realness of reality remains unverified, although the sentiment is already real enough. Interestingly, this passage was deleted when the story was reissued in 2019. This editorial choice may or may not indicate that the Cold War is no longer relevant, but it does suggest that the sentiments are not real anymore.

What is the relevance of a story like this to Sinophone Malaya/Malaysia or Singapore literature? How do we discuss the politics of this specimen of Cold War culture? We could of course consider this story as a case study of cultural circulation in the shadows of the Cold War, as a few recent studies have already shown.[6] But literary historians have largely failed to account for a text like this, or the overall regional cultural infrastructures that it signifies. Popular literature, particularly the market-driven kind, has been a symptomatic lacuna in scholarly studies that testifies to the different social conditions that shape literary history writing in disparate Sinophone spheres. Even as modern literary histories from Hong Kong and Singapore/Malaysia have pushed back against a prioritization of the May Fourth Movement, the alternative discourses are differentially treated in these two localities, particularly where it pertains to the status of popular literature. Hong Kong literary histories written after the 1980s have adopted a receptive attitude toward mass market popular literature, but a similar tendency cannot be found in current discussions of Sinophone Singapore and/or Malaysia literary histories.

This article will utilize popular literature as a wedge to pry open some foundational critical discourses that inform existing locality-focused literary histories. This new line of inquiry aims to make way for a more robust discourse of cultural politics in tandem with a regional conceptualization of Sinophone cultural production. Popular forms such as romance fiction, I argue, arise from and coconstitute a regional Sinosphere that can only be understood, following Laura Doyle's recent study, as inter-imperial. In the first half of this article, I discuss three ways that this concept of inter-imperiality can offer a new understanding of regional political dynamics in the shadow of the Cold War, which in turn informs the aesthetic condition of popular literature and the Hong Kong–Southeast Asia connection facilitated by the travels of writers and the circulation of literary works. In the second part, I discuss how the exemplary writer Liu Yichang reflected on and engaged with inter-imperial positionality in his romantic fictions.

Cold War Inter-imperial Politics and Cultural Infrastructure

Writing popular literature back into literary history is not just a question of genre, since its omission reveals a particular way of conceptualizing cultural politics. Eminent Singapore literary historian Fang Xiu 方修 acknowledged in 1959 that popular literature existed in the public culture of Singapore and Malaya, and he mentioned a Hong Kong detective fiction magazine called the *Blue Cover Detective Magazine* 藍皮書 in that year's annual review of the state of Mahua 馬華 (Malayan Chinese) literature and arts. For him, this is an example of the unhealthy "yellow culture" against which the Singaporean state had launched a successful campaign. Fang Xiu's description of this example of yellow culture is rather specific:

> [In 1959], not only have writings that promote promiscuity or depict violence and superstition disappeared after various tabloid publications were shut down, the self-congratulatory Hong Kong stories that used to be published in major newspapers have also become scarcer. This type of urban legend used to come out once a day. Sometimes when the newspapers encounter slow days, publishers would repackage the stories from the *Blue Cover Detective Magazine*. The content is simply about a man and a woman, meeting inadvertently at the beach, in a park, or on a bus, and then a love affair ensues miraculously. With an appropriate introduction from the editor, these will all be a *good story*.

> 不但那些誨淫誨盜，偵探打鬥，鬼神迷信的文字，隨着若干小報的被禁止出版，失去了孳息蔓延的窩窟，就是一些在大報上自鳴得意的港派傳奇，也見機斂跡了。這類傳奇，從去年底起，就每日出品一篇，遇到 '難產' 的時候，便把 '藍皮書' 裏面的東西拿來改頭換面，內容無非是一男一女，在海濱，公園，或車上邂逅，於是產生了 '奇異的愛情' 。據編者鄭重介紹，這些都是 "good story" 呢。[7]

As Fang Xiu was a left-leaning literary critic, his dismissal of popular literature is not surprising but troubling. Many of the same arguments had already emerged before the onset of the Asia-Pacific War, in the context of a discussion of the popularization of Nanyang literature. Influenced by the May Fourth Movement, most writers who participated in this discussion held that "popularization is not equivalent to vulgarization" 通俗化绝不是庸俗化,[8] and they claimed that "to insist on the pleasure of popular literature does not mean turning ourselves into the likes of Zhang Henshui or Buxiaosheng, those who merely cater to lower tastes" 至於 '通俗文學' 讀物的有趣,我們不是要像張恨水和不肖生的一類的作家,他們是低級趣味的作家.[9]

Popular literature's occlusion from literary historiography, however, does not line up neatly with existing political divisions. The "nonleft" or "right" circles of literary critics also seemed to have a hard time accepting the proliferation of popular literature of the 1950s and 1960s. With respect to the Hong Kong–Singapore/Malaya connection, the literary publications that have so far received the most attention are the journal *Chao Foon* 蕉風, which championed *chun wenxue* 純文學 (pure literature), and *Student Weekly* 學生週報, both of which were published by the Union Press 友聯出版社 and were backed by funding from the Asia Foundation. Scholars have frequently discussed the political orientation and literary quality of *Chao Foon*, but they have not really touched the issue of the division between *chun wenxue* and *su wenxue* 俗文學 (popular literature).[10] I propose that we address the occlusion of popular literature by rethinking the literary region informed by the discussions of inter-imperiality pertaining to the Cold War.

Laura Doyle explores the concept of inter-imperiality by drawing on recent world history scholarship about empires (particularly earlier and non-Western ones) and the phenomenological discourses of existential relationality.[11] As Doyle explains: "Despite the familiar rhetoric of rise and fall, world empires with their various projects of modernization have not existed simply sequentially. They have overlapped with each other, battled each other, and borrowed from each other, forming each other through processes of transculturation."[12] Although Doyle applies the term *inter-imperiality* to a variety of historical situations, I am specifically interested in examining the mid-twentieth-century Sinophone spheres from this perspective. As I see it, Doyle's discussion helps deepen our understanding of the Cold War and the cultural dynamics on both interregional and intraregional scales, in three ways.

First, Doyle's perception of vying empires' power dynamics is most explicitly manifested in terms of their competing "wish to manage and 'conquer' the volatile terrain of existential relationality," and not just their "desire for profit."[13] This observation can help us understand the position of Chinese in Hong Kong and Southeast Asia within a field of geopolitical relationality. Second, the term *inter-imperiality* describes the relationship not only between contemporaneous empires but also between empires from different periods. The sedimented history of earlier empires, their alliances or competition with other empires, can be accessed by examining their traces left in human memory or the materiality of technological or cultural forms. The so-called shatter zones—"strategic inter-imperial zones, again and again vied over for their resources and their geographic location"—provide a particularly rich reserve of these memories and cultural forms.[14] Third, Doyle suggests that the concept "beckons critics to study the ways that literatures have continually reshaped the geopolitical economies that catalyzed their creation."[15] At the same time, she offers a renewed understanding of geopolitics, moving it away from a domain solely reserved for national or state actors, and instead acknowledging individual agency both in terms of one's ability to recognize the entangled power relations in which he or she is situated, and the everyday struggles that prevent one from becoming a mere pawn of superpower struggles or interstate politics. According to Doyle, the inter-imperial condition is "a fraught position, lived all at once in the neighborhood, at the imperial court, on the road, in the body, and amid the invasive stream of political events and news."[16] The rootedness of inter-imperiality in a philosophy of existential relationality leads to an understanding of agency "not as an aspect of autonomy, nor as primarily individual or unidirectional, but rather as dialectical: always already arising interdependently."[17] This relational approach to agency, I suggest, can greatly enrich and add nuance to our understanding of Cold War cultural politics. In the remainder of the article, I explore the implications of this concept for an exploration of Sinophone cultural production in Hong Kong and Southeast Asia during the Cold War.

Viewing the world according to a set of rigid binary oppositions, which is how we conventionally perceive the Cold War, cannot capture the palimpsest of relationality in the social world. The political power play during this period consists of not just the negotiation of and collaboration between old and new empires, or top-down implementation of imperial infrastructures at a regional scale. There were also the lateral networks that were created by and also resisted imperial distribution of power. Many historians have studied the political structures of Hong Kong, Singapore, and Malaya in the Cold War, the configurations of which go beyond immediate localities. I draw on this existent scholarship to chart a regional political force field impacting Sinophone cultural production.

For instance, historian Prasenjit Duara has argued that the Cold War witnessed a new configuration of imperialism, one that "no longer emphasized conquest on the basis of innate differences among peoples and their inevitable destinies of superiority and exploitation" but was instead "development oriented." The imperialist factor lay in the imposition of designs for enlightenment upon emergent nations by an enormously superior national power backed by military force.[18]

While the US role in the Cold War fits this description of new imperialism, the British empire as an older form of imperialism certainly did not fade out in places like Hong Kong and Singapore/Malaya. Historical studies by Chi-kwan Mark, Priscilla Roberts, and Tracy Steele provide numerous examples showing how the colonial government in Hong Kong sought US assistance in some matters while also working to undermine its influence in others, thereby performing what Roberts calls an "acrobatics of balancing" in order to sustain British control of the city.[19] But the inter-imperial position of Hong Kong during the Cold War did not pertain just to Anglo-American interactions, which both provoked and reacted to the colonial city's relationship with mainland China and Taiwan at given moments of history. The fact that Hong Kong's geographical position and infrastructure allowed it to play important roles in wars with other Asian nations—it functioned as a military base for British soldiers who fought in the Korean War and provided the US with a much-needed location for R&R and acquiring vital war supplies during the Vietnam War—suggests that regional relationality was also established due to this colonial city's embeddedness in multiple imperial circuits.[20]

That the "overseas Chinese" were viewed by new and old empires as the political fulcrum during the Cold War is amply demonstrated in Grace Chou's study of the founding of the Chinese University of Hong Kong. Chou details the complex process of how New Confucianist scholars both conciliated and resisted the anti-Communist political agenda of the US and the colonialist mentality of the British in their debates about the university's goals, medium of instruction, and social standing.[21] Chou tells a story of the coformation of Chineseness defined from the perspective of New Confucianism within Cold War political structures, which in turn made the dualism of colonialism versus Chineseness untenable. Chou's history charts a regional scope beyond Hong Kong by showing that colonial officers frequently cross-referenced between different localities in the map of the British empire, specifically Singapore and Hong Kong, in order to assess the political impact of Chinese postsecondary institutions.

For the Southeast Asian nation-states caught in the fervor of decolonization, the keyword was "independence." Yet Christopher Goscha and Christian F. Ostermann have argued that the histories of decolonization and the Cold War are connected in myriad and complex ways, so that attaining independence does not mean we can overlook the regional and global power structures at play.[22] Joseph M. Fernando's description of how the newly independent government led by Tunku Abdul Rahman pushed back against British and American pleas to join the Southeast Asia Treaty Organization, a Cold War alliance, demonstrates that decolonization translates not so readily into autonomy, but more immediately to "acrobatics"—the juggling of power and play with semantics in order to stay in a neutralist position that avoids "being drawn directly into the extended Cold War proxy confrontations in Southeast Asia."[23] Fernando's comment that

"Malaya's campaign for independence did not take place in a vacuum"[24] echoes Doyle's observation that it is precisely the desire to "manage and 'conquer' the volatile terrain of existential relationality" that most clearly reflected the inter-imperial power dynamics of this period. "Relationality" here pertains to Malaya/Malaysia's relationship not just with the major players in the Cold War (i.e., the US, the Soviet Union, and China), but also with fellow new states in Southeast Asia, specifically Indonesia and the Philippines. As the above discussion shows, viewing the Cold War from the perspective of inter-imperiality allows us to chart the multiply vectored relationality across hierarchies of power.

The ethnic Chinese sat uneasily across different lines of relationality in the interregnum period between World War II and the 1960s. My current book project, which examines an American-backed cultural organization, the Union Press (UP), shows that the United States was eager to tilt the political orientation of the "overseas Chinese" (a term that inadequately accounts for the heterogeneity of the Chinese in Southeast Asia but was widely used during the Cold War) in a specific direction by intervening in cultural production. From the perspective of the Asia Foundation, which provided funding for the UP, Hong Kong had an advantageous position when it came to cultural production and circulation due to the historical trade networks with Southeast Asia and the influx of cultural workers from China after 1949. At the same time, the Asia Foundation was concerned that the movement of Chinese cultural workers and products from Hong Kong to Southeast Asia did not pose a threat to the sovereign boundaries of the Southeast Asian nation-states.

I cite below a series of exchanges in the Asia Foundation archives to show that the relationality of the UP's diasporic leaders to their motherland and to Singapore/Malaya were factored into a consideration of winning Chinese students over from Red China, a political exigency that made this Chinese-language organization valuable in the first place. The meaning of diaspora was a political topic debated and settled in a geopolitical field, never a purely cultural issue pertaining to "ancestral ties" or individual choice. In October 1958 the Asia Foundation invited Richard J. Coughlin, a sociologist whose research focused on Chinese communities in Thailand, to evaluate the UP's performance in Singapore/Malaya and Bangkok. Coughlin criticized the leaders of the UP for not doing enough to promote local talent, saying, "I think local leadership should be identified and promoted, and feel that the UP has been derelict in not doing so long ago." He observed that "the present Hong Kong people . . . seem intent . . . to run the show in Southeast Asia ad infinitum," although he "seriously doubt[ed]" whether they eventually wanted to settle down in Southeast Asia or Hong Kong.[25] He also cited their current leadership's reluctance to learn local languages, noting that "many of the present UP leaders have lived there for several years, without making an effort to learn even bazaar Malay, perhaps one of the easiest languages in the world." Responding to this criticism, one of the UP's founding directors, William Hsu, "agreed . . . that the present directors in Singapore, Malaya, and Bangkok should probably learn the local languages, but with qualification. Some . . . are not adept at learning languages. Moreover, the UP's work in Singapore and Malaya is almost entirely with Chinese, and here a knowledge of Mandarin is sufficient usually." [26]

After this report was sent to the foundation's headquarters in San Francisco, John Sullivan, the director of programs, considered point by point the criticisms Coughlin leveled against the UP before concluding that "when looked at from the light that the Union Press is a Chinese organization working with Chinese students in Malaya/Singapore, it would appear that its programming is proceeding in the right direction." Sullivan clarified that he reached this assessment by reminding himself and his colleagues in the Asia Foundation of the political objectives of a cultural organization such as the UP. As the memo states, under the "Malaya/Singapore Level III objectives under the heading of Students (Chinese)," to which Sullivan drew the reader's attention, "the danger of orientation to the communist motherland is sharpened by the dearth of available and useful sources of information in Chinese that are not tinted with pro-Peking attitudes."[27]

This series of exchanges underscores the significance of a number of entangled cultural infrastructures—the Chinese language in written and oral forms being one of them, another being UP's circulatory network between Hong Kong and Southeast Asia—that provided a foundation for political regionalism in the Cold War. William Hsu's attempt to remind the Asia Foundation that written Chinese could facilitate a form of communication between the editor and the reader differing from spoken Chinese—a reminder that fell on deaf ears—is a good example of the multiple and proliferating forms of relationality that people and culture on the move often step into. In conventional studies of the Cold War and Chinese communities outside the People's Republic of China, we tend to evoke binary oppositions of left versus right, sojourn versus settlement, hegemony versus resistance, and modernism versus realism. The concept of inter-imperiality, by juxtaposing cultural infrastructures with empires, can render more dynamic interpretations than these terms of binarism. This concept also opens up a discussion of less examined trajectories of movement and more subtle forms of connectivity (such as the connection of Hong Kong and Singapore/Malaysia or Southeast Asia as a whole), not just those that run with or against the path of Cold War. It implicitly addresses the question of periodization, a key issue of debate in Cold War studies, by attending to the accrued histories of earlier imperialisms, particularly the earlier war wrought by the Japanese empire, which configured Chinese imaginaries of the Cold War.

Below, I will suggest that popular literature—a cultural field that scholars such as Sai-shing Yung and Christopher Rea have convincingly shown to fit uneasily within models of national or local literature—proves to be another fertile ground to observe the negotiation of Sinophone literature with its inter-imperial positionality.[28]

Liu Yichang's Romantic Fiction

During a five-year period between 1952 and 1957—when Liu Yichang, a writer who emigrated to Hong Kong from Shanghai in the late 1940s, was working as a newspaper editor in Singapore and Malaya—he published between three and ten stories per month in *Nanyang Siang Pau* 南洋商报, a leading Chinese-language newspaper in the region, using the pen name Ge Li Ge 葛里哥. These stories are indeed the type of "good story" and romantic fantasy that Fang Xiu described in the passage cited above. Around the same time, Liu also contributed stories to the USIA-sponsored Hong Kong popular literature magazine *The Story Paper*. Other contributors included writers such as Ma Lang 馬朗, Li Weiling 李維陵, Wan Fang 萬方, and Huang Sicheng 黃思騁, who, along with Liu Yichang, were also key figures in an early phase of Hong Kong literary modernism.[29] The stronghold for this modernist movement was a magazine called *Wenyi xinchao* 文藝新潮 (Literary New Wave), supported by Law Bun's 羅斌 enterprise, Universal Publishing House 環球出版社. When Fang Xiu, in his annual review, mentioned the *Blue Cover Detective Magazine*, a pulp fiction magazine also published by Law Bun, he probably did not realize that he had engaged an important literary network that disobeyed the rigid division between highbrow "pure literature" and middle- or lowbrow popular literature, and that this network was connected to both political forces and commercial interests in an intricate manner.

Deciphering this network's relationality to Cold War politics on the one hand and capitalistic cultural industry on the other would have fit well with the political agendas of the left in Singapore and Malaya in the late 1950s and 1960s, but leftist critics at that time did not consider fully the complexity of this transnational network. As shown in their critique of the American-sponsored magazine *Chao Foon* in 1960, the left tried to fit a multifaceted and fluid cultural field into a binary opposition between a doctrine of art for art's sake (deemed as bourgeois) and an ideology of socialist realism (deemed as proletarian). As a result, it became impossible for leftist critics to reflect on their own positionality in an inter-imperial force field. It is no surprise that someone like Liu Yichang, who was mostly operating under the radar as far as any strict definition of serious literature or any explicit political propaganda is concerned, would be considered insignificant by critics on the left.

Wang Mei-hsiang quoted an authorization form filed for Liu Yichang's publication of "Singapore Story" in the *Story Paper*, in which it is stated that "the story is written in response to the suggestion of USIS Singapore that there be more stories with Malayan Chinese settings and the anti-communist theme treated in a subtle manner to avoid being branded as 'sheer propaganda.'"[30] The fact that the USIA encouraged writers to make the setting, characters, or certain aspects of the plot closely related to Southeast Asia reflected American empire's "wish to manage and 'conquer' the volatile terrain of existential relationality," in the words of Laura Doyle. The diasporic relationality of the Chinese vis-à-vis their Communist homeland and their adopted homes in the so-called free world was subject to reconfiguration by the US as the new imperial power with complex interactions with the newly decolonized states. The dominant discourse of regionalism defined by the USIA is not overly concerned with how much individual writers knew about Southeast Asia or even whether they had any experience living there. Yet Liu Yichang, compared to the other Hong Kong contributors to the *Story Paper*, was more keenly interested in writing about migrant laborers and sojourning intellectuals, as we can see from his short fictional pieces published in *Nanyang Siang Pau* in 1958–59.

If we cross-reference between the romantic fiction Liu wrote for the *Story Paper* and the fiction he published in the local newspaper *Nanyang Siang Pau* around the same time, we find they have a similar underlying pattern that juxtaposes subjects of migration, exile, and diaspora against Confucian moralism. The same narrative form shows how Liu Yichang translated his own experience of sojourning between different localities: Singapore, Malaya, and Hong Kong.

Compared to the *Story Paper* pieces, the stories published in *Nanyang Siang Pau* have few literary embellishments. They seem to have been derived from formulaic accounts of a typical immigrant experience, and it is not hard to imagine the author having overheard the stories from casual conversations at tea houses or having read about them in some tabloid publications. For instance, "Guofan mousheng ji" 過番謀生記 (An Account of Making a Living in a Foreign Land) depicts immigrant laborer Ah Xiang's lament over the fate of his abandoned wife left behind in a home village in China.[31] "Niucheshui zhi chen" 牛車水之晨 (Morning in Kreta Ayer) and several other stories focus on men addicted to gambling or who have been arrested for committing petty crimes. The stories typically convey the men's palpable sense of repentance and regret when it is expressed to a female member of the family, such as a mother or daughter. Another recurring theme in Liu's stories involves a lonely man's chance encounter with a mysterious and seductive woman in an exotic modern city. In most of these stories, the female characters recount heart-wrenching stories about having been driven into prostitution by poverty or by their abusive husbands.

Most of these stories contain a surprising twist or an added layer of complexity, and these elements can grab the reader's attention and alleviate their boredom with the formulaic elements. For instance, in "Huangjia shan yanyu" 皇家山艳遇 (An Amorous Encounter at Fort Canning), a country boy coming to Singapore for the first time meets an attractive woman and follows her into a lavish residence. Just as their relationship is about to pick up speed, he discovers that she has supernatural power, and the teardrops she has left on his shirt turn out to be blood. In "Relan wusha zhi ye" 惹兰勿刹之夜 (A Night at Jalan Besar), a man goes in search of a prostitute who turns out to be a former schoolmate and lover. While we expect this to be a standard sentimental tale about a woman's downfall, the ending reveals that the story actually depicts a scheme to crush prostitution, and the man, who is a police chief working undercover, is in a double bind about where to direct his sympathies and sense of justice. Similarly, "Guofan mousheng ji" has a conventional plot about a hardworking immigrant who picks a Malay woman for his wife after having made a fortune, but the end of the story becomes more complex, with a depiction of the delusional psychological state of the wife left behind.

If we follow John Cawelti's argument that formulas "can speed up the communication between writer and reader . . . because formulas work by reflecting values and assumptions shared by a community of readers within a culture,"[32] then it is not difficult to understand why Liu's immigrant narratives are often moral tales revolving around the virtues of being a loyal husband, a responsible father, and a righteous man. Liu Yichang did not fundamentally change the formula of writings about immigrant experience. Surprising turns such as those discussed above might be interpreted as an indication of the flair of an ingenious writer who simply wants to grab his reader's attention while not deviating too far from formulaic storylines. However, it is also possible to consider Liu's knack for innovation as more than narrative hooks to engage the reader but rather as a sign of negotiation on the level of social forms and social sanctions in migrants' lives. Scholars Theo D'haen, Rainer Grübel, and Helmut Lethen argue that "every court case involving a literary work shows time and again that it is a very thin line indeed between literary conventions and social norms, and that this proves a continuous source of contention."[33] In other words, even though we cannot directly equate literary form, such as genre, with social form, the two are not entirely unconnected, though it is often indeterminate where they will intersect or overlap with each other.

When rewriting these formulatic immigrant tales into the more complexly woven stories in the *Story Paper*, the sliding scale between convention and innovation tilts toward the end of innovation.[34] And innovation is usually manifested in Liu's depiction of female characters who are set up against Confucian moral conventions. In these stories, Liu provides an abundant supply of female characters cast in the stereotypical roles of prostitute, taxi dancer, escort lady, and nightclub singer, following the generic pattern of popular romantic fiction of the 1950s and 1960s. Instead of expelling these women from the moral center and showing how they have been corrupted by capitalism and have succumbed to their own vanity, Liu gives them greater latitude by endowing them with more spatial mobility, as if suggesting that despite their inability in the end to counter Confucian expectations that they behave like a proper woman and a dutiful wife, they can at least move away or step aside, even if temporarily. For instance, the female protagonist of "Lanse xingqiliu" 藍色星期六 (Blue Saturday) travels between Vietnam, Malaya, Singapore, and Hong Kong after leaving mainland China. Here and elsewhere, Liu flirts with convention—including Confucian moralism—just as his stories both reproduce and renew the aesthetic convention of the romantic fiction genre. The surprising twists in his storylines are therefore not simply an indication of a talented author; rather, they reveal the writer's reading of the patterns in the cultural field in which he was embedded.

Commentators have noted that Liu was fond of repetition. Lim Fong Wei 林方偉, for example, points out that two *Story Paper* stories, "Yeshu xia zhi yu" 椰樹下之慾 (Desire under a Coconut Tree) and "Singapore Story," are actually rewritings of stories previously published in *Nanyang Siang Pau*.[35] Ackbar Abbas, in his analysis of Wong Kar-wai's movie 王家衛 *Huayang nianhua* 花樣年華 (In the Mood for Love)—which is loosely based on one of Liu's novellas from the early 1970s—also argues that repetition is what accounts for both how the protagonists' affair began and how it ended. "Every repetition has a certain 'originality' to it," Abbas asserts.[36] As I read it, originality can be understood as a driver for innovation, sometimes manifested as a compulsion. "Blue Saturday," an "innocuous story" written for the *Story Paper*, is all about a compulsive desire that eventually leads the narrator, who is a writer, into a tragic pattern of repetition. The narrative begins on a spooky note, describing the narrator's chance encounter at a racecourse with our heroine, Xia Meixian. He soon finds out, after visiting Meixian's home, that the courtyard has a tombstone with her name inscribed on it. Is Meixian, whom the narrator has just met, a dead woman? Is she a revenant? Liu resists closing off the story with a conventional frame of a ghost story, and instead he reveals that the narrator visits the racecourse again four years later, with the ostensible aim of fleshing out a short story he is crafting. The story happens to be inspired by his discovery of the tombstone four years earlier. Not surprisingly, he bumps into Meixian again and recognizes her instantly because she is wearing the same blue dress with a flower pinned to it, just like four years earlier. What a lasting impression Meixian must have made on the narrator—he remembers her appearance to the last detail! The story presents a series of uncanny repetitions, allowing disparate occurrences to double and mirror each other. At the same time, what appears at first to be an innovative twist turns out to be rather conventional. For instance, we finally find out that Meixian has deliberately sought the narrator out from the beginning because he bears a strong physical resemblance to her dead husband. She intends to instrumentalize this encounter so that she may then relive her past, in order to repent the earlier wanton behavior that she believes caused her husband's death. In the end, however, by making the narrator play the role of her former husband, Meixian indirectly causes his child to die and his marriage to fall apart, in effect turning the man's life into a mirror image of her own.

The story turns the Confucian expectation for a woman to be proper and duty-bound upside down because Meixian's desire to be good (by remedying the damage she has wrought) is what turns her into a literal femme fatale. The story is in essence a metaphor about the diaspora, not for the least because there is an abundant amount of movement depicted in this story. Meixian moves about restlessly and compulsively—we are told that after leaving China for Hong Kong, she takes off again for Saigon—as if trying to escape from the rationality and inevitability of social conventions.

However, morality is not left far behind, and instead it haunts the footloose character, turning her into someone like a racehorse on a predestined course.

"Blue Saturday" obviously contains no reference to any political theme. A USIA memo in August 1956 provides an explanation why the agency would be interested in funding the publication of a story like this. Seeking approval for publishing four titles of *Story Paper* from USIA Washington, the Hong Kong office stated, "All these four are innocuous stories to be interjected into the *Story Paper* series at appropriate intervals to avoid having this popular publication being recognized as a USIS [USIA] vehicle for propaganda purposes."[37] What justifies our reading "Blue Saturday" as in some way connected to "Singapore Story"? I find in both stories a similar tension between innovation, which is associated with movement, and some underlying patterns charted by forces beyond the individual's control. This tension is manifested at the end of "Singapore Story," when the narrator laments: "When will it be possible for me to freely stroll into the forests of Malaya for a break?" 幾時才可以自由地走入馬來亞的森林里去散步[38] When the story was republished in the collection *Lanse xingqiliu* 藍色星期六 (Blue Saturday, 2019), however, the last sentence was changed into a lover's lament: "Wider than heaven and the earth, this endless feeling of regret is boundless" 天長地久有時盡，此恨綿綿，無盡期.[39] Could the deliberate avoidance of a hot spot in the Cold War—the Malayan jungles—be interpreted as a negotiation between abiding by conventions (including the generic conventions of romantic thrillers) and responding explicitly to the political agenda defined by the USIA for the *Story Paper*? I suggest that the author was keenly aware of the geopolitical sphere that structured the production of popular literature during the Cold War. Even an "innocuous story" cannot transcend the existential relationality configured by Cold War forces. Rather, the story could show the inter-imperial positionality of mainland émigrés in the 1950s and 1960s, revealing their careful navigation through a moral and political minefield.

Conclusion

To conclude, we may return to the question of how to discuss the politics of this specimen of Cold War culture. Wang Mei-Hsiang analyzed the different strategies employed by the Chinese authors recorded in the USIA archives to fit their stories into the political aims of the US government. Some of the writers set their stories against the backdrop of contemporary events—such as Li Weiling's story "The Red Lantern," which uses the Hungarian Revolution of 1956 as a backdrop—and developed explicitly counter-Communist themes based on the depictions of these events. Other writers, meanwhile, developed love stories and political discussions as separate but parallel threads; and in some works, the romantic plotlines contain hidden political narrative, but others do not address politics at all.[40] Similarly, Kenny Ng revealed that the USIA was sensitive to the risk of the *Story Paper* sounding too politicized and instead preferred "a balanced output in which 'three out of four stories use anti-communist themes. The fourth is innocuous,' while the writing should be maintained at 'popular low level.'"[41] Despite this diversity of subject matter, both Wang and Ng suggest that it is the content of a story that performs its political work. What I have proposed above is a broader structural interpretation of Cold War cultural politics. I suggest that we read popular literature in relation to an inter-imperial forcefield, in which the ethnic Chinese were deemed to be a moving piece that nonetheless had a significant impact on the overall political configuration of the Cold War in Asia. I detect in Liu's stories, whether or not they contain direct allusions to Communism, a similar pattern that sets the diasporic subject's compulsion for mobility against the dead weight of routine, to which characters repeatedly return. Singapore, Malaya, and Southeast Asia offer an exotic background—a new frontier of sorts—that forms a necessary ingredient for a chronotope illustrating this tension. I propose that Liu's engagement with literary patterns mirrors the well-patterned world in which existential relationality is managed by major Cold War political forces. This mirroring suggests to me Liu's cognizance of the political conditions in which he was embedded and signifies a geopolitical reckoning with the real world at large, even when Liu's work failed to fulfill the USIA's propagandistic agenda. This perspective gives us more room to incorporate those hitherto neglected cultural productions into the histories of Sinophone Singaporean and Malayan literature. It offers more ways for us to evaluate how the regional literary field intersected with the Cold War beyond the singular defense of its "literariness." Liu Yichang's case demonstrates that being embedded in a political force field and offering a pleasurable reading experience certainly do not have to contradict each other. Recognizing the connection between literary ecology and the global sociopolitical condition would allow us to rethink certain literary movements in both Hong Kong and Sinophone Southeast Asian literatures, such as modernism and its mythologized opposition to realism.

SHUANG SHEN is associate professor of comparative literature and Asian studies at Penn State University. She is the author of *Cosmopolitan Publics: Anglophone Print Culture in Semicolonial Shanghai* (2009) and coeditor of a special issue of *Social Text* on "China and the Human" (2011–2012) and a special issue of *Verge* on "Asian Urbanisms" (2015). She has published articles and essays in *Comparative Literature*, *MLQ*, *Modern China*, *MCLC*, *PMLA*, *Xinmin Weekly* (in Chinese), and *Wanxiang* (in Chinese). She is currently working on a book project that studies trans-Pacific circulation of Sinophone literature during the Cold War.

////////////////////////////////

Notes

1   Wang, "Mei yuan wenyi tizhi xia," 22.
2   Boltanski, *Mysteries and Conspiracies*, 16.
3   Ibid., 18.

4   Ng, "Soft-Boiled, Anti-Communist Romance," 104.

5   Liu, "Xinjiapo gushi," 12.

6   Scholarship that focuses on Hong Kong–Singapore connections in the 1950s and 1960s, such as the work of Lanjun Xu and Grace Mak, is mainly historical and privileges visual culture. More conceptualization of this connection, particularly where it pertains to literature and literary history, is necessary.

7   Fang, "Yijiuwujiu nian," 122.

8   Shi Jun, "Nanyang de tongsu wenyi," 108.

9   Nan Ao, "Zhanshi tongsu wenxue," 94–95.

10   See Lim, *Chao Foon*, 43–69, for a survey of contemporary reception of the *Chao Foon* magazine.

11   See Doyle, "Toward a Philosophy," "Inter-imperiality," "Modernist Studies," and *Inter-imperiality.*

12   Doyle, "Modernist Studies," 672.

13   Doyle, *Inter-imperiality*, location 186 of 10464, Kindle Book.

14   Doyle, "Inter-imperiality," 163.

15   Doyle, *Inter-imperiality*, location 1586 of 10464, Kindle Book.

16   Ibid., location 184 of 10464.

17   Ibid., location 161 of 10464.

18   Duara, "The Cold War," 90.

19   Roberts, "Cold War Hong Kong," 13.

20   Ibid., 26.

21   Chou, *Confucianism*, chapters 2 and 3.

22   See Goscha and Ostermann, *Connecting Histories.*

23   Fernando, "Cold War," 75.

24   Ibid., 68.

25   Although many leaders of the Union Press were sent from the organization's Hong Kong headquarters, they were originally from China or Taiwan, not Hong Kong.

26   Dick Coughlin's evaluation of the Union Press, dated October 1, 1958, is attached to Pat Judge's memo to the president of the Asia Foundation, dated October 9, 1958. Box P-135, File: MEDIA Publishers Union Press General I.—1959, Malaya/Singapore, Program. Hoover Institution.

27   Sullivan's response to Judge appears in a memo dated October 24, 1958. Box P-135, File: MEDIA Publishers Union Press General I.—1959, Malaya/Singapore, Program. Hoover Institution

28   Yung and Rea, "One Chicken."

29   Wang, "Literary Field."

30   Ibid., 32.

31   For Liu's stories published in *Nanyang Siang Pau*, I refer to a recently edited volume *Redai fengyu* 熱帶風雨 [Tropical Storms].

32   Cawelti, "Formulas and Genre Reconsidered Once Again," 134.

33   D'haen, Grübel, and Lethen, *Convention and Innovation*, xvi.

34   Here I am referencing Calwelti's argument that "there are formulaic aspects to almost any sort of literature, just as there are probably aspects of artistry or creativity in the most tired of standardized romances or mystery stories." See Cawelti, "Formulas and Genre Reconsidered," 131.

35   Lim Fong Wei, "Chongfu de shuxie."

36   Abbas, "Wong Kar-wai's Cinema," 125.

37 Memo from USIS HK to Washington, dated August 14, 1956. National Archives, College Park, MD. RG0306, Entry 61, Box #2, Series: East Asia and Pacific Country Files, 1948–1960. Folder: Hong Kong, Hong Kong, July–December 10, 1956.

38 Liu, "Xinjiapo gushi," 12.

39 Liu, *Blue Saturday*, 106.

40 Wang, "Literary Field," 22–23.

41 Ng, "Soft-Boiled, Anti-Communist Romance," 96.

References

Abbas, Ackbar. "Wong Kar-wai's Cinema of Repetition." In *A Companion to Wong Kar-wai*, edited by Martha P. Nochimson, 115–34. Malden, MA: Wiley Blackwell, 2009.

Boltanski, Luc. *Mysteries and Conspiracies: Detective Stories, Spy Novels and the Making of Modern Societies*, translated by Catherine Porter. Malden, MA: Polity, 2014.

Cawelti, John. "Formulas and Genre Reconsidered Once Again," in *Mystery, Violence, and Popular Culture*, 130–40. Madison: University of Wisconsin Press, 2004.

Chou, Grace Ai-Ling. *Confucianism, Colonialism and the Cold War: Chinese Cultural Education at Hong Kong's New Asia College, 1949–1963*. Leiden: Brill, 2011.

D'haen, Theo, Rainer Grübel, and Helmut Lethen, eds. *Convention and Innovation in Literature*. Philadelphia: Benjamins, 1989.

Doyle, Laura. "Inter-imperiality: Dialectics in a Postcolonial World History." *Interventions*. 16, no. 2 (2014): 159–96.

Doyle, Laura. *Inter-imperiality: Vying Empires, Gendered Labor, and the Literary Arts of Alliance*. Durham, NC: Duke University Press, 2020, Kindle for Macbook.

Doyle, Laura. "Modernist Studies and Inter-imperiality in the Long Duree." In *The Oxford Handbook of Global Modernisms*, edited by Mark Wollaeger and Matt Eatough, 669–96. New York: Oxford University Press, 2012.

Doyle, Laura. "Toward a Philosophy of Transnationalism." *Journal of Transnational American Studies* 1, no. 1 (2009). https://doi.org/10.5070/T811006941.

Duara, Prasentjit. "The Cold War and the Imperialism of Nation-States." In *The Oxford Handbook of the Cold War*, edited by Richard M. Immerman and Petra Goedde, 86–102. New York: Oxford University Press, 2013.

Fang Xiu 方修. "Yijiuwujiu nian de Mahua wenyijie" 一九五九年的馬華文藝界 [The Sinophone Malayan Cultural Field in 1959]. In 新馬文學史論集 [Collected Articles on the Literary Histories of Singapore and Malaysia], 116–30. Hong Kong: Sanlian Shudian Xianggang Fengdian, 1984.

Fernando, Joseph M. "The Cold War, Malayan Decolonization and the Making of the Federation of Malaysia." In *Southeast Asia and the Cold War*, edited by Albert Lau, 66–84. New York: Routledge, 2012.

Goscha, Christopher E., and Christian F. Ostermann, eds. *Connecting Histories: Decolonization and the Cold War in Southeast Asia, 1945–1962*. Washington, DC: Woodrow Wilson Center Press, 2009.

Lim Choon Bee 林春美. <Jiaofeng> : *Feizuoyi de Mahua wenxue* 《蕉風》：非左翼的馬華文學 [Chao Foon and Nonleftist Mahua Literature]. Taipei: Shibao chuban, 2021.

Lim Fong Wei 林方伟. "Chongfu de shuxie, fanfu de huiwang: Liu Yichang de bianzou qingjie" 重複的書寫，反复的回望：劉以鬯的變奏情結 [Rewritings and Revisits: Variations in Liu Yichang's Writings]. In *Lanse xingqiliu* 蓝色星期六 [Blue Saturday], 309–14. Hong Kong: Huoyi chubanshe, 2019.

Liu Yichang 刘以鬯. *Lanse xingqi liu* 蓝色星期六 [Blue Saturday]. Hong Kong: Huoyi chubanshe, 2019.

Liu Yichang 刘以鬯. *Redai fengyu* 熱帶風雨 [Tropical Storms]. Hong Kong: Huoyi chuban-she, 2010.

Liu Yichang 刘以鬯. "Xingjiapo gushi" 星加坡故事 [Singapore Story]. *Xiaoshuobao* 小説報 [The Story Paper], no. 36 (1956 or 1957):

Mak, Grace Yan-yan 麥欣恩. *Xianggang dianying yu Xinjiapo: Lengzhan shidai Xinggang wenhua lianxi, 1950–1965* 香港電影與新加坡：冷戰時代星港文化連繫, 1950–1965 [Hong Kong Cinema and Singapore: A Cultural Ring between Two Cities, 1950–1965]. Hong Kong: Hong Kong University Press, 2019.

Nan Ao 南鰲. "Zhanshi tongsu wenxue de liangsan wenti" 戰時通俗文學的兩三問題 [A Few Questions about Popular Literature during the War]. Reprinted in *Mahua xinwenxue daxi* 馬華新文學大系 [Compendium of Malayan Chinese Literature], *Lilun piping yiji* 理论批评一集 [Collection of Theoretical Treatises, Volume 1], edited by Fang Xiu, 94–95. Singapore: Xingzhou shijie shuju, 1972.

Ng, Kenny K. K. "Soft-Boiled, Anti-Communist Romance: *The Story Paper* and Liu Yichang's *A Singapore Story*," In *Chineseness and the Cold War: Contested Cultures and Diaspora in Southeast Asia and Hong Kong*, edited by Jeremy E. Taylor and Lanjun Xu, 94–109. London: Routledge, 2021.

Roberts, Priscilla. "Cold War Hong Kong: Juggling Opposing Forces and Identities." In *Hong Kong in the Cold War*, edited by Priscilla Roberts and John M. Carroll, 26–59. Hong Kong: Hong Kong University Press, 2016.

Shi Jun 實君. "Nanyang de tongsu wenyi" 南洋的通俗文藝 [Popular Literature and Arts in Nanyang]. Reprinted in *Mahua xinwenxue daxi* 馬華新文學大系 [Compendium of Malayan Chinese Literature], *Lilun piping yiji* 理論批評一集 [Collection of Theoretical Treatises, Volume 1], edited by Fang Xiu, 108. Singapore: Xingzhou shijie shuju, 1972.

Steele, Tracy. "Hong Kong and the Cold War in the 1950s." In *Hong Kong in the Cold War*, edited by Priscilla Roberts and John M. Carroll, 92–116. Hong Kong: Hong Kong University Press, 2016.

Wang Mei-Hsiang 王梅香. "Mei yuan wenyi tizhi xia de Tai, Gang, Mahua wenxue changyu: yi yishu jihua <Xiaoshuo bao> wei li" 美援文藝體制下的台、港、馬華文學場域：以譯書計畫《小說報》為例 [The Literary Field in Taiwan, Hong Kong, and Malaysia under the US Aid Literary Institution: A Case Study of the Book Publication Program of *The Story Paper*]. *Taiwan shehui kexue yanjiu jikan* 台灣社會科學研究季刊 [Taiwan: A Radical Quarterly in Social Studies] no. 102 (2016): 1–40.

Xu, Lanjun. "The Southern Film Corporation, Opera Films, and the PRC's Cultural Diplomacy in Cold War Asia, 1950s and 1960s." *Modern Chinese Literature and Culture* 29, no. 1 (2017): 239–82.

Yung, Sai-Shing, and Christopher Rea. "One Chicken, Three Dishes: The Cultural Enterprise of Law Bun." In *The Business of Culture: Cultural Entrepreneurs in China and Southeast Asia, 1900–65*, edited by Christopher G. Rea and Nicolai Volland, 150–80. Vancouver: University of British Columbia Press, 2015.

NICHOLAS Y. H. WONG

Inter-imperial, Ecological Interpretations of the "Five Coolies" Myth in Penang and Medan

ABSTRACT This article proposes resource extraction politics as a lens to analyze the relationship between Malaysian Chinese (or Mahua) literature and the global literary economy. Rather than ascribe Mahua literature to its present national boundaries and diasporic communities, the article locates its formation in inter-imperial nodes of trafficked labor and art production, as well as a global system of colonial plantations. The article revisits Zeng Huading's 曾華丁 (1906–1942) short story (1928) and Ba Ren's 巴人 (1901–1972) historical drama (1949) about the myth of five Chinese coolies and their execution in 1871 for murdering a Dutch foreman in a Deli tobacco plantation in East Sumatra. The Anglo-Dutch migration corridor, or the cross-straits coolie trade between the two imperial jurisdictions of Penang (Straits Settlements) and Medan (East Sumatra), now part of Malaysia and Indonesia respectively, was one Nanyang connection, but these writers have been discussed separately within Mahua and Yinhua 印華 (Indonesian Chinese) contexts. Ba Ren, in particular, is studied as a leftist writer who contributed artistically to the Indonesian and Chinese revolutions in the 1940s and 1950s. Here, the article rethinks Ba Ren's legacy within a Mahua corpus, and Zeng Huading's fiction within a cross-straits history of labor. This ecological reading of their works also highlights their critique of Mahua's peripheralization within a world economy and global literature.

KEYWORDS Mahua literature, Ba Ren, plantation labor, coolie trade, inter-imperiality

Resource Extraction Politics and Inter-imperial Circulation of Myth

Having witnessed rising inequalities amid trends of rapid deglobalization during our transformative COVID-19 moment, I found it untenable to write about geopolitical rhythms of literature without considering material forms such as interrupted supply chains, tightened labor control, and migrant surveillance, which phenomena might consolidate new imperial forces of capitalist over-accumulation. If literary historians have linked geopolitical shifts with literary-cultural transformations while also decoupling them, why not expand an analysis of state power to include market forces by examining, for example, literary-intellectual responses to what Marxist geographer David Harvey calls capitalist "spatio-temporal fixes," which offset economic cycles of boom and bust?[1] Furthermore, how do a minor literature and its histories register threats of a different order, such as ecological threats arising from the extraction and

PRISM: THEORY AND MODERN CHINESE LITERATURE • 19:2 • SEPTEMBER 2022
DOI 10.1215/25783491-9966667 • © 2022 LINGNAN UNIVERSITY

processing of minerals or commodity crops, or policies of land redistribution and Indigenous displacement?

Historians and literary scholars alike have drawn on concepts of transimperial circulation and inter-imperiality to loosen our conceptual reification of physical borders. Border production by empires has nudged the writing of literature and its histories in territorial directions, which prompts us to ask: what does it mean to write a transimperial perspective of literature, considering that literary circulations and ideas migrate on different time scales and meet different kinds of resistance, compared to commodities, labor, and capital? Even when literary subjectivity is settled, it is always already on the move, according to Laura Doyle's definition of inter-imperiality: "In all cases, authors not only write back to or negotiate a relation to one empire; they negotiate a position *between and among* empires."[2]

The Anglo-Dutch "migration corridor," or the cross-straits coolie trade between the two imperial jurisdictions of Penang (Straits Settlements) and Medan (East Sumatra), now part of Malaysia and Indonesia respectively, helped to provide much-needed labor for Deli tobacco plantations after their opening in the mid-1860s. But the Treaty of 1871 demarcated the Anglo-Dutch border between Penang and Medan, and both sides began to regulate the numbers and types of Chinese laborers leaving the British-controlled Malay Peninsula and entering Dutch Sumatra. Drawing on the lessons of British plantation ambitions in Sri Lanka and Mauritius a few decades earlier,[3] promoters of British liberalism in the Straits Settlements sought to protect British subjects (who nominally included coolies) by setting up the Chinese Protectorate in 1877. When indentured Chinese migration to South America was abolished in 1874, Southeast Asia absorbed the labor supply, and Deli was one such place. In the 1880s, Dutch planters bypassed Chinese brokers in the Straits Settlements to directly solicit coolies from Qing China with the help of German shipping companies.[4] Therefore, we can update the binary figures of the coolie and the *towkay* (boss) under an interimperial gaze.[5] Chinese coolies who ended up in Deli faced competing figures who delimited their freedom of movement in late nineteenth-century East Sumatra, including planters, the colonial government in Batavia, Chinese brokers and depot keepers, Straits Chinese tycoons, Malay sultans, Dutch sinologists, British colonial officials who promoted "free" labor, and Qing diplomats who set up consuls to protect them and use the injustices of the coolie trade as an alibi to assert China's sovereignty using international law, to name but a few stakeholders.[6]

Decades of border control and migrant surveillance have disaggregated the spaces of literary production and reception in line with national and transnational interests. The term *Mahua* 馬華, or "Malayan/Malaysian Chinese," can be traced back to the 1920s and 1930s, where *Ma* in *Mahua* generally referred to peninsular Malaya and invoked the conditions and legacies of colonial

British rule and its capitalist structures in the region.[7] By this point the British had already consolidated their rule, and quite a few Chinese-language writings in Malaya during that period dealt with attendant social issues and labor unrest. Mahua literature in its early years defined itself as an anticolonial critique of capitalism. But such a critique, and indeed, the continual task of intellectual decolonization, feels incomplete when an explanation for Mahua literature's thematic and stylistic development is confined to a tripartite colonial British–diasporic Chinese–national Malay framework. So, rather than ascribe Mahua literature to its present national boundaries and diasporic communities, I locate its formation in inter-imperial nodes of trafficked labor and art production, as well as a global system of colonial plantations.[8]

This essay revisits the inter-imperial circulation of the myth of five ancestors as an intermedial (prose and drama) response across several decades to the coolie trade across the Straits of Malacca. The myth goes that in 1871, five coolies took the blame for the murder of a Dutch foreman in a tobacco plantation and were executed. Temples in Medan and Kedah, constructed in their name, deify them in the pantheon of Chinese folk religion.[9] But writers who celebrate them have been discussed separately within Mahua and Yinhua 印華 (Indonesian Chinese) contexts. Ba Ren 巴人 (the pen name of Wang Renshu 王任叔, 1901–1972) is often studied as a leftist writer who contributed artistically to the Indonesian and Chinese revolutions in the 1940s and 1950s. Here, I rethink Ba Ren within a Mahua corpus, and conversely, I rethink Zeng Huading 曾華丁 (1906–1942) within a cross-straits history of labor, to study Mahua literature within regional forces that mark its peripheralization within a global economy and global literature.

That the Five Coolies myth is produced "*between* and *among* empires" but is remembered via a segmented ecology along national lines inspires my rethinking of Mahua literary history. First, I understand *ecology* as what Amitav Ghosh calls a "form of emplacement in which the landscape, and its hidden forces" create "commonalities between the people who dwell in it, no matter what their origin."[10] Minor history and literature, in response to this ecology, perform what Fernando Coronil calls *counterfetishism*—a double move that goes upstream to examine relations of labor and nature behind their product's smooth appearance and exchange, and downstream to extract imaginative mileage out of such transformations.[11] Using Walter Benjamin's montage method, unfairly disparaged by Adorno as being "located at the crossroads of magic and positivism," my essay explores the tensions and links between unmasking the "commodity fetish" of tobacco and allegorizing such a commodity to arrive at other possible human relations.[12] Second, I use ecologies as a method for writing literary history. Rather than choosing texts that discuss environmental changes and writers' responses to resultant social phenomena, I instead argue that ecological thinking has been foundational to the formation of what we now call Mahua literature and Nanyang studies. But this thinking remains submerged; hence, the task of the Mahua critic is to uncover the *inter-imperial ecologies* of art and labor. In doing so, discussions of minor literature can bypass any national imperative to assimilate to its frameworks of colonial modernity or to prove allegiance to dominant versions of the local.[13]

For example, I trace the origins of Mahua literature and Nanyang studies not to declarations of local consciousness and style, but to the discovery and interiorization of the productive landscapes of tin and rubber (among other commodity export industries), borrowing Kojin Karatani's argument on the origins of modern Japanese literature.[14] The encroaching ubiquity of mines and plantations that created towns and villages across the colonial-national peninsular landscape presented urgent artistic and intellectual options for writers and intellectuals who either benefited from and supported the colonial structure and economy, or who were disenfranchised by and resisted them. Often the latter, Mahua writers and Nanyang historians developed a specific point of critique. Granted, these thinkers who were close to or part of the laboring class desired a strong Chinese nation, like the tin and rubber industrialists and barons, though the barons felt that such a dream was easier to achieve by co-opting the colonial structure. By foregrounding this class distinction within the colonial hierarchies of Malaya's export economy and the resulting armed capitalist-communist struggle, I move away from stereotypical discourses of good-versus-bad ethnic Chinese who either assimilated or resisted assimilation—discourses that were internalized by Mahua writers and Nanyang intellectuals in their debates about local-sojourner identities and realist-modernist aesthetics and their attempts to write indigenous, Chinese-language histories of Southeast Asia from the 1930s through the 1990s.

Arguing against a Cold War interpretive framework of post–World War II national development in Sinophone studies, I revisit the colonial legacies of ecological change and infrastructural development on the Malay Peninsula, and Mahua writers' literary-intellectual strategies for decolonizing the market and state. Also, since resource procurement chains long antedated any formal nations in Southeast Asia, the idea of "national literatures" looks like a label thinly pasted on at a late date.[15] With attention to slow and quick industrial processes, short and long periods of planting and harvesting a crop, and the *longue durée* spatial transformations of a territory due to foreign capital and international demand, I introduce *inter-imperial ecologies* as a new "minor" spatiotemporal response to literary-intellectual projects previously read as anxious responses to flashpoints of China's political turmoil, as well as the wax and wane of ethnic discrimination experienced by these writers in their adopted or birth countries.

Beyond National Ecologies: A Wider Literary-Historical Framework

Behold the product label "Made in Malaya" on the corners of rubber sheets produced from latex, bound for export to US industries. In the metropolitan market, the commodity evokes a far-flung place, while locally its demand is taken as a form of national pride. Often these imaginations obscure the historical processes by which the construction of networks such as roads and railways facilitated the movement of a commodity from its extraction site to cities and ports, and the extension of state power over frontiers and borderlands via institutions like forestry departments, not to mention legal mechanisms like gazetting the land in the name of protecting Indigenous territories. But histories of infrastructure have challenged the seemingly inevitable territorialization and integration of space around colonial-national time. Resource extraction, as these histories reveal, involves different technologies and forms of capital, regimes of control and the use of other commodities, a mixing of speech patterns and religious practices by local and foreign, state and nonstate actors, across centuries.

On the Malay Peninsula, tin mines and rubber estates and, more recently, rare earth refineries and oil palm plantations represent this marginal excess in the national imagination. Even though they involve workers, investors, and observers differently, these commodities and industries have solidified an imagined community around the necessity of national exports. However, for me, their uniform appearances as trees on a highway next to piles of infertile dirt evoke buried histories and produce a sense of national despair. If print capitalism, for Benedict Anderson, fosters national belonging around a common discourse and language, extractive capitalism during the same age has only produced diffuse, stratified modes of representation and critique.[16] This essay goes against the disorienting effects and legacy of a segmented, racialized colonial-national society by excavating moments and movements of anticolonial environmental critique of capitalism that transcend spaces of nations and empires.

My main challenge here is to convey a sense of narrative contingency to the events leading up to a total colonization of the Malay Peninsula, and the role of trade and industries in fostering integration as well as disintegration of empire, through liberal neglect of parts of Malaya and other colonies, or the different forms of rule on the peninsula, unevenly applied, but measured against the efficacy of resource extraction across different geographical terrains. Without this element of commodity histories, Mahua literary history would be a more straightforward account of the evolution of literary coteries and journals or academic societies out of tin-mining towns and plantation villages, where they gained visibility due to easy access to education, radio, assembly places, publication houses, and academic institutions. Adding a geoeconomic layer would be to consider late-empire intellectual formations in light of nonnational, "disintegrative" frontier economies: the Dutch, British, and French trying to gain a foothold over seventeenth-century Phuket's tin trade, overland and sea routes of the tin trade in northern Malaya and southern Siam, details such as the Siam-Malaya cross-border railway schedule, or the fact that tin products in the nineteenth century had to be transported by elephants overland to the ports. Later, the dominance of British capitalists in Malayan tin and rubber industries after the 1870s coincided with the end of the Larut Wars and colonial British economic consolidation of the peninsula through direct and indirect rule (via the Straits Settlements and the Federated and Unfederated Malay States), where their "too big to fail" investments necessitated empire's return to Malaya after the Japanese interregnum in order to use its natural wealth to revive the UK's postwar economy. Subsequent forms of political integration such as the Malayan Union and the Federation of Malaya paved the way for postindependence Malaya, and later Malaysia (which aroused controversy in neighboring Indonesia and the Philippines for representing protectionist capitalist interests), to redistribute land to Malay peasants via smallholdings, the gazetting of Indigenous land, and the nationalization of foreign tin and rubber conglomerates in the 1970s and 1980s.

Hence, to write a history of minor literature and its complex relation to state power and market forces during Malaya's transitional period from colony to nation is to reintroduce views by a nonelite, diasporic intellectual class into the geoeconomic colonial-national space of Malaya's decolonization. The result is a reorganization of the spatial flows of colonial state capitalism after independence. This story is appealing, but it does not allow us to think of Mahua literature as a nonnational category.[17] National biases are everywhere: Shahua 砂華 (Sarawak Chinese) literature was assimilated into the category of Mahua literature after Sarawak joined Malaysia, according to the same logic by which Xinhua 新華 (Singapore Chinese) literature stopped being Mahua literature after Singapore was expelled from the merger. Because of Singapore's intertwined histories of governance, immigration, and extractive capitalism as part of Malaya, Xinhua writers could stake a larger claim to Mahua literature than could Shahua writers, who sometimes reject the label of Mahua literature based on historical experience. We might also consider the proposition that Mahua literature is a separate entity from Taihua 泰華 (Thai Chinese) literature by dint of a border.[18] This article challenges such national definitions of Mahua literature by turning to literary responses to the inter-imperial management of Chinese laborers for the East Indies tobacco trade across the two imperial jurisdictions of Penang (Straits Settlements) and Medan (East Sumatra), now part of Malaysia and Indonesia respectively, suggesting that similar geoeconomic spaces of literature can be drawn for other commodities such as pepper, gambier, sugar, and coffee.

Maps and other technologies that consolidate land and frontier regions make the nation visible. Plantation economies based around efficacy and streamlined relationships to the land through settlement and extraction evict other forms of Indigenous and migrant circulations. In the following pages, I argue for a fluid category of Mahua literature that critiques this utilitarian concept of land.

Ecology and Repetition: "Where Can the Coolie Speak?"

In the two texts about the myth that I will analyze, Zeng Huading's short story set in the Straits Settlements (1929) and Ba Ren's historical drama set in East Sumatra (1949), both advance a nonnational ecological critique of extractive capitalism. These stories re-create from the migrant laborer's perspective what is scantily available from court testimonies, police interviews, contract signatures, and *qiaopi* 僑批 (letters and remittances). From these two texts, we expect the Five Coolies' heroic confession to murdering a European foreman in a tobacco plantation and their subsequent execution. However, the stories are also interested in the meanings that artistic repetition can bear on the inter-imperial ecology of Nanyang. Both authors are aware of their outsider statuses in representing the plight of tobacco plantation workers, so they present artistic forms as a response to the question "Where can the coolie speak?"[19] Through art, as I will show, ecology repairs and nurtures the coolies' relationship to the land to which they are bound. Rather than animalizing their being, ecology imbues them with agency. A historical parallel would be Javanese laborers, who also came to work in these plantations, becoming smallholders on the peripheries of their former estates in East Sumatra.[20]

Labor's resistance against the temporality of surveillance and regimented plantation work are represented in the forms of strikes, destruction of crops, and most interestingly, song and dance. Embodied rhythm, and repetition of artistic forms as labor, substitute for the mundane repetition of plantation labor. As Amitav Ghosh muses about peasant resistance, its "challenges to the capitalist and imperialist order" come "from what W. E. B. Du Bois described as 'part legend, part whimsy, part art.'"[21] The inter-imperial ecology of art and labor is key: Ba Ren reminds us that folk songs were brought from Penang (and Singapore) to Sumatra, and not just laborers.[22] Such repetition also troubles the dialectic of work and art. In Zeng Huading's story, the workers in nature and their living quarters resemble words in a newspaper, consumed during a reader's leisure time. In Ba Ren's play, laborers adapt and sing songs, sometimes during work, and get punished for it. As Ba Ren's preface explains, the New China Drama Club in Medan performed his piece as a street play for Indonesians and Chinese alike, according to the tradition of *wayang* (street opera) troupes being brought in from the Straits Settlements to Deli, as entertainment for coolies after work, in different Chinese topolects.[23] Art produces inter-imperial, ecological meaning for workers: "Revolutionary leaders argued that travelling theatre shows which attracted labouring audiences had more impact than their speeches."[24]

Zeng Huading's Anticolonial Ecological Critique

How is Zeng Huading's work usually understood? When we encounter Mahua literature from the 1920s and 1930s, some of its local writing visibly takes a stand against the colonial structure involving Chinese capitalism that exploits migrant laborers. But received wisdom in Mahua literary history prizes a "localization" narrative that culminated in the debates of 1948, which naturalize "local color" as local style, grammar, and linguistic inflection, as well as a shift away from a diasporic concern for mainland China to a local concern for colonial Malaya without the reference point of China.[25] Because of the civil war then ongoing in China, the framing of this debate regrettably presented an either-or option of representation and implied a China referent that needed to be invoked in order to be banished. This specter of *Chineseness* as nation haunts discussions of the origins and development of Mahua literature to this day. Rather than the opposite of *diasporic*, I explore the local as a geoeconomic space of contestation. From Zeng's work, we see that Mahua self-definition was already present decades earlier in the struggle of labor and capitalist relations within colonial Malaya's "extractive, plantation-based economies oriented toward the resource and market needs of the industrializing West."[26]

The literary historian Fang Xiu's 方修 two-volume anthology of Mahua short stories from 1919 through 1942, curated several years after Malaya's independence, pays attention to this fact.[27] Quite a few stories depict the harsh conditions of plantation work, which drive laborers to revolt against the Chinese owners and managers who work closely with them on site, in the forms of murder, sabotage of cash crops, and suicide. For example, Rao Chuyu's 饒楚瑜 "Qiulong" 囚籠 (Prisoner's Cage) depicts scenes from rubber plantations wherein employment and retrenchment follow the vicissitudes of global prices of rubber or "golden trees" 黃金樹.[28] Income from gambling dens shields plantation owners and managers from fluctuations in rubber prices, as the short story ends with their dissolute merrymaking. Yicun's 一村 "Xianglin shenchu" 橡林深處 (Deep in the Rubber Plantation) is another straightforward, rousing depiction of labor misery as a result of gambling addiction and extortionist loans. The story follows the protagonist, Ya Cai, who borrowed five dollars from his boss to repatriate himself home. He later hangs himself from a tree, though a fellow worker rescues him. Workers then mobilize to demand an increase in their minimum wage.

The standout from Fang Xiu's collection is Zeng Huading's "Wuxiongdi mu" 五兄弟墓 (The Grave of Five Brothers). The story of a plantation owner's murder, which ends in the execution of the five who confessed, is sustained by a metonymic realism that is missing from the anthology's other stories. Similes of animals and nature are rhythmically repeated across objects following a logic of contagion, rivaling the unbridled, imperceptible transformation of material in the processes of colonial capitalism. Here's an example:

> Their towkay, a rich man of the tropics, bound them up as reptiles using words tougher than iron in a tobacco plantation wider than the sky and as blue as the night sky. Some were hedgehogs, some were ants, while some

were tiny earthworms. Hence the tobacco slowly grew out of the reptiles' heads like human hair. The rich man of the tropics plucked the gold from the heads of the reptiles. Hence cast aside with the tobacco stems in the tobacco plantation that was wider than the sky and bluer than the night sky were coolies of the tobacco plantation.

Compared to the scale of the plantation, only as large as characters on a newspaper, as numerous as characters on a newspaper, using a few leaves from reeds to put together the flat surface of leaves to build that burrow of a beast that accommodated one human back in the shape of a drawn bow to revolve inside, were the living quarters of the Chinese coolies. . . .

Compared to the scale of the plantation, only as large and numerous as characters on a newspaper, the house that accommodated one human back to revolve inside in the shape of a drawn bow was similarly expectant.

牠們的頭家，熱國的闊人，用比鐵還要硬的說話把牠們綁在比天還要寬闊，藍得和夜裏的天空一樣的菸園裏做爬虫。有的是刺蝟，有的是螞蟻，有的是小蚯蚓。於是菸在爬虫的頭上，緩緩地，人類的頭髮似的長出來了。熱國的闊人在爬虫頭上拔了菸葉上的金子，於是和菸的幹子委棄在比天還要寬闊，比夜還要藍的菸園裏的也是菸園的豬仔。

和菸園比例起來，衹有和報紙上的字一樣大細，和報紙上的字一樣多少的，只用幾片蘆荻的葉子編成的葉扁搭就的只容得一個彎弓樣的背脊在裏邊旋轉的獸窠，就是中華的豬仔的寄宿舍了. . . .

和菸園比例起來，衹有和報紙上的字一樣大細，一樣多少的只容得一個彎弓似的背脊在旋轉的屋子也一樣在期望着。[29]

In this passage, the cramped living quarters on the tobacco plantation are compared to small Chinese characters in the newspaper, inviting the reader to consider the medium of the story, which was published on February 22, 1929, in an issue of *Art and Literature Weekly Supplement* (文藝周刊), as either complicity or intimacy.

In a mythical expression of capitalist exploitation in the passage above, coolies who harvest tobacco leaves are *described as being*—and not just resembling—"reptiles," whose labor is indistinguishable from their bodies: "tobacco slowly grew out of the reptiles' heads like human hair." They are similarly described as animals as diverse as hedgehogs, ants, and earthworms. Such depersonalization places the story's laborers in a separate metaphorical structure that is bound to the natural world. In two instances, when objects are said to resemble animals, the simile transfers to the five "brothers." First, the figure of the dog: "the car leapt and jumped about like a dog from the side of the body of the field of tobacco plants, carrying on its back his master, the rich man from the hot country" 汽車狗似的從菸草的身畔躍着跳着，馱着他的主人，熱國的闊人。[30] But then, the five "brothers" refute and update the narrator's choice of a happy description of a dog beholden to its master: "we place in front of you our five dog-like lives that bear less honor than the squirrels on coconut trees, even though we are Chinese brothers, even though we kill to avenge the brutal lives of our brothers" 我們五條狗似的比椰樹上的松鼠還要不名譽的生命就擺在這裡，雖然我們是中華的手足，雖然也是為着我們的手足的殘酷的生活而殺人.[31]

Second, when they were sentenced to death by hanging, the hemp ropes around their necks were like "five evil snakes" 五條惡蛇, and upon their deaths, they look as though they are "suspended like snakes" 蛇似的吊着.[32] Zeng Huading's metonymic realism of oppressive plantation work and resistance against it uniquely centers a natural world that blends the human and the animal, thus prefiguring postwar Mahua modernist works that foreground the lush, tropical Malayan landscape, such as the unexplored jungle, the plantation, the mine, or other geographic spaces, as a site for exploring the characters' identity or origins, the legacies of colonial-capitalist oppression, and so on. By depicting human forms as mutable into insects and nature, Zeng Huading also resists the categorizing impulse in the development of British natural history in the region.

Besides "reptiles," Chinese coolies are described in the story as *chusheng* 畜生, which can mean domestic animal or, with a vulgar connotation, a beast or dirty swine. In contrast, the Chinese literati's act of writing to earn a living, referred to in the pun on "crawling over squared or lined paper" (爬格子), is rather tame. This analogy of plantation living quarters to written characters reappears, but before that the reader witnesses laborers dancing to the whipping motion of the cane and shoes pelting on their bodies, and then to clandestine scenes of sharpening knife blades, which culminates in a "similarly expectant" atmosphere, like words on a page. Words like "expectation" (*qiwang* 期望 and *qipan* 期盼) are repeated to convey different meanings: for profit, to eke out a bare living, or to conduct an assassination, while the dancing is conveyed through words like "dancing" (跳舞) or "waving in the wind" (飄舞). Characters in the story are given monikers as identification, for example, "rich man of the tropics" (熱國的闊人), the Chinese "owner of glass factory" (玻璃主) who has a heart made of "earth" (土), who contrasts with the five "brothers" who met in Huangquan, their "bodies thick with blood" (充實着血的軀體).[33]

Despite its trenchant critique of Malaya's plantation economy, Zeng's story provides a satisfying ending for both oppressor and oppressed. The five perpetrators' martyrdom by hanging is presumably a fit punishment from the perspective of colonial British authorities, who were on another occasion displeased by Huan You's 寰遊 *Crossroads* 十字街頭 (1930), a poetic play about unemployed plantation workers and tin miners who organized a street march. In the latter case, the playwright was expelled from British Malaya, and the publication that published it, *Fanxing* 繁星, and other Chinese newspaper supplements were ordered to shut down.[34] Overall, Zeng's adaptation of the Five Coolies myth, though set in an unnamed location, speaks to the widespread inter-imperial circulation of the horrors of the tobacco trade. For me, the literary-historical significance of Zeng's story is not only its insightful use of human-animal metaphors to depict how tobacco transforms the bodies of those who extract it. It is also Zeng's attention to art and labor, which allows readers to perceive the Mahua local as what "landscape, and its hidden forces" do to those who encounter it. The Mahua local is *not* the result of a conscious nurturing of identity through dogmatic prescriptions of literary style and content, concocted in a writer's leisurely time. Such alchemical desire of the local is already present on ecological bodies; one could just find and record its stultifying repetitions and sinewy mutations—or oppression and resistance—as Zeng Huading did.

An Inter-imperial, Ecological Reinterpretation of Ba Ren's Historical Drama

Unlike Zeng Huading, Ba Ren approaches the Five Coolies myth with the acumen of a literary theorist and takes pains to reflect his research into the histories of the Deli tobacco plantation murders in various versions of his play. In their own ways, both writers reveal an inter-imperial, ecological dimension to the original myth and to Mahua literature. In this section, I trace how local deities like the Five Coolies become national heroes and anticolonial martyrs, but underlying this transformation is Ba Ren's ecological critique of extractive capitalism, in feudal and colonial forms, through song and repetition. Ba Ren had asked his friend, who later wrote the introduction to the play, to visit the Medan temple to collect historical material about the Five Coolies, which helped him edit the 1949 version.[35] When the New China Drama club performed the play, one of the club's organizers excised its Indonesian characters in order to streamline the dramatic action, muddling Ba Ren's intentions of "portraying a united struggle by various races against imperialism."[36] But in the printed edition I use here, especially in the paratext and off-stage descriptions, the inter-imperial transformations of land, labor, and commodity in eastern Sumatra during the Aceh War (1873–1904), which the Dutch won, are unmistakable. In his preface, Ba Ren outlines the history of the Deli plantation estates and connects Chinese labor in Southeast Asia to its histories in Cuba, Peru, Chile, and Hawai'i, all the while addressing his audience as "dear readers" (親愛的讀者與觀眾).[37] As I will show, ecological alienation—which is to say, the seizure of Indigenous land by plantation estates—though involving local rulers, set up the main reason for the violent murder committed by Chinese coolies in the first act, and later an uprising by Gayos and Malays in the second. My reading adds a new dimension to current assessments of Ba Ren's legacy: he was the first ambassador from the People's Republic of China to Indonesia in 1950, he had witnessed and supported the Indonesian National Revolution (1947), and he asserted Third World solidarity as part of pre-Suharto, post-Bandung Indonesia-China diplomacy through socialist-realist writing.[38] In other words, he worked secretly on behalf of the Chinese Communist Party to stage a Marxist play in Medan as a means to garner left-wing support against the Chinese Nationalists there.[39] Artistically, he redefined diasporic collectivity and the dramatic conventions of Chinese-language spoken theater in the wake of Indonesia's independence.[40]

I find Ba Ren's script to yield more meanings—in the same way that Ann Stoler finds opacity and doubt in the colonial archives—when Frans Carl Valck (1835–1892), assistant-resident on the eastern coast of Sumatra, blames tobacco planter J. Luhmann, rather than the attacking Gayos and Malays, for his family's murders in 1876.[41] Interestingly, Ba Ren combined the events from 1871 and 1876; that is, he starts off the play with the plot of five coolies murdering a Dutch foreman, after which a trial at the sultan's court is followed by Hei Er 黑二, the coolies' friend, banding together with Gayos and Malays to take out Luhmann, but not before singing revolutionary and worker songs based on Indonesian poems. The Gayo was none other than the historical Panglima Selan (沙畬), "feared by the local Bataks," and the Malay was Sjahrir (拉迦爾), a poignant name in Indonesian history.[42] By suturing together instances of labor unrest from different times and places, Ba Ren articulates an inchoate concept of Indonesian nationalism where Chinese migrants, indigenous Bataks and Malays, and the highland Gayos are bound together by their oppression and experience of Dutch imperialism.

As Ba Ren makes clear, the case of the five coolies was but an alibi for the colonial government in Batavia to institute Dutch extraterritoriality in East Sumatra, on the pretext that the sultan's use of the death penalty was too harsh; to the Dutch, the sultan's court executed Chinese migrants whose jurisdiction it did not cover.[43] This new colonial overreach angered plantation managers, who argued that the sultan had conferred upon them legal rights over their employees.[44] Ba Ren responds to this complex situation with a dual critique of feudal and imperial powers: he outlines the legal and extralegal means by which sultanate elites and planters in East Sumatra alike grabbed land along the Sumatran coast and expelled Indigenous communities, while local rulers fended them off.[45] An example of Ba Ren's feudal critique:

> Even though the foundation of society has not totally changed, the Deli sultanate, in order to seize tribal lands and put down various agricultural communes, rented out large quantities of land, collected taxes on local products of the communes, and set up a burgeoning state-form of tools of oppression. Armies, policemen, and courts were aimed toward implementing the autocratic rule of the sultan.

> 雖然社會的基礎還沒有完全改變，但日里蘇丹為爭奪部落土地和鎮壓各個農村公社，以便出租大批土地和徵收村社土產，已建立了初具規模的國家形式的鎮壓工具。軍隊、警察和法院就已執行蘇丹的專制統治為目的了。[46]

However, in a few scenes where two local policemen debate the legitimacy of impending Dutch extraterritoriality, Ba Ren supports the side of Usman 烏斯曼, who thinks he should serve the sultan: "yes, our Sultan rented out the land, but it's because the government in Batavia is in control! In one stroke of the law, it's a long-term lease of seventy-five years" 咱們蘇丹租出地去，也因為那個巴達維亞的政府，是他頂頭上司哪！一道法律下來，七十五年的長期租借.[47] The other policeman, Mathi 馬奇, professes his loyalty to the Dutch queen, and in the end is stabbed for taking the wrong side, recalling an earlier scene when Gaosheng 高升, a Chinese recruiter of laborers who wears a Napoleon hat, meets his demise at the hands of his nephew Hei Er.

I end this section by briefly noting that laborers' songs in the play mark patterns of dissent in this history of inter-imperial, ecological transformation. For example, Sjahrir modifies the song of the Chinese from Penang to reflect Deli conditions, but it is revealed that Hei Er had taught the song to Pangkor Tawar (Pang'e tawa 龐額塔瓦), revealing tobacco's transculturation of art and labor; by turns she and another Malay woman, Melati 茉拉蒂, sing for their friends who commiserate about life on the estates, or as requested by Luhmann 魯曼 and other foremen, who critique their choice of adapting certain words.[48] Before the coolies' trial, Panglima Selan performs a Malay and Batak dance associated with crops, weddings, burial, and sickness as a masked demon in front of the courthouse. A judge chases them away, symbolizing the policing powers over plantation employees that Dutch extraterritoriality reshapes.[49] Poignantly, Ba Ren's play ends with an image of ecological sacrifice, in which diasporic labor secures neither livelihood nor acculturation in the face of extractive capitalism that takes on feudal and colonial forms:

> You landed in my country just like beans sown in foreign soil. Mother earth is as loving in this land and as benevolent as mothers everywhere. You were supposed to grow, blossom, and bear fruit here. You were also the sons of our mother earth. But our mother earth is a victim. . . . Exhausted, she cannot give you any reward.

> 你們就像豆子一樣落在咱們的土地上來了。我們的土地，像天下的慈母一般的仁愛，本來是可以讓你們生活下來，抽芽，長葉，開花和結果的。你們原始打底母親的兒子呵！可是我們的大地母親，卻也是一個受罪的人呀 [. . .] 也不能給你們應得的報酬了。[50]

National independence in Indonesia, whose fight Ba Ren joined in, would augur well, or at least transform the terms, for diasporic labor transcending its ecological alienation and exhaustion. While Zeng Huading's coolies become the very commodity crops they were planting and harvesting at the quick turn of a phrase, Ba Ren's coolies are compared to a food source that abides by nature's maturation cycles, though these are unfulfilled. Details like these—the slow and quick industrial, natural, or magical processes of becoming a plant—make these inter-imperial, ecological scenes come alive and bear fruit for Mahua literary studies much later.

Plantation Narratives: Mahua Literature in a Global Literary Economy

What is the global significance of tobacco plantation narratives from the Nanyang? What does it mean to call Zeng Huading a Mahua writer, given that definitions of *Mahua* were emerging in the 1920s and 1930s, when Zeng was writing his anticolonial short stories about British Malaya and Borneo? One notes the proliferation of plantation narratives during a time when writers tentatively defined the term *Mahua*. But rather than seek out literary origins—that is, to find when the term *Mahua* first appeared and was discussed, or to trace the Mahua ur-text, which can be alternately attributed to the first local-born writer who writes in Chinese, a foreign-born writer who writes about local topics, or someone who writes using Malayan language and style, loosely defined—my essay instead revisits the inter-imperial, ecological contexts in which Malaya emerged on the literary map by way of the nation's material significance for commodity production for the world market.

To revisit the Nanyang plantation system now when borders are closed and when commodity chains and labor markets are disrupted reminds us that Mahua is a node in the global economy, a point of access that also receives, re-creates, and reexports literary ideas and myths, unconstrained by national boundaries and origins. This is how I understand the minoritizing impulse in Deleuze and Guattari's theorization of minor literature: the *minor* is a response to state power and market forces.[51] Thus, our decolonial impulse does not take at face value a national inheritance of colonial mapping, but instead questions a theory of minor literature that is wedded to a critique of, and hence forever bound to, the majoritarian impulse of national literature. Zeng Huading's and Ba Ren's works are pointed literary responses to the persistence of extractive capitalism and the struggle of Chinese labor in plantation estates. For them, inscribed at the origins of the Mahua and Yinhua projects is a dialectic of revolution and empire in starkly ecological terms, rather than a colonial-national territorial space for minorities to map their ethnicity, language, and belonging. One sees their Sinophone accounts sitting alongside Malay, Batak, Gayo, and Javanese accounts of the same history of labor unrest and revolt against plantation estate foremen and owners.

NICHOLAS Y. H. WONG is assistant professor in the School of Chinese at the University of Hong Kong. He teaches Chinese-English translation and is writing a book on the relationship between extractive capitalism and minority writing in Chinese-language literary and historical accounts from Malaysia, Singapore, Thailand, and Indonesia.

Acknowledgments

This essay evolved out of a conversation with David Xu Borgonjon and notes by Matthew Shutzer. I thank them, as well as the Society of Fellows in the Humanities, the University of Hong Kong, for giving me space to write. I also thank my two reviewers and the organizers and participants of the following workshops for their feedback: "Between Mobility and Place-Making: The Worlds of Southeast Asia in Modern Chinese Literature," Faculty of Arts and Social Sciences, National University of Singapore and Duke University; the 2020 InterAsia Academy: Integration and Disintegration in InterAsian Perspective, Social Science Research Council; and "Doing Theory in Southeast Asia," Centre for Cultural Studies, Chinese University of Hong Kong.

Notes

1   See Harvey, "'New' Imperialism."
2   Doyle, "Thinking Back through Empires." I thank Shuang Shen for this reference.
3   See Sivasundaram, *Waves across the South.*
4   Jany, "Imperial Crossings," 8. For the migration route from Shantou/Swatow and Fuzhou via Singapore to Deli, see Macauley, *Distant Shores*, 189.
5   Lombard-Salmon, "Taoke or Coolies?" 184n33.
6   Jany, "Imperial Crossings," 12, 17, 42, 47, 48, 57. By the 1880s indentured migration to the East Indies was reminiscent of Cuba and Peru, and the harsh treatment of coolies was seen in the same light as anti-Chinese laws in the United States and Australia.
7   See Tee, "Sinophone Malaysian Literature."
8   See Shih, "Comparison as Relation," and Doyle, *Inter-imperiality*, 21.
9   Jany, "Imperial Crossings," 38. Also, in the Kedah Gurun Goh Chou Temple, the five coolies, now deities, are dressed in bourgeois dress.
10   Ghosh, *Nutmeg's Curse*, 220–21.
11   On counterfetishism, see Coronil, "Introduction."
12   Theodor Adorno's correspondence with Walter Benjamin, November 10, 1938. See Benjamin, *Selected Writings*, 4, 102.
13   For a version of this argument in political science, see Mamdani, *Neither Settler nor Native.*
14   See Karatani, *Origins of Modern Japanese Literature.*
15   I thank Haun Saussy for this insight.
16   See Anderson, *Imagined Communities.*
17   Recent attempts to denationalize the spaces of Mahua literature include Chan, "Indigeneity."
18   For an inter-imperial analysis of a historian who lived in the frontier region of the Thai south and Malay north, see Wong, "Thai, Chinese and Malay Modern."
19   Jany, "Imperial Crossings," 59.
20   See Stoler, *Capitalism and Confrontation.*
21   Ghosh, *Nutmeg's Curse*, 237.
22   Ba Ren, *Wuzu miao*, 147.
23   Jany, "Imperial Crossings," 37–38.
24   Harper, *Underground Asia*, 70.
25   See Tee, "Sinophone Malaysian Literature."
26   *Encyclopaedia Britannica*, "The Impact of British Rule."
27   Fang Xiu, *Mahua xin wenxue xuanji (yi)* and *Mahua xin wenxue xuanji (er).*

28 Fang Xiu, *Mahua xin wenxue (er)*, 96.

29 Fang Xiu, *Mahua xin wenxue (yi)*, 114–16.

30 Ibid., 116.

31 Ibid., 117.

32 Ibid., 119–20.

33 Ibid., 118–19.

34 See Seah, "<Shizi jietou> shijian."

35 Ba Ren, *Wuzu miao,* 5–6.

36 Ibid., 283. At another point Ba Ren laments that "the play became solely about the struggle of Chinese laborers against Dutch imperialism" (劇本的內容就成為單純的華工反抗荷蘭帝國主義的鬥爭). Ibid., 142.

37 Ibid., 137, 144.

38 See Zhou, *Migration*, 34–51; Ba Ren, *Wuzu miao*, 142.

39 Jany, "Imperial Crossings," 53.

40 See Stenberg, *Minority Stages*, 76–95.

41 For details of the Luhmann family murders and the skeptical aftermath of colonial documentation, see Stoler, "'In Cold Blood.'"

42 Ibid., 173. Panglima Selan led raids on plantations in Luhmann's estate. Sutan Sjahrir (1909–1966) was Indonesia's prime minister and independence leader. I follow Zhou's rendering of *La jia er* 拉迦爾 as Sjahrir in *Migration*. For the postdating of the 1871 event, as well as a genetic criticism of Ba Ren's play that brings together the myth, archive, and architectural memory of the five ancestors, see Stenberg and Minasny, "Coolie Legend."

43 Ba Ren, *Wuzu miao*, 139, 284.

44 Jany, "Imperial Crossings," 16.

45 Ba Ren, *Wuzu miao*, 138.

46 Ibid., 200–201.

47 Ibid., 211.

48 Ibid., 148–51; 181–94.

49 Ibid., 202.

50 Ba Ren, *Wuzu Mao*, 258. The English translation is Zhou's, from Zhou, *Migration*, 48.

51 See Deleuze and Guattari, *Kafka*.

References

Anderson, Benedict. *Imagined Communities: Reflections on the Origin and Spread of Nationalism*. Revised and enlarged. London: Verso Books, 1991.

Ba Ren 巴人. *Wuzu miao* 五祖廟 [The Temple of Five Ancestors]. Guangzhou: Huacheng chubanshe, 1986.

Benjamin, Walter. *Selected Writings*, vol. 4, *1938–1940*. Cambridge, MA: Harvard University Press, 2006.

Chan, Cheow Thia. "Indigeneity, Map-Mindedness, and World-Literary Cartography: The Poetics and Politics of Li Yongping's Transregional Chinese Literary Production." *Modern Chinese Literature and Culture* 30, no. 1 (Spring 2018): 63–86.

Coronil, Fernando. "Transculturation and the Politics of Theory: Countering the Center, Cuban Counterpoint." In *Cuban Counterpoint: Tobacco and Sugar*, by Fernando Ortiz, xxvi–xxx. Durham, NC: Duke University Press, 1995.

Deleuze, Gilles, and Félix Guattari. *Kafka: Toward a Minor Literature*, translated by Dana Polan. Minneapolis: University of Minnesota Press, 1986.

Doyle, Laura. *Inter-imperiality: Vying Empires, Gendered Labor, and the Literary Arts of Alliance*. Durham, NC: Duke University Press, 2020.

Doyle, Laura. "Thinking Back through Empires." *Modernism/modernity* 2, cycle 4 (2018). https://modernismmodernity.org/forums/posts/thinking-back-through-empires.

Encyclopaedia Britannica. s.v. "The Impact of British Rule." Accessed September 15, 2021. https://www.britannica.com/place/Malaysia/The-impact-of-British-rule.

Fang Xiu 方修, ed. *Mahua xin wenxue xuanji, xiaoshuo (er)* 馬華新文學選集，小說(二) [Selections of New Mahua Literature, Fiction: Volume 2]. Singapore: Xingzhou shijie shuju, 1969.

Fang Xiu 方修, ed. *Mahua xin wenxue xuanji, xiaoshuo (yi)* 馬華新文學選集，小說(一) [Selections of New Mahua Literature, Fiction: Volume 1]. Singapore: Xingzhou shijie shuju, 1967.

Ghosh, Amitav. *The Nutmeg's Curse: Parables for a Planet in Crisis*. London: Murray, 2021.

Harper, Tim. *Underground Asia: Global Revolutionaries and the Assault on Empire*. Cambridge, MA: Harvard University Press, 2021.

Harvey, David. "The 'New' Imperialism: Accumulation by Dispossession." *Socialist Register* 40 (2004): 63–87.

Jany, Gregory. "Imperial Crossings: Chinese Indentured Migration to Sumatra's East Coast, 1865–1911." BA thesis, Yale University, 2021. https://elischolar.library.yale.edu/ceas_student_work/12.

Karatani, Kojin. *Origins of Modern Japanese Literature*, translated by Brett de Bary. Durham, NC: Duke University Press, 1993.

Lombard-Salmon, Claudine. "Taoke or Coolies? Chinese Visions of the Chinese Diaspora." *Archipel* 26 (1983): 179–210.

Macauley, Melissa. *Distant Shores: Colonial Encounters on China's Maritime Frontier*. Princeton, NJ: Princeton University Press, 2021.

Mamdani, Mahmood. *Neither Setter nor Native: The Making and Unmaking of Permanent Minorities*. Cambridge, MA: Harvard University Press, 2020.

Seah, Cheng Ta 謝徵達. "<Shizi jietou> shijian" 《十字街頭》事件 [The *Crossroads* Incident]. *Lianhe zaobao* 聯合早報, February 27, 2018. https://www.zaobao.com/news/fukan/literary-writings/story20180227-838313.

Shih, Shu-mei. "Comparison as Relation." In *Comparison: Theories, Approaches, Uses*, edited by Rita Felski and Susan Stanford Friedman, 79–98. Baltimore: Johns Hopkins University Press, 2013.

Sivasundaram, Sujit. *Waves across the South: A New History of Revolution and Empire*. Chicago: University of Chicago Press, 2021.

Stenberg, Josh. *Minority Stages: Sino-Indonesian Performance and Public Display*. Honolulu: University of Hawai'i Press, 2019.

Stenberg, Josh, and Budiman Minasny. "Coolie Legend on the Deli Plantation: Tale, Text and Temple of the Five Ancestors." *Bijdragen tot de Taal-, Land- en Volkenkunde* 178 (2022): 159–91.

Stoler, Ann Laura. *Capitalism and Confrontation in Sumatra's Plantation Belt, 1870–1979*. 2nd ed. Ann Arbor: University of Michigan Press, 1995.

Stoler, Ann Laura. "'In Cold Blood': Hierarchies of Credibility and the Politics of Colonial Narratives." *Representations* no. 37 (Winter 1992): 151–89.

Tee, Kim Tong. "Sinophone Malaysian Literature: An Overview." In *Sinophone Studies: A Critical Reader*, edited by Shu-mei Shih, Chien-hsin Tsai, and Brian Bernards, 304–14. New York: Columbia University Press, 2013.

Wong, Nicholas Y. H. "Thai, Chinese and Malay Modern: Civilisational and Textual Discourses in Hsu Yun-Tsiao's 1933 Diaries in Patani." In *Chapters on Asia: Selected Papers from the Lee Kong Chian Research Fellowship, 2017–2018*, 49–70. Singapore: National Library Singapore, 2019.

Zhou, Taomo. *Migration in the Time of Revolution: China, Indonesia, and the Cold War*. Ithaca, NY: Cornell University Press, 2019.

NICOLAI VOLLAND

Fluid Horizons
Oceanic Epistemologies and Sinophone Literature

ABSTRACT This article revisits Sinophone literature from the archipelagic region of the western Pacific to understand how thinking with and through the ocean shapes patterns of place-making and identity formation. Scrutinizing stories by Syaman Rapongan and Ng Kim Chew, the article shows how the ocean figures on several distinct registers: as the locale where these works unfold, as the object toward which their characters' yearnings and reflections are directed, and as a condition of being. Alternatively, the ocean can be read in the metaphorical and allegorical sense, as a device that allows their authors to critique (neo)colonial violence, the irruption of modernity, and especially the rigors of land-based and supposedly stable epistemologies. Against these, Rapongan and Ng posit what I call oceanic epistemologies, that is, systems and methods of knowledge drawn from and intertwined with the ocean as a condition of being on a terraqueous globe. The oceanic epistemologies in Sinophone literatures from littoral East and Southeast Asia allow us to rethink fundamental questions of being, identity, and history. They build upon, but methodologically move beyond, the critical apparatus offered by Sinophone literature.

KEYWORDS Oceanic epistemologies, oceanic literature, Syaman Rapongan, Ng Kim Chew, Sinophone literature

> My mind began to melt into imaginings of the world at the bottom of the sea. . . . So
> many scenes of my time underwater began to float across the textures of my mind, so
> beautiful and startling that they made me tremble.
>
> 我的心開始溶解於對海底世界的幻想. . . . 好多好多美好、驚險的令人振奮的影幕開始
> 浮現在我的腦海紋路
>
> —Syaman Rapongan, "Cold Sea, Deep Feeling"

> When I enter the ocean, my indigenous identity emerges. I become a historical being
> riding waves, running as a liquid mass, pulled up from the deep and thrown forward
> with a deafening roar. I disappear with fish and strands of seaweed as I course through
> veins of ocean currents.
>
> —Karin Amimoto Ingersoll, *Waves of Knowing*

Syaman Rapongan's 夏曼·藍波安 (1957–) work centers on what he calls "oceanic literature" (*haiyang wenxue* 海洋文學). A member of the Tao people, an ethnic

PRISM: THEORY AND MODERN CHINESE LITERATURE • 19:2 • SEPTEMBER 2022
DOI 10.1215/25783491-9966677 • © 2022 LINGNAN UNIVERSITY

group native to Lanyu 蘭嶼 (Orchid Island), Rapongan is usually classified as a Taiwanese Indigenous author. Categories like this, however, obscure more complex patterns in the making of identity. Not only does Taiwan figure in oppositional terms in much of Rapongan's fiction; the author's discursive constructions of identity are at once distinctly place-bound, revolving around Lanyu, a small island forty miles off Taiwan's southeast coast, while at the same time dissolving this geoliterary bondedness by immersing Lanyu in an oceanic expanse that stretches across much of the Pacific Ocean and extends to archipelagic Southeast Asia and onward into the Indian Ocean.[1] The ocean, for Rapongan, is not an empty, watery void, separating continents and coastal communities; it is, rather, both a space of sensory experience central to meaning-making for the inhabitants of Rapongan's literary world, and a canvas for projections of kinship. This kinship, in Rapongan's stories, extends far beyond Lanyu's shores, and reaches outward to other ocean-based communities. The oceanic imaginaries of Rapongan's work propose forms of knowledge and identity that defy rigid norms and that in themselves remain fluid and flexible, operating in ways that resemble not so much hard and supposedly reliable patterns of logic and reason, but rather the waves and ocean currents so central to his fiction.

Syaman Rapongan's oceanic epistemologies challenge land-based forms of thinking and writing, and their associated registers of meaning, drawing attention to alternative modes of meaning-making situated at the littoral peripheries of the Sinophone world. In its own civilizational imaginary and much of its literature, China has been construed in continental terms, as a land-based entity—an empire situated on terra firma, the center of a world on its own, bounded by deserts, mountains, jungles, and oceans—places inhabited (if at all) by semibarbaric or barbaric peoples. This civilizational self-understanding entails more than a sense of firm ground and clearly identifiable territorial delineations. It has also engendered a belief in ancient and reliable categories of thought and knowledge. The growth of critical interest in Chinese literatures from beyond and outside the Chinese mainland, as well as the rise of Sinophone studies, have exposed the artificiality and partiality of these notions and revealed them to be less stable than they may appear.[2] Literary and critical interventions from Sinophone Southeast Asia, in particular, have forced a productive reckoning with the underlying assumptions of the field.

Southeast Asia, like Syaman Rapongan's Lanyu, is an archipelagic region, bounded and intersected by maritime spaces. Hence, oceanic epistemologies are key to rethinking the region's situatedness within the larger literary and thought worlds on a global scale. In his classic essay "Our Sea of Islands," Epeli Hauʻofa challenges his readers to reimagine the "small islands" of the Southern Pacific as a "sea of islands."[3] It was imperialist expansion in the eighteenth and nineteenth centuries that had shattered "a large world in which peoples and cultures moved and mingled unhindered by boundaries of the kind erected much later by imperial powers."[4] Hauʻofaʻs project, accordingly, is to decolonize the minds of the Pacific's Indigenous denizens and reclaim the ocean, in its expansive and intellectually productive vastness, as their natural home and state of being. Hauʻofaʻs estimation of Oceaniaʻs ability to extricate itself from the socioeconomic chokehold of empire may have been overly optimistic. Syaman Raponganʻs fiction, as we shall see, presents a decidedly more sober account of the economic and ecological challenges faced by Oceaniaʻs denizens. Hauʻofaʻs epistemological intervention, however, his reconceptualization of a maritime world in maritime terms, offers a productive point of departure for reimagining transoceanic Chinese literatures.

Like Hauʻofa, Édouard Glissant foregrounds the connectedness of the Antillean islands of the Caribbean. Glissantʻs archipelagic imagination, too, is grounded in history, though for him a rejection of colonialismʻs violent irruption cannot possibly lead to a return to the status quo ante. Rather, the archipelagic imaginary is predicated upon the very memory of this colonial violence, in particular the legacies of the slave trade across the Black Atlantic.[5] It is what unites the inhabitants across all that divides them—languages, (post)colonial regimes, islands—and it leads Glissant to argue for a "poetics of relation," a poetics "that is latent, open, multilingual in intention, directly in contact with everything possible" and that "interweaves and no longer projects. . . . It inscribes itself in a circularity. . . . Trajectory, even bent or inflected, no longer applies."[6] The archipelagic imaginary, then, no longer just acknowledges and affirms its own geospatial situatedness. It also talks back to patterns of thought that are themselves legacies of colonialism, and it posits alternative modes of meaning-making that are inspired by the oceanic world from which they have emerged. Thus, for both Glissant and Hauʻofa the ocean represents not what divides and separates, but what unites; it is the constitutive element of their worlds, the source of its critical and emancipatory potential. Identifying themselves as islanders in a maritime world does not marginalize their voices, but rather lends them flexibility and fluidity, an epistemological vantage point from which they confront the intellectual, economic, and political powers that be.

The ocean, however, is arguably not only a space that challenges the dominant geopolitical imaginary and binary notions such as land/water, center/periphery, and domination/subjugation. It is also a physical presence that can and needs to be encountered in sensory ways. This sensory experience is, according to Karin Amimoto Ingersoll, central to what she calls a "seascape epistemology": "Ke kai [the sea] enables an autonomous reconnection, recreation, and reimagination for all Kanaka Maoli [Indigenous Hawaiians] through an ocean-based epistemology."[7] Her people activate this embodied potential through immersing in it (see the epigraph of this article). Ingersoll engages with the medium of the ocean through her surfboard, and by doing so, unlocks her own past and that of her people. This bodily engagement activates a set of literacies, "an oceanic knowledge that privileges an alternative political and ethical relationship with the surrounding physical and spiritual world."[8] Acknowledging Hauʻofa's intervention, Ingersoll nonetheless critiques his tendency to romanticize and essentialize Pacific Islanders' relationship with the ocean. Instead, she proposes to "expand the notion of seascape into a methodology about the movement of theories, realities, and identities."[9] In Ingersoll's account, identities—like the forms of knowledge and constructions of meaning they are composed of—are never stable. They exist in dynamic and decentral patterns of interaction with their oceanic environment. While she is concerned chiefly with Indigenous epistemologies, Ingersoll's move to shift focus to the ocean as a simultaneously conceptual and physical entity is instructive for literary projects that critically engage the aqueous realm, projects located at the intersection of the littoral and the literary.

Compared to the Caribbean, the South Pacific, and even the Indian Ocean, the western Pacific—the maritime region that includes the littoral areas of China, Taiwan, and much of Southeast Asia—has received little critical attention. A long tradition of literary studies has, in principle, accepted the continental and civilizational paradigm of China as a unified and centralized entity, situated on the East Asian landmass and, if facing outward at all, turning its gaze toward inner Asia. Since the late nineteenth century, this gaze has shifted, not so much to the ocean and China's coastal areas but rather across the ocean, to North America or Western Europe, almost invariably to the neglect of the intervening maritime spaces. These geospatial imaginaries have direct bearing on the very terms and categories in which Chinese literature is discussed. Going back to C. T. Hsia's "obsession with China," much of the critical literature henceforth has focused on questions of the nation, ethnicity, history, and identity—a conceptual and critical vocabulary that takes for granted the unitary and stable nature of its world.[10] Constitutive of a theoretical and methodological paradigm, these land-based epistemologies have remained firmly in place, even where they entail patterns of limited variability through modes of dialectic binaries, producing a sense of order and reliability, continuity and analytical soundness that governs both the public and the private realms. Central categories of social thought and organization all affirm and perpetuate this continental, landed tradition of both literary and critical writing.

Sinophone studies, with its emphasis on marginality, diaspora, and responses to multiple forms of colonialism, has pushed back forcefully against China-centrism in spheres ranging from the political through the linguistic to the literary. Refocusing critical attention to the periphery, to the minor Sinitic literatures of Taiwan, Hong Kong, Southeast Asia, and diasporic communities, Sinophone studies has productively reconceived especially "the conjuncture of China's internal colonialism and Sinophone communities everywhere immigrants from

China have settled," thus "disrupt[ing] the chain of equivalence established, since the rise of nation-states, among language, culture, ethnicity, and nationality."[11] Geospatially, Sinophone studies has highlighted literary regions that can all be described as maritime or littoral. This overlap has been occasionally acknowledged.[12] Most notably, Brian Bernards draws on Glissant to delineate the notion of Nanyang/South Seas, foregrounding the archipelagic nature of Southeast Asia. However, Bernards primarily focuses on "interregional relations and exchanges in Southeast Asia" and the ways in which such connections have fostered processes of Sinophone creolization that are "transcolonial, transnational, [and] translingual" in nature.[13] He is less concerned with the watery element that enables these connections, the ocean itself, and with the epistemological implications of this littoral consciousness. Sinophone studies shares an intellectual genealogy with some of the oceanic studies literature discussed above, drawing on the same critical resources—no more so than in their shared emphasis on decentral networks, their interest in peripheral viewpoints and communities, and their counterhegemonic agenda.[14] At the same time, certain propositions articulated by Sinophone studies have met with resistance, especially in Southeast Asia, where some observers have found Sinophone studies' bird's-eye view difficult to reconcile with locally developed concepts and approaches. Oceanic studies and its conceptual frameworks, I propose, may allow us to build on the critical contributions of Sinophone studies, while avoiding some of its pitfalls, by rethinking Sinophone literatures from a maritime perspective.

In this article, I revisit Sinophone literature from the archipelagic region of the western Pacific to understand how thinking with and through the ocean shapes patterns of place-making and identity formation. In the works under scrutiny here, the ocean functions on several distinct registers. It may, as in Syaman Rapongan's work, figure in the literal sense, as the locale where his fiction unfolds and as the object toward which his characters' yearnings and reflections are directed. Alternatively, such as in the work of Ng Kim Chew 黃錦樹 (1967–), it may constitute a condition of being, the central conceit on which his stories are predicated. Finally, both Rapongan's and Ng's work display what I will call oceanic epistemologies: systems and methods of knowledge drawn from and intertwined with the ocean as a condition of being on a terraqueous globe. The oceanic epistemologies in the Sinophone literatures from littoral East and Southeast Asia—or, rather, the western Pacific—allow us to rethink fundamental questions of being, identity, and history. They move us beyond continental paradigms, both epistemologically and methodologically.

The article first turns to Syaman Rapongan's short stories. In his work, Rapongan immerses his reader in the ocean, gazing at the sea from his home on the shore and taking us on extended diving trips. The practice of spearfishing in particular emerges as a conjuncture of bodily/sensory experience and social as well as metaphysical praxis. It is embedded in traditional hierarchies of value and meaning that ritually reconnect him to his ancestry and the spiritual world of his people. At the same time, it enacts an oppositional stance, an articulation of his characters' rejection of both the political economy of the "mainland" (here, Taiwan) and the epistemological structures imposed upon his people.

I will then turn to Ng Kim Chew and the island world of the Nanyang. Rereading one of Ng's better-known stories, "Ala de zhiyi" 阿拉的旨意 (Allah's will), I propose that the story represents an extended meditation on the problem of identity, hinging on the story's locale—an island the narrator is forbidden to leave. During his island exile, as I will show, Ng's narrator sees his own language, and with it his very identity, dissolving into the surrounding oceanic expanse. Rather than being fixed in time and place, identity in this maritime environment becomes fluid, liquefying old bonds while allowing for new connections and networks of meaning to take shape. Both Ng's and Rapongan's fiction challenge land-based systems and categories of thought; in their work, we see oceanic epistemologies at work.

Syaman Rapongan's Immersive Logic

In the introduction to his 1997 collection of stories *Leng hai qing shen* 冷海情深 (Cold Sea, Deep Feeling), Syaman Rapongan recounts constant quarrels with his wife and his children:

> Having failed to extract ten yuan from me, the kids accused me: "Dad, you are so lazy, you don't go to earn money for us."
>
> I replied confidently: "Your dad goes spearfishing and gives you fresh fish to eat, that's earning money, too."
>
> They rejected me out of hand: "What nonsense!"[15]

> 孩子們從我身上搜刮不到十塊錢時，說：「爸爸，你最懶，你都不賺錢給我們。」
>
> 我很自信地回道：「爸爸射新鮮魚給你們吃就是賺錢呀。」
>
> 「才怪呢！」孩子們反駁道。

This episode, which reappears in lightly fictionalized form in the collection's title story, pits two sets of logic against each other. Rapongan's wife and children, just like the narrator's family in "Cold Sea, Deep Feeling," have internalized the socioeconomic conventions and value systems of modernity. A man's worth, for them, is calculated in accordance with his ability to provide for the sustenance of his family; his success or failure is measurable in monetary terms. His wife's and children's complaints about the narrator's refusal to work in the regulated modern economy mark socioeconomic and personal failure in the eyes of mainstream society. The alternative that Rapongan holds to against this land-based logic remains sheer nonsense (*guai* 怪) to his addressees. But Rapongan is unde-terred and insists on his own logic. At the end of the introduction, his exasperated mother offers to hide his spear gun. But, counters the author, "when I heard this I just laughed. For I would build a new spear gun" 我聽了之後，笑了起來，因爲我還是會再做一個魚槍的.[16] Rapongan's oceanic epistemology is resilient and self-confident; it will not be subdued easily.

The ocean figures prominently in most of Rapongan's stories. It is a constant sensory presence, either gazed at from ashore or experienced through immer-sion, by the swimmers and divers who populate his stories. The sea is introduced at the outset of "Cold Sea, Deep Feeling," when the narrator observes the murky, gray waters from his porch, through the persistent drizzle of the winter rains. His diving gear sits next to him on his porch, his spear gun "pointed toward the sea" 槍頭朝海.[17] He will soon give in to his yearning for the sea, leaving behind his household's nagging women and embarking on yet another spearfishing expedi-tion. Swimming, diving, and fishing—the narrators' immersion in the ocean—constitute the narrative core of Rapongan's stories. "Cold Sea, Deep Feeling" recounts a single spearfishing trip. In "Feiyu de huhuan" 飛魚的呼喚 (The Call of the Flying Fish), a Tao youth gains permission to accompany his father on what will be his maiden fishing expedition. And "Haiyang chaoshengzhe" 海洋朝聖者 (The Ocean Pilgrim), a capsule maritime bildungsroman, depicts a returnee from Taiwan documenting the rediscovery of his roots and his personal pride through a series of spearfishing trips.

Spearfishing is a recurring element that offers both a degree of suspense and a site of philosophical deliberation for Rapongan. In "Cold Sea, Deep Feeling," the narrator dives beyond the windswept ocean surface down into the calm shadows of the reefs, following schools of fish that drift suspended in the ocean currents. In contrast to fishing with nets, during which fishermen remain dry in their boats, spearfishing requires them to physically enter the ocean and encounter their prey at a short distance. It requires substantial skill and as much knowledge, which can be acquired only through extended practice in the company of experienced elders. It is also inherently dangerous. The divers find themselves face to face with sharks and need to swim against strong and treacherous ocean currents. Keeping calm and not showing fear in such circumstances count as proof of a diver's matu-rity. In Rapongan's stories, then, spearfishing is at once a sensory experience, of the kind outlined by Ingersoll, and a social and metaphysical practice. It activates registers of social being and identity on a range of levels, including gender, clan, and ethnicity. Manhood in particular figures prominently in Rapongan's stories. The transformation of social and economic life is threatening customary forms of identity, and spearfishing is a means to reassert gendered claims to respect and social standing.[18] In "The Ocean Pilgrim," the narrator returns to Lanyu from Tai-wan and is ridiculed by other men for his inability to dive and hunt in the ocean;

in their eyes, his integration into the modern economy has emasculated him. To regain his pride and his social position, he needs to relearn spearfishing from his cousins and uncles. Diving and fishing thus are embedded in the larger oceanic logic that underlies Rapongan's fiction.

The practice of spearfishing is regulated by an elaborate set of customary practices and taboos, and disrespect for these ritual practices will trigger a crisis. This happens in "Cold Sea, Deep Feeling," where it is the epistemic crisis, rather than the fishing expedition itself, that constitutes the story's narrative focus. The epistemological significance of spearfishing, Rapongan suggests, outweighs the sensory gain of the immersive oceanic experience. Diving among the reefs, the narrator gets carried away by excitement or greed and does not cease his pursuit until his fishing net is filled with fish. By the time he returns to shore, night has fallen, and he has violated the most central taboo of the Tao people: the prohibition against nighttime fishing. Reaching home, he finds his family in mourning. He has been presumed dead and, in accordance with custom, his clan members have swarmed out to recover his body from the fangs of the angry spirits. It takes a night of exorcising ritual and collective storytelling to reestablish the ritual order and for the narrator to regain admission to his community. Hence, the sensory and experiential immersion in the water is but a function of the ritual and metaphysical order that regulates life in the oceanic world of Lanyu.

What is at stake in Syaman Rapongan's works, then, is the question of identity. The Indigenous, non-Sinitic names in his stories are markers of resistance against a mainstream culture. Their transliterations break up the homogeneity of the Chinese textual surface and become rem(a)inders of alterity from an author writing in what is, essentially, the language of his colonizer.[19] Yet while indigeneity is undoubtedly an important concern for Rapongan, as observers such as Kuei-fen Chiu and Hsin-ya Huang have claimed, it is not the only source of identity in Rapongan's fictional world.[20] Other categories, such as gender hierarchies and politics, are equally central. As noted above, gender differences are hierarchies (sometimes bordering on the misogynist) that are marked throughout his short stories. Ultimately, however, it is the ocean itself that emerges as the masculine principle in Rapongan's stories. In contrast, the land—and land-based modern occupations such as teaching—are perceived as female. In this sense, then, the oceanic world of Lanyu emerges as masculine, while Taiwan is feminized.

Taiwan, throughout the stories in *Cold Sea, Deep Feeling*, functions as an Other, an alternative mode of being and reasoning that Rapongan's oceanic epistemology subverts and opposes. Taiwan is characterized as a disruptive influence in the oceanic world, associated with experiences and practices that corrode the Indigenous culture of the Tao people. Its political economy marginalizes Lanyu, but its people are no longer silent—Lanyu is talking back from the periphery. In "The Ocean Pilgrim," the narrator's uncle says a prayer before their dive in which he addresses the fish: "Don't be afraid of the [flash]lights in our hands; these things are what the outsiders (i.e., the Han people) have given to us. I pray for the good spirits of our ancestors to protect your descendants" 不要驚訝我們手裡的燈光，這個玩意是異族（指漢人）送給我們的，祈求善良的祖靈護佑你們的後裔。[21] What Rapongan glosses as "Han people" are "outsiders," ethnically alien to Lanyu. The consequences of Taiwan's exploitation of Lanyu are to be seen everywhere. While fishing offshore, Rapongan and his cousins swim amid debris and unexploded ordnance; the ocean floor is littered with thousands of bomb craters left behind by Taiwan's air force, which had used the area as a bombing range for target practice.[22] The cousin concludes bitterly, "In this country, we Yamei are being thoroughly humiliated. How can we still love the Republic of China [Taiwan]?" 我們雅美人在這個國家，真的是被徹底的羞辱，叫我們如何熱愛中華民國呢?[23] Rapongan does not provide an answer. In his stories, Taiwan is presented as a land-based power, oblivious if not hostile to the maritime environment of Lanyu and its Indigenous inhabitants.

The identification of Taiwan with land and power is ironic, as Taiwan perceives itself as an island nation (*daoguo* 島國), a periphery in the shadow of a continental great power—China.[24] In Rapongan's work, Taiwan's status is inverted; vis-à-vis Lanyu, the ultraperiphery, Taiwan becomes a colonial regime that threatens the livelihood and identity of Lanyu's inhabitants, destroying Lanyu's ecology and overwhelming its ritual economy with the demands of a modern state.[25] In this light, Rapongan's oceanic epistemology becomes a source of resistance, an alternative structure of thinking and knowledge that allows him and the inhabitants of his story world to talk back to Taiwan. The ocean is a resource that allows the Indigenous people of Lanyu to assert their own distinct identity and to reclaim their own logic against the homogenizing violence emanating from the Taiwanese mainland. The ocean defines Lanyu's alterity and provides the basis of its identity.

Ng Kim Chew and the Fluidity of Being

Syaman Rapongan's mobilization of the ocean as a source of alternative identity comes at a price. In the course of constructing the Indigenous identity of the Tao people, as expressed in their rituals and their traditional way of life and work, Rapongan invariably objectifies this identity—and, arguably, the very notion of identity itself. His ethnographic project, as critics have pointed out, is in fact a *re*construction of identity, made possible through the anthropological lens of a semi-outsider.[26] The protagonists of Rapongan's stories are returnees to Lanyu, men who make self-conscious decisions to rediscover and relearn the mode of being a Tao islander. Ironically, the essence, as it were, of Tao indigeneity and its oceanic roots can be perceived only after being filtered through the lens of modernity and its landed conceptual apparatus.[27] More importantly, the very concept of identity turns into a monolithic, unchanging, primordial entity that manifests itself in a set of binaries—Lanyu and Taiwan, ocean and land, tradition and modernity, men and women. These binaries seem at odds with the sort of relational thinking that is commonly associated with archipelagic and oceanic epistemologies. Are there ways, then, to think about identity in oceanic terms, without succumbing to the allure of entrenched patterns of thought that are themselves attributable to a land-based logic? It is in this regard that Ng Kim Chew appears much more skeptical of the existing epistemic horizons than Rapongan. Identity is a recurring theme, an obsession even, in Ng's fiction. His stories are set within and engage with the island world of archipelagic Southeast Asia, even if they do not appear to be "oceanic literature" in the narrow sense. Ng's approach to the problem of identity and his take on the ocean, however, both differ radically from Rapongan's. What becomes fluid in Ng's stories is the very nature of identity as an epistemic category.

In Ng's short story "Allah's Will," the narrator recounts, on his deathbed, the story of his life and travails on a remote island. In his youth, he gets caught up in Malaya's (mostly ethnically Chinese) Communist insurrection, is arrested, and is sentenced to death. On the execution ground, he faints when the firing squad ready their guns, only to awaken on a boat delivering him to a remote island, inhabited by some of Malaya's ethnic minority peoples. He learns that a "most cherished friend" belonging to the royal family has secretly intervened to spare his life, but only on the condition that he sign a pledge to live forever on the island, to never again contact his friends and family, to never again speak Chinese, and instead to convert to Islam and found a new family. In other words, he must start a new life under a new name and leave behind his former self. The story then tells of the narrator's circumcision and his conversion, and of a lifetime spent on the island, but also of little acts of what he calls "stubborn resistance" 頑抗, symbolic clandestine reassertions of his Chineseness. His final, and most momentous, act of defiance is writing down the story of his life, and doing so in Chinese. "I am very aware of the fact," he declares at the outset of the narrative, "that, if the story I will tell below were revealed to the world, it would cause a major storm" 我清楚的知道，以下所講述的故事如果被披露於世，將會引起多大的風波 and implicate his wife, children, grandchildren, as well as his "most cherished friend."[28]

Ng's story has been variously read as a critique of Chineseness, a depiction of linguistic anxiety, and an inquiry into the cultural meanings of script. Carlos Rojas highlights the author's playful interrogation of the "conditions of intelligibility" raised by the story.[29] Alison Groppe foregrounds "the fear of losing the Chinese language" that constitutes one of the "deepest anxieties" of Sinophone Malaysian communities.[30] And for Andrea Bachner, the story represents "a desperate act of scriptural loyalism" in which the protagonist faces up to the precarity of diasporic

Chineseness.[31] All these readings are plausible and offer helpful insights about Ng's fictional strategies and his commentary on the existential anxieties of Sinophone communities in Southeast Asia. The allegoric thrust of Ng's story, however, seems to aim higher yet. Chineseness, language, and script are all markers of identity, pointers toward a more fundamental concern. In what follows, I will instead read "Allah's Will" as an extended meditation on the very nature of identity itself, a bold critique of a notion that is so central to the politics of East and Southeast Asia. This critique, I will show, hinges on the symbolic conceit of the island and its maritime environment, and presents itself as inspired by an oceanic mode of thinking.

A key scene in "Allah's Will" is the narrator's circumcision, carried out shortly after his arrival in his abode of exile. The circumcision ceremony denotes his symbolic conversion to Islam and the literal shedding of his former identity. The ritual constitutes a prominent marker that distinguishes the Muslim and non-Muslim (i.e., ethnically Chinese) populations of Southeast Asia and hence signals a crucial and allegedly traumatic moment in the narrator's transition. To undergo circumcision, as a Chinese individual, is a transgressive act:

> Before and after the ceremony, and even during the procedure, I kept remembering my parents' exhortations since I was a child: Chinese are Chinese, foreigners are foreigners; you can play together and go to school together, but a Chinese can never become a foreigner, and neither can a foreigner become Chinese.[32]

> 在手術完成之前之後，甚至在手術中，一直憶起父母親自小灌輸的觀念：唐人就是唐人，番仔就是番仔，可以一起玩，一起念書，可是唐人不能變成番仔，番仔也不能變成唐人。

This same exhortation is repeated, again and again, throughout the story. It recurs at strategic moments as reassertions of ethnic identity, whenever this identity may be threatened. Ethnic difference is essentialized, and identity is cast into absolute terms. The transgression of this taboo, hence, is likened to an acute and painful loss of identity, an act of emasculation. At his circumcision ceremony, "the village chief produced a small knife (similar to the knife my father used to castrate pigs)" 村長掏出了一把小刀(和父親所用的閹豬刀類似) (119). And a few lines later, the narrator comments on the smell of the bandage applied to his penis after the procedure: "This smell was similar to that of the traditional medicine used to stop bleeding that my father applied after castrating young pigs" 那股氣味，也和父親閹完小豬後傷口止血所用的土方近似 (119). The narrator, then, leaves little doubt that his circumcision is, for all practical purposes, an attempt to castrate him—to emasculate him and his ethnic being. It is an assault against the very Chineseness he keeps reasserting during the procedure.

The newly circumcised—or, in his own words, emasculated or castrated—narrator is made to marry the village chief's daughter. In a surprising turn of events, he goes on to father an ever-growing number of children: "'The number of your children will be determined by Allah's will.' In no time, and in accordance with Allah's will, my sons alone were numerous enough to field a soccer team. Following the island's custom, I planted a coconut tree after the birth of each child, and by now our house is surrounded by a veritable forest" 「有多少孩子,那是阿拉的旨意。」一轉眼,依阿拉的旨意,單單是男丁足以組成一個足球隊。依照島上為每個降生的孩子種上一棵椰子樹的習俗,屋子周邊如今已是一大片椰林 (135). The narrator's astonishing fertility obviously puts the lie to his insistence that his conversion is an act of castration. To the contrary, his numerous offspring are living proof of the resounding success of his conversion. Rather than destroying his ability to procreate, his adoption of a new identity has fantastically boosted the narrator's fertility. And it is precisely here that Ng's sarcastic take on the issue of identity lies. For all the narrator's protestations to the contrary, identity emerges as a highly malleable, fluid construct. The story's protagonist is, accordingly, outed as an unreliable narrator.

The suspicion that we cannot trust the narrator's confessions of his primordial and unchangeable Chineseness is confirmed in accounts of his small acts of defiance, designed to secretly reassert his Chinese identity. To memorialize himself, he decides to erect a stele and composes an inscription. Knowing that he is not allowed to write Chinese, he opts for the ancient Chinese seal script with its pictographic characters, which offer him plausible deniability. Trouble is, "I had never learned the seal script, and I could hence rely only on my imagination" 我並不識篆文,只能憑想象而會意 (129). Accordingly, he invents his own "characters," pictograms of a pig, oxen, and cowrie shells. Yet what he draws are characters only in his own imagination; they are illegible to anyone with knowledge of Chinese seal script. The scheme sounds improbably complex, and the more obvious explanation appears to be: has the narrator simply forgotten how to write Chinese after all his years on the island, his cultural identity vanishing in the sea surrounding him? The story then describes his discovery of stone fragments with an ancient inscription. Yet the pieces contained just two "fragmentary characters" 不完全的字, incomplete and hence unreadable, as are those on porcelain shards he finds on the island's beaches. His attempts to piece them back together are to no avail—"Everywhere were critical pieces missing" 處處是致命的失落的環節 (130). Once again, Ng forces us to question the narrator's reliability. Is it the texts that are incomplete and hence unreadable—or has the narrator simply forgotten how to read Chinese?

The single most enigmatic line of "Allah's Will" is the story's opening sentence (after the epigraph, a quotation from the Quran): "(Originally written in Malay)" (原文為馬來文) (109). The sentence in parentheses acquires meaning only in light of the pointers that Ng plants at key moments in the story, strategically casting doubt on the narrator's reliability and the veracity of his account. In this light, then, the opening line affirms the suspicions detailed above. For, right after that line, the narrator, now on his deathbed, explains the motivations for composing an account of his life, and the difficulties he faces:

> I haven't written Chinese for almost thirty years, and I can't recall the precise look of many characters (I may miss strokes or add some, or mistake one character for another one, or have just the vaguest recollection of its shape, or recall just its pronunciation . . .). But no matter what, *I steadfastly refuse to transliterate any of them into Malay*; I'd rather substitute a homonymic character [for one I forgot].

> 將近三十年沒寫中文字，許多字的形體要嘛記不全(少一筆或多幾筆或記成別的形體或竟只是個朦朧的印象，或只記得它的聲音......)，不管怎樣,非不得已我絕不用馬來拼音替代，而寧願用同音之字。(109; emphasis added)

The narrator insists he is writing in Chinese. It is difficult, and he has to come up with ways to make up for his deficiencies, but what he writes is Chinese, and nothing else. He adamantly refuses to write in Malay. Or so he tells us. Yet the story's very first sentence laconically cancels all his elaborate professions. No matter how hard he tries and what he says, the text he produces is not Chinese: "Originally written in Malay." The narrator has, after all, failed in his final, most consequential attempt to reassert his Chinese identity via the medium of the Chinese script. His ability to write Chinese has vanished, dissolved in the long years of island life.

For the narrator of "Allah's Will," the Chinese script is a central marker of identity, a symbolic medium that reconnects the diasporic Chinese populations of Southeast Asia with their imagined homeland and their "native" culture. In the story, however, this pillar of identity has eroded, gradually washed away by the waves that lap at the island's shore. Despite the narrator's protestations to the contrary, identity itself has been exposed as a malleable, fluid entity. It is not set in stone, unchangeable and absolute, but rather subject to the forces of time and the environment. The much-repeated strict separation of Chinese and Malay people—who, as the narrator keeps reminding us, cannot be turned into one another—is exposed as a fiction. For the narrator's own experience is living proof of the very feasibility of changing one's identity, of transgressing the fetishized boundaries between different ethnic groups. His conversion—from a Chinese into a Malay man, from a Communist rebel into a respected village elder and teacher—is, all things considered, a resounding success. His numerous offspring, in accordance with Allah's will, demonstrate this much—thus the story's title. "Allah's Will," in other words, is Ng Kim Chew's sarcastic (and self-reflexive) answer to essentialized and rigid notions of identity, which he shows to be untenable, at least in archipelagic Southeast Asia.[33]

The maritime world of Southeast Asia is, of course, central to Ng's fiction, and the trope of the island is key to "Allah's Will." The entire story, with its meditation on the nature and character of identity, hinges on this trope, on the island as a microcosmos. Yu-ting Huang has noted that "islands are in Ng's stories artificial spaces; isolated and bounded, they are laboratories for psychological drama."[34] More is at stake, however, than mere satirical allegorization. In *Modernity at Sea*, Cesare Casarino proposes the notion of the ship as "the heterotopia par excellence" (following Foucault), an imagined space that allows authors to think through problems still on the threshold of imagination, for which no conceptual language as yet exists.[35] An analogous case can be made about Ng's use of the island in "Allah's Will." It is a heterotopic space allowing Ng to interrogate the notion of identity. The island is a confined space that the narrator is not allowed to leave, an experimental, hypothetical space that allows Ng to dissolve the notion of identity and demonstrate its untenability. The island is a site separate from the mainland, but, as Epeli Hauʻofa has reminded us, it is not an isolated space; rather it is connected to a larger island-world, an oceanic expanse that operates by its own rules and that generates epistemologies distinct from those of the continents beyond the horizon. Ng's story is a powerful demonstration of how oceanic epistemologies, with their foregrounding of the fluid, decentral, and counterhegemonic, help to critique established patterns of thinking and reasoning.

Conclusion

Central to "Allah's Will," and to much of Ng Kim Chew's other fiction, is the maritime environment of archipelagic Southeast Asia. Creatively deploying the fluid logic of this aqueous region, he mocks and challenges the epistemic order of land-based regimes. Like other authors on the maritime (ultra)periphery of the Chinese literary world, Ng draws attention to alternative modes of thinking and being. Where Syaman Rapongan uses the reconnection with the ocean as a strategy to push back against a violent colonial modernity (which, ironically, is associated with the self-professed island nation of Taiwan), Ng targets the epistemological foundations of this modernity itself. And while Rapongan engages with the ocean in a literal sense, Ng focuses on immersion and fluidity in a more abstract, allegorical manner. Thus, both Ng and Rapongan draw upon the ocean, the "sea of islands," to reformulate the terms of their literary enterprises, whether through the corporeal and sensory reassertion of identity, or instead, its deconstruction via the fluid horizons of logic. In this sense, both prove themselves to be connected, related to an expansive body of maritime literature that defies the categorizations imposed on it by continental structures of political and epistemic power.

The methodologies and approaches of oceanic and maritime literary studies, and the conceptual apparatus offered by the growing field of the "blue humanities," allow us to rethink the geoliterary positioning of fiction from the western Pacific and its adjacent littoral areas. As I have argued in this article, oceanic epistemologies empower Sinophone writers along lines similar to those proposed by Sinophone studies, all the while retaining flexibility—fluidity indeed—when confronted with issues such as diasporic connections or Indigenous identities. They confront the violence emanating from colonial and neocolonial projections of empire, interrogate the power structures inherent in language and script, and reclaim material and sensory regimes for their literary projects. The maritime environment forges new possibilities of thinking about issues such as home and space, connections and trajectories, belonging and becoming. The intersection of the littoral and the literary, as it were, is central to creative production from the region, and to the region itself.

NICOLAI VOLLAND is associate professor of Asian studies and comparative literature at Penn State University. His research interests include modern Chinese literature and culture, cosmopolitanism, transnationalism, Sinophone Studies, and oceanic studies, and he is the author of *Socialist Cosmopolitanism* (2017). He is a past president of the Association of Chinese and Comparative Literature.

////////////////////////////////

Notes

1   Transoceanic connections figure most prominently in Rapongan's most ambitious literary project, his 2014 novel *Dahai fumeng* 大海浮夢 (Ocean of Floating Dreams). The Tao are an Austronesian people speaking a Malayo-Polynesian language, with ethnic and linguistic links to groups in maritime Southeast Asia, the Central and South Pacific, and the Indian Ocean.

2   For a critical engagement with this problem see Wang, "Hua-yi zhi bian."

3   Hauʻofa, "Our Sea of Islands," 7.

4   Ibid., 8.

5   "The unconscious memory of the abyss," writes Glissant, "served as the alluvium for these metamorphoses. The populations that then formed, despite having forgotten the chasm [of the Middle Passage], despite being unable to imagine the passion of those who foundered there, nonetheless wove this sail." Glissant, *Poetics of Relation*, 7.

6   Glissant, *Poetics of Relation*, 32.

7   Ingersoll, *Waves of Knowing*, 3.

8   Ibid., 5.

9   Ibid., 18.

10 See Hsia, "Obsession with China"; Wang, *Monster That Is History*; and Ban Wang, *Illuminations from the Past*, among others.

11 Shih, "Concept of the Sinophone," 710. Strictly speaking, Shih excludes from the Sinophone those locales where settler colonialism has made Chinese the dominant language at the expense of Indigenous languages. This narrow definition has remained contentious. See Tsu and Wang, *Global Chinese Literature.*

12 Shu-mei Shih notes—though only in passing—the potential of the maritime to disrupt continental paradigms of China. See Shih, "What Is Sinophone Studies?," 2.

13 Bernards, *Writing the South Seas*, 15, 20–24.

14 Aside from Glissant, Françoise Lionnet's work has influenced both Sinophone Studies and oceanic studies. Glissant and Lionnet in turn both draw on Deleuze and rhizomatic modes of thought, as does Shu-mei Shih.

15 Rapongan, "Guanyu leng hai yu qing shen," 11–12. All translations in this article are my own.

16 Ibid., 14.

17 Rapongan, "Leng hai qing shen," 17. For an English translation of the story by Terence C. Russell see "Cold Sea, Deep Feeling."

18 It is debatable to what degree such attempts can be successful. As Gwennaël Gaffric notes, Rapongan's narrators tend to be returnees from Taiwan who consciously reject the corruptions of modern life, in search for a purer, traditional life. Gaffric's identification of these positions as "primitivism" and "cosmopolitanism," however, is problematic. See "Do Waves Have Memories?" More accurately, the Lanyu islanders' perception of tradition may be described as an indirect one, mediated through the encounter with modernity.

19 See, for instance, "Call of the Flying Fish." A similar function can be attributed to romanized sentences and exclamations of Tao language. Interspersed within the Chinese text, they disrupt the flow of reading and call attention to their own alterity. See "Feiyu de huhuan," 78, 84.

20 See Chiu, "Production of Indigeneity," and Huang, "Representing Indigenous Bodies." Gaffric has pointed out the need to move beyond reading Rapongan under the label of Indigenous literature. See "Do Waves Have Memories."

21 Rapongan, "Haiyang chaoshengzhe," 103.

22 Not visible—and not mentioned in these stories—but no less pernicious and harmful to the island environment—is the nuclear waste storage facility built by the Taiwanese government on Lanyu. One of the focal events of Taiwan's Indigenous movement were the 1988 protests against this facility. See Guan Xiao-Rong, *Lanyu baogao.*

23 Rapongan, "Haiyang chaoshengzhe," 109.

24 On Taiwan's internal heterogeneity and Syaman Rapongan's critical stance toward Taiwan, compare also Huang, "Archipelagos."

25 I am borrowing the concepts of ultraperipherality and ultramarginality from Lionnet and Jean-François, "Literary Routes." On Taiwan as a colonial power see also Gaffric, "Do Waves Have Memories."

26 See Gaffric, "Do Waves Have Memories." Rapongan holds a BA in French from Tamkang University. Shortly after the publication of the stories discussed above, he returned to Taiwan, to earn an MA degree in Anthropology from National Tsinghua University.

27 Pointedly, those islanders who have remained "untainted" by the culture of the colonizers—especially women—are also those who most fiercely resist his narrators' "return" to tradition.

28 Ng, "Ala de zhiyi," 109. For an English translation by Carlos Rojas, see Ng, "Allah's Will."

29 Rojas, "Introduction," xx.

30 Groppe, *Sinophone Malaysian Literature*, 92.
31 Bachner, *Beyond Sinology*, 140.
32 "Ala de zhiyi," 119; hereafter cited in the text.
33 The story may be read also as a comment on Ng's own hyphenated identity as an immigrant Malaysian-Taiwanese. See the postscript to the 2001 edition of *Ke bei* 刻景, the collection in which "Allah's Will" appeared.
34 Huang, "Archipelagos," 92.
35 Casarino, *Modernity at Sea*, 19–44.

References

Bachner, Andrea. *Beyond Sinology: Chinese Writing and the Scripts of Culture*. New York: Columbia University Press, 2014.

Bernards, Brian. *Writing the South Seas: Imagining the Nanyang in Chinese and Southeast Asian Postcolonial Literature*. Seattle: University of Washington Press, 2015.

Casarino, Cesare. *Modernity at Sea: Melville, Marx, Conrad in Crisis*. Minneapolis: University of Minnesota Press, 2002.

Chiu, Kuei-fen. "The Production of Indigeneity: Contemporary Indigenous Literature in Taiwan and Cross-Cultural Inheritance." *China Quarterly* 200 (2009): 1071–87.

Gaffric, Gwennaël. "Do Waves Have Memories? Human and Ocean Issues in Taiwan Indigenous Writer Syaman Rapongan's Writing." *TRANS—Revue de littérature générale et comparée* 16 (2013). https://doi.org/10.4000/trans.867.

Glissant, Édouard. *Poetics of Relation*, translated by Betsy Wing. Ann Arbor: University of Michigan Press, 1997.

Groppe, Alison M. *Sinophone Malaysian Literature: Not Made in China*. Amherst, MA: Cambria, 2013.

Guan Xiao-Rong 關曉榮. *Lanyu baogao, 1987–2007* 蘭嶼報告1987–2007 [Lanyu Report, 1987–2007]. Taipei: Renjian chubanshe, 2007.

Hauʻofa, Epeli. "Our Sea of Islands." In *A New Oceania: Rediscovering Our Sea of Islands*, edited by Eric Waddell, Vijay Naidu, and Epeli Hauʻofa, 1–6. Suva, Fiji: University of the South Pacific School of Social and Economic Development, 1993.

Hsia, C. T. "Obsession with China." In *A History of Modern Chinese Fiction*, 3rd ed., 509–32. Bloomington: Indiana University Press, 1999.

Huang, Hsinya. "Representing Indigenous Bodies in Epeli Hauʻofa and Syaman Rapongan." *Tamkang Review* 40, no. 2 (2010): 3–19.

Huang, Yu-ting. "The Archipelagos of Taiwan Literature: Comparative Literature and Island Writings in Taiwan." In *Comparatizing Taiwan*, edited by Shu-mei Shih and Ping-hui Liao, 80–99. Abingdon, UK: Routledge, 2014.

Ingersoll, Karin Amimoto. *Waves of Knowing: A Seascape Epistemology*. Durham, NC: Duke University Press, 2016.

Lionnet, Françoise, and Emmanuel Bruno Jean-François. "Literary Routes: Migration, Islands, and the Creative Economy." *PMLA* 131, no. 5 (2016): 1222–38.

Ng Kim Chew 黃錦樹. "Ala de zhiyi" 阿拉的旨意 [Allah's Will]. In *Ke bei* 刻背 [Back Inscriptions], rev. ed., 109–36. Taipei: Maitian chuban, 2014.

Ng Kim Chew. "Allah's Will," translated by Carlos Rojas. In *Slow Boat to China and Other Stories*, 121–47. New York: Columbia University Press, 2016.

Rapongan, Syaman 夏曼·藍波安. "Cold Sea, Deep Feeling," translated by Terence C. Russell. *Taiwan Literature: English Language Series* 17 (2005): 15–42.

Rapongan, Syaman. "Feiyu de huhuan" 飛魚的呼喚 [The Call of the Flying Fish]. In *Leng hai qing shen* 冷海情深 [Cold Sea, Deep Feeling], 69–87. Taipei: Lianhe wenxue chubanshe, 1997.

Rapongan, Syaman. "Guanyu leng hai yu qing shen" 關於冷海與情深 [On Cold Sea and Deep Feeling]. In *Leng hai qing shen* 冷海情深 [Cold Sea, Deep Feeling], 11–14. Taipei: Lianhe wenxue chubanshe, 1997.

Rapongan, Syaman. "Haiyang chaoshengzhe" 海洋朝聖者 [The Ocean Pilgrim]. In *Leng hai qing shen* 冷海情深 [Cold Sea, Deep Feeling], 97–129. Taipei: Lianhe wenxue chubanshe, 1997.

Rapongan, Syaman. "Leng hai qing shen" 冷海情深 [Cold Sea, Deep Feeling]. In *Leng hai qing shen* 冷海情深 [Cold Sea, Deep Feeling], 15–48. Taipei: Lianhe wenxue chubanshe, 1997.

Rojas, Carlos. "Introduction: Ng Kim Chew and the Writing of Diaspora." In Ng Kim Chew, *Slow Boat to China and Other Stories*, translated and edited by Carlos Rojas, vii–xxi. New York: Columbia University Press, 2016.

Shih, Shu-mei. "The Concept of the Sinophone." *PMLA* 126, no. 3 (2011): 709–18.

Shih, Shu-mei. "What Is Sinophone Studies?" In *Sinophone Studies: A Critical Reader*, edited by Shu-mei Shih, Chien-hsin Tsai, and Brian Bernards, 1–16. New York: Columbia University Press, 2013.

Tsu, Jing, and David Der-wei Wang, eds. *Global Chinese Literature: Critical Essays*. Leiden: Brill, 2010.

Wang, Ban. *Illuminations from the Past: Trauma, Memory, and History in Modern China*. Stanford, CA: Stanford University Press, 2004.

Wang, David Der-wei 王德威. "Hua-yi zhi bian: Huayu yuxi yanjiu de xin shiye" 華夷之變：華語語系研究的新視界 [Sinophone/Xenophone Studies: Toward a Poetics of Wind, Sound, and Changeability]. *Zhongguo xiandai wenxue* 中國現代文學 34 (2018): 1–27.

Wang, David Der-wei. *The Monster That Is History: History, Violence, and Fictional Writing in Twentieth-Century China*. Berkeley: University of California Press, 2004.

CHEOW THIA CHAN

Off-Center Articulations
Social Class, Postcolonial Singapore, and Reorienting Southeast Asian Chinese Literary Studies

ABSTRACT Recent studies on Singapore Chinese literature have employed analytical lenses such as the Sinophone and postloyalism, which are exogenous to the historical and everyday experiences in the region that produced the texts. This article proposes using the lens of the Chinese-educated to bridge local self-understandings with extralocal modes of interpretation, in order to better illuminate place-specific writing practices. As a salient category of both lived experience and analysis by local researchers, the category of the Chinese-educated occasions a form of "off-center articulation" that maintains strategic distance from Sinophone studies while also enriching the field's conceptual repertoire. Specifically, this analytical perspective highlights how literary representations of social class play a significant role, alongside language and ethnicity, in registering the historical diversity of the Singapore Chinese community. Through examining Singaporean Chinese writer Chia Joo Ming's novel *Exile or Pursuit* (2015), this article reinterprets the novel's gallery of characters and depictions of interpersonal relations to elicit fading memories of socioeconomic divides and gaps in cultural attainment among ethnic Chinese Singaporeans and their migrant predecessors. It ends by charting future directions for Southeast Asian Chinese literary studies that collectively track a broader locus of "Chinese-educated" literary and cultural practices, and that promote critical inter-referencing within the region.

KEYWORDS Sinophone, postloyalism, the Chinese-educated (*huaxiaosheng*), off-center, social class

In 2016, the *Oxford English Dictionary* (*OED*) sparked a controversy by adding the Singapore English term *Chinese helicopter*.[1] Defined by the authority on the English language as "a Singaporean whose schooling was conducted in Mandarin Chinese and who has limited knowledge of English," the compound derives from a mispronunciation of the word "educated" (which apparently sounded like "helicated" to those from Chinese-medium schools, and later morphed to become "helicopter").[2] In circulation since the 1970s, the term has become a label that demeans Chinese-educated Singaporeans for their inadequate command of English, casting them as lower members of society. To those who recall the indignities suffered by the Chinese-educated, the term's inclusion in the *OED* promotes acceptance of the derogatory expression, which one critic compares to "rubbing salt into an old wound that never healed."[3]

PRISM: THEORY AND MODERN CHINESE LITERATURE • 19:2 • SEPTEMBER 2022
DOI 10.1215/25783491-9966687 • © 2022 LINGNAN UNIVERSITY

In Chinese, the corresponding term used for referring to the Chinese-educated is *huaxiaosheng* 華校生, a word that carries connotations that go beyond the literal meaning of "students of Chinese-medium schools." Huang Jianli specifies that *huaxiaosheng* (hereafter "the Chinese-educated") refers to students "who did not go to English-medium schools but were educated through the Chinese-medium secondary schools and Nanyang University."[4] Evident in Huang's definition is a comparison to the *yingxiaosheng* 英校生, those Singaporean Chinese who were educated in English (hereafter "the English-educated"). Akin to topolectal group differences among Singaporean Chinese, this bifurcation into opposing educational circles disrupts the myth of a homogenous Singapore Chinese community. Functioning as identification labels to position school graduates from one language stream in relation to the other, the two terms jointly allude to divergent values, cultural dispositions, social statuses, political affinities, and worldviews. Scholars such as Huang Jianli and Lau Wai Har contend that the outlook on life of the Chinese-educated is primarily conditioned by language and culture rather than by ethnicity, which is taken as a given. The group members perceive themselves as embodiments of pure and thus authentic Chineseness whose cultural Other is not the other ethnic groups who also live in Singapore, but the English-educated Chinese who stands for all things Western.[5]

Prior to the *OED*'s inclusion of *Chinese helicopter*, the plight of the Chinese-educated in Singapore had largely receded from local memory.[6] In this essay, I revive the intellectual and literary discourses of the Chinese-educated, the purpose of which is certainly not to further remind the historical actors of their pain. Dissociation from its derisive rhetorical twin in English is possible, as the term *Chinese-educated* evokes a broader emotional overtone of *beiqing* 悲情 (sorrow) rather than a singular sense of humiliation. In my view, the term is particularly helpful for bridging local self-understandings with extralocal lenses of interpretation, such as Sinophone or postloyalist approaches, which recent studies on Southeast Asian Chinese literature have employed to illuminate place-based writing practices.[7] In the abutting context of Malaysian Chinese literary studies—where the choice of adopting native or nonnative categories of thought as analytical frames is a long-standing issue—Ng Kim Chew has elaborated on the merits of shifting between the use of "experience-near" 貼近感知經驗 and "experience-distant" 遙距感知經驗 concepts.[8] Following Ng's spirit of creating a productive dialectic rather than a reductive binary, I contend that while exogenous approaches offer important ideas to grasp the historical and everyday human experiences of the literary region, it is time to reintroduce the concept of the *Chinese-educated* to describe specific social practices and perform pertinent cultural analyses. Specifically, the term can complement the nonlocal frameworks by showing the strong mutual connections between the term's practical and discursive uses.

One way of framing the reciprocal influences between this social group's historical experiences and their literary representations conceptually is to read the resultant gestalt as what I have called "off-center articulations."[9] In the context of Singapore Chinese literature (locally called *Xinhua wenxue* 新華文學, hereafter "Xinhua literature"), authors and critics foster these articulations in two senses. First, given that the Chinese-educated is a literary and analytical parameter readily understood by members of the Singapore Chinese society, it serves as a *joint* to moderate the presiding concepts of Sinophone studies whose proponents are more often knowledge specialists whose ideas have not quite played important roles in the cultural politics of the postcolonial nation. Foregrounding the long-standing presence of the *Chinese-educated* trope in local discourses also throws into relief the historical and ideological circumstances under which concrete linkages are made between social forces and rhetorical forms.

Second, by focusing on a term that circulates in the grassroots, narratives of the Chinese-educated reveal the Singapore Chinese cultural milieu at an unprecedented resolution by indexing the group's sense of alienation despite being part of the majority ethnic community. The positionality of its members therefore marks a paradox, as grievances about social estrangement are more often associated with minorities. To account for this atypical psychology of estrangement from one's own ethnic community requires parsing social class—compared to race, a hitherto little-adopted analytical scale for examining Southeast Asian Chinese literature—within the Singapore Chinese community. By "class," I mean the social stratification that divides people into groups who occupy hierarchical structural positions in society, rather than the collective self-awareness of groups differentiated according to their relations of production, and the actions groups take to advance their common economic interests. As a category of lived experience, the Chinese-educated reveals how linguistic marginalization (vis-à-vis the English-educated) masks class marginalization that offsets ethnic majority privilege at specific historical moments. As a category of cultural analysis, it disrupts the veneer of common ethnicity by demonstrating how the space of Singaporean Chineseness is neither monolithic nor transparent. Suspending the customary focus on race in Sinophone studies, and embodying class-related issues that matter to situated social actors and the local Chinese community, stories about the Chinese-educated in Singapore deviate from both abstract nostalgia for China and anti-Sinocentrism to *express* an alternative form of localized Chinese cultural identity.

To illustrate how off-center articulations function in a Southeast Asian milieu, this article will start by elaborating on the sociohistorical background of the Chinese-educated and how the group has been conceptualized in Singaporean intellectual and literary discourses. It then uses Singaporean Chinese writer Chia Joo Ming's 謝裕民 2015 novel *Fangzhu yu zhuizhu* 放逐與追逐 (Exile or Pursuit) to exemplify not just a type of writing that spotlights the quasi-central subject position within a dominant ethnic group, but also a compositional mode that can be read productively through a blending of global and local critical vocabularies.

The Chinese-Educated in Singaporean Intellectual and Literary Discourses

No postcolonial account of the Singapore Chinese community is complete without considering the Chinese-educated. To better understand narratives about the group and their deprivileged lives, it is necessary to know Singapore's longer history of vernacular education. From the colonial period to the post–World War II period, education on the island was divided into separate language streams with uneven support from the British government. Unsurprisingly, the British favored English-medium education, as it preferred to nurture an English-educated elite that best served metropolitan interests. Although Chinese education in Singapore dates back to the early nineteenth century, *Chinese-educated* and *English-educated* became recognizable social labels only in the wake of the 1956 *All Party Report on Chinese Education*. The report promulgated bilingual education whereby Chinese, Malay, and Tamil schools adopted English as a second language, while English schools did the opposite. As Sai Siew Yee notes, the Chinese-educated category is generation-specific. The identity of the group is most pronounced among those who attended *huaxiao* 華校 (Chinese-medium schools) up through the 1970s, before the state prioritized English for education in the 1980s.[10] The closing of Nanyang University—the sole Chinese-medium university outside China, Hong Kong, and Taiwan—in 1980 dealt a tremendous blow to the Chinese-educated, as it symbolized the fall of a cherished fortress of Chinese culture in Singapore. By 1987, the government mandated that all schools adopt English as the principal medium of instruction for all subjects except for "mother tongue" courses—which were assigned by the state according to its prescribed race for students—thereafter relegating Chinese to the margins of the national education system and the society at large. The decline in Chinese-language education meant that the Chinese-educated lost out in life chances. They lost their voices in nation-building despite forming the greater constituency among the ethnic Chinese. Sidelined in the country's English-dominant economic modernization, they became occupationally disadvantaged and turned into a social minority in the 1980s.

Apart from being marginalized in terms of socioeconomic status, the Chinese-educated were also displaced in the political sphere. Since the early twentieth century, Chinese-educated youths and adults had constituted a critical force in place-based political activism ranging from anti-Japanese movements to decolonization efforts. They were heavily involved in leftist anticolonial politics after World War II, causing different state authorities to associate them with leftist radicalism and ethnic chauvinism.[11] However, after Singapore gained independence, it was the

English-educated who became the political elites of the postcolonial state. Kwok Kian-Woon summarizes how the two social groups therefore also operate as political categories:

> The "Chinese-educated" as a social collectivity and as social construction was forged out of both the development of Chinese education and the politics of decolonization. In the process, the Manichean divide of non-communist/multiracialist versus communist/chauvinist tended to privilege the English-educated as a harbinger of modernization and to demonize the Chinese-educated as a danger or obstacle to progress. To the extent that there was a clear political divide between the English-educated and Chinese-educated, it may be more useful to consider each group as propounding a vision and version of modernity.[12]

Earlier competing visions of Singapore's modernization route are now increasingly foreign to young Singaporean Chinese immersed in an English-dominant schooling system. Many of them were born in the 1990s after the closure of Chinese-medium schools and thus have not heard of the term *Chinese-educated*; much less do they sympathize with the emotional angst the identity generates among their ethnic predecessors.[13] They are also far more familiar with the state-driven approach to organize the population through the reductive racialized formula of "Chinese, Malays, Indians, and Others." Against this particular backdrop of an Anglophone Singapore, where at the same time the younger generation views the makeup of the national community primarily in terms of race, Xinhua literature preserves the record of such social trauma and offers a site of resistance against historical amnesia.

Indeed, the topic of the Chinese-educated in academic discourses also appears in the literary sphere. However, there is as yet no genre called *huaxiaosheng wenxue* 華校生文學 (literature of the Chinese-educated). The historical strands of Chinese-language literature by or about the Chinese-educated have stayed separate arguably because some works are read more as leftist literature penned by participants in student movements with deep associations with Chinese-medium schools. For instance, the trope of the Chinese-educated can be traced to works such as "Qingchun qu" 青春曲 (Song of Youth) and "Shen Yulan tongxue" 沈郁兰同學 (Fellow Student Shen Yulan), both of which were written amid the fervor of decolonization in the 1950s by He Jin 賀巾, a student activist who later joined the Malayan Communist Party. Composed in the vein of socialist realism, the two short stories, which portray the idealism of the Singaporean Chinese-educated who strove for fundamental changes in their lives and mindsets, enjoyed tremendous popularity and evoked deep emotional identification among readers in Singapore and Malaya.[14]

Useful for tracking the relationship between Chinese-medium education and literary production more holistically, a "literature of the Chinese-educated" can bring together the left-leaning works in the late colonial period and works associated with the group in the postcolonial period. After Singapore gained independence in 1965, the waves of societal changes, especially in the education sector, catalyzed a new genre of literary writings that critics have characterized as "Xinjiapo shanghen wenxue" 新加坡傷痕文學 (Singapore scar literature), referencing a mainland Chinese literary trend from the late 1970s and early 1980s that focuses on the trauma and injustices suffered during China's Cultural Revolution (1966–1976). In a non-China context, Teo Sum Lim 張森林 traces the genesis of the critical rubric in Singapore to 1992 and contends that "as long as the creative works—including poetry, prose essays, fiction, drama, and cross-talk—touch upon the decline of Chinese-language education and culture during this period, regardless of whether their fundamental spiritual tone is forlorn or vehement, they belong to the category of 'Singapore Scar Literature'" 凡是在這個期間內容觸及新加坡華文教育或文化式微問題的文學創作，包括詩歌、散文、小說、戲劇、相聲， 無論它們的精神基調是悲涼的或激越的，都屬於新加坡傷痕文學的範疇.[15] According to Teo, the localized category can be applied retrospectively to cover literary production from 1981 to 2007, the period when Chinese-language education in Singapore saw a marked decline after the closure of Nanyang University in 1980 and the abolition of non-English-stream schools in 1987, which resulted in heightened authorial awareness of the need to preserve Chinese culture.[16]

Literary works classified as Singapore Scar Literature inscribe the psychological turmoil of the Chinese-educated years after their personal and collective trauma have passed. To Gabriel Wu, the conspicuous theme of exclusion and discrimination in postcolonial Xinhua literature—which arises from how the Chinese-educated belong to the majority race in the country, and yet embody the figure of an alien—can be analyzed through the notion of "expressive otherness," which conveys how the Chinese-educated nurses a "deep regret arising from his perceived inferiority in the economic, social and cultural realms as Singapore undergoes rapid modernization."[17] In Yeng Pway Ngon's 英培安 novels, the pathos of "expressive otherness" is often channeled through jaded male protagonists who tend to compare class superiority to racial superiority. For instance, the main character in *Guji de lian* 孤寂的臉 (Lonely Face) complains via free indirect speech that "having graduated from Nanyang University, he lives like a person of color in a society dominated by white people, and appears both incompetent and clumsy" 他這個南大生， 就像活在白人社會裡的有色人一樣， 顯得既低能又笨拙.[18] In a later novel, the first-person narrator makes this even more explicit: "Though the country has achieved independence . . . we [the Chinese-educated] are still governed by an English-educated elite, except that the skin color of the elites who govern us has changed" 國家獨立了 . . . 我們 [華校生] 還是由一群

受英文教育的精英統治，統治我們的精英只是換了膚色罷了。[19] In both works, Yeng's protagonists conflate race and language to construct a hierarchy of class relations, whereby the English-educated and the white colonialists are cut from the same cloth. Resonating with sociological accounts, these literary narratives reflect a kind of enduring multiracial oblivion, whereby the cultural Other of the Chinese-educated is not the Malays or the Indians who live alongside them in Singapore, but the English-educated.

As seen in Yeng's novels, attaining university-level education does not preclude the Chinese-educated from feeling inadequate. The sense of inferiority is also harbored by intellectuals, including university graduates, teachers, and journalists. Besides Yeng, Zhang Hui 張揮 and Teoh Hee La 張曦娜 have also contributed to the corpus of literary works on Chinese-educated intellectuals. Zhang Hui is well known for his 1990 collection of flash fiction titled *45.45 Huiyi jimi* 45.45 會議機密 (45.45: The Classified Secret of the Meeting), which portrays the plight of Chinese-educated teachers who were forced to navigate radical linguistic changes in work settings due to the sweeping education policy reforms. In the 1980s, many of these teachers had to switch to conducting lessons in English after the non-English medium schools were phased out in 1987. In the collection's title story, a school principal holds these Chinese-educated "converted teachers" responsible for the students' poor English results at the national examination, claiming that the teachers' bungling English instruction adversely influenced the students' English proficiency.[20] What Zhang Hui's story withholds from readers is the crushing pressure caused by the new linguistic demands on the Chinese-educated teachers. The tragic fate of *huaxiaosheng* school instructors who could not adapt to the fully English teaching environment is poignantly depicted in Teoh's acclaimed "Ren Muzhi" 任牧之 (The Educator Jen Mu Chih). In the short story, two educators with a common Chinese school background suffered from such a deep sense of shame and intense emotional agony that they committed suicide.[21]

It is in the context of this Singaporean Chinese intellectual and literary climate that I wish to examine Chia Joo Ming's novel *Exile or Pursuit*. The author is no stranger to the Chinese-educated label, for he himself is a member of the group. Born in 1959, he experienced the gradual decline of Chinese-medium schools while witnessing the ascendance of English in local education and in society. In the Singaporean Chinese-language literary scene, Chia first achieved acclaim in the 1980s for his works that limn the detrimental impact of urbanization on the island state.[22] His shift to portray a Chinese-educated man's life in *Exile and Pursuit* thus deserves attention for the ways in which the novel weaves his concerns in the 2010s for the social group with historical reflections on institutions such as family, tradition, and government, which are already discernible in his 1999 short story collection *Yiban shifei* 壹般是非 (The Insignificance of Being) and his 2005 novellas included in another collection, *Chonggou Nanyang tuxiang* 重構南

洋圖像 (A Reconstruction of the Nanyang Picture). Overall, I contend that Chia's novel uses the figural tropes of the *huaxiaosheng* and the *houyimin* 後遺民 (post-loyalist) to negotiate between two modes of representing Singaporean Chinese, which jointly serve to elicit social class as a hidden parameter of distinction for the local Chinese community. The characters' varied class standings show how Chinese linguistic and cultural identities are differentially cultivated in the only Southeast Asian country with an ethnic Chinese majority.

When the Chinese-Educated Meets the Postloyalist: Decentering Class Privilege within the Xinhua Community

As an anomalous tale of the Chinese educated's upward social mobility, *Exile or Pursuit* fits uneasily in the lineage of Singapore Scar literature, which often features characters trapped in unhappy marriages and unsatisfying jobs. Configured as a bildungsroman spanning from the 1970s to the 1990s, the novel depicts how the protagonist Hok Leong 福良, who is derided as a "Chinese helicopter," achieves success despite harsh societal treatment.[23] Moving through various formal education stages, he drifts apart from friends made in different settings—public housing estates, schools, mandatory military service, and so forth—and finally improves his social status through marriage and professional recognition.

The multiple facets of Hok Leong's off-center positionality in the local Chinese community is manifested through his romantic relationships. At first, Hok Leong, who comes from a working-class family background, falls in love in middle school with Chiu-yun 秋雲, an Indonesian Chinese girl whose businessman father belongs to the financial elites often featured in scholarly studies on the Chinese overseas. When they are dating, he is keenly aware that they are "not the same" (*buyiyang* 不一樣) (27; 39), even though they met in a Chinese-medium school.[24] The critic Sim Wai Chew rightly contends that the romance between the two characters signifies a form of "cross-class solidarity."[25] However, contrary to Sim's view, the relationship cannot fully account for Hok Leong overcoming his disaffinity for English and "significantly improv[ing] his life chances," which Sim further reads as depicting "a rapprochement between the so-called 'English-' and 'Chinese-speaking' sections of the Singapore ethnic Chinese population."[26] Though Hok Leong does learn to appreciate English pop songs from Chiu-yun, thereby demonstrating that he is not impervious to heterocultural influences, he also picks up Chinese songs and classical poetry from her. Tellingly, the lyrics of the farewell song he sings publicly to Chiu-yun come from a Christina Georgina Rossetti poem translated by the famous mainland Chinese poet Xu Zhimo 徐志摩. The performance suggests Hok Leong's limited gravitation toward Anglophone culture.

The extent to which Chia fashions Hok Leong as a foil against stereotypical impressions of the Chinese-educated as ethnically and linguistically chauvinistic can be seen in the protagonist's subsequent relationship. While undertaking

Singapore's compulsory military service, Hok Leong dates Eileen, a woman from a working-class family, who attended English-medium schools. They break up eventually, as Eileen holds relatively liberal attitudes toward socializing in order to realize her professional aspirations. In emphasizing the rift between Hok Leong and Eileen despite their similar class background, the novel foregrounds the substantive gap in value systems between the Chinese-educated and the English-educated, and shows the heterogeneity of the Xinhua community, especially in terms of how two groups cannot be easily generalized based solely on race, language, or class.

For the rest of the story, Hok Leong remains very conscious of his Chinese-educated identity. He enters the local university but drops out because of his inadequate English proficiency. He adopts the label of *Chinese helicopter* self-deprecatingly when he is penalized for his English handicap during military service or in jobs. All these instances demonstrate that despite his open-minded experiences with linguistic and cultural differences in his love life, Hok Leong eventually remains in a primarily Chinese-language realm. His contact with the English-educated world can be compared to a tangent that touches the side of a circle but does not penetrate it.

Contrary to Sim's contention, then, the novel never truly "spurns the cultural marginalization meme that is a distinct leitmotif of Singapore Sinophone writing"; neither does it "signal the end of mourning" for the sense of estrangement that is prevalent in Chinese-educated discourses.[27] Using Chia's own words, *Exile or Pursuit* extends his authorial approach in "Anwen jiaqi" 安汶假期 (Ambon Vacation) and *m40*, which fashions an "Other as protoganist" (*tazhe zhujiao* 他者主角) who interprets the alienating times he lives through (233). Marking a hyperreflexive self, Hok Leong harbors a sense of enduring otherness, which he expresses through constant internal comparisons between his own life and the lives of people he encounters, resulting in a ceaseless assessment of his self-image, self-efficacy, and self-esteem.

In the novel, Hok Leong cuts a figure of loneliness. He uses the word *juli* 距離 (distance) repeatedly to gauge his interpersonal intimacies (127, 145). His earlier relationship with Chiu-yun is just a prelude to his ongoing sense of alienation. Later in the narrative, he again contemplates the socioeconomic disparity between him and his third girlfriend, Hsiao-yuan 小願, never relinquishing the awareness that they were brought up in "different worlds" 不同的世界 (138; 190), despite both of them being Chinese-educated. In contrast to his life that revolves around public housing estates and crowded food centers, Hsiao-yuan comes from a family of educators who lead a middle-class lifestyle that includes regular restaurant meals and leisurely get-togethers.

At the same time, Hok Leong feels another kind of distance vis-à-vis his middle school friends. Over the years, they drifted apart after his friends took on blue-collar jobs and Hok Leong progressed along the education ladder. At one point, he ran away after spotting from afar his childhood friend working at a food center, indicating not just his upward class mobility; the truth is that he does not wish to remember his wayward youth, which he hesitates to share with Hsiao-yuan, for fear of being reminded of his incompatibility with her. His reflections at his middle school friend's wedding poignantly reveals that their friendship has lost the sense of emotional proximity:

> Amid the merriment and banter, Hok Leong felt strongly that this was *his* level. He belonged here. Fu *laoshi*'s level was too high for him. But he also discovered that Ying-jun and the others were drifting further and further from him. He did not have any company.
>
> 福良在笑聲話語裏深覺，這裏才屬於他，傅老師太高了；只是他發現，英俊他們離他越來越遠。沒有人和他在一起。(184; 254)

Jointly considered, Hok Leong's friendships and romantic relationship point toward an even finer social boundary than the one between the English-educated and the Chinese-educated, which highlights the inner fissures that exist within the latter. Besides socioeconomic class differences, such as the one that exists between Hok Leong and his friends, the worlds of Hsiao-yuan and Hok Leong are further separated by a gap in cultural capital. Whereas Hsiao-yuan's parents were graduates of Amoy University in China who moved to Singapore and became members of the local Chinese intellectual class, Hok Leong's father traveled southward from British Malaya in order to escape the life of a rubber tapper. That Hok Leong and Hsiao-yuan eventually got married therefore symbolizes not just another instance of cross-class solidarity, but also how the class diversity of Southeast Asian Chinese societies intersects with the temporal contingencies of broader Chinese migration.

In the extract quoted above, Hok Leong's inner voice also tells him that the sophisticated cultural taste of "Fu *laoshi*" (Teacher Fu) is out of reach. Hok Leong's rumination on his compounded solitude thus discloses how he has to negotiate a third form of distance that arises from his misgivings about dating Hsiao-yuan while being largely ignorant of high Chinese culture. The "Fu *laoshi*" in Hok Leong's thought refers to Fu Ting 傅淳, a friend of Hsiao-yuan's father, who plays a pivotal supporting role in the novel. Through interactions with Fu Ting, as with Hsiao-yuan, Hok Leong realizes the stark deficit in his Chinese cultural knowledge. Given his working-class background, Hok Leong does not belong to the group that the sociologist Kwok has discussed under the rubric of *huawen zhishifenzi* 華文知識分子 (Chinese-educated intellectuals). These intellectuals are highly literate in and deeply attached to Chinese language and culture. As Kwok notes, many of them commit themselves to "the legacy of Chinese education as part of their autobiographical past and socio-cultural formation (in the Chinese sense of *xiuyang* 修養)."[28] His inadequacy and relatively weak sense of social mission gainsay the common perception that every Chinese-educated person is necessarily well immersed in Chinese history, literary arts, and intellectual discourses, and feels responsible for shoul-dering the work of cultural transmission.

What makes Hok Leong an unusual Chinese-educated figure is that he was also a *gongkesheng* 工科生—that is, a student channeled into the technical educa-tion track as postindependence Singapore sought to create manpower for rapid industrialization. According to Chia, who drew from his own student experience of undergoing such vocational training, these technical-stream schools—which incorporated craft subjects such as carpentry, electrical fitting and installation, welding, and mechanical drawing—used English textbooks, while classroom instruction was carried out in Chinese.[29] In the 1970s, when Hok Leong enrolled in technical education, schools that provided practical training were afflicted with social stigma as Singapore's emerging middle class deemed vocations that entailed technical expertise and manual labor to be less prestigious.[30] Hok Leong manages to leave the technical track later and rejoins the academic track for high school. This twin identity caught in between two different education routes proves hugely consequential later for his achieving success in life. Nonetheless, as a Chinese-educated *gongkesheng* more oriented toward technical subjects, Hok Leong's rudimentary knowledge of Chinese history falls short in understanding concepts such as *wusi yifeng* 五四遺風 (the May Fourth legacy), which Hsiao-yuan uses to describe the mental disposition of her parents and Fu Ting.

Hok Leong's thought-provoking relationship with Fu Ting can be charac-terized as an encounter between the Chinese-educated and what David Wang calls the *hou yimin* 後遺民 (postloyalist). Wang's theory of postloyalism revolves around a politics of time and memory enacted by the implications of three hom-onyms: the alien-*yimin* 夷民, the migrant-*yimin* 移民, and the loyalist-*yimin* 遺民.[31] In the story, Fu Ting presents a layered identity that encompasses this poly-semy of *yimin*. First, though he is considered "Chinese" in Singapore, Fu is actu-ally an ethnic Manchu who is distantly related to Pu Yi, the last Qing dynasty emperor, thereby making him an "alien" to the Han majority in China. This por-trait shades into the second referent: he left China to work and study in Eng-land, but he eventually settled down in Singapore, making him both an "alien" and a "migrant" to the nonnative places he visited. Finally, he has been sinicized but also turned into an Anglophile after his English sojourn. Yet he calls himself "an old fogey from the previous dynasty" (*qianchao yilao* 前朝遺老) (177; 244), referring ambiguously to either the late Qing or the *minguo* 民國 (Republican China) period, which oddly hints at a Sino-Southeast Asian temporal continuity.

In addition, despite liking Taiwan for its atmosphere of the Republican era, during which he was born, he could not quite accept the place as Republican China, and he indulges in his imaginary nostalgia for that era through the conscious cultivation in Singapore of an intellectual lifestyle steeped in the appreciation of music and the arts. In this way, the complex blend of spatiality and temporality in Fu's biography fashions him as a special kind of "loyalist," a sociopolitical subject out of touch with his times.

Building on Wang's theory, Chien-hsin Tsai notes how loyalism is almost always postloyalism, as loyalists often expand their definitions of loyalism after they survive state crises and settle down in foreign lands.[32] At one significant plot point, Fu Ting shares with Hok Leong that it is impossible for him to relinquish the May Fourth legacy, speaking as if the cultural inheritance is a burden:

> That May Fourth legacy thing. Who cares about that? . . . What's the use of finding a boyfriend who knows these things? What, in reality, are these passed-down customs and habits? Basically things that we can't cast off! . . . Look at you, clean as a whistle. No cultural baggage to speak of. Isn't that better than Hsiao-yuan? Because of her background she's poisoned by this cultural legacy business. . . . You can make up for each other's shortcomings. You have a technical background, you can help pull us humanities types out of our imaginary universe and back to reality.

> 像那天說什麼"五四遺風,"誰管這些啊?...找個知道什麼是"五四遺風"的男朋友來幹嘛?遺留下來的風尚有什麼用?我們是擺脫不了啊....我看你,乾乾淨淨的,什麼包袱都沒有,多好啊!像她,因爲家裏的關係,中了我們的毒。...你們能互相填補對方的不足,特別你是工科的,能把我們這些學文的人,從一廂情願里拉回現實。(129; 177–78)

Here, one can say that in becoming a reluctant loyalist, Fu has simultaneously become a postloyalist. The postloyalist's inadequate understanding of the Xinhua cultural ecology is exposed when Fu considers the two young people's relationship merely from the perspective of cultural capital and heritage concerns, but is blind to the place-specific class differences that pose the more substantive barrier. Regrettably, the novel never allows access to Fu Ting's deeper interiority. To read the way in which a person like Fu Ting, who is so deeply attached to the Republican era, expresses such capitulatory sentiments reinforces our understanding of how becoming "Chinese" in a Southeast Asian locale can involve multivalent postloyalism. As the site where China interfaces with the larger Sinophone world, Singapore hosts Fu Ting's rupture with his past peregrinations—he realized he had nowhere else to go after arriving in the British colony—and his conversion from a Manchu *alien* to a sinicized *migrant*. Harboring a discrepant scale of exile—a keyword in the novel's title that refers to the characters' pervasive sense of displacement—compared to Hok Leong, Fu Ting registers the hidden diversity of the local Chinese community as a non-Han person and a Republican *loyalist* from China.

As the novel enters the 1990s toward the end, Hok Leong is selected to be stationed in Shanghai to expand his company's business due to his Chinese proficiency and technical knowledge, both of which have ironically become assets. It was no coincidence that Singapore's government renewed its emphasis on Chinese language and culture to accommodate the economic rise of China in the last decade of the twentieth century.[33] In other words, the state's reengagement with Chineseness as a sociocultural resource for political and economic development purposes offers the backdrop for Hok Leong, with his unique background in Chinese and engineering, to improve his social standing at the turn of the twenty-first century. By this point, Fu Ting has already passed away. In the last instance, then, *Exile or Pursuit* can be read as a social allegory of how postcolonial Singapore's homegrown technical-oriented Chinese modernity transcended the cultural modernity derived from links with China.

Conclusion

By using the double lenses of the Chinese-educated and the postloyalist, my reading of Chia's *Exile or Pursuit* evinces a form of situated Chineseness in Singapore shaped by intersectional forces of race, class, and migration. The analysis shows how Xinhua literature can be studied through a meaningful amalgam of critical vocabularies selected near and far. Examining Chinese cultural ecologies in this way stays close to historical actors' self-understandings of discursive representations in non-China settings. It also bolsters ties with local scholarly discourses and cultural politics that advances knowledge-making traditions on site.

The two lenses prove illuminating for studying Chia's other works, because they converge further in his 2018 novel *Jianguo* 建國 [Kian Kok]. Set in 2015—the year when Chia's *Exile or Pursuit* was first published, and when Singapore celebrated fifty years of independence—the eponymous Chinese-educated protagonist, whose name (and hence the title of the novel) also means "the founding of a country," is confused about why the state changed the starting point of its sovereignty. Kian Kok vividly remembers that Singapore celebrated the twenty-fifth anniversary of its establishment in 1984, which meant that at that time the state located the country's genesis in 1959, when Singapore was granted full internal self-government by the British colonial administration. Yet, the 2015 state-directed celebrations were based on a founding date of 1965, the year when Singapore left Malaysia and gained full independence. Reconciling the two temporalities felt important to Kian Kok, because his parents named him after the first event that celebrated national autonomy, and he had always felt some pride in sharing the same age as the new country. Notably, the decline of Chinese-medium schools and Chinese-language newspapers compounded his sense of becoming out of step with the times: whereas both he and Singapore were twenty-five years old in 1984, in 2015 he was already fifty-six while Singapore was only fifty. The feeling of temporal disorientation resulted in him addressing himself as a *qian "chao" yilao* 前 "潮" 遺老, a term that describes an old-fashioned person left behind by the waves of time. Coincidentally, the term is homonymous with a phrase that refers to a loyalist, which the character Fu Ting used on himself in *Exile or Pursuit*.[34]

Extrapolating from the Singapore case, this article proposes a larger project of tracking Southeast Asian Chinese literary and cultural practices through the Chinese-educated, as the trope that represents a social group of substantial scale is prominent in genealogies of Chineseness in the region but in different ways. Given how ethnic Chinese communities in sites such as Malaysia and Indonesia have also faced schooling interruptions due to war, colonialism, independence struggles, and other forms of social tumult, the comparative project can be built on the common ground of parsing what Sai has called in the Singapore context the "ruptured identit[ies]" caused by "discontinuous Chinese educational experience[s]."[35]

For instance, the "Chinese-educated" approach can uncover neglected fault lines in local Chinese life-worlds. I have in mind creative writings associated with the *duli zhongxue* 独立中學 (independent middle schools), the type of Chinese-medium schools in postcolonial Malaysia that rejected state funding in order to continue using the Chinese language as the medium of instruction. The positionalities of these schools in a Malay-partisan country are entangled , with their pasts caught in between Nationalist versus Communist political leanings during the late colonial period and the two world wars.[36] Indonesia also witnessed the competition for overseas Chinese students' support mounted by the two Chinas during the Cold War. The complex streams of vernacular and colonial Chinese schools in Indonesian history, and the ways in which their wide-ranging cultural activities intersected with local sociopolitical dynamics—which were linked either to Taiwan or to the mainland state—await further study.[37]

In this light, the expanded project can enrich Sinophone studies in two ways. First, drawing the Southeast Asian locus of the Chinese-educated will suspend the well-worn cataloguing of variations from the originary Chineseness of China by establishing a gallery of representational *huaxiaosheng* writers and characters who are *hua* in multiple respects historically, depending on colonial and postcolonial ethnic, linguistic, gender, class, and political relations embedded in their respective milieus. Expanding from the Singapore context, where Chinese constitute the majority ethnic group, to other Southeast Asian locations will enable the exploration of the ways in which Chinese communities embody different shades of alterities as minority or assimilated populations. The endeavor can then change the axis of comparison and promote more inter-referencing of localized undertakings among this set of identified places in the south.

Second, this newly identified orbit of Southeast Asian Chinese cultural production accentuates not just differences across national contexts, but also differences *within* local worlds. As seen through the anomalous literary representations in *Exile or Pursuit*, a focus on "*hua*-as-ethnicity" can obscure a focus on "*hua*-as-social-class" in Singapore. Chia's novel therefore supplements discursive place-making by surfacing historical memories of internal diversities within the same ethnic group, which in turn contribute toward the overall differentiation of Southeast Asian locales. In other words, for the broader regional scale, the concept of *Chinese-educated* and its cognate *Chinese-medium schools* can function as significant literary portals of varying temporal horizons to access the inner pluralities of Southeast Asian Chinese societies, their respective historical constitutions, and their multivalent cultural expressions of Chineseness.

Collectively, the literary discourses by and about the Chinese-educated, which document and portray hybridized Chinese cultural institutions in colonial and postcolonial locations in Southeast Asia, will enable us to grasp the dialectics between structures of feeling—the competing modes of emergent thought orientations—and aesthetic forms of social history that prompt new reflections on communal trauma, diasporic imagination, and localization. By focusing on the very same categories of difference related to place, ethnicity, and language that Sinophone studies has productively explored, and by unlocking new analytical parameters such as class and temporality—for instance, writers' differential approaches to perpetuating the cultural ideals of Republican China[38]—narratives of and by the Chinese-educated will yield similar yet also divergent off-center articulations that mark Southeast Asia as a highly significant region of global Chinese literary production.

CHEOW THIA CHAN is assistant professor of Chinese studies at National University of Singapore. His research interests include modern Chinese-Sinophone literature, Southeast Asian studies, and diaspora studies. He is the author of *Malaysian Crossings: Place and Language in the Worlding of Modern Chinese Literature* (forthcoming, 2022) and has edited "Transregional Singapore Chinese Literature," a special section in *Renditions: A Chinese-English Translation Magazine* (2021).

////////////////////////////////

Notes

1   Leong, "Petition to Remove 'Chinese Helicopter.'"
2   See *OED Online*, s.v. "Chinese," https://www-oed-com.libproxy1.nus.edu.sg/view/Entry /31770?redirectedFrom=chinese+& (accessed July 15, 2022); and Chen, "'Chinese Helicopter.'"
3   Leong, "Petition to Remove 'Chinese Helicopter.'"

4   Huang, "Dilemma and Anguish," 336.

5   Lau observes how the Chinese-educated think of the English-educated as "arrogant, open, modern, Westernized and easygoing," whereas the latter regards the former as "conservative, parochial, chauvinistic, politicized and hard-working." See Lau, "Bridging the Gap," 201.

6   Chen, "'Chinese Helicopter.'"

7   See relevant sections in edited volumes such as Shih, Tsai, and Bernards, *Sinophone Studies*, and Rojas and Bachner, *Oxford Handbook*.

8   Ng, "Fansi 'Nanyang Lunshu,'" 21–31.

9   I first used "off-center articulations" to frame Malaysian Chinese (Mahua) literature in my book *Malaysian Crossings: Place and Language in the Worlding of Modern Chinese Literature* (forthcoming) and to discuss the writer Li Yongping's transregional negotiation of his positionality in the margins of both Mahua and Taiwan literary spaces. Here, I extend the concept to Xinhua literature, which is located in a different geographical context (Singapore), in order to illustrate how "off-centeredness" can occur within the cultural ecology of a place rather than translocally. As noted in my book, Masao Miyoshi had employed the term "off-center" earlier in his monograph *Off Center: Power and Culture Relations between Japan and the United States* for literary and cultural analyses of asymmetrical historical encounters.

10   This condensed history of Chinese and bilingual education is distilled from Sai, "Post-independence Educational Change," 80–83, 91, and Purushotam, *Negotiating Language*, 50–74.

11   For more on the Chinese-educated as political actors, see Kwok, "Chinese-Educated Intellectuals in Singapore," 496–98.

12   Ibid., 499.

13   Chen, "'Chinese Helicopter.'"

14   The two stories are collected in He Jin, *He Jin xiaoshuo xuanji*, 1–39, 40–59. The collection reveals that the former was written under the pseudonym Wei Jia 韋嘉. Fang Xiu points out that "Fellow Student Shen Yulan" attracted twenty to thirty pieces of literary criticism after it was published. See Fang Xiu, *Zhanhou Mahua wenxueshi chugao*, 113. For a reading of these works as Singapore Chinese leftist literature, see Ngoi, "Qingchun, geming yu lishi."

15   Teo, "Dangdai Xinjiapo shanghen wenxue," 99.

16   Ibid., 98–100.

17   Wu, "Expressive Otherness," 46. Wu also writes creatively under the name "Wu Yeow Chong" 吳耀宗. His works are discussed in Brian Bernards's article in this issue.

18   Yeng, *Guji de lian*, 25.

19   Yeng, *Wo yu woziji de ersanshi*, 26.

20   Zhang Hui, *45.45 Huiyi jimi*, 1–4.

21   Teoh, "Ren Muzhi," 155–72.

22   See Wong and Xu, *Xinjiapo huawen wenxueshi chugao*, 309–10.

23   Chia, *Fangzhu yu zhuizhu*, 87, 155. All subsequent references from the novel will be presented as in-text citations.

24   Extracts from *Exile or Pursuit* in English translation are modified from Chia, *Exile or Pursuit*, trans. Sim, and the page numbers are cited in the text following the page reference from the original novel in Chinese.

25   Sim, "Becoming Other," 5.

26   Sim, "Overlapping Scriptworlds," 3.

27 Ibid., 4.

28 Kwok, "Chinese-Educated Intellectuals in Singapore," 502.

29 Chia Joo Ming (pers. comm., June 22, 2021). On Chia's education trajectory, see Chia, *Fangzhu yu zhuizhu*, 232.

30 For an overview of this specialized facet of Singapore's education history, see Chong, "Vocational Education in Singapore."

31 Wang, *Huayifeng qi*, 14.

32 Tsai, "Distant Shore," 842.

33 For a commentary on Singapore's state attitudes toward Chinese language and culture in the 1990s, see Tan, "Chinese-Singaporean Identity," 333.

34 Chia, *Jianguo*, 10.

35 Sai, "Post-independence Educational Change," 89.

36 See L. E. Tan, *Politics of Chinese Education in Malaya* and Y S. Tan, *Development of Chinese Education in Malaysia*. For an example of poetry written during wartime in Malaya, see Ko Chia-cian's article in this issue.

37 Existing studies include Huang, *Yindunixiya huawen jiaoyu fazhanshi*, and Zhou, *Migration in the Time of Revolution*, 89–96.

38 Chong Fah Hing identifies two diasporic literary temporalities related to Republican China (*minguo* 民國). Following the establishment of the People's Republic of China in 1949, one *minguo* literary lineage took flight to Taiwan and extended its tradition, whereas the other group of literati traveled to Singapore and Malaya via Hong Kong and promoted their cultural practices in the fields of education, media, and publishing. As Chong points out, many writers from Republican China migrated and taught in Singapore and Malayan Chinese-medium schools, and also nurtured the first generation of postindependence Mahua writers. See Chong, "Zhanhou Mahua," 11, 22. Given how some Chinese schools in Indonesia and the Philippines also maintained connections with Taiwan's Chinese Nationalist government after 1949, the *minguo* literary lineage in Southeast Asia is very likely more complicated and well worth investigating.

References

Chen, Heather. "'Chinese Helicopter': Singlish OED Entry Baffles Singaporeans." BBC News, May 13, 2016. https://www.bbc.com/news/world-asia-36283670.

Chia Joo Ming. *Exile or Pursuit*, translated by Sim Wai Chew. Singapore: Balestier, 2019.

Chia Joo Ming 謝裕民. *Fangzhu yu zhuizhu* 放逐與追逐 [Exile or Pursuit]. Singapore: Full House Communications, 2015.

Chia Joo Ming 謝裕民. *Jianguo* 建國 [Kian Kok]. Singapore: Full House Communications, 2018.

Chong Fah Hing 莊華興. "Zhanhou Mahua (Minguo) wenxue yizhi: Wenxueshi zaikancha" 戰後馬華(民國)文學遺址： 文學史再勘察 [Chinese Malaysian Literature of Republican Traces in Post War Era: Literary History Revisited]. *Taiwan Dongnanya xuekan* 台灣東南亞學刊 [Taiwan Journal of Southeast Asian Studies] 11, no. 1 (2016): 7–30.

Chong, Terence. "Vocational Education in Singapore: Meritocracy and Hidden Narratives." *Discourse: Studies in the Cultural Politics of Education* 35, no. 5 (2014): 637–48.

Fang Xiu 方修. *Zhanhou Mahua wenxueshi chugao* 戰後馬華文學史初稿 [A Preliminary Draft of Postwar Malayan Chinese Literary History]. Singapore: T. K. Goh, 1978.

He Jin 賀巾. *He Jin xiaoshuo xuanji* 賀巾小説選集 [A Short Story Collection by He Jin]. Singapore: Xinhua wenhua shiye youxian gongsi, 1999.

Huang Jianli. "Dilemma and Anguish of the Chinese-Educated." In *Impressions of the Goh Chok Tong Years in Singapore*, edited by Bridget Welsh, James Chin, Arun Mahizhnan, and Tan Tarn How, 336–49. Singapore: NUS Press, 2009.

Huang Kunzhang 黃昆章. *Yindunixiya huawen jiaoyu fazhanshi* 印度尼西亞華文教育發展史 [The History of Chinese-Language Education Development in Indonesia]. Kuala Lumpur: Malaixiya huaxiao jiaoshihui zonghui, 2005.

Kwok, Kian-Woon. "Chinese-Educated Intellectuals in Singapore: Marginality, Memory and Modernity." *Asian Journal of Social Science* 29, no. 3 (2001): 495–519.

Lau, Wai Har. "Bridging the Gap between the Two Worlds: The English-Educated and the Chinese-Educated." In *Our Place in Time: Exploring Heritage and Memory in Singapore*, edited by Kwok Kian-Woon, Kwa Chong Guan, Lily Kong, and Brenda Yeoh, 199–207. Singapore: Singapore Heritage Society, 1999.

Leong, Weng Kam. "Petition to Remove 'Chinese Helicopter' from Oxford English Dictionary." *Straits Times*, May 28, 2016. https://www.straitstimes.com/singapore/petition-to-remove-chinese-helicopter-from-oxford-english-dictionary.

Miyoshi, Masao. *Off Center: Power and Culture Relations between Japan and the United States*. Cambridge, MA: Harvard University Press, 1991.

Ng Kim Chew 黃錦樹. "Fansi 'Nanyang lunshu': Huama wenxue, fuxitong yu renleixue shiyu" 反思 "南洋論述" ： 華馬文學、複系統與人類學視域 [A Reflection on "Nanyang Discourses": Chinese Malaysian Literature, Polysystems, and Anthropological Horizons]. In Tee Kim Tong 張錦忠, *Nanyang lunshu: Mahua wenxue yu wenhua shuxing* 南洋論述： 馬華文學與文化屬性 [Studying Southeast Asian Chinese: Essays on Chinese-Malaysian Literature and Cultural Identity], 11–37. Taipei: Maitian, 2003.

Ngoi Guat Peng 魏月萍. "Qingchun, geming yu lishi: He Jin xiaoshuo yu Xinjiapo zuoyi huawen wenxue" 青春、革命與歷史： 賀巾小說與新加坡左翼華文文學 [Youth, Revolution, and History: He Jin's Novels and Singapore Chinese Leftist Literature]. *Zhongguo xiandai wenxue* 中國現代文學 [Modern Chinese Literature], no. 23 (2013): 29–47.

Purushotam, Nirmala. *Negotiating Language, Constructing Race: Disciplining Difference in Singapore*. Berlin: Mouton de Gruyter, 1998.

Rojas, Carlos, and Andrea Bachner. *The Oxford Handbook of Modern Chinese Literatures*. New York: Oxford University Press, 2016.

Sai, Siew Yee. "Post-independence Educational Change, Identity, and 'Huaxiaosheng' Intellectuals in Singapore: A Case Study of Chinese Language Teachers." *Southeast Asian Journal of Social Science* 25, no. 2 (1997): 79–101.

Shih, Shu-mei, Chien-hsin Tsai, and Brian Bernards. *Sinophone Studies: A Critical Reader*. New York: Columbia University Press, 2013.

Sim Wai Chew. "Becoming Other: Literary Multilingualism in the Chinese Badlands." *Textual Practice* 34, no. 2 (2018): 1–19. https://doi.org/10.1080/0950236X.2018.1509117.

Sim Wai Chew. "Overlapping Scriptworlds: Chinese Literature as a Global Assemblage." *CLCWeb: Comparative Literature and Culture* 21, no. 4 (2019): 1–11. https://doi.org/10.7771/1481-4374.3206.

Tan, Eugene. "Chinese-Singaporean Identity: Subtle Change Amidst Continuity." In *Impressions of the Goh Chok Tong Years in Singapore*, edited by Bridget Welsh, James Chin, Arun Mahizhnan, and Tan Tarn How, 328–40. Singapore: NUS Press, 2009.

Tan, Liok Ee. *The Politics of Chinese Education in Malaya, 1945–1961*. Kuala Lumpur: Oxford University Press, 1997.

Tan, Yao Sua. *The Development of Chinese Education in Malaysia*. Petaling Jaya, Malaysia: SIRD, 2021.

Teo Hee La 張曦娜. "Ren Muzhi" 任牧之 [The Educator Jen Mu Chih]. In *Beiwanglu: Xinjiapo huawen xiaoshuo duben* 備忘錄： 新加坡華文小說讀本 [Memorandum: A Sinophone Singaporean Short Story Reader], edited by Quah Sy Ren 柯思仁 and Hee Wai-Siam 許維賢, 155–72. Singapore: Nanyang Technological University Center for Chinese Language and Culture, 2016.

Teo Sum Lim 張森林. "Dangdai Xinjiapo shanghen wenxue de faren" 當代新加坡傷痕文學 的發軔 [The Genesis of Contemporary Singapore Scar Literature]. *Huawen wenxue* 華 文文學 [Literatures in Chinese], no. 109 (February 2012): 98–105.

Tsai, Chien-hsin. "A Distant Shore: Migration, Intextuation, and Postloyalism in Chia Joo Ming's 'Ambon Vacation.'" In *The Oxford Handbook of Modern Chinese Literatures*, edited by Carlos Rojas and Andrea Bachner, 832–46. Oxford: Oxford University Press, 2016.

Wang, David Der-wei 王德威. *Huayifeng qi: Huayu yuxi wenxue sanlun* 華夷風起： 華語 語系文學三論 [When the Sinophone Wind Blows: Three Disquisitions on Sinophone Literature]. Kaohsiung: Guoli zhongshan daxue wenxueyuan, 2015.

Wong Meng Voon 黃孟文 and Xu Naixiang 徐迺翔, eds. *Xinjiapo huawen wenxueshi chugao* 新加坡華文文學史初稿 [A Preliminary Draft of Singapore Chinese-Language Literature]. Singapore: National University of Singapore Department of Chinese Studies and Global Publishing, 2002.

Wu, Gabriel. "Expressive Otherness: A Dominant Theme of Xinhua Literature since 1965." *Asian Culture* 27 (June 2003): 46–57.

Yeng Pway Ngon 英培安. *Guiji de lian* 孤寂的臉 [Lonely Face]. Singapore: Caogen shushi, 1989.

Yeng Pway Ngon 英培安. *Wo yu woziji de ersanshi* 我與我自己的二三事 [Trivialities about Me and Myself]. Taipei: Tangshan, 2006.

Zhang Hui 張揮. *45.45 Huiyi jimi* 45.45 會議機密 [45.45: The Classified Secret of the Meeting]. Singapore: Xinjiapo zuojia xiehui, 1990.

Zhou, Taomo. *Migration in the Time of Revolution: China, Indonesia, and the Cold War.* Ithaca, NY: Cornell University Press, 2019.

BRIAN BERNARDS

Iridescent Corners
Sinophone Flash Fiction in Singapore

ABSTRACT Starting in the 1970s, flash fiction developed into an outsized literary practice relative to other Sinophone forms in Singapore. Flash fiction's smallness and brevity cohere with the fast pace of urban Singaporean life and transformation of its cityscape, the compartmentalized relationship between the nation's four official languages, the marginality of literary spaces and challenges to maintaining literature as a profession, and Southeast Asia's relative obscurity as a world literary center (with Singapore as a small but important connective hub). Taking Yeng Pway Ngon's fleeting scene of Speakers' Corner (a flash platform of "gestural politics") as a point of departure, this article charts a short history of Sinophone flash and its relationship to literary community building in Singapore through integrative readings of representative works by Jun Yinglü, Ai Yu, Wong Meng Voon, Xi Ni Er, and Wu Yeow Chong, recognizing their formal and thematic intersections not as "big ideas in tiny spaces" but as iridescent corners that traverse the state's cultural, political, and geographical out-of-bounds (OB) markers. Rather than privileging professional mastery, their works trace flash fiction's iridescent literariness and worldliness to hyperlocality (the physical and literary "corners" they illuminate), compressed temporality, a participatory culture of authorship, and a spirit of amateurism. This amateurism is derived not from a sense of linguistic underdevelopment or technical lack among these authors, but from their passionate and vulnerable engagement with the flash form, as well as the dissident moral conscience of their thematically and stylistically intersecting critiques of Singapore's sociopolitical OB markers.

KEYWORDS flash fiction; Sinophone literature; Singapore; Singaporean literary history; participatory authorship

"Feibang" 誹謗 (Defamation Suit), a 2003 work of flash fiction by the award-winning Sinophone Singaporean author Yeng Pway Ngon 英培安 (1947–2021), describes a parrot that escapes its cage at a pet shop and flies to a nearby assembly place where an opposition party member is speaking out against Singapore's ruling People's Action Party (PAP). The man's slogan, "Down with autocracy!" 打倒獨裁政權, fails to rile anyone in the crowd besides the parrot, which loudly mimics the speaker. Secret police in the audience use an audio recording of the speech to level a defamation suit—based on the rationale that since the government is popularly elected, Singapore "can't possibly be an autocracy" 不可能獨裁—against not just the opposition party speaker but also the parrot, who receives "a one-year prison sentence for its mimicry" 鸚鵡因為學舌，坐牢一年, and against its owner "for failing to properly discipline the bird he raised" 沒

PRISM: THEORY AND MODERN CHINESE LITERATURE • 19:2 • SEPTEMBER 2022
DOI 10.1215/25783491-9966697 • © 2022 LINGNAN UNIVERSITY

有好好管教他養的鸚鵡.[1] Yeng's story satirizes the PAP's knee-jerk recourse to defamation lawsuits to silence its critics and blunt an opposition party's ability to mount a serious political challenge by ultimately bankrupting them. "Defamation Suit" relies on the punchy and cleverly ironic twist 轉折—in this case, the government's punishment of the parrot and its owner by association—a technique common to flash fiction.

Yeng's story reflects flash fiction's assumption of a platform for spontaneously incisive sociopolitical commentary that ironically falls on passively indifferent ears. The assembly place Yeng mentions in the story is likely Speakers' Corner, a six-thousand-square-meter section of Hong Lim Park in Singapore that first opened in September 2000 at the government's direction, then under the leadership of Goh Chok Tong (prime minister 1990–2004), to "help develop civil society by making active citizenship more visible."[2] Hailed as the city-state's only "free-speech venue," Speakers' Corner requires no assembly permits for use, though the government demands proof of Singaporean citizenship and advance registration at a nearby police post of all speakers. However, because all speech must observe vaguely defined out-of-bounds (OB) markers that prohibit public discussion of sensitive racial, religious, and political issues, Speakers' Corner is an example of what Terence Lee calls Singapore's "gestural politics," a type of liberal democratic window dressing to maintain the good graces of the foreign visitors, investors, and dignitaries upon whom the nation relies to maintain its stature as a dependable and welcoming global hub.[3] Lee Hsien Loong, son of Lee Kuan Yew (prime minister 1959–1990) and Goh's successor, described the significance of Speakers' Corner as more "emblematic" than "practical," prompting the PAP's political opponents to declare the space a "political farce" that "makes a mockery of Singapore's constitutional right to free speech."[4]

By exaggerating the degree to which Singapore polices the OB markers of sociopolitical speech—extending the coverage to a bird and its hapless owner—Yeng's "Defamation Suit" satirizes the impotency of the "gestural politics" that Speakers' Corner emblematizes as a physical space. At the same time, Yeng's narrative is self-reflexive, as Singapore's Sinophone flash fiction operates as a sort of literary Speakers' Corner: it is a platform that invites amateur, informal, collaborative participation. It provides a stage for the momentary auditioning of microhistories or counternarratives that scope out or test the bounds of the state's OB markers, even while acknowledging such counternarratives are likely to be met with indifference by a larger public generally presumed to be avoidant of political speech and uninterested in literary pursuits. After all, the guiding logic of the Singaporean developmentalist state is that politics is best left to the professional technocratic class, while literary pursuits have traditionally been branded as "a luxury we cannot afford."[5]

Leading from Yeng's "Defamation Suit," this article charts a short, translingual genre history by considering the sociocultural factors that have made flash fiction a central practice in Sinophone Singaporean literature, itself a compartmentalized corner of the larger regional Sinophone and translingual Singaporean literary spaces it connects and inhabits. Integrative readings of the formal and thematic intersections and departures of representative flash fiction by Jun Yinglü 君盈綠, Ai Yu 艾禺, Wong Meng Voon 黃孟文, Xi Ni Er 希尼爾, and Wu Yeow Chong 吳耀宗 demonstrate how the smallness and brevity—or compressed temporality and spatiality—of the form cohere with several relational aspects of Singapore's brand: the pace of urban life and constant transformation of the cityscape, a pace that is hard to grasp or halt except in a type of quick capture or momentary archival snapshot; the unevenly compartmentalized yet culturally translational relationship between the nation's four official languages; the marginality of literature as a profession in Singapore; and Southeast Asia's relative obscurity as a world literary center (with Singapore as a territorially miniscule city-state functioning as a connective hub for the larger region). Taken collectively as a participatory practice that welcomes amateur experimentalism, these works of flash fiction read as small-scale, iridescent primers—or hyperlinked corners (indicating the compressed and compartmentalized spaces—both physically and figuratively—that they illuminate, which are linked by theme and style)—of Singapore's Sinophone literary scene. The notion of the amateur here comprises two semantic layers: it refers both to unremunerated literary community-building that is unconcerned with professional mastery, as well as the passion of the practitioner who, without expectation of reward or notoriety, uses the form as a tool of sociopolitical insight and commentary.

Sinophone Flash: A Spirit of Amateurism

Known by countless names across a vast swath of languages and literary cultures, flash fiction is a niche form and technique. Serious interest in flash fiction—including scholarly analysis, global conferences among practitioners, and literary histories devoted to the practice—is a more recent phenomenon spanning the last three decades, intensified by the form's technological compatibility with mobile devices that have helped expand its global reach. Both New Zealand and the UK have declared National Flash Fiction Days.[6] The Flash Fiction Academy of China 中國微型小說學會 has grown increasingly active since it was first established in 1992.[7] Amid its translingual global convergences, flash fiction (or simply *flash*) has become a catch-all term in English for the practice, encompassing various other subgeneric monikers that reference varying lengths ranging from as few as six (!) words to more than a thousand.

Comparative literary studies theorize flash in ways that notably reflect the traits and practice of flash fiction itself: short, anecdotal, often allegorical, and collaborative. In the introduction to their 2015 *Flash Fiction International* anthology (which includes stories by authors from over fifty countries and Anglophone translations from nearly twenty languages), James Thomas, Robert Shapard, and Christopher Merrill describe flash as "big ideas in tiny spaces," be they "deep, outrageous, humorous, or in the best cases iridescent,"[8] reflecting multiple shades, angles, and perspectives despite—or perhaps due to—their compact form. As the Sinophone Singaporean examples discussed below demonstrate, the so-called iridescence of flash is derived from not only the different perspectives that various practitioners offer on a similar theme or issue, but from the distinct effects produced by a wide range of approaches to the form's space limitations: for example, a frantic pace versus a deliberate deceleration of the reader through elusive implication rather than direct forthrightness; objective realism versus poetic abstraction; or an ironic subversion of meaning and syntax versus a more conventional use of prose.

Addressing flash fiction's specific appeal in contemporary China, Aili Mu and Julie Chiu attribute the increasing practice of the form to its compatibility with mobile technology and device independence, suggesting that flash fiction offers "relative freedom from censorship not enjoyed in other media."[9] In the Sinophone literary world outside mainland China, flash fiction's emergence is regionally and transnationally linked according to analogous timelines, yet its developmental trajectories are distinctly localized with content tailored to their historical, translingual, and sociopolitical contexts. In Taiwan, where Sinophone flash fiction perhaps achieved its earliest popularity, its publication has bridged both commercial and literary presses, while in Hong Kong the form is, according to Shouhua Qi, "retiring from popular media to the ivory tower of serious literature."[10] In Southeast Asia, the inaugural World Sinophone Flash Fiction Conference 世界華文微型小說研討會 was held in Singapore in 1994. Since then, numerous Southeast Asian cities, including Manila, Kuala Lumpur, Jakarta, and Bangkok have hosted the conference.[11]

The relatively novel use of *shan xiaoshuo* 閃小說 (a literal translation of *flash fiction*) since the mid-2000s in mainland Chinese and Sinophone literary contexts should not overshadow the distinctive literary histories of *weixing xiaoshuo* 微型小說 (literally "microfiction"), particularly in Southeast Asia. In an environment where Sinophone literature itself is already a niche industry, *weixing xiaoshuo* has by no means been a sideshow that occupies only a small sliver of the overall literary scene.[12] In Singapore, flash fiction has been on the vanguard of local Sinophone literary activity since shortly after national independence in 1965. Both Wong Meng Voon and Lai Shihe 賴世和 trace the emergence of Singaporean *weixing xiaoshuo* to the early 1970s.[13] Lai also points out that its modern roots are planted in the Sinophone Malayan New Literature movement dating to the 1920s, when stories that now resemble flash were categorized under "short fiction," or *duanpian xiaoshuo* 短篇小說. From 1919 to 1965, the short story was Sinophone Malayan fiction's dominant form: novels were remarkably few, while hundreds of short-fiction collections (some including flash-length stories) were published. Responding to their readers' preferences, editors of Sinophone Malayan newspaper literary supplements, journals, and magazines—the common forums of initial literary publication—favored short stories publishable in one issue over serialized narratives. Moreover, when publishers produced anthologies of works that first appeared in these forums, short fiction volumes containing stories from multiple authors were far more common than the collected works of a single author, which, until much more recently, usually only saw publication after an author's output spanned multiple decades. Sinophone Malayan short fiction represents the fertile soil from which Singapore's flash initially sprouted, with the term and category of *weixing xiaoshuo* becoming, according to Lai, "independent" 獨立 from the broader category of Sinophone Malayan *duanpian xiaoshuo* only after Singapore broke from Malaysia in 1965 following a failed two-year merger.[14] The coincidence between the independence of the *weixing xiaoshuo* category and that of Singapore as a nation-state suggests that developments in Singapore's Sinophone literary scene postpartition are crucial to understanding that scene's coalescence around flash fiction as arguably its most prolifically practiced form of narrative fiction.

Singapore's newspaper literary supplements and magazines played an indispensable role in fostering *weixing xiaoshuo* as an independent form in the 1970s. By the 1980s, Singaporean flash had garnered international attention in Sinophone literary circles, appearing in special issues of journals like *Hong Kong Literature* 香港文學. In 1988, Zhou Can 周粲 (the pen name of Chew Kok Chang 周國燦, 1934–) became the first Singaporean to publish a single-authored volume of Sinophone flash. Sinophone flash truly flourished in the 1990s: from 1992 to 1998, Singapore published its own *Flash Fiction Quarterly* 微型小說季刊.[15] The decade witnessed greater genre variation in flash, including science fiction and postmodernist play with the boundaries of what counts as narrative in such a compact form.

Since this flourishing occurred before the Internet was a widespread forum for literary output and prior to the existence of smartphones—the flash-compatible technologies to which flash fiction's global rise has been attributed—what explains Sinophone flash fiction's appeal at these distinct moments in Singapore's history? First, the threat to Singapore's Sinophone education—namely, institutions of higher education like Nanyang University, which the government forcibly closed in 1980—under a bilingual, English-first education policy implemented in 1966 following independence cannot be discounted. From its founding in 1956 through the 1970s, Nanyang University not only cultivated its own Sinophone authors from among its faculty and student body but also sponsored literary activity that brought together aspiring Sinophone authors from various schools and cultural industries. As these threatened spaces contracted, flash fiction stood out as an easily and quickly producible, draftlike, familiar format to sustain local Sinophone literary activity and networks. Coupled with the intensification of the government's Speak Mandarin campaign targeting Chinese Singaporeans in the 1980s and 1990s—which carved out "mother tongue" corners within English-first educational institutions—Sinophone flash assumed the role of not just a literary form but a creative pedagogical tool for Sinophone literacy in the classroom. Some Mandarin instructors viewed reading and writing flash fiction as facilitating language learning (in an environment where Mandarin is arbitrarily racialized as a mother tongue but is practically spoken as a second or third language), while also allowing for localized expressions from other Sinitic heritage languages threatened under Lee Kuan Yew's dialect media ban (chiefly targeting Hokkien, Teochew, Cantonese, and Hakka) to filter through as a topic and entry point for intergenerational communication. This is evident in the young adult short stories fictionalizing the teaching experiences of You Jin 尤今 (the pen name of Tham Yew Chin 譚幼今, 1950–), a former high school Mandarin teacher and arguably Singapore's most popularly consumed Sinophone author.[16]

Flash fiction's proliferation in the 1980s and 1990s coincided with Singapore's emergence as one of the four Asian Tiger economies. With multinational investment and neoliberal development rapidly transforming Singapore's cityscape into the PAP's vision of a "First World" oasis in Southeast Asia, the cost of living—along with sociocultural expectations around the pace of one's economic productivity—rose dramatically. Xi Ni Er (the pen name of Chia Hwee Pheng 謝惠平, 1957–), one of Singapore's most prolific flash practitioners since the 1980s, correlates Sinophone flash fiction's flourishing during this period with Singapore's rapid economic transformation:

> Amid post-1980s urbanization, Sinophone writers seem to have found a new literary form that suits them: flash fiction. The elements of precision, quickness, simplicity, and brevity have enabled authors working in different literary genres to make flash fiction their "sword-making ground."

> 在80年代以後的城市化過程中，華文作家似乎找到了一個適合他們書寫的新興文體：微型小說。精、速、簡、短等元素讓從事不同文體的作者都以微型小說為"造劍地"。[17]

Compounded by Singapore's historical self-perception as a literary and cultural desert (tied to its former colonial status as a mercantile trading port settled by migrants from elsewhere in Asia), the challenge to make ends meet in an environment where literature is largely considered a luxury for a relatively small or indifferent local readership made it increasingly difficult to maintain literary authorship as a profession, especially in non-Anglophone circles (given the official privileging of English as the preferred medium of interethnic communication and the first language of public education in Singapore).

Yet important contemporary resonances between Sinophone flash fiction and the broader multilingual Singaporean literary ecosystem encourage a more integrative translingual reading across what Weihsin Gui aptly identifies as the official "four-corner" siloing of Singapore literatures in English, standard Chinese (Mandarin), Malay, and Tamil.[18] As with Sinophone flash fiction, Anglophone flash fiction in Singapore has also served as a venue for pedagogical practice and invitation to collaborative, amateur participation. The National Library Board's Read! Singapore campaign, for example, held flash fiction contests over three years beginning in 2012 and published the winning entries in a collection titled *33 Flash Fiction Stories* (2015).[19] Due to the racialized linguistic structuring of Singaporean education, the voices and perspectives of ethnic and racial minority authors in Singapore are more prominent in Anglophone flash than in Sinophone, but asymmetrical analogies between the class- and cultural-inflected marginalization of the Sinophone and the racial minoritization of Malay and Indian communities can be drawn between the two spheres. Anglophone Malay Singaporean writer Alfian Sa'at's 2012 flash collection, *Malay Sketches*, reveals solidarities with contemporary Sinophone flash in terms of the author's use of the flash form to convey a particular affect (claustrophobic, cramped, cornered, fleeting) and his mode of speaking between the lines to implicitly critique a sense of politically engineered cultural confinement. In her article "A Delicate Pellet of Dust" (drawn from a line in Alfian's story "Overnight" that draws attention to the ephemeral yet delicately small archival quality of flash fiction), Joanne Leow identifies *Malay Sketches* as a "dissident text" in "both form and content." She describes how Alfian's use of flash reflects the "cramped spaces of everyday life in Singapore," especially for the Indigenous minority Malay community. Taken together, the stories hyperlink the cramped or lost spaces of their individual settings—including military camps, marital beds, public housing estates, and "memories of demolished villages"—to create openings and trace "the effect of fraught histories of displacement and racialized policies."[20]

According to Malay literature scholar Nazry Bahrawi, the type of flash fiction showcased in Alfian's *Malay Sketches* is rarer in the Malay-language (or Bahasa) literary scene in Singapore, though the *cetera* form is an example of a Malay genre that resembles flash fiction and that generally falls under the broader category of *cerpen* (short fiction),[21] which, like Sinophone flash, emerged in the 1920s in the local Malayan newspaper scene.[22] Translingual analogies can further be drawn between scholarly discourses on Tamil Singaporean literary history and the types of historical developments that led flash fiction to be a popular form in the Sinophone literary scene. These include the role of vernacular newspapers in the development of local Tamil literature (especially short fiction); the persistence of a socioeconomic gulf between the English-educated and Tamil-educated communities (as it was working-class Tamils, from port workers to hairdressers to schoolteachers, who sustained the Tamil literary scene from the 1960s through the 1970s); the predominance of collaborative anthologies over sole-authored volumes; and the reinvigoration of the literary scene through the arrival of a new, educated Tamil diaspora in the 1990s that was more steeped in Tamil literary language and that participated in literary creation while maintaining and advancing professions in other industries.[23]

Sinophone authors in Singapore and throughout Southeast Asia have primarily made their living in fields like journalism, education, business, and civil bureaucracy, so creative writing is generally a passion project sustained in one's spare time with little monetary return. A corollary to Singapore's economic emergence continually attracting many Chinese Southeast Asians from elsewhere in the region as a work or study destination has been the development of Singapore as a regional hub and collaborative network of amateur Sinophone literary production centered around flash fiction. In 1995, Wong Meng Voon (1937–), cofounder of the Singapore Writers Association, compiled *ASEAN Youth Flash Fiction* 亞細安青年微型小說, a volume of Sinophone contributions by young authors from various Southeast Asian countries. In 1996, the Malaysian author Meng Sha 孟沙 (the pen name of Lim Meng Sai 林明水, 1941–2020) and Thai author Sima Gong 司馬攻 (the pen name of Kriangchao Durongsang เกรียงเชาว์ ดุรงค์แสง, 1933–) collaborated to compile the Singapore volume in the *Masterpieces of World Sinophone Flash Fiction* 世界微型小說名家名作 series.[24]

While flash is a flexible form open to aestheticization cultivated through practice and experimentation, its requisite brevity generally favors economical bluntness over rhetorical refinement. This creates the perception of a more level playing field between the amateur and the professional, a field where experienced and inexperienced practitioners alike can be playfully vulnerable, less seriously concerned with their sense of linguistic and artistic mastery. Though the flash form—through the types of pedagogical implementations noted above—has continually recruited new Singaporean participants, it is necessary to distinguish between the connotation of the amateur as a novice to literary creation and the *spirit of amateurism* with which Sinophone Singaporean flash is frequently imbued, even by those experienced authors whose finely honed examples are cited as "masterpieces." This latter signification draws from Roland Barthes's theorization of *l'amateur* in 1975: noting its etymology from the Latin *amator* as "one who loves and loves again," Barthes defines the amateur as someone who repetitiously engages in a hobby or project without a "spirit of mastery or competition," not with the expectation of reward or return but simply to "renew" one's "pleasure," graciously and "for nothing."[25] In *Representations of the Intellectual*, Edward Said furthers Barthes's definition by distinguishing between the professional, which implies narrow specialization favoring the marketing of oneself as "uncontroversial" and "unpolitical," and the amateur, who performs an activity or task out of "care and affection." For Said, the amateur spirit is a type of moral conscience that bears the potential to transform the technical profession into something "lively" and "radical."[26] The spirit of amateurism informs not only how Sinophone flash practitioners passionately and affectionately approach literary creation but also how they contest, satirize, creatively repurpose, subvert, or obliquely implicate political dictates by Singapore's technocratic and governing professional class, including the suggestion that literary pursuits are "a luxury we cannot afford."[27]

Through its refusal of mastery, Sinophone flash—in its prolific, collaborative, and abundant smallness—carves out a corner for decolonial thinking that intersects with proposals by Anglophone authors like Alfian Sa'at who have called on Singapore to address its all-too-comfortable relationship with discursive legacies of imperial mastery that survive relatively unchecked in the city-state's postcolonial institutions and monuments.[28] I read cultural and literary value—particularly for Chinese Southeast Asian communities whose sense of inherent "possession" of vernacular Chinese as a literary language has frequently been questioned, tentative, insecure, and uncertain—in Sinophone Singaporean flash fiction's spirit of amateurism, which involves what Julietta Singh, in *Unthinking Mastery*, calls practices of "unmasterful" or "vulnerable" textual engagement; for Singh, this is "a practice of opening ourselves up to our dependence on other discourses, peoples, beings, languages (that we know and do not yet know), and things that give rise to the ways that we think and the claims that we make."[29]

Sinophone Singaporean flash alchemizes the vulnerability and insecurity of smallness, brevity, amateurism, and multidirectional cultural and linguistic dependency on the "other" into a signature asset, as Lai Shihe suggests: "Singapore is small in territory and population, yet its writers are not discouraged by this. . . . They use the small to overcome the big and the many, making flash fiction Sinophone Singaporean literature's trademark brand" 新加坡地方小，人口少，作家們並不因此而氣短. . . . 以小勝大，以少勝多，使新華微型小說，成為新華文學的品牌.[30] Beyond smallness, Sinophone flash's themes of brevity, transitoriness, marginality, efficiency, and compactness that cohere with the form's materiality and formal affect are coupled with a desire to use flash as a mode of quick capture (like a Polaroid snapshot) to preserve and archive that sensibility, experience, and memory before it is wiped away, even if that archive is tiny and gets tucked away in the back pages of an anthology that most readers never discover. Invitations to amateur practice, often extended by experienced and distinguished practitioners through educational pedagogy or patronage of public literary events, are delivered through expressions of empathy for a shared sense of insecurity over one's linguistic "mastery" or inheritance. Combined with these traits, representations of itinerant crossings in the Southeast Asian region, with

Singapore functioning as a connecting hub rather than a miniscule territory, are abundantly traceable in the works of numerous authors, such as those described below. Often flirting with Singapore's OB markers, these flash stories individually cast unique light on such themes, but their respective authorial imprints are often fragmentary and interdependent, and their iridescence is best illuminated through a dialogic and intersectional analysis.

Integrative Readings of Singaporean Flash

"Guo Guan" 過關 (Passing through Immigration, 2013), a work of flash by Jun Yinglü 君盈綠 (the pen name of Low Siew Tin 劉秀珍, 1949–),[31] illuminates a transient intersection of the national, local, and regional. The story juxtaposes two Singaporean families simultaneously making a routine border crossing, with one from Singapore to Malaysia and the other from Malaysia to Singapore, on opposite sides of the Singapore-Johor Causeway over the Strait of Johor, by addressing parallel questions that are asked in each family vehicle at the time of crossing. In the first vehicle (returning to Singapore), an eight-year-old boy and his ten-year-old sister sitting in the backseat complain that they are deprived of spending their weekends with their friends. They ask their parents why the family always goes to Johor Bahru (JB) to eat and shop, since, according to the children, Singapore's supermarkets offer more than JB's. In the second vehicle (leaving for Johor), an elderly mother, seated in the back with her husband, asks their adult children (a brother and sister): "Why must we send your father to a nursing home in JB? There are many in Singapore too!" 為什麼一定要把老爸送去JB的療養院？ 新加坡也有很多間嘛![32] In each vehicle, the two questions elicit the same response: things are cheaper in JB. While critiquing the high cost of living in Singapore, Jun Yinglü's story—juxtaposing JB's supermarkets with its elderly care facilities—uses the itinerant crossing (the simultaneous arrival and departure) of the two family vehicles to indict the materialism of the adult children who cast off an elderly parent for the sake of a deal, even when it separates that parent from his spouse during their golden years. Yet the story's simple style is noteworthy: the one-page flash is constructed almost entirely of dialogue, set up by a paragraph break in which skeletal details are provided to switch the scene from one vehicle to the next. The language is direct and concise, but the critique is oblique, established only by a juxtaposition of the adjacent conversations that are partitioned within each vehicle but that are linked for the reader. This type of juxtaposition is instructive as a method for a syncretic reading of the various Singaporean "corners" illuminated by Sinophone flash.

For example, Jun Yinglü's commentary on the utilitarian materialism informing intergenerational breakdown (especially in terms of the treatment of the elderly in Singapore) is given adjacent treatment in the flash story "Chonghuo xinsheng" 重获新生 (A New Lease on Life, 2013) by Ai Yu (the pen name of

Liew Kwee Lan 劉桂嵐, 1956–), which appeared in the same 2013 volume as Jun Yinglü's story and is similarly constructed primarily as dialogue. An unnamed man returns home from a Sunday shopping trip to tell his wife how he saw his mother's previously discarded chair now being resold at the market. The man confirmed it was indeed his mother's chair by inspecting it for an image of a turtle he carved on one of its legs as a child. Even though his wife describes the chair as a worthless piece of rubbish, the man describes feeling moved by seeing the chair being given the opportunity for a new lease on life in the marketplace. Yet when his wife suggests retrieving his mother from the nursing home on Sundays, the man's attitude shifts to resemble his wife's view of the old chair, as he responds: "Let that old trash come home?" 讓那個老廢物回家?[33] Whereas Jun Yinglü's "Passing through Immigration" uses the obsession over a cheap deal in her materialist framing of intergenerational breakdown, Ai Yu's more biting satire—voiced through the words exchanged by her protagonists—indicts the cruel discarding of the elderly as garbage, redeemable or "recyclable" only if they serve an economically productive function. In this case, the man's wife has a more utilitarian rationale for bringing home his mother each Sunday: it will give the family maid a day off, meaning they intend to task his mother with housecleaning and childcare duties to save money. The wife ironically throws her husband's words back at him when he worries this would be unduly cruel to his mother: "We're not bullying her. We're allowing her to get out, be active, and do things again. It's like what you just said, this is called a new lease on life" 不是欺負她，我們是讓她能再出來活動做點事，你剛才說的，這叫重獲新生！[34]

Given flash fiction's utility in Singapore's Mandarin mother tongue language pedagogy (which is also tasked with inculcating Chinese Singaporean students with ethnocultural values), it is easy to read these compressed anecdotes—in their plain and straightforward language—as cautionary tales about heartless urban cruelty that runs counter to Confucian filiality.[35] Yet Ai Yu's momentary paralleling of the couple's abuse of the man's mother and the family's maid (hinting that the maid is currently required to work every day of the week) extends the story's primary critique of the unfilial treatment of elderly parents to Singapore's outsourcing of domestic labor to migrant workers. This type of momentary paralleling of marginalized figures (the elderly and the maid), much like the momentary juxtaposition of two compressed spaces in "Passing through Immigration," is another common strategy of Sinophone Singaporean flash that similarly invites integrative readings. Foreign domestic workers have been a prominent subject in Singaporean popular culture since the nation's emergence as an Asian Tiger economy in the 1990s led to a rapid increase in the number of dual-income families and foreign domestic workers (primarily from the Philippines and Indonesia). Despite only 20 percent of households employing domestic help as of 2019,[36] foreign domestic workers have become a fixture in Singaporean cultural production, with numerous films, literary works, and staged dramas portraying the relational dynamics—running the spectrum from intimacy and affection to psychological alienation and physical abuse—between Singaporean families and their domestic help.[37]

Wong Meng Voon's flash story "Di 'san' zhong yuyan" 第 "三" 種語言 (A "Third" Kind of Language, 2013) indicts the verbal abuse of Singapore's foreign domestic workers while playfully addressing the interlingual dimensions of the transnational, interpersonal communications and intimacies between such workers and their employers. This half-page narrative captures a telling moment in the relationship between a wealthy, new immigrant family from China in Singapore and the Filipina maid they hire to look after their newborn baby. The Filipina maid, with experience working for different Chinese Singaporean families and possessing a "natural gift" for languages, has a solid grasp of common, everyday vocabulary in Singaporean Mandarin. When the madam of the household discovers the Filipina maid behind their residence one night chatting with a friend while holding the employer's baby haphazardly, she instinctively curses the maid with a foul stream of Mandarin invective but then catches herself, spontaneously replacing her words for "fucking bullshitting" 說他媽的蛋 (literally "speaking his mother's eggs")—whose meaning the maid would likely understand—with classical literary Chinese approximations, *yun qi mu zhi luan* 云其母之卵. The stiff formality of the literary terms comically inoculates the ferocity of the verbal abuse because their meaning is only likely to be understood when read: when heard, they form seemingly incoherent babble. In this sense, Wong Meng Voon's "third" kind of language is spontaneously concocted to avoid intelligibility in the domestic intimacy of Singapore's interethnic and translingual spaces. It also alludes to the oblique form of critique that Singaporean flash fiction adopts: a type of coded language that must be used so the object of the critique is unable to catch the meaning.

This type of flash has pedagogical value in Singapore's Mandarin mother tongue classrooms, as it gives students a humorous translational entry point into more challenging literary Chinese. It does this while also drawing attention to the divisions between the everyday Mandarin—often inflected by English, Malay, and other Sinitic languages—spoken by Chinese Singaporeans and the formality of the written vernacular learned in the mother tongue classroom. In this sense, the story hints at some of the larger translingual dynamics that shape everyday Singaporean reality, magnifying while also generating friction with the compartmentalization of official languages through mother tongue education that tends to be racially exclusive—a classroom in which a Filipina domestic worker, should she find entry, would likely feel marginalized and out of place.

This compartmentalization mirrors the position of Sinophone literature (including flash) within the larger multilingual Singaporean literary ecosystem.

In a compressed form like flash, quick and clever wordplay (such as puns) is more common than intricate and ornate rhetoric. Across the multilingual terrain of Singaporean flash, a distinct feature of its clever wordplay is its translingual quality.[38] Even the pen name of one of its most prolific Sinophone practitioners, Xi Ni Er, is a transliteration of the English "Senior," a title emphasizing not his individuality but rather his relationship to his younger brother, fellow author and journalist Chia Joo Ming 謝裕民. Sinophone Singaporean flash foregrounds the translingual hierarchy between Mandarin and other subordinated Sinitic languages like Hokkien, Cantonese, Teochew, and Hakka, which were commonly spoken as native tongues before the government's implementation of its racialist mother tongue policy, its Speak Mandarin campaign, and its media broadcast policy in 1979, which has effectively functioned as a dialect ban in mainstream media (precisely the time when the practice of Sinophone flash was gaining traction).[39]

Xi Ni Er's flash story "Dajia xue Chaoyu" 大家學潮語 (Everyone Learns Teochew, 2003) is a satirical exposé of the consequences of Singapore's dialect media ban after nearly two decades in effect, tying this issue to the critique of economic utilitarianism, materialism, elderly care, and intergenerational breakdown foregrounded in the stories discussed above.[40] The story features two relatives who only want to learn Teochew so they can communicate with a dying ancestor, not to learn about the man's life or to connect with their family history before he dies but so they can bargain with him to be included in his will, which will only be communicated orally (again reflecting the division between written and spoken language):

> The old ancestor in the intensive care unit would soon update his will—his posthumous letter, no, his dying words. Those who did not understand his Teochew dialect would be unable to learn his wishes or communicate with him and would have to stand off to the side, with no chance to bargain.[41]

> 躺在加護病房的老祖公就快要重新確定他的 will——就是遺書，不，是遺囑的時刻。聽不懂他的潮語，不了解他的願望，無法與他溝通者，都一律靠邊站，而且，也無從 bargain。[42]

Suddenly, learning Teochew—which the story, in a cleverly packaged defiance of state dictates, proclaims as "the old ancestor's mother tongue" 老祖公的母語—has an urgent, utilitarian function in the modern Singaporean economy: appropriating the technocratic English idiom of the PAP (like the author's use of *will* and *bargain* above), the two relatives give the study of Teochew "first priority."[43]

Yet the two protagonists know no one else who still speaks this "ancestral tongue," and due to the dialect media ban, they discover their only way to access Teochew media is to listen to a daily twenty-minute FM radio news broadcast. To keep elderly Chinese Singaporeans who are not fluent in any of the nation's four official languages updated on important state policies and current events, the Singaporean government allows short evening news broadcasts in the commonly spoken Sinitic languages besides Mandarin as an exception to the dialect ban. However, these programs are compact and compressed, occupying a small corner of the media scene, much like flash fiction itself. One of the protagonists—invoking the invitation to offer feedback on quality of service that a technocratic Singapore takes pains to maintain—suggests lodging an official complaint with the government over the lack of time and space available for learning Teochew, but the other responds: "You should count yourself lucky that there's even such a program. If you *complain*, you may be regarded as interrupting, no, interfering with government *policy*" 老弟，有得聽就 '偷笑' 了。你去 complain，弄不好變成 干擾——不，干涉政府的 policy 了。[44] This admonition demonstrates a fear of reprisal for questioning state policy and satirically indicts the patronizing father-knows-best tone of the state, suggesting that the opportunity to access Teochew media is simply a courtesy that the government extends, a privilege it could easily revoke. Implicating state policy as a kind of window dressing (the compressed space allowed for dialect media), Xi Ni Er's "Everyone Learns Teochew" returns us to the type of gestural politics that Yeng Pway Ngon satirizes in his depiction of Speakers' Corner in "Defamation Suit." Invoking the insecurity or vulnerability of one's linguistic inheritance under the utilitarian governing language ideology and policies of the state, the story also invokes a common theme of lacking the time—or the desire—to cultivate meaningful and lasting connections in a society obsessed with productivity and material gain.

Offering a cleverly playful and experimental take on this theme, "Wuyan gongyu" 無言公寓 (The Speechless Apartment) by Wu Yeow Chong (1965), which appears in his 2002 Hong Kong–published flash volume *Huo ban leng* 火般冷 (As Cold as Fire), also departs from the punchier, more straightforward language of flash outlined above. The challenging postmodernist, metafictional style of the twenty-seven flash stories in *As Cold as Fire* generated much interest and debate in the Sinophone Singaporean literary scene when they were first published. Favoring atmosphere over plot and character, the stories convey a simulated reality that blurs boundaries between realism and illusion; frequently employ second-person narration; "subvert the textual structure of words and deliberately distort the original meaning of idioms" 顛覆文字的結構與刻意扭曲成語的原意; aim to slow down the reader's pace (forcing one to linger on the fragmentary and the fleeting); and combine vague abstraction regarding the setting with an uncanny sense of subliminal hyperlocality. For example, the abstract names "KS" and "GB" that Wu often gives his characters likely imply the Singlish (Singaporean English pidgin) term *kiasu* (originally from Hokkien, roughly meaning "fear of missing out," but usually used in the pejorative to critique materialist behavior) and the English phrase *good boy*.[45]

The title of Wu's "The Speechless Apartment" ironically subverts the notion of "speechless," since—much like the dialogue-heavy examples discussed above—it is an entirely verbal (or quoted-speech) text: the playing of telephone messages by family members trying to reach each other through the home answering machine but never catching someone on the receiving end, so the messages echo around an empty apartment. The story's first line is the outgoing message recorded by the father, KS, on the home voice mail system: "This is KS. It's not convenient to answer the phone now. Please leave your name and phone number and I will contact you as soon as possible. Thank you. Beep" 我是 KS，現在不方便接電話。請留下您的姓名和電話號碼，我會盡快和您聯絡。謝謝。嘟.[46] The message repeats throughout the story, often getting cut off in midsentence, indicating that the caller chose not to leave a message and hung up in frustration after discovering no one was home, with Wu's avoidance of quotation marks forcing the reader to identify changes in speaker. All the other lines of the story are messages that each caller leaves. There are a total of five callers: KS calling home looking for his wife to tell her he will be late because he has to work into the night in advance of the next day's stockholders' meeting; his wife calling home looking for their son, GB; a call from the "Golden Radiance Super Lucky Draw" 金光燦爛超級幸運大抽獎 informing KS that he has won their contest and needs to call back within three days to claim his prize; GB calling to let his parents know that he is at his uncle's playing on the computer and will be home soon; and finally a call from the police, which leaves a suspenseful cliffhanger: "Is this KS's family? This is the police station . . ." 請問您是 KS 的家人嗎？這裡是警察局 . . .[47] When considered as a fragment within the darker subject matter that populates much of As Cold as Fire—such as adultery, a murder trial, a suicide, and a drowning, wherein names like KS and GB are used repeatedly—the ending of "The Speechless Apartment" can only leave the reader feeling uneasy that something terrible has happened. In this way it demonstrates Wu's more implicit use of the ironic twist technique, which is used more explicitly in the other examples of flash discussed here. The recorded message—the quick capture of a fleeting moment archived in a corner of a compact space—becomes the family's main mode of (mis)communication and is indicative of intergenerational breakdown.

Mapped onto the handful of examples detailed here, the distinct treatments of themes of materialism, the discarding and denigration of the nonutilitarian (including the elderly), the fraught transnational and translingual intimacies with and abuses of foreign domestic workers, official versus nonstandard multilingualism, and intergenerational communication breakdown collectively illuminate Sinophone flash fiction's intertextual reflections of and responses to its compressed, cornered, and compartmentalized space of literary production as it edges up to and sometimes cleverly traverses the OB markers that govern cultural, artistic, and political discourse in the city-state. The authors' experimental use of language, whether terse and direct or abstract and elusive, and their polyvocal techniques of producing sociocultural commentary (as through stories fashioned almost entirely as dialogue or quoted speech) draw self-reflexive attention to practices, spheres, and contexts for producing, circulating, and consuming flash fiction itself.

Hyperlinked Arrivals and Departures

Reflecting the compressed spatiality and temporality of the flash form, the Sinophone Singaporean stories discussed above feature transitory episodes—covering only the span of a parrot's mimicry of a single line of politically inflammatory speech, the crossing of a bridge by two family vehicles traveling in opposite directions, or the playback of disembodied voices on a home answering machine—in hyperlocal settings: small, compact corners within the already small, compact city-state. Rather than individual examples of "big ideas in tiny spaces," Sinophone Singaporean flash fiction's worldliness, literariness, and conceptual force is not drawn from a bound, singular, masterful instantiation of the flash form but through its narrative adjacencies and intertextual intersections and departures for which multiple stories (by multiple practitioners) and integrative readings serve as hyperlinks. As individually compact yet distinctly iridescent corners, these episodes cumulatively prod the state's OB markers around political speech, language policy, race, ethnicity, and the nation's reliance on foreign workers. Yet their critiques are not just composed as responses to state policy, as they implicate broader sociocultural concerns, like the discarding or exploitation of elderly relatives simply for the sake of a deal.

Ironically, the modern historical factors that partitioned, compartmentalized, and marginalized Sinophone literature in postcolonial Singapore inspire much of the generative force behind the emergence, distinction (especially from its short fiction foundations in colonial Malaya), robustness, and vitality of the city-state's Sinophone flash fiction and its practitioners. The rise of the internet and mobile media formats have only opened more channels through which authors and readers may connect to flash. Rather than privileging professional mastery (the discursive legacies of colonialism and common organizing principles for the formation of contemporary world literary canons), Sinophone Singaporean flash fiction's iridescent literariness and worldliness are traced to its itinerant locality (at the nexus of the local, national, and regional) and compressed temporality (generating correspondence between physical spaces and literary practices), its open and participatory collective of practitioners, and its amateur spirit of vulnerability or nonmastery—a spirit not defined by crudeness, inexperience, or lack of style but by passion, resistance to professionalization, and a sociopolitically dissident moral and civic conscience.

BRIAN BERNARDS is associate professor of East Asian languages and cultures and comparative literature at the University of Southern California. He is author of *Writing the South Seas: Imagining the Nanyang in Chinese and Southeast Asian Postcolonial Literature* (2015) and coeditor of *Sinophone Studies: A Critical Reader* (2013).

////////////////////////////

Acknowledgments

This research was assisted by an Advancing Scholarship in the Humanities and Social Sciences Research Grant from the Office of the Provost at the University of Southern California. The author wishes to thank the special-issue editors, Carlos Rojas and Cheow Thia Chan, as well as the two anonymous reviewers, for their generous and constructive feedback on prior drafts.

Notes

1   Yeng, *Bu cunzai de qingren*, 122. An English translation of the story by Goh Beng Choo appears in Yeng, *Nonexistent Lover*, 126. The translation here is a slight modification of Goh's version.
2   Lee, "Gestural Politics," 145.
3   Ibid., 135.
4   Ibid., 146.
5   In 1969, Lee Kuan Yew famously referred to poetry as "a luxury we cannot afford" to encourage Singaporeans to "prioritize science and technology to modernize the nation," as Weihsin Gui points out ("Contemporary Literature from Singapore").
6   Thomas, Shapard, and Merrill, *Flash Fiction International*, 22.
7   Qi, preface, 11.
8   Thomas, Shapard, and Merrill, *Flash Fiction International*, 23.
9   Mu and Chiu, introduction, xxi–xxii.
10 Ibid., xx–xxi; Wong, "Zongxu," 5.
11 Zuojiawang bianji, "Shijie huawen weixing xiaoshuo 40 nian."
12 Xi Ni Er, "Shanzhe weiliang de guangmang," 8–9.
13 Wong and Xu, *Xinjiapo huawen wenxue shi chugao*, 257; Lai, *Xinjiapo huawen weixing xiaoshuo shi*, 16.
14 Lai, *Xinjiapo huawen weixing xiaoshuo shi*, 17–23.
15 Ibid., 25–28.
16 See, for example, the numerous classroom anecdotes in You Jin's *Ting, qingchun zai kuqi!* 聽，青春在哭泣！(Listen, the Youth Are Crying! 2004), which has been translated into English by Sylvia Li-chun Lin under the title *Teaching Cats to Jump through Hoops* (2012).
17 Qtd. in Chen, "Chaoyue yizuo shan."
18 Gui, "Contemporary Literature from Singapore."
19 Ibid.
20 Leow, "'Delicate Pellet of Dust,'" 724–27.
21 Bahrawi, pers. comm., August 13, 2021.
22 Jaffar, Ahmad, and Hussein, *History of Modern Malay Literature*, 86.
23 Mani, "Fifty Years of Singapore Tamil Literature," 51–54.
24 Lai, *Xinjiapo huawen weixing xiaoshuo shi*, 28–29.

25 Barthes, *Roland Barthes*, 52.

26 Said, *Representations of the Intellectual*, 74, 82–83.

27 In 2014, Christine Chia and Joshua Ip repurposed Lee Kwan Yew's pronouncement that "poetry is a luxury we cannot afford" to ironically title an anthology of Anglophone Singaporean poetry (Gui, "Contemporary Literature from Singapore").

28 The flash fiction in Alfian's *Malay Sketches* highlights examples of these discursive legacies.

29 Singh, *Unthinking Mastery*, 90–91.

30 Lai, *Xinjiapo huawen weixing xiaoshuo shi*, 29.

31 A freelance writer and former television screenwriter in Singapore, Jun Yinglü has served as director of the World Sinophone Flash Fiction Academy.

32 Jun, "Guo guan," 87.

33 Ai Yu, "Chonghuo xinsheng," 32–33.

34 Ibid., 33.

35 In his reading of Ai Yu's flash, Ng Heng Teong 黃興中 interprets "A New Lease on Life" in this way, suggesting that the man's carving of a turtle on the leg of his mother's chair as a child serves as an early sign of his filial deficiency ("Chonghuo xinsheng de bei'ai," 34).

36 Awang and Wong, "As Maids Become a Necessity."

37 For a discussion of such cultural representations in film, see McKay, "Politics of Mirrored Metaphors"; Ho, "Desiring the Singapore Story"; and Bernards, "Mockumenting Migrant Workers."

38 Alfian Sa'at's *Malay Sketches*, for example, includes a glossary of terms from numerous languages, including multiple Malay dialects.

39 Liew, "Limited Pidgin-Type Patois?" 217.

40 An English translation of this story by Howard Goldblatt and Sylvia Li-chun Lin appears in Xi Ni Er, *Earnest Mask*, 176–77. The translations I cite are from that volume, with some slight modifications.

41 Ibid.

42 Xi Ni Er, *Xi Ni Er weixing xiaoshuo*, 128–29.

43 Ibid., 129.

44 Ibid., 128; Xi Ni Er, *Earnest Mask*, 176.

45 Tong, Lin, Xi Ni Er, and Hong, "Siren huayu," 105–17. In his short preface to the volume, Hong Kong writer P. K. Leung 梁秉鈞 (using his pen name Ye Si 也斯) writes that Wu's "flash fiction experimentations contain his Singaporean background, his response to Hong Kong and Taiwan literature, and his gradual broadening of his horizons and maturation of his skills before and after going abroad" to obtain his doctorate at the University of Washington in Seattle ("Xiao xu," 8).

46 Wu, *Huo ban leng*, 69.

47 Ibid.

References

Ai Yu 艾禺. "Chonghuo xinsheng" 重獲新生 [A New Lease on Life]. In *Xingkong yiran shanshuo: Xinjiapo shanxiaoshuo xuan* 星空依然閃爍：新加坡閃小說選 [The Stars Still Twinkle in the Sky: Selected Singaporean Flash Fiction], edited by Xi Ni Er 希尼爾 and Xue Feng 學楓, 32–33. Singapore: Lingzi chuanmei, 2013.

Awang, Nabilah, and Wong Pei Ting. "As Maids Become a Necessity for Many Families, Festering Social Issues Could Come to the Fore." *Channel News Asia*, November 4, 2019.

https://www.channelnewsasia.com/singapore/maids-foreign-domestic-workers-singapore-necessity-families-847201.

Barthes, Roland. *Roland Barthes by Roland Barthes*, translated by Richard Howard. New York: Hill and Wang, 2010.

Bernards, Brian. "Mockumenting Migrant Workers: The Inter-Asian Hinterland of Eric Khoo's *No Day Off* and *My Magic*." *positions: asia critique* 27, no. 2 (2019): 297–332.

Chen Yong 陳勇. "Chaoyue yizuo shan—Xinjiapo Xi Ni Er Fangtanlu" 超越一座山——新加坡希尼爾訪談錄 [Passing over a Mountain: An Interview with Singapore's Xi Ni Er]. *Zhongguo zuojiawang* 中國作家網 [ChinaWriter.com], January 17, 2012. http://www.chinawriter.com.cn/2012/2012-01-17/113238.html.

Gui, Weihsin. "Contemporary Literature from Singapore." *Oxford Research Encyclopedia of Literature*, November 20, 2017. https://oxfordre.com/literature/view/10.1093/acrefore/9780190201098.001.0001/acrefore-9780190201098-e-189?rskey=zUcZEy&result=1.

Ho, Michelle H. S. "Desiring the Singapore Story: Affective Attachments and National Identities in Anthony Chen's *Ilo Ilo*." *Journal of Chinese Cinemas* 9, no. 2 (2015): 173–86.

Jaffar, Johan, Mohd. Thani Ahmad, and Safian Hussein. *History of Modern Malay Literature*, vol. 1, translated by Hawa Abdullah. Kuala Lumpur: Dewan Bahasa dan Pustaka, 1992.

Jun Yinglü 君盈綠. "Guo guan" 過關 [Passing through Immigration]. In *Xingkong yiran shanshuo: Xinjiapo shanxiaoshuo xuan* 星空依然閃爍：新加坡閃小說選 [The Stars Still Twinkle in the Sky: Selected Singaporean Flash Fiction], edited by Xi Ni Er 希尼爾 and Xue Feng 學楓, 87. Singapore: Lingzi chuanmei, 2013.

Lai Shihe 賴世和. *Xinjiapo huawen weixing xiaoshuo shi* 新加坡華文微型小說史 [The History of Sinophone Singaporean Flash Fiction]. Singapore: Lingzi chuanmei, 2004.

Lee, Terence. "Gestural Politics: Civil Society in 'New' Singapore." *Sojourn: Journal of Social Issues in Southeast Asia* 20, no. 2 (2005): 132–54.

Leow, Joanne. "'A Delicate Pellet of Dust': Dissident Flash Fictions from Contemporary Singapore." *Journal of Postcolonial Writing* 51, no. 6 (2015): 723–36.

Liew Kai Khiun. "Limited Pidgin-Type Patois? Policy, Language, Technology, Identity and the Experience of Canto-Pop in Singapore." *Popular Music* 22, no. 2 (2003): 217–33.

Mani, A. "Fifty Years of Singapore Tamil Literature." In *50 Years of Indian Community in Singapore*, edited by Gopinath Pillai and K. Kesavapany, 51–55. Singapore: Singapore World Scientific Publishing, 2016.

McKay, Benjamin. "The Politics of Mirrored Metaphors: Flor Contemplacion and *The Maid*." *positions: east asia cultures critique* 19, no. 2 (2011): 463–98.

Mu, Aili, and Julie Chiu. Introduction to *Loud Sparrows: Contemporary Chinese Short-Shorts*, translated by Aili Mu, Julie Chiu, and Howard Goldblatt, xii–xxiii. New York: Columbia University Press, 2008.

National Library Board. *33 Flash Fiction Stories: From Read! Singapore's Flash Fiction Contest*. Singapore: National Library Board, 2015.

Ng Heng Teong 黃興中. "Chonghuo xinsheng de bei'ai: Du 'Chonghuo xinsheng'" 重獲新生的悲哀——讀《重獲新生》 [The Sorrow of Rebirth: Reading "A New Lease on Life"]. In *Xingkong yiran shanshuo: Xinjiapo shanxiaoshuo xuan* 星空依然閃爍：新加坡閃小說選 [The Stars Still Twinkle in the Sky: Selected Singaporean Flash Fiction], edited by Xi Ni Er 希尼爾 and Xue Feng 學楓, 34–35. Singapore: Lingzi chuanmei, 2013.

Qi, Shouhua. Preface to *The Pearl Jacket and Other Stories: Flash Fiction from Contemporary China*, edited and translated by Shouhua Qi, 11–14. Berkeley, CA: Stone Bridge, 2008.

Sa'at, Alfian. *Malay Sketches*. Singapore: Ethos Books, 2012.

Said, Edward W. *Representations of the Intellectual*. New York: Vintage Books, 1996.

Singh, Julietta. *Unthinking Mastery: Dehumanism and Decolonial Entanglements.* Durham, NC: Duke University Press, 2018.

Thomas, James, Robert Shapard, and Christopher Merrill, eds. *Flash Fiction International: Very Short Stories from around the World.* New York: Norton, 2015.

Tong Noong Chin 董農政, Lin Gao 林高, Xi Ni Er 希尼爾, and Hong Zhenlong 洪振隆. "Siren huayu: Tan Wu Yaozong de weixing xiaoshuo" 四人話語：談吳耀宗的微型小說 [Four-Person Discussion of Wu Yeow Cheong's Flash Fiction]. In *Huo ban leng* 火般冷 [As Cold as Fire], by Wu Yeow Chong (Wu Yaozong) 吳耀宗, 103–26. Hong Kong: Qingwen shuwu, 2002.

Wong Meng Voon 黃孟文. "Di 'san' zhong yuyan" 第 "三" 種語言 [A "Third" Type of Language]. In *Xingkong yiran shanshuo: Xinjiapo shanxiaoshuo xuan* 星空依然閃爍：新加坡閃小說選 [The Stars Still Twinkle in the Sky: Selected Singaporean Flash Fiction], edited by Xi Ni Er 希尼爾 and Xue Feng 學楓, 77. Singapore: Lingzi chuanmei, 2013.

Wong Meng Voon 黃孟文, ed. *Yaxi'an qingnian weixing xiaoshuo* 亞細安青年微型小說 [ASEAN Youth Flash Fiction]. Taipei: Yuanshan fulunshe/Singapore: Xinjiapo shicheng fulunshe/Xinjiapo zuojia xiehui, 1995.

Wong Meng Voon 黃孟文. "Zongxu" 總序 [Preface]. In *Xinjiapo huawen weixing xiaoshuo shi* 新加坡華文微型小說史 [The History of Sinophone Singaporean Flash Fiction], by Lai Shihe 賴世和, 5–6. Singapore: Lingzi chuanmei, 2004.

Wong Meng Voon 黃孟文 and Xu Naixiang 徐迺翔, eds. *Xinjiapo huawen wenxue shi chugao* 新加坡華文文學史初稿 [A Preliminary History of Sinophone Singaporean Literature]. National University of Singapore, Department of Chinese Studies and Global Publishing, 2002.

Wu Yeow Chong (Wu Yaozong) 吳耀宗. *Huo ban leng* 火般冷 [As Cold as Fire]. Hong Kong: Qingwen shuwu, 2002.

Xi Ni Er. *The Earnest Mask: Stories*, translated by Howard Goldblatt and Sylvia Li-chun Lin. Singapore: Epigram Books, 2012.

Xi Ni Er 希尼爾. "Shanzhe weiliang de guangmang" 閃著微亮的光芒 [Flashing a Faintly Bright Radiance]. In *Xingkong yiran shanshuo: Xinjiapo shanxiaoshuo xuan* 星空依然閃爍：新加坡閃小說選 [The Stars Still Twinkle in the Sky: Selected Singaporean Flash Fiction], edited by Xi Ni Er 希尼爾 and Xue Feng 學楓, 7-10. Singapore: Lingzi chuanmei, 2013.

Xi Ni Er. 希尼爾. *Xi Ni Er weixing xiaoshuo* 希尼爾微型小說 [Xi Ni Er's Flash Fiction]. Singapore: Lingzi chuanmei, 2004.

Ye Si 也斯. "Xiao xu" 小序 [Short Preface]. In *Huo ban leng* 火般冷 [As Cold as Fire], by Wu Yeow Chong (Wu Yaozong) 吳耀宗, 6–9. Hong Kong: Qingwen shuwu, 2002.

Yeng Pway Ngon 英培安. *Bu cunzai de qingren: Duanpian xiaoshuoji* 不存在的情人：短篇小說集 [The Nonexistent Lover: Collected Short Fiction]. Taipei: Tangshan chubanshe, 2007.

Yeng Pway Ngon 英培安. *The Nonexistent Lover and Other Stories*, translated by Goh Beng Choo. Singapore: City Book Room, 2017.

You Jin. *Teaching Cats to Jump through Hoops*, translated by Sylvia Li-chun Lin. Singapore: Epigram Books, 2012.

You Jin 尤今. *Ting, qingchun zai kuqi!* 聽，青春在哭泣！ [Listen, the Youth Are Crying!]. Singapore: Lingzi chuanmei, 2004.

Zuojiawang bianji 作家網編輯. "Shijie huawen weixing xiaoshuo 40 nian 40 jian dashi pingxuan zhaixiao" 世界華文微型小說 40 年 40 件大事評選揭曉 [Forty Major Events in the Forty Years of World Sinophone Flash Fiction]. *Zuojiawang* 作家網 [Writers' Net], December 21, 2018. http://m.zuojiawang.com/html/wentandongtai/35788.html.

KO CHIA-CIAN

Translated by Sun Pingyu

Chinese-Language Memories under the Conflagration of War
On the Martyrdom of Chung Ling High School's Teachers and Students

ABSTRACT As a Chinese-medium educational institution, Chung Ling High School (CLHS) in Penang enjoyed an illustrious reputation in the Malayan era. During the fall of Penang in World War II, the deaths of eight teachers and forty-six students from CLHS marked a painful episode in the history of Penang's intellectual community, manifested in their sense of trauma and reflections on the crisis of Chinese education. After CLHS was reopened during the postwar period, the school set up a committee to commemorate the sacrifices of its teachers and students through memorial services, erection of a monument, and publication of tribute books. Applying the theories of French historian Pierre Nora, this article discusses how the ensuing *les lieux de mémoire* (sites of memory) formed through the sacrifices of CLHS teachers and students, inscribing the plight of literary lineage and cultural severance, which in turn takes on the role of reviving and perpetuating the ethnic Chinese spirit. In this sense, the sacrifices of the CLHS teachers and students as "sites of memory" have become a part of the ethnic community's collective memory. When we examine how war memory texts are constructed, the CLHS tragedy embeds the connections between Chinese education and the ethnic sentiments of the Chinese community during the Japanese occupation.

KEYWORDS Chinese-medium schools, Chung Ling High School (Penang), Guan Zhenmin, traumatic memory, anti-Japanese

War and Chinese-Medium Schools

In the early hours of December 8, 1941, the Japanese military launched an assault on the Kelantan state in the northern part of the Malay Peninsula. After landing, the Japanese took over this northern region within a day, which marked the beginning of the Greater East Asia War. On December 11, Japanese fighter planes conducted air raids over Penang Island. For the first time since the establishment of Penang as a port city, the shadows of war and death loomed over the prosperous island. After a few days of large-scale bombing, British officials and garrisons retreated, leaving Penang in a state of anarchy. Different local ethnic communities sent representatives to form the Penang Service Committee for the maintenance of temporary public order. However, the bombings did not stop. On December 19, the committee had to broadcast news of the British retreat to the Japanese that

PRISM: THEORY AND MODERN CHINESE LITERATURE • 19:2 • SEPTEMBER 2022
DOI 10.1215/25783491-9966707 • © 2022 LINGNAN UNIVERSITY

had occupied other parts of northern Malaya, pleading with them to end the air raids. On the same day, Japanese soldiers entered the city and officially initiated what would become three years and eight months of Japanese colonial occupation.

Since the beginning of maritime trading in the eighteenth century, Penang Island has been of strategic importance to the Malay Peninsula. This island—which, under British colonization, opened for trade in 1786, earlier than Singapore—was a Chinese migrant society replete with talent and culture. The five major Chinese families and British colonial merchants formed Penang's booming commercial scale. Coexisting with the business scene was the spread of Chinese clan associations and other organizations; influential newspapers like *Penang Sin Poe* 檳城新報 and *Kwong Wah Yit Poh* 光華日報; and an assortment of southbound scholars, revolutionaries, and reformists. It was a typical Nanyang city that hosted the ethnic Chinese. After conquering Singapore in February 1942, the Japanese military launched the "Sook Ching" 肅清, a massive inspection operation that was conducted in Singapore and various states in the Malay Peninsula, during which Penang was given the Japanese name Penan (彼南). The purge spread to Penang in April, particularly affecting the Chinese community and leaving deep scars. Among those impacted was the renowned Chinese-medium Chung Ling High School 鍾靈中學 (CLHS). Many of the school's teachers and students were arrested on the charges of being communists and anti-Japanese, and were subsequently interrogated and tortured. A total of eight teachers and forty-six students were killed.[1] These events marked a painful episode in the history of Penang's intellectual circle and devastated the local Chinese community, leaving traumatic memories of the killings and destruction during the so-called Penan Times.

During the initial period of the Japanese occupation, the Japanese destroyed Chinese schools and libraries across the Malay Peninsula.[2] After the war, the CLHS Incident marks the historical memory of the local Chinese during the occupation, as it involves the fatal sacrifices of intellectuals and relates to the broader trauma of the intellectual community and the local Chinese education crisis. Readings of the crisis gesture toward the ideal of cultural continuation through Chinese-language education, as well as the sustaining of the literary lineage or medium embedded in the ethnic Chinese spirit. As part of the historical experiences of the Penang Chinese during the war, the sacrifices of the CLHS group are conspicuous for their symbolic significance. After the war, several CLHS teachers produced historical testimonies and traumatic accounts in the form of survivors' accounts and denunciations, all of which are historical memories of trauma rooted in contemporary sentiments. After the postwar reestablishment of CLHS, the school established a Committee to Commemorate the Deceased Teachers and Students of Chung Ling and organized a memorial service, erected a monument, and published a collection of tributes. In addition, the Chinese-language teacher Guan Zhenmin 管震民 (1880–1962) composed elegies, prefaces to monument inscriptions, and the lyrics for "Fuxing ge" 復興歌 (Song of Reestablishment), the "Zhuidaohui ge" 追悼會歌 (Memorial Service Song, and the song written for the "Binlangyu Huaqiao kangzhan xunnan jigong ji linan qiaobao jinianbei" 檳榔嶼華僑抗戰殉職機工暨罹難僑胞紀念碑 (Monument for the Sacrificed Overseas Chinese War-Resistance Mechanics and Perished Compatriots in Penang). Functioning as both historical record and lyrical expression, Guan's compositions documented the plight of his fellow teachers and students.

In addition, Guan himself encountered great family misfortune during the occupation. His classical-style poems are melancholic and powerful records of the period, resonating with the adversities faced by the school's teachers and students. Drawing from the ideas of French historian Pierre Nora, all the aforementioned forms of memory, be they tangible or intangible, can be viewed as "sites of memory" (*les lieux de mémoire*) formed after the sacrifices of the CLHS teachers and students, constituting a nodal point linking memories of Malayan Chinese-education movements and Chinese schools. As Nora points out, the existence and perpetuation of sites of memory depend on the creation of physical archives, the sustainment of anniversary events, the organization of celebratory activities, the delivery of eulogies, and the witnessing of such actions. If people lacked the ability to commemorate, history would sweep away everything, resulting in the erasure of memories.[3] The CLHS calamity evokes the destruction of lives and its attendant suffering. In this sense, the status of the sacrifices of the CLHS members as "sites of memory" has become a part of the community's collective memory.

As we consider how these war memory texts were constructed, it is hard to deny that CLHS, one of the top Chinese schools in prewar Malaya, endured a tragedy that became embedded in the connections between Chinese education and the Chinese community's ethnic consciousness under Japanese occupation. The narration of this period of CLHS history informs how we regard the collective memories of the Chinese during the occupation, and in particular, the impact and appeal of these memories to Chinese education. The position of these teachers before and after the war, when considered alongside their bitter experiences during the war itself, projects the cultural identities and cultivated virtues of a generation of Chinese-language educators. Given the school's status as a site for the community bound by memories of Chinese education, its positionality is worth exploring for its resonance with the sacrifices of the CLHS's members.

Chinese-Language Teachers and Chinese-Language Imagination before and during the War

The flourishing of new education in Malaya and Singapore was closely linked to the late Qing reform and revolutionary movements. Revolutionaries had settled in Penang by the early twentieth century, and CLHS was established in 1917, at a moment when China was still reeling from the failed attempt to overthrow President Yuan Shikai 袁世凱, and the Nationalist Party realized that education was the only way to save the nation. Followers of Sun Yat-sen 孫逸仙—including Khoo Beng Cheang 邱明昶, Xu Shengli 許生理, and Tan Sin Cheng 陳新政 of the Penang Philomathic Union—responded to the call to help educate a new generation of youth by establishing Chung Ling School, which initially included a lower and upper primary school. The binome *zhongling* 鍾靈, from which the school takes its name, comes from the idiom *zhonglingyuxiu* 鍾靈毓秀, meaning "to gather heavenly and earthly essences to nurture outstanding talents." In 1923, the secondary school section was established, and the institution was renamed Chung Ling High School, making it the first Chinese high school on the Malay Peninsula.[4] Because the ethnic consciousness shared by the school's board of directors, teachers, and students was close to the political stance of the Nationalists, many teachers and students joined the party. The revolutionaries also set up schools with far-reaching influences, and soon new-style schools began appearing in the Chinese districts of many cities and towns. These schools became bases from which it was possible to promote Chinese culture and instill local Chinese with national, ethnic, and cultural identity.

Looking back at the initial implementation of Chinese-language education in Singapore and Malaya, we must not overlook the nineteenth-century appointment of Qing envoys or the turn of the century of Confucianism movement. In 1881, Tso Ping Lung 左秉隆 was designated the first Chinese consul of Singapore. Coordinating with local efforts to establish private schools and literary societies, he organized literary societies, recruited and selected outstanding works, and encouraged newspapers and journals to publish articles about writing and lists of award winners. Although the topics are beyond the traditional topics of the Confucian Four Books and Five Classics, his efforts nevertheless helped create a literary field that became an alternative to the newspapers and journals that consisted predominantly of news articles and official announcements. Between 1891 and 1894, the next consul, Huang Zunxian 黃遵憲, established the Southern Society and continued the practice of recruiting and selecting literary submissions. His topics were more relatable as they concerned local realities in Nanyang. In 1904, the vice consul of Penang, Cheong Fatt Tze 張弼士, facilitated the establishment of Chung Hwa Confucian School 孔聖廟中華學校, the first Chinese school in Penang. Over the next twenty years, schools, libraries, newspapers, publications, and Confucianism movements flourished and completely altered the face of local Chinese communities in Singapore and the Malay Peninsula by shaping new intellectual classes and their literary education within the immigrant societies.

The political and cultural identities of the consuls highlight the agency of their diplomatic and enlightenment missions, thereby expanding the Singaporean and Malayan Chinese imagination about the role of consuls, sentiments towards China, and cultural education. From this perspective, the Singapore and Penang consuls transformed the immigrant community's sojourner mentality and established a "Chinese language" (*huawen* 華文) space within the local environment. The ecology helped to forge a common ideological identification for the overseas Chinese by creating a space for the intermingling of culture and literature, which enabled Chinese language to take root. At that time, the late Qing reformer Chen Chi 陳熾 (1855–1900) advocated for the establishment of schools in ethnic Chinese communities, saying: "If the West learns and Chinese people do not, then we will always be their servants. Accordingly, we will spend several thousand taels each year to attract talent from overseas, and when things change in the West, talented individuals are bound to appear, meaning that there will be people who will defend China abroad" 西人皆學而華人不學，故終為人役耳。歲費數萬金以羅海外之才，以待歐西之變，他日必有奇才碩彥應運而生，為海上之夫餘以藩屏中國者。[5] The strategic distribution of educational support for the overseas Chinese was closely aligned with the Qing court's diplomatic priorities. However, one should not overlook the fact that in the Straits Settlements, overseas Chinese communities' demand for education revealed the tensions found in multiethnic communities. Consular appointments, Confucianism movements, and Chinese schools helped promote a sense of *zhonghuaxing* 中華性 (Chineseness) within these communities. In the growing Chinese communities in Singapore and Malaya, the interplay between Chinese ethnic and cultural sentiments suggest that *Chinese language* was not simply transmitted from the May Fourth Movement or new styles of education, nor does it simply mark the spirit of modernity that enlivens a national imagination. Instead, it represented an inheritance of a Chinese literary heritage.

Since the late nineteenth century, Penang had been a city where the humanities thrived. Li Jun's 力鈞 *Binlangyu zhilue - yiwenzhi* 檳榔嶼志略-藝文志 (A Short Account of Penang Island—A Treatise on Arts and Letters) and Thio Chee Non's 張煜南 *Binlangyu liuyu shige* 檳榔嶼流寓詩歌 (A Sojourner's Poetry about Penang Island) recorded the refined cultures of the south. Journalists and teachers also left behind poems and artworks in native place guilds, ancestral halls, temples, cemeteries, and schools. There were also literary societies established before the war, such as the Hut of Goose and Snow Poetry Society 鴻雪廬詩社 and the Penang Poetry Recital Society 檳榔吟社, as well as special issues devoted to classical-style poetry, all of which contributed to early Penang's literary and cultural environment. These writing practices encouraged a broader Chinese-language consciousness.

In 1924–1925, when the secondary school section was first introduced into CLHS, there were only three or four Chinese-language teachers in total for the primary and secondary sections. By 1938, when the first cohort of high school students graduated, the number of Chinese teachers grew to twenty-three.[6] This was the largest number of teachers before the war. The increase in teaching strength indicates not only the growth in student numbers but also the high frequency of scholars who sought refuge southward amid the war in China. Due to the lack of local-born Chinese language teachers in Nanyang, southbound teachers became the driving force in Chinese-language education.[7] The sense of unity that the Chinese community and Chinese schools had toward the Chinese language reflected the emotional persuasion of the overseas Chinese who provided aid to China's war resistance efforts. The performance of anti-Japanese operas, patriotic songs, and roving choirs from China that promoted anti-Japanese sentiments and raised funds for war refugees on the mainland also fueled passion toward Chinese language and the sense of ethnic sentiments enfolded within.

Teachers prior to World War II were basically *nanlai wenren* 南來文人 (southbound scholars). Their worlds of poetry often encapsulated their nostalgic melancholy and an attendant sense of entrapment as they helplessly watched battle flames engulf their homeland from their barren locales in the tropical south. In 1923, Chen Shaosu 陳少蘇 accepted an appointment to teach Chinese at CLHS, making him part of the school's earliest cohort of Chinese-language teachers. Many of the works in his posthumous anthology *Shengchuntang ji* 生春堂集 (The Hall of Spring Arrival Collection) express regret for a life in displacement, but he also penned works about the local landscape, such as *Bincheng bajing* 檳城八景 (The Eight Scenes of Penang), and about his cultural interactions with local communities. Such were the complex sentiments of the early southbound scholars who were often caught in a conflict of *shuangxiang qinghuai* 雙鄉情懷 (double-homeland belonging).

Guan, Chen, and Wang Qiyu 汪起予, who also taught at CLHS, were hailed as the Three Masters of Chung Ling. They were well-versed in classical literature and contributed to the school's vibrant poetry-writing atmosphere. In addition, Chen's brother-in-law Li Ciyong 李詞傭, who was also a Chinese-language teacher at CLHS and had been a member of a literary research group under the China New Literature and Art Society 中國新文藝社團, composed *Binlang yuefu* 檳榔樂府 (Penang Ballads) and *Yeyin sanyi* 椰陰散憶 (Scattered Thoughts under the Palm Shade). The former is a collection of lyrics about the Penang landscape and local histories, written in melodic elegance and interthreaded with diasporic sentiments. His style is graceful, restrained, and beautiful. The classical poetry of CLHS teachers reveals the importance of the Chinese school system—which existed separate from the newspapers, the other important instrument—in perpetuating the lineage of classical-style writings in the Mahua literary tradition. Residing in the far-flung equatorial islands, their nuanced and delicate but nevertheless agitated sentiments can easily be imagined. Conveyed through the medium of literature, they share an indignation about the times, and their writing practices inaugurated a southern literary style that combines diasporic nostalgia with a dedicated concern for China.

In the mid-1930s, CLHS teachers became very responsive to various anti-Japanese resistance and Chinese aid (AJCA) rallies. Less than two months after the Marco Polo Bridge Incident, the Penang Fundraising Committee was formed under the leadership of the CLHS board of directors. The committee and its efforts were planned and mounted by the Penang Philomathic Union. As one of the CLHS's founding organizations, the union illustrates how the interconnected social network could greatly mobilize the Chinese community. The committee's fundraising events included donations, charity performances, sales, and the purchase of government bonds, which involved not just the teachers and students but also the directors. In other words, what the scholar Wong Hong Teng views as the tripartite ACJA endeavors of the board directors, teachers, and students was not solely a tribute to the CLHS, but was also a point of rallying ethnic sentiment for the Penang Chinese community.[8]

During the anti-Japanese movement in Penang, Guan occasionally experienced the sorrow of a sojourner but was also energized with passion for the war resistance. Guan was born in China in 1880 in Huangyan County, Taizhou Prefecture, Zhejiang Province, and was hired as a teacher at CLHS in December 1934. Together with his good friend, the poet Xu Xiaoshan 許曉山, they established the Penang Poetry Recital Society to express their aspirations through poetry. Guan commemorates the occasion in a grandiose fashion: "Who will continue the *Guangling* san, a zither tune that is now lost? / Even in blazing barren lands in the remote frontier, there lie undiscovered talents" 誰續廣陵散亡曲，炎荒尚有不遺才.[9] The Chinese-language education system in the British colony was frequently inspected by education officials from China. These schools used China-published textbooks that often carried anti-British and anti-Japanese instructional material,[10] thereby helping to shape and cultivate a Chinese identity. However, the colonial government subsidized Chinese schools far less than government schools, and parents who sent their children to Chinese schools did it out of two reasons: an affinity for the mother tongue, and an evocation of ethnonationalist sentiments. Hence, we can see that when teachers joined the AJCA movement, the Chinese ethnic sentiments in the world of poetry and prose demonstrate a strong faith in the power of words.

During the three years and eight months of Japanese occupation, Guan lost almost his entire family. The CLHS's administration was terminated, while the campus was sealed off and plundered. Guan's poems from this period were frequently records of bloodshed and tears: "Like multiple flocks of birds, the fighter jets crowd the skies, / Like deafening beads, the bullets fire nonstop. . . . Wandering souls roam here and there, ghost-fires accumulate into green jade/ Tears fused with blood, turning the surroundings red" 飛鳶陣陣布天空，彈

似連珠聲更隆．．．　游魂到處燐成碧，淚血交流色映紅.[11] Under the aggressive Japanese language policy implemented during the occupation, Guan also expresses the vulnerability of carrying on with the cultural lineage that Chinese schools and Chinese languages symbolize: "My words lack spirit, while vainly filled with regret, / Who would take pity on heroes in miserable impasses" 文字無靈空有恨，英雄末路孰相憐.[12]

In April 1942, when the Sook Ching operation was launched, CLHS teachers and students were among the first group to be impacted. Eight teachers and forty-six students were interrogated, tortured, and eventually killed. In particular, several CLHS Chinese-language teachers were either tortured to death or survived but suffered a miserable fate. Wang Qiyu died of illness during the throes of passionate support for the anti-Japanese movement among the Singapore-Malayan Chinese. Guan's son Guan Lianggong, an athletics instructor at CLHS who was among the CLHS members arrested, died in prison on a hunger strike. Guan's wife and granddaughter became extremely distressed and passed away around the same time. Chen Shaosu, after receiving news of CLHS teachers' and students' plight with no hopes of rescue, passed away in 1943 due to illness (resulting perhaps from pent-up indignation). Li Ciyong, meanwhile, died in prison after being tortured and interrogated.

The Chinese teachers' war experiences evoked their "Chung Ling anti-Japanese spirit" that had been fostered during the AJCA rallies and the occupation period. Hence, their poetry embodies personal hardships while presenting their living conditions during the war, combined with an underlying ethnic spirit. In a commemorative article, Wang Qiyu's son Wang Kaijing 汪開競—who was also a Chinese teacher at CLHS—quoted an impassioned poem by his father:

> The vital energy of the sword congeals into a white rainbow,
> Its blade has been sharpened ten thousand times.
> Sorghum reeds, like green veils, masquerade the evil forces,
> Leaving students displaced and departed spirits terrorized.
> Singing fervently the tales of the three clans that jointly toppled the Qin state,
> Even if the initial mission failed, it has ignited a flame in the rest of us.
> We shall attack the core of the enemy quarters,
> then celebrate by drinking to our hearts' content.

> 劍氣凝虹白，曾磨十萬橫。青紗連帳隱，墨水旅魂驚。慷慨歌三戶，焚沈激眾生。黃龍終直搗，有酒快同傾.[13]

The allusion to the "vital energy of the sword" 劍氣 points to the youth's talent honed through hardships, while "green veils" 青紗 is short for the "green veil masquerade" 青紗障—an allusion to how, in northeastern China, crops such as sorghum grow tall and dense, forming screens of green veils that make it easy for bandits to hide themselves. This metaphor suggests the danger-filled surroundings that hampered young students in their knowledge-seeking journey. Wang Kaijing, hoping the students would maintain their will to fight, also used an allusion to how "three clans toppled the Qin" 三戶亡秦, referring to how the Qin dynasty could be overthrown by the unified efforts of survivors in the state of Chu. Hence the two couplets following the word *kangkai* 慷慨 (fervently) emphasizes that with determination, they would achieve victory despite only having limited strength.

Accordingly, in Wang Kaijing's narration of the martyrdom of the CLHS group, what arouses people is still the emphasis on the sacrificial dedication with which the teachers and students pursued their objective of saving the nation. All the personal strands of writing constitute the imprint of the times: in terms of the politics of affect for the local Chinese community, the "Chinese" imagination shaped by the Chinese schools contribute to a "history of pain" that combines prewar patriotic sentiment with traumatic wartime suffering. The form of classical-style poetry, as a part of the literary lineage, can be compared to the "force" (原力) of the Chinese language. In the postwar memorial practices that include elegies, monuments, and prefaces to monument inscriptions, the power of words was harnessed to commemorate a harrowing period of the school's history. This is a "site of memory" that was born out of a series of commemorative rituals and which has become a symbol for the Chinese community to express their identification with and belonging to Chinese education.

The Martyrdom of Chung Ling Teachers and Students: The "Scar Writings" of Poetry and History

After CLHS was reestablished following the war, Wang Kaijing, writing under the pseudonym Yi Teng 依藤, published *Bi'nan jiehui lu* 彼南劫灰錄 (A Record of the Penang Catastrophe) in September 1957. Using prose narration that doubled as historical documentation, he preserved a precious and authentic record of Penang during the Japanese occupation. However, with respect to activating historical memories, it is important to note how classical literary forms such as rhapsody, poetry, and prose may shape historical memories by contributing to a reimagination of the Chinese language. Poetry is commonly regarded as a literary form of refined elegance, yet poetic compositions during times of crisis shuttle between testimonials that seek to record reality and lyrical expressions of emotive indignation.

As for Guan's war-related writings that subtly convey the lingering pain of losing his son, they are also works on trauma suffered by the victims' family members. In other words, Guan's pain from losing his son does not only represent personal trauma; it also uses the suffering of Chinese school communities—consolidated through the historical experiences of CLHS—to trace the panic-stricken atmosphere in Penang during the occupation.

If Sook Ching was a brutal massacre that the Japanese military inflicted upon the local Chinese community and on students at Chinese schools, the motivation behind the persecution could be related to how CLHS was a key base for AJCA rallies prior to the invasion. The Japanese regarded the school as the base camp for the Malayan Communist Party forces involved in the anti-Japanese movement. Guan wrote a set of poems denouncing the Japanese by depicting the harsh realities during the Sook Ching operation, which included the lines: "The thoroughfares and alleyways were all cordoned off / The crowds' eyes displayed terror when the masked informants arrived / Fearing a mere nod in their direction, / will then leave them with a chalked mark on their back" 通衢小巷斷人行，蒙馬虎皮眾目驚。祇恐當前頭一點，便將粉筆背書名.[14] The Japanese military, with the help of Chinese interpreters, identified Malayan Communist Party members and supporters of other anti-Japanese movements. Backed by the Japanese military, the interpreters terrorized the crowds as they identified the targets. Those identified would be marked and would be unable avoid their fate. Guan's denunciations are not righteous condemnations on ethnic grounds; instead he compares the young students and teachers to "helpless calves injured by rabid dogs, / Callously imprisoned and killed without restraint" 犢子偏遭猘犬傷，無情縲絏肆摧戕. This is a documentation of unlivable or ungrievable lives, which points to the precarity, insignificance, and fragility of the collective sacrifice of CLHS members. It is an epistemology of traumatic memories due to war or persecution.[15] The line "staying close and on guard, looking out for more traps ahead, / Fearing that someone might know that we were from Chung Ling" 跬步不離防觸阱，鍾靈二字怕人知 is especially vivid, as it inscribes the trauma and fear that the Sook Ching caused.

Hence the phrase *fenkeng zhi can* 焚坑之慘 (the horror of book burning and literati burial) in the poem's title could be read as Guan's oblique commentary embedded in his documentary mode of composition, which preserves a profound imagery that can recall traumatic memories of the group of persecuted and sacrificed teachers and students. There were corresponding measures in reality. After the fall of Penang, the Japanese military instructed the bureau of education to order all bookshops to send in their Chinese-language books for inspection. Later, over two hundred thousand Chinese-language books were destroyed, which was tantamount to exterminating the Chinese language itself (only maps and dictionaries were exempted). In addition, newly opened schools were only allowed to teach in Japanese, while all other languages were banned.[16] Speaking to the survival crises of individual and mother tongue language education, the poem's allusion to *kengru* 坑儒 (burying literati alive) expresses the intellectuals' historical grievances. In some ways, the tragedy of the CLHS teachers and students represents the severance of prewar Chinese education and intellectual tradition. If we look from the perspective of the ethics and the entanglements among the poet, the war, and the memories of violence, the name *Chung Ling* in the poem is elevated to a symbol of victimhood that incorporates the subjectivities and spirit of the Chinese community, and as a result of a "Chinese language complex," it thereby becomes a part of the local Chinese historical memory.

Guan personally witnessed Chung Ling's tribulations, which projected the crises and fear of educational and cultural ruptures. His postwar poems written in the classical style, elegies, and prefaces to monument inscriptions focused on the period's grievances and created a prototype for the trauma that befell Chinese education. On February 28, 1946, during the CLHS memorial service, he composed the Memorial Service Song. The plaintive and melancholic lyrics recorded the victims' spirit of sacrifice for Penang's Chinese education history:

> Listen to the mourning melodies, soaring far and high,
> Elegiac banners and couplets fill the hall.
> Rest in peace, watch the sun set in the Eastern Ocean,
> Whereas our Republic of China shines gloriously.
> With utmost reverence, we offer incense to our deceased teachers and students,
> Who bravely sacrificed for education under cruel oppression.
> Also, on this monument your names will be preserved in history,
> Summoning souls to return and behold this sincerity together.

> 聽哀悼樂聲悠揚，哀輓聯幛掛滿會場。
> 安眠吧，看日落東洋。我中華民國大放榮光。
> 敬為我們殉難師生謹掬心香，在鐵蹄下為教育而犧牲。
> 還有豐碑青史永留姓氏芬芳，魂兮歸來同鑒此衷藏。[17]

Even more moving are the elegy and preface to the monument inscription he composed for the deceased CLHS teachers and students in spring 1946. Written in parallel prose, the words contain denunciations that convey national and personal animosity or tributes to the deceased teachers and students, which strike a chord in readers' hearts. The most unique aspect of such works lies in how they set the ground for proclaiming the integration of Chinese education and ethnic spirit. By using rhetorical parallelisms and oppositions, Guan detailed the chain of events leading to the purge and its aftermath, as well as the values shared by CLHS: "Patriotic sentiments should never be forgotten, be it night or day. A frugal lifestyle should be regarded as the norm. One should always donate generously to every disaster relief program" 愛國觀念，昕夕不忘。縮衣節食，視為經常。凡逢賑災，慨解義囊. This was the consensus shared by the Nanyang Chinese in support of their homeland's anti-Japanese war resistance efforts. Next, Guan tirelessly recounted the destruction and brutalities inflicted by the Japanese military on the Chinese schools, as well as the literary teachers and students during the southern invasion that was part of their Greater East Asia domination plan:

> Chinese schools were destroyed and scholars were arrested. Our teachers and students have nowhere to seek justice. More than several hundred people were arrested, tied up, and confined; imprisoned and coerced into false confessions—be it through fire burning or water curing, or through bills and clauses—the inhumanity is so cruel that spirits wail and deities weep. Not to mention the atrocities of book burning and burying of intellectuals, which cannot be exhausted through writing. Sigh! Our young men of Chung Ling, strong and determined, who are well versed in both literary and military affairs, their good reputations travel far and wide. . . . What the Japanese bandits saw resulted in subjecting the students to more enmity. They were whipped and interrogated without valid reasons, and later buried alive or died of malnourishment, with bones exposed on the mountain hills. Such tragedy leaves both men and deities indignant, both heaven and earth sorrowful. . . . A few strikes of the atomic bombs have pacified the Fusō land. One who does not reflect on its moral conduct would be the architect of his own downfall. Both personal woes and national crises are avenged once and for all. With the rebirth of the school, in honor of the preceding circumstances.

> 摧殘華校，逮捕文人。我校師弟，有口難伸。奚啻百數，縲絏羈身。殆入囹圄，逼供承招。火灼水灌，種種科條。慘無人道，鬼哭神號。焚坑之虐，罄竹難描。嗟我多士，鍾中錚錚。文才武學，遐爾蜚聲。. . . 倭寇視之，更若仇讎。鞭笞拷撲，不問情由。活埋瘦斃，暴骨山坵。人神共憤，天地 為愁。. . . 幾聲原子，底定扶桑。不自度德，宜至滅亡。家仇國恥，一舉肅清。復興黌學，眷念前情。[18]

Elegies are primarily a tribute to the deceased. However, Guan Zhenmin's writing is not only a tribute and a commendation; it also contains criticism and condemnation. The target recipients of his writing have extended beyond the deceased and reached the living, and by extension, readers not acquainted with the deceased or the work's context. In his analysis of the aesthetic attributes of elegies ("tribute texts"), Ko Ching-ming mentioned that when one considers the work's implied reader, the ritualistic form of "narration" will transform and expand into an amalgamation of complex content that embodies traits of "memorialization" 祭, "libation" 奠, "commendation" 讚, and "lamentation" 哀, which also takes on the characteristics of a literary work.[19] It is therefore not difficult to view Guan's elegy as a memorialization of the past. On that basis, it displayed the jolting and contemplative orientation of war trauma in order to introduce the galvanizing and touching nature of the Chinese education experience, which touches upon the essence of Chinese cultural continuity and propagation.

Extending the spirit and rhetorical strategies of his other writings, Guan contributed the preface to the memorial inscription for the deceased teachers and students. With the stone memorial as a medium to transmit historical memories, the preface was able to achieve the enduring effect of propagating the discourse. Once again, the preface emphasizes how the teachers and students of CLHS "would express their passionate patriotism and swear to be the underlying support for the nation from start to end. They rallied public appeal and always received responses in return, and they dared to step up and be heard. Out of all the Chinese schools, ours has been the most vocal, so the Japanese hated us to the core" 愛國之熱忱，自始至終誓為後盾，前呼後應，敢作先聲，由華校而言，以我校為最，而日敵視之，則恨之刺骨. He continued to inscribe the scars of war:

After [the Japanese] arrived from across the oceans and occupied this lonely island, institutions of higher education were the first to be targeted, followed by the arrests of innocent teachers and students, who were either regarded like officials involved in the Yuanyou factionalism, or treated like literati of the Donglin movement, with their names recorded, in a plan to capture them all. Tortured repeatedly and imprisoned without escape, they were incriminated just like Gong Ye Chang. History repeats itself in neverending cycles of book-burning and burying of intellectuals, the atrocities committed would put even Emperor Qin to shame. Spirits howled and deities wept, men seethed and heaven raged. With corpses left exposed and bones lying barren, where should the wandering souls go? Sacrificing their own lives in the name of education—who could have ever envisioned this? Alas! With a few atomic blasts, the archipelago is now in ruins. All of the nation's humiliations and personal enmities have been washed into the ocean. To the noble sacrifices made for a righteous deed, we have erected a memorial in the middle of the courtyard, which is no different from the historical offerings that would commemorate their ancestors for generations thereafter. Such customs would be forever preserved and never replaced, thus providing solace that shall travel miles beyond and retain the goodness of the names.

迨偷渡重洋，首淪孤島，先毀最高之學府，大捕無辜之師生，非稱元祐之黨人，即置東林之名籍，為一網打盡之計，用百般殘酷之刑，縲絏同羈，罪非公冶，焚坑重演，毒過嬴秦，鬼哭神號，人天共憤，暴屍露骨，魂夢何安？為教育而捐軀，豈生人所逆測乎？噫！幾聲原子，三島為墟，國恥家仇，共洪流而逝東海，成仁取義，貞石而樹中庭，何殊血食千秋，永保馨香之勿替，且慰藉遊萬里，長留姓氏之同芳。[20]

When the elegy and the preface to the inscription are read together, it becomes apparent that both texts center on the traumatic memory of Chinese education. What is memorialized are the educators' sacrifices, as they have become heroic souls in the crisis of national and community survival. Similar imagery is blended into the poetry, the elegy, and the inscription's preface. Each component is interconnected with the next, yielding a musical triptych of plaintive tunes.

Conclusion

The traumatic memory of the martyred CLHS teachers and students is closely linked to corresponding developments in the Chinese community and in Chinese education. For a long time after the 1940s, the AJCA movement and the postoccupation trauma constituted the ethnic and cultural source of the Chinese community's emotional identification. On that account, Penang and CLHS have jointly become a site of memory that is of important and decisive significance. The significance does not lie in the specificity of the site, but rather in its anchoring effect, which marks the reference point of the survivors of catastrophic events, which, in turn, becomes the reference point for people born long after the events occurred.[21] From the perspective of postmemory, the succeeding generations can only pursue their predecessors' recollections through the sites of memory. The CLHS sacrifices thus become a metaphor that permits the cultural and literary shaping of trauma, thus enabling the larger sacrifices of Chinese education and the Chinese community to occupy a noble moral position indicative of the ethnic spirit.

KO CHIA-CIAN is associate professor in the Department of Chinese Literature, National Taiwan University. His works include *Loyalists, Boundary and Modernity: The Southbound Diaspora and Lyricism of Sinitic Poetry, 1895–1945* (2016), *The Metaphors of Nation and History: An Intellectual History Survey on Modern Martial Arts Fiction, 1895–1949* (2014), and *Compendium of Malaysian Chinese Literary Criticism: Volume on Ko Chia-Cian* (2019).

SUN PINGYU holds a BA (Hons) in Chinese studies from the National University of Singapore. She provides freelance translation services to Singaporean arts institutions.

///////////////////////////////

Notes

1 See *Bincheng zhongling zhongxue*.
2 Besides the massacre of CLHS members, teachers and students at other Chinese schools and members of the education sector were also killed. See Tay, *Malaixiya Huawen*, 412–15.
3 Nora, "Jiyi yu lishi," 10–11.
4 Yeap, *Bincheng zhongling zhongxue shigao*, 15–25; Tan, "Chunfeng huayu sishi nian," 1–45.
5 Chen C., "Nanyang lun," 145.
6 Wong, "Wencai fengliu," 110–64.

7   According to Wong Hong Teng's calculations, a third of prewar Chinese teachers were born in China, while only 6 percent were born locally. Prewar southbound teachers were primarily from Jiangsu and Fujian, while postwar southbound teachers were mostly from Guangdong and Fujian. See Wong, "Wencai fengliu," 115–16.

8   For more on AJCA rallies, see Wong, "Dongjiaoxue sanweiyiti."

9   Guan, *Lütianlu yincao*, 1. In what follows, titles of poems from this anthology will be cited in the notes with title and page number.

10   For more information on the state of Chinese schools before the war, see Chen Y., "Binzhou bainianlai de jiaoyu," 398–405.

11   Guan, *Lütianlu yincao*, 7.

12   Guan, *Lütianlu yincao*, "Bumian bingshi chuke" 不眠並示楚客 (Several Sentences for Sojourn Dwellers on a Sleepless Night), 17.

13   Wang Yang, "Zhongling zhongxue yuansheng xunnanji," 23.

14   Guan, *Lütianlu yincao*, 7.

15   For a discussion of Judith Butler's work on living conditions under violence and war, see Lee, *Jiyi zhengzhi*, 37–38.

16   Wu, "Lunxian shiqi de bincheng jiaoyu," 524–25, and Yiteng, "Fenshu," 95–98.

17   Guan, "Zhuidaohui ge," 21.

18   Guan, *Lütianlu shiwenji*, 22–23.

19   Ko, "'Diao,' 'ji,'" 210–11.

20   Guan, *Lütianlu shiwenji*, 6.

21   Winter, "Jiyi zhi chang," 80.

References

Bincheng zhongling zhongxue xunnan shisheng rong'ailu 檳城鍾靈中學殉難師生榮哀錄 [A Collection of Tributes to Martyred Chung Ling High School Teachers and Students]. Penang: Committee to Commemorate Martyred Chung Ling Teachers and Students, 1947.

Chen Ciliang 陳次亮. "Nanyang lun" 南洋論 [On Nanyang]. In *Haiguo gongyu jilu* 海國公餘輯錄 [Collected Off-Duty Thoughts on Maritime Nations], edited by Thio Chee Non 張煜南, 145. Shanghai: Shanghai Chinese Classics Publishing House 上海古籍出版社, 2020.

Chen Yijing 陳翼經. "Binzhou bainianlai de jiaoyu" 檳州百年來的教育 [100 Years of Education in Penang]. In *Bincheng huaren dahuitang qingzhu chengli yibai zhounian - xinsha luocheng kaimu jinian tekan* 檳州華人大會堂慶祝成立一百週年-新廈落成開幕紀念特刊 [Special Issue: Centennial Anniversary of Penang Chinese Town Hall and Inauguration Ceremony for the New Building], 398–405. Penang: Penang Chinese Town Hall 檳州華人大會堂, 1983.

Guan Zhenmin 管震民. *Lütianlu shiwenji (wenchao)* 綠天廬詩文集(文鈔) [A Collection of Poems and Works of Lütianlu]. Penang: Lütianlu, 1955.

Guan Zhenmin 管震民. *Lütianlu yincao* 綠天廬吟艸 [Lütianlu anthology]. Penang: Guan Zhenmin xiansheng qinian rongshou jinian shouguan weiyuanhui, 1949.

Guan Zhenmin 管震民. "Zhongling zhongxue shilue" 鍾靈中學史略 [A Brief History of Chung Ling High School]. *Zhongling zhongxue jikan (fuxing tehao)* 鍾靈中學季刊(復興特號) [Chung Ling High School Quarterly (Reestablishment Issue)], 1946, 50–51.

Guan Zhenmin 管震民. "Zhuidaohui ge" 追悼會歌 [Memorial Service Song]. In *Bincheng zhongling zhongxue xunnan shisheng rong'ailu* 檳城鍾靈中學殉難師生榮哀錄 [A Collection of Tributes to Martyred Chung Ling High School Teachers and Students], 21. Penang: Committee to Commemorate Martyred Chung Ling Teachers and Students, 1947.

Ko Ching-ming 柯慶明. 'Diao,' 'ji' zuowei wenxue leixing zhi meigan tezhi" 「弔」、「祭」作為文學類型之美感特質 [The Aesthetic Perception of the Writings of "Mourning" and "Tributes" as Literary Genres]. In *Gudian zhongguo shiyong wenlei meixue* 古典中國實用文類美學 [The Aesthetics of Classical Chinese Practical Writings], 205–97. Taipei: National Taiwan University Press 國立臺灣大學出版中心, 2006.

Lee Yu-cheng 李有成. *Jiyi zhengzhi* 記憶政治 [The Politics of Memory]. Kaohsiung, Taiwan: National Sun Yat-sen University Center for the Humanities, 2020.

Li Ciyong 李詞傭. *Binlang yuefu* 檳榔樂府 [Penang Ballads]. Nanjing: Lianhua yinshu guan 聯華印書館, 1936.

Li Ciyong 李詞傭. *Yeyin sanyi* 椰陰散憶 [Scattered Thoughts under the Palm Shade]. Shanghai: Zuozhe shushe 作者書社, 1937.

Lam Lap 林立. "Yishi yishi: Miaoshu xinjiapo rizhan shiqi de jiuti shiji *Xiehai*" 亦詩亦史:描述新加坡日佔時期的舊體詩集《血海》 [*Sea of Blood*: A Classical-Style Chinese Poetry Collection about the Japanese Occupation in Singapore]. *Tsing Hua Journal of Chinese Studies* 清華學報 47, no. 3 (2018): 547–89.

Nora, Pierre. "Jiyi yu lishi zhijian: changsuo wenti" 記憶與歷史之間：場所問題 [Between Memories and History: A Question of Sites], translated by Huang Yanhong 黃艷紅. In *Jiyi zhi chang* 記憶之場 [Sites of Memory], edited by Pierre Nora, 3–28. Nanjing: Nanjing University, 2015.

Tan Chee Seng. "'Sook Ching' 1942 Dan Penglibatan Sekolah Menengah Chung Ling Pulau Pinang: Suatu Interpretasi Baru." *Kajian Malaysia* 37, no. 1 (2019): 51–82.

Tan Eng Chaw 陳榮照. "Chunfeng huayu sishi nian: Zhongling 1917–1957" 春風化雨四十年：鍾靈 1917–1957 [Through Forty Years of Education and Nurture: Chung Ling 1917–1957]. In *Bincheng zhongling zhongxue xiaoshi lunji* 檳城鍾靈中學校史論集 [A Collection of Penang Chung Ling High School Historical Essays], edited by Tan Eng Chaw, 1–45. Singapore: Chung Ling High School (Singapore) Alumni Association, 2007.

Tay Lian Soo 鄭良樹. *Malaixiya Huawen jiaoyu fazhanshi* 馬來西亞華文教育史 [The Historical Development of Chinese Education in Malaysia], vol. II. Kuala Lumpur: United Chinese School Teachers' Association of Malaysia 馬來西亞華校教師會總會, 1999.

Wang Yang 汪洋. "Zhongling zhongxue yuansheng xunnanji" 鍾靈中學員生殉難記 [A Record of the Martyred Chung Ling High School Staff and Students]. In *Bincheng zhongling zhongxue xunnan shisheng rong'ailu* 檳城鍾靈中學殉難師生榮哀錄 [A Collection of Tributes to Martyred Chung Ling High School Teachers and Students], 23. Penang: Committee to Commemorate Martyred Chung Ling Teachers and Students Committee, 1947.

Winter, Jay. "Jiyi zhi chang yu zhanzheng yinying" 記憶之場與戰爭陰影 [Sites of Memory and the Shadow of War], translated by Li Gongzhong 李恭忠 and Li Xia 李霞. In *Wenhua jiyi yanjiu zhinan* 文化記憶研究指南 [A Companion to Cultural Memory Studies], edited by Astrid Erll and Ansgar Nünning, 78–94. Nanjing: Nanjing University, 2021.

Wong Hong Teng 王愼鼎. "Dongjiaoxue sanweiyiti de kangri yundong (1937–1945)" 董教學三位一體的抗日運動 (1937–1945) [The Trinity of School Directors, Teachers, and Students during the Anti-Japanese War Resistance Movement (1937–1945)]. In *Bincheng zhongling zhongxue xiaoshi lunji* 檳城鍾靈中學校史論集 [A Collection of Penang Chung Ling High School Historical Essays], edited by Tan Eng Chaw 陳榮照, 284–363. Singapore: Chung Ling High School (Singapore) Alumni Association, 2007.

Wong Hong Teng 王愼鼎. "Wencai fengliu de huawen jiaoshi" 文采風流的華文教師 [The Talented and Brilliant Chinese-Language Teachers]. In *Bincheng zhongling zhongxue xiaoshi lunji* 檳城鍾靈中學校史論集 [A Collection of Penang Chung Ling High School Historical Essays], edited by Tan Eng Chaw 陳榮照, 110–64. Singapore: Chung Ling High School (Singapore) Alumni Association, 2007.

Wu Tiren 吳體仁. "Lunxian shiqi de bincheng jiaoyu" 淪陷時期的檳城教育 [Penang Education during the Japanese Occupation Period]. In *Xinma huaren kangri shiliao 1937–1945* 新馬華人抗日史料 1937–1945 [Anti-Japanese War Resistance Efforts by Singapore-Malayan Chinese 1937–1945], edited by Hsu Yun Tsiao 許雲樵 and Chua Ser Koon 蔡史君, 524–25. Singapore: Wenshi chuban 文史出版, 1984.

Yeap Chong Leng 葉鍾鈴. *Bincheng zhongling zhongxue shigao (1917–1957)* 檳城鍾靈中學史稿 (1917–1957) [Historical Manuscripts of Penang Chung Ling High School (1917–1957)]. Singapore: Chinese Heritage Centre, 2009.

Yiteng 依藤 [Wang Kaijing 汪開競]. "Fenshu" 焚書 [Burning Books]. In *Binan jiehui lu* 彼南劫灰錄 [Penang Catastrophe Records], 95–98. Penang: Penang High School, 1957.

NG KIM CHEW

Translated by PO-HSI CHEN

Why Does a Failed Revolution Also Need Fiction?
On the Mahua Genre of Failed Revolutionary Historical Fiction

ABSTRACT The historical relationship between the categories of Malayan Communist fiction and People's Republic of China revolutionary historical fiction remains to be clarified, just as the Malayan Communist revolution was covertly, but undeniably, connected to the Chinese Communist Party. This essay attempts to take the PRC's revolutionary historical fiction as a reference point to reinvestigate Malayan Communist fiction, which was characterized as "historical fiction" by left-wing writers. Examples include Jin Zhimang's *Hunger*, Liu Jun's *Wind Blowing in the Woods*, and Tuo Ling's *The Hoarse Mangrove Forest*. The key issue is that the PRC's revolutionary historical fiction is premised on triumphalism, to authenticate the revolution's legitimacy, while Malayan Communists' revolutionary historical fiction hinges instead on the *failure* of revolution—though it cannot be recognized as such. How do these latter works contemplate and represent revolution? Does fiction have to rationalize the legitimacy of a failed revolution (or one mired in predicaments)? Or does fiction attempt to accomplish something else? These questions may concern the raison d'être of Malayan Chinese literary realism, which takes representing reality as its mission and investigates its underlying paradoxes.

KEYWORDS Malayan Communist fiction, historical fiction, revolutionary historical fiction

> The failed revolution does not have a history.
>
> 失敗的革命沒有歷史。
>
> —Huang Ziping 黃子平, *Geming, lishi, xiaoshuo* 革命.歷史.小說 [Revolution, History, Fiction]

Malayan Communist Historical Fiction

As is well known, Malayan Communist fiction—fictional works about the revolutionary activities of the Malayan Communist Party (MCP, 1930–1989)—can be divided into three types based on the authors' relationships to the MCP: (1) works by former MCP members (including Jin Zhimang 金枝芒 [Chen Shuying 陳樹英, 1912–1988], He Jin 賀巾 [Lin Jinquan 林金泉, 1935–2019], and Hai Fan 海凡 [Hong Tianfa 洪添發, 1953–]); (2) works by non-MCP realist writers, both leftists and non-leftists (including Tuo Ling 駝鈴 [Peng Longfei 彭龍飛, 1936–], Liu Jun 流軍 [Lai Yongtao 賴湧濤, 1940–], Yu Chuan 雨川 [Huang Junfa 黃俊發, 1940–], and Ding Yun 丁雲 [Chen Chun'an 陳春安, 1952–]); and (3) works by modernism-inclined writers who are neither leftists nor MCP members (including Xiao Hei 小黑

PRISM: THEORY AND MODERN CHINESE LITERATURE • 19:2 • SEPTEMBER 2022
DOI 10.1215/25783491-9966717 • © 2022 LINGNAN UNIVERSITY

[Chen Qijie 陳奇傑, 1951–], Li Zishu 黎紫書 [Lim Pow Leng 林寶玲, 1971–], and Ng Kim Chew 黃錦樹 [1967–]).[1] Of these, Tuo Ling and Liu Jun are the only two who explicitly called their own work historical fiction.

For instance, in the preface to a collection of his writings, Tuo Ling mentions that some Chinese scholars classify his novels *Xiaoyan sanjin shi* 硝煙散盡時 (When the Gunpowder Smoke Dissipated), 沙啞的紅樹林 *Shaya de hongshu-lin* (The Hoarse Mangrove Forest), and *Jimo xingzhe* 寂寞行者 (Lone Walker) as political fiction, and he responds:

> Such categorization is extremely misleading, especially with respect to the first two works. Although I describe political struggle at some length, my goal is to reflect the social transformations and differences among various ethnic groups before and after independence. Therefore, they could be more accurately called "historical fiction."
>
> 這樣的歸類是極具誤導性的，尤其是前兩部更是如此。儘管我用了一些篇幅來描寫那場政治鬥爭，但目的卻在於反映國家獨立前後的社會變遷和各族人民面貌的差異，準確一點的說：這是「歷史小說」。[2]

However, Tuo Ling does not clarify exactly what he means by historical fiction. Liu Jun, in contrast, offers a more specific definition in the postscript to his novel *Zai senlin he yuanye* 在森林和原野 [In the Forest and Wilderness]:

> Historical fiction can be divided into two types. The first takes historical events and figures as its objects and then fictionalizes within the confines of historical facts. For the narrative plotline to unfold, a certain degree of artistic processing—including fictionalization, imagination, and character depiction—is necessary. . . . The second type draws on a certain historical event and then artistically refashions it such that it has an entirely fictional plot but a combination of real and fictional characters—though the real characters are not necessarily entirely real, just as the fictional characters are not necessarily entirely fictional.
>
> 歷史小說有兩種表現手法，一是以歷史事件和人物為對象，在史實框架內進行創作，為展開故事貫串情節，適當的虛構、想像、刻劃等藝術加工是必要的。
> ……二是取材於某個歷史事件，從而進行藝術處理，故事情節純屬虛構，人物有真有假，真的未必全真，假的未必全假。[3]

Liu Jun believes his works belong to the second type, for which "the historical background is real, the location and time span are exact, whereas the characters and plot are half real and half fictional" 時代背景是真實的，發生地點和時間跨度是確切的，人物和故事則真假參半.[4] In reality, the only difference between these two types of historical fiction involves the degree of fictionality, though both remain highly dependent on historical facts. Although the passage quoted above emphasizes how the two types of historical fiction are artistically processed, the truth is that this sort of artistic processing has long been the weakness of this type of Malayan Communist fiction. This weakness can be observed in Liu Jun's own description of *In the Forest and Wilderness*, in which he writes:

> [This novel's] main storyline focuses on the heroic MCP-led resistance against Japanese invasion and British colonial rule. The historical background is real, the location and time span are exact, while the characters and plot are half real and half fictional. The defection of the MCP state secretary of Johor, the clandestine collaboration between the MCP General Secretary Lai Teck and the Japanese Special Higher Police, the New Village policy and the villagers "eating from a common pot," and the Batu Cave Massacre of September 1, 1942, are all based on true characters and incidents. However, the political prisoners' prison break, the guerillas' ambush of the enemy's firewood carts, and the shooting of helicopters with AK-47s are 30 percent real and 70 percent fictional.

> (本書)內容以馬來亞共產黨帶領民眾反抗日本侵略、反英殖民統治的英勇事跡為主線。時代背景是真實的,發生地點和時間跨度是確切的,人物和故事則真假參半。馬共柔佛州州委投敵背叛、馬共總書記萊特和日本特高科暗中勾結、新村政策和村民吃大鍋飯,九一黑風洞慘案等都是真有其人確有其事;政治犯越獄、游擊隊伏擊敵人運薪車、以AK步鎗射擊直升機等章節卻是三分真實和七分虛構。[5]

Readers familiar with the history of the MCP will see that this account hews very close to "history."

In addition to the preface quoted above, Tuo Ling later supplemented his idea of historical fiction in another short essay. He was well aware that historical fiction cannot be treated as official history, and when Chen Jian 陳劍 asked him, "Can 'stories' distort historical facts? Should literature be a faithful reflection of historical facts?" "故事" 可否歪曲歷史事實?文學是否必須老老實實反映歷史事實, Tuo Ling replied:

> While historical facts must be respected, historical fiction cannot be treated as official history, just as *Sanguo zhi* 三國志 (History of the Three Kingdoms) is distinct from *Sanguo yanyi* 三國演義 (Romance of the Three Kingdoms). To foreground characters' images, fiction tends to embellish and exaggerate. To attract readers, authors are allowed to devise events and developments not documented in the official history. These approaches, however, should be rational and correspond to the characters' thoughts and personalities. In other words, historical fiction is the artistic creation that takes history as its skeleton, and literature its flesh and blood. Hence, history is history, and fiction is fiction; the two cannot be conflated, and there is no need for dispute. What I write is fiction that is simi-

lar to *yanyi* [historical romance], which should not be judged by the standard of an official history. As for the biggest difference between historical narrative and literary narrative, I think it is that while the former seeks truth and is based on evidence, the latter pursues not only "truth" but also "goodness" and "beauty." The former belongs to academia, whereas the latter belongs to art.

史實必須尊重。不過，歷史小說畢竟不能當正史看，就如《三國志》和《三國演義》一樣。小說為了人物形象的突出，免不了誇張和渲染。為了吸引讀者，作者也允許自行設計正史中沒有記載的事件和情節。但這也須合情合理，符合人物的思想性格。換句話說，歷史小說是以歷史為骨架文學為血肉的藝術創造。因此，歷史是歷史，小說是小說，不能混為一談，更不需要爭論。我寫的是類似演義的小說，不能當作正史來指指點點。至於歷史敘述與文學敘述的最大不同點，我認為前者求真，言必有據；後者除了「真」之外，還要加上「善」與「美」。前者屬於學術的範疇，後者屬於藝術的天地。⁶

Like Liu Jun, Tuo Ling understands literary works to be distinct from historical narratives, since they are artistic creations that require fictionalization. As he suggests above, when scholars critique his works for falling short of historical authenticity, he claims that they are just fiction, not history; yet when they critique his works from a literary standpoint, he defends his works by pointing to their historicity.

All of Liu Jun's works were composed after 2002, while Tuo Ling's novels about the MCP were composed between 1991 and 2004. Like most Malayan Communist fiction, these works were written not long after the official end of the Malayan Communist revolution with the Hat Yai Peace Agreement of 1989 and the subsequent lifting of the ban on works about the MCP that had been in place since the beginning of the Malayan Emergency in 1948. Of course, modern fiction will focus on contemporary subject matter, given that modern consciousness and the sense of modernity are both directly related to the time setting of the theme. Given that Singapore and Malaysia were not established until the 1950s and 1960s, the histories of both nation-states are comparatively short, and therefore stories about the Malayan Communists are also relatively contemporary. Why then are these works set in the recent past called "historical fiction"? Neither author provides a definitive answer, but judging from the fact that leftism in the region from the 1930s to the contemporary period relied on the Chinese Communist Party's (CCP) intellectual resources, their most relevant references were the CCP's post-1950s revolutionary historical fiction. And indeed, in the preceding passage Liu Jun mentions the novel *Hongyan* 紅岩 [Red Crag], which was one of the seminal titles in the quartet of revolutionary works known as "three reds and one forest," the others being *Hongri* 紅日 [Red Sun], *Hongqi pu* 紅旗譜 [Keep the Red Flag Flying], and *Linhai xueyuan* 林海雪原 [Tracks in the Snowy Forest].

Whether or not Liu Jun and Tuo Ling explicitly mentioned having been influenced by these latter works is not particularly important; instead, one should draw connections between these works on a methodological or theoretical basis. My claim for their literary associations is derived from two sources. First, the MCP had long received support from the CCP. In particular, in the late 1950s, due to the Briggs Plan launched by the British colonial government, the MCP kept retreating as its food supply and logistical support were cut off, but in the early 1960s, most MCP officials were protected by the CCP and sought asylum in Hunan.[7] As a result, the MCP emulated the CCP's ideology, strategies, and organization. Second, since the 1930s, revolutionary literature imported from China (often called "realism") has been passed down in Malaya, and Mahua literary realism was undoubtedly inspired by the CCP's revolutionary literature. This can be clearly seen in how Fang Xiu 方修 (1922–), Fang Beifang 方北方 (1918–), and Wu An's 吳岸 (1937–) ideas about realism tracked those of the CCP. Hence, one can infer that the first two types of MCP fiction are emulations of the CCP's revolutionary historical fiction because of their shared ideology and literary views—though the emulation is not necessarily intentional. As the two worldviews, historical views, and literary views share the same blood relations, when their experiences are also similar, so will the fiction bear resemblance, thus yielding a valuable comparative perspective.

Revolutionary Historical Fiction

China's revolutionary historical fiction is part of the literature from the Seventeen-Year Period (i.e., the seventeen years from the establishment of the People's Republic of China [PRC] in 1949 to the beginning of the Cultural Revolution in 1966) and has gained substantial traction in contemporary literary studies. Huang Ziping uses the label *revolutionary historical fiction* (革命歷史小說) to describe these works,[8] though some of them could also be classified as "revolutionary popular literature" (革命通俗文學), while others are closer to bildungsromans and legendary tales.[9] Nevertheless, Huang argues that the function of these works is similar:

> To canonize recent "revolutionary history"—they narrate the origins of revolutionary myths, heroic romances, and ultimate promises. In so doing, they maintain the grandiose hopes and fears of their countrymen and prove the legitimacy of contemporary realities. Through narrating and reading practices at the national scale, they may construct the national subjective consciousness in the new order established by the revolution.

> 將剛剛過去的『革命歷史』經典化──它們講述革命的起源神話、英雄傳奇和終極承諾，以此維繫當代國人的大希望與大恐懼，證明當代現實的合理性，通過全國範圍內的講述和閱讀實踐，建構國人在這革命所建立的新秩序中的主體意識。[10]

To achieve this objective, the works must be institutionalized as part of the ideological superstructure, which means entering the educational system (as assigned readings), the discourses of literary criticism (with guarantees of garnering acclaim), and contemporary literary history (as part of the literary canon), and so forth. Only a state apparatus, seized by a triumphant revolutionary regime, can achieve these objectives. On the other hand, literary works belong to the people—and even if they actually correspond to a specific class (the proletariat) and ethnicity (the Han, who tend to use the Chinese language), they are nevertheless undoubtedly part of the PRC's *national literature*. When Chinese scholars discuss revolutionary historical fiction, they do not pay attention to these "inconsequential" questions, which are mere residual observations after the PRC case is compared to Malayan Communist fiction as a formation of "failed revolutionary historical fiction." By contrast, the MCP never gained control of the political regime or of the state apparatus. In Malaysia, which only recognizes Malay as its national language, writing in Chinese is not inevitable and might even appear politically incorrect. At the level of their content, almost all those narratives focus on ethnic Chinese, meaning that they may be critiqued for having insufficient "national character." The existential conditions of those Chinese stories can be compared to the New Villages (where the inhabitants were mostly of Chinese descent) under the Briggs policy, and their situation indexes the larger predicament of Mahua literature.

However, the PRC's revolutionary historical fiction differs from Mahua literature in the sense that it belongs to, and is possessed by, the state. Since such works carry an ideological function, it is little wonder that they are strongly controlled by the state. Among relevant works, revolutionary popular literature that "uses traditional fictional techniques, such as vernacular language and engaging storylines, to represent the theme of 'revolution'" 以傳統小說的手法來表現 "革命" 的主題，語言通俗，具有很強的故事性 and that is "widely welcomed by readers" 很受讀者歡迎—such as *Tracks in the Snowy Forest* and *Tiedao youjidui* 鐵道游擊隊 [Railroad Guerillas][11]—has no counterpart in Malayan Communist fiction, and hence can be set aside. (Malayan Chinese realists are in general very "serious" and decline to write enjoyable novels.) Chronologically and logically speaking, such fictional works should include not only the prehistory and the history of the revolution, but also a microhistory in which individuals and the masses participate in the revolution because of their "enlightenment."[12] The two scales are often intertwined and overlapping, enfolding a bildungsroman within. Liang Bin's 梁斌 *Keep the Red Flag Flying* and Yang Mo's 楊沫 *Qingchun zhi ge* 青春之歌 [Song of Youth] are commonly recognized as examples of red bildungsromans. The former is a "novel that aims at revealing the process whereby Chinese peasants, under the CCP's leadership, spontaneously moved toward self-conscious revolutionary struggles" 旨在揭示中國農民在中共領導下由自發走向自覺革命鬥爭歷程的小說,[13] while the latter describes the three stages of a young educated woman's growth into a red "typical character."

Among other examples of revolutionary historical fiction, *Red Crag* is recognized as a "Red Bible." Based on a true story about actual human suffering, the original story is as follows:

> During the period of political transition in the 1940s and 1950s, a large number of revolutionaries who had fought to overthrow the Kuomintang (KMT) regime were imprisoned in a concentration camp called the Sino-American Cooperative Organization. On the eve of the collapse of the Nationalist army and the occupation of Chongqing by the Liberation Army, some of the revolutionaries (such as the authors of *Red Crag*) escaped from prison, but most were secretly killed.
>
> 四五十年代政權交替時期,被稱為「中美合作所」的集中營裡,關押著許多為推翻國民黨政權而鬥爭的革命者。在國民黨政府軍隊潰散,山城重慶為解放軍攻佔的前夕,他們中有人越獄而出(如《紅岩》的作者),而多數被秘密殺害。[14]

Red Crag was first published in 1961; by the 1980s there were more than eight million copies in circulation, setting a record for the most widely distributed novel since the beginning of China's New Literature. Although attributed to Luo Guangbin 羅廣斌 and Yang Yiyan 楊益言, this "communist textbook" was actually a collective work coauthored by "a group of writers who collaborated to serve the same ideological objective" 一群為著同一意識型態目的而協作的書寫者們.[15] The coauthors were the survivors of the incident that inspired the work, and they describe actual events. The coauthors include a party cadre (Ma Shitu 馬識途, 1915–]), a senior editor (Zhang Yu 張羽), and an experienced author (Sha Ting 沙汀), while the work itself was published by a large postliberation publisher (China Youth Press).[16] In terms of artistic criteria (such as literary language, scene descriptions, characterization, dialogue, and quality of plot) and ideological demands (such as the recounting of faith and belief), the work's completion was based on the best efforts of collective collaboration. Hence, it could serve as a "textbook of revolutionary lives" 革命生活的教科書, in that it is rich in ideologically correct content yet is still highly readable.[17]

According to Zhu Chengfa's 朱成發 *Hongchao* 紅潮 [Red Tide], by the end of the Cultural Revolution, many youth of Chinese descent in the Singapore-Malaysian region had turned to leftism. Publications from communist China were not hard to come by, including revolutionary historical fiction.[18]

The Allegory of Besiegement or Breaking Through

When making a comparison with the CCP's revolutionary historical fiction, we find an intriguing phenomenon wherein Jin Zhimang's 1961 novel *Ji'e* 饑餓 [Hunger] is the work most comparable to *Red Crag*, though its editorial preface juxtaposes *Hunger* with the Soviet writer Alexander Fadeyev's novel *The Rout*:

> *Hunger* vividly describes a brutal incident where fourteen revolutionary fighters persisted under a blockade of food supplies by the British colonial authorities. It reveals the nobility of revolutionary fighters amid cruel conditions, and even in a desperate situation, they still see rays of hope. . . . Although only five fighters eventually survive, they do not relent. What they see, after all, is the prospect of the revolution that ends with them breaking through layers of besiegement alongside relocating until victory is attained. . . . It is just like *The Rout*, the well-known novel from the Russian October Revolution, which describes the dauntless sacrifice of the guerilla fighters amidst struggles so brutal that ultimately only a few fighters remain. Mournful and tragic, the story enables the readers to experience the noble revolutionary spirit and quality of the fighters, thus enhancing their revolutionary will to fight.

> 《饑餓》形象地描繪了14位革命戰士在英殖民當局嚴厲封鎖糧食的饑餓線上堅持鬥爭的慘烈事跡，從殘酷的一面反映出革命戰士的高貴品質，在絕望的境地仍然看到曙光。......雖然最終只剩下5位戰士，但他們毫不動搖，看到的畢竟是革命的前景，終於突破重圍轉移勝利。......正如蘇聯十月革命時期的著名小說《毀滅》，敘述一個游擊隊的勇士們在殘酷的鬥爭中英勇犧牲，最後只剩下幾個戰士，故事悲切壯烈，卻也使讀者體會到勇士們高貴的革命精神和品質，從而增強革命的鬥志。[19]

At the level of its plot, *Hunger* shares many similarities with Fadeyev's *The Rout* in that both involve guerilla fighters besieged and sacrificed, while survivors break through the encirclement. The similarity with *Red Crag* (in which CCP members are held captive and sacrificed, while survivors break through the siege) is structural. But the rhetoric of "enhancing revolutionary will to fight" has to reckon with the hurdle that is the historical outcome.[20] If one uses historical outcome as the context to interpret revolutionary historical fiction, then both *The Rout* and *Red Crag* are works of historical fiction about the success of the revolution. Under these circumstances, the survivors' breakthrough serves to "enhance the revolutionary will to fight." However, if it were a failed revolution—and note that when *Hunger* was first published, there were already signs of the MCP's impending defeat—the survivors' breakthrough serves more like a heavy-handed intervention to provide a positive denouement to the story, which is not as representative as the preceding sections on siege and sacrifice.[21]

All things considered, as a member of the MCP, the author might have intended initially to write this novel to inspire others. For instance, the last paragraph of the work reads:

> This struggle was difficult and challenging, but they persevered through the brutal hunger while enduring immense hardship during the guerilla warfare in the forest. However, these challenges were not enough to halt their efforts to advance. Under the party leadership and with support from the masses, our contingent has been slowly growing again. Hoisting the dazzling flag of national liberation, forward we march.

> 這一場鬥爭，也是困難和艱苦的。但他們從殘酷的饑餓中過來，經歷了森林游擊隊戰爭中的最大的困難和最高的艱苦，這也不足以阻止他們的鬥爭的前進的步伐了。在黨的領導和群眾的支持下，隊伍又慢慢壯大起來，高舉著民族解放的光輝燦爛的旗幟，勇往向前了。[22]

This ending, in fact, is not far from that of *Red Crag*:

> A beam of red light gradually appeared on the eastern horizon, gradually shimmering above the green Jialing River. Blue is the cloudless sky. The gorgeous morning clouds radiate numerous beams of light.

> 東方的地平線上，漸漸透出一派紅光，閃爍在碧綠的嘉陵江上；湛藍的天空，萬裏無雲，絢麗的朝霞，放射出萬道光芒。[23]

Hunger was published nineteen years before the end of the MCP revolution, by which point the MCP army had already been forced to withdraw from the northern border of the Malayan Peninsula and retreat to southern Thailand. Of course, had the revolution succeeded, it would have meant that the difficulties depicted in *Hunger* were ultimately overcome, in which case *Hunger*, like *Red Crag*, would have been regarded as a model for overcoming obstacles. However, given that in reality the revolution failed, the novel can only be an allegory of failure.

An Elegy of Youth

He Jin, born in Singapore, grew up in the age of "red tide." In his twenties he penned several works that depicted how youths of Chinese descent embraced leftist beliefs, including "Qingchun qu" 青春曲 [Song of Youth] and *Shen Yulan tongxue* 沈玉蘭同學 [Fellow Student Shen Yulan]. The overall "rewriting" of the social realities seen in his earlier works occurs in his novel *Julang* 巨浪 [The Mighty Wave], which he wrote after the end of the revolution. His entire oeuvre bears no traces of influence from the CCP's revolutionary historical fiction.

The Mighty Wave takes Singapore's May Thirteenth Incident of 1954 as its point of departure, depicting the fight against the British colonial government by a group of left-wing middle-school students of Chinese descent. The colonial authorities cracked down on the student movement because they viewed it as a threat. These harsh external conditions also placed pressure on the movement's internal organization, which in turn presented considerable challenges to their faith and camaraderie. The youthful comrades collaborated and helped one another but also had numerous conflicts and romantic entanglements. Some were arrested, while others were forced underground. Eventually they developed from inexperienced students into proletarian fighters who walked among workers and peasants. Most notably, in the (anti)climactic scene, the leader, Li Xin, betrays his comrades. He was already of questionable character, having raped a female subordinate. There is no denying that the "revolution plus love" formula exists, but what we find in He Jin's work is neither romance nor passion, just nerve-wracking mundane existence. The amalgamation of loosely structured trivial details stems less from fictional motivations than from historical ones.

This attempt to "document history" is clearly articulated in the work's postscript.[24] Because the author personally experienced the events and adopted a realistic style, Phoon Yuen Ming 潘婉明 argues that the work "to some extent provides a 'powerful' testimony of the May 13th Student Movement, representing those who were directly involved" 在某種程度上為『五一三學運』提供了『有力』的當事人說法.[25] In other words, whatever He Jin wrote was probably based on historical occurrences, although they are not mentioned in official party history.

The Mighty Wave is set between 1954 and 1959, when He Jin would have been aged between nineteen and twenty-four. By the time he finished the work, however, he was over seventy, and the novel recalls the golden era of the educated youth of Singapore more than fifty years earlier. This suggests that He Jin had no regret for his youthful years, though those who could sympathize with him are mostly his contemporaries who shared the same memories.

In *Liuwang* 流亡 [Exile], which was written shortly after *The Mighty Wave*, the narrative horizon narrows. While *The Mighty Wave* is told from the perspective of several young students, *Exile* instead uses the protagonist Chen Tianzhu's limited viewpoint to depict the experience of being forced into exile in Indonesia. Although this exile has an autobiographical dimension,[26] it only reflects the experience of a small minority of the MCP. Perhaps constrained by He Jin's own empiricism, *Exile* reveals that the author has no intention to speak for the entire MCP. Ironically, after the failure of the revolution, his failed revolutionary historical fiction is manifested as a failure of fiction. *Exile* is an extreme example of low-quality fictionalized history—a memoir written under the guise of fiction—while also signaling the limits of the MCP's intellectual elites' reflection.[27] In contrast to the revolutionary historical fiction of the CCP's successful revolution, the style of *Exile* is characterized by a virtual lack of style.

An Alternate History

This lack of style is precisely the main stylistic characteristic of the second type of MCP fiction, which does not have a self-conscious sense of form or genre but does have a sense of mission. Dubbing it *historical fiction* proves this point. Both Tuo Ling and Liu Jun mention historical romance when they discuss historical fiction, revealing their awareness that, as Tuo Ling puts it, "historical fiction is the artistic creation that takes history as its skeleton, and literature its flesh and blood" 歷史小說是以歷史為骨架文學為血肉的藝術創造.[28] However, neither author seems to be aware that historical romance is, in fact, highly dramatized, to the extent that historical facts are reduced to the background. In the preface to a collection of his works, Tuo Ling comments on fictional writing in relation to historical fiction:

> I have been very serious about literary composition. From the outset, I have thought that fiction must be a poeticized painting of life. Not only should its content conform to the tenets of truth, goodness, and beauty, its structure and plot development should also follow the natural laws. I understand the Western term *fiction* as referring to purely fictional work. This does seem to be the case, given that their plots often contain unexpected elements and do not avoid "dramatization." I have always been very hesitant about this kind of technique.
>
> 對於文學創作的態度，我是很認真的。一開始便認為，小說應該是一幅詩化的人生圖景，不但內容要符合真善美的條件，而且佈局結構和情節發展都要順乎自然規律。對西方的 "fiction" 這個字眼，我的理解是純粹虛構的故事。事實似乎也是如此，他們所設計的情節變化，往往出人意表，全然不避『戲劇性』之嫌。對於這種創作手法，我一直頗為躊躇。[29]

This passage invites a symptomatic reading. First, perhaps only some Beijing School (*Jingpai* 京派) writers would hold the view that "fiction must be a poeticized painting of life." Second, it is even harder for content to "conform to truth, goodness, and beauty," because what is true and good is not necessarily beautiful, and what is good is not necessarily true and beautiful. Goodness is a moral requisite, while truth concerns factuality. Generally speaking, only a highly politicized Confucianist or political propagandist would make such demands. Furthermore, beauty often stems not from content but from mode of expression. Third, it is even more bizarre to demand that structure and plot development "follow the natural laws." What are these natural laws? Judging from Tuo Ling's fiction, these laws seem to refer to a chronology of real-life events, as seen in *The Hoarse Mangrove Forest*, where the plot roughly mirrors the author's own biography. Perhaps this is how Tuo Ling understands the deeper meaning of realism that is tasked with "reflect[ing] reality"?

It has always been a mystery to me why Mahua realists produce such mediocre works yet nevertheless continue to write nonstop—producing an endless stream of meaningless repetition and repetitive meaninglessness, much like Kafka's hunger artist. Tuo Ling is one of the very Mahua few authors who can clearly articulate how they have been (perhaps inadvertently) trapped in the intellectual dilemma; yet even he, in the passage cited above, seems to ignore a stock phrase used by traditional Chinese storytellers: "There is no story without artifice" 無巧不成書. These authors do not realize that good fiction requires a creative reconfiguration of so-called reality, and they were evidently unaware that both Mark Twain (1835–1910) and Jorge Luis Borges (1899–1986) had already observed that truth is stranger than fiction. That is to say, fiction must avoid clichés and follow the rules of art, while reality does not face the same restrictions and can instead follow the laws of contingency. Apparently, authors like Tuo Ling live in an entirely orderly universe, and therefore his "natural laws" are bland and uneventful. His universe is transparent and can be fully comprehended, with no secrets or mystery. It is no wonder that the plots of his works are so stiff and rigid.

In "Guanyu lishi xiaoshuo" 關於歷史小說 (On Historical Fiction), Tuo Ling criticizes the authors of the third type of MCP fiction for "knowing nothing about history yet regarding themselves as avant-garde" 對歷史一無所知偏又自視前衛. He also thinks that "in the end, they can only work behind closed doors" 到底只能閉門造車 and their works are "not worth reading, and there is even less need to study them" 既沒有甚麼閱讀的價值,更沒有進行研究的必要.[30] Apparently, he has a fixed opinion about what "history" is, and he feels that only the things that accurately convey the "truth, goodness, and beauty" of history are valuable. On the same page, he states: "We hope more people who have endured the stormy epoch take up their pens and engage in deeper and more delicate characterization. Not only should we add beautiful essays to the literary corpus, but we should also rectify the distorted history" 我們所期望的是,更多曾經時代的風口浪尖者拿起筆來,作更深入更細緻的刻畫。我們不僅要為文學添華章,也要糾正被歪曲了的歷史.[31] What is "distorted history"? Is it the positioning of the MCP by the Malaysian government? Tuo Ling does not specify. He evidently believes that the eyewitness accounts by those "who have endured the stormy epoch" 經時代的風口浪尖者—which is to say, those who have lived through history—represent "undistorted history." However, whether it be He Jin's novels or MCP members' memoirs, these works all reveal that historical actors possess limited perspectives.

Liu Jun's case should be similar. In the postscript to *Wind Blowing in the Woods*, he notes that "this is a historical topic, the artistic image depicted should therefore not deviate too much from the historical facts. I proceeded with caution and restrained my own imagination to prevent fictionality from trespassing the boundary" 這是歷史題材，所刻畫的藝術形象不能離史實太遠。我小心謹慎，克制懸想，不讓虛構越界.[32]

The "historical facts" to which Liu Jun's fiction limits itself remain to be determined. But all these authors assume that they understand the relevant history and that their fictional works can even replace history. Liu Jun goes so far as to claim that "those who wish to understand the MCP will have to read my novels" 將來要瞭解馬共,要讀我的小說. However, unlike the CCP's revolutionary historical fiction that spares no effort to mobilize resources from local literary forms and popular literature, their novels offer no novelistic pleasure whatsoever, perhaps because they opted for a low level of dramatization. The gap in *literariness* is stark. Though they hope to replace history with fiction, they end up sacrificing fiction for the sake of what they perceive to be authentic history.

Failed Revolutionary Fiction

In theory, when it comes to the failure of left-wing revolution in the Chinese-language world, there is another type of failed revolutionary historical fiction. The latter can be found in Taiwan, and it involves the failure (and purging) of the Taiwanese Communist Party and CCP-organized underground campaigns. Interestingly, authors responded to these events by composing not historical fiction, but rather lyrical fiction imbued with modernist pathos. Examples include Chen Yingzhen's 陳映真 (1937–2016) "Xiangcun de jiaoshi" 鄉村的教師 (The Countryside Teacher), "Lingdang hua" 鈴鐺花 (Bellflowers), and "Shanlu" 山路 (Mountain Path); Guo Songfen's 郭松棻 (1938–2005) "Yue yin" 月印 (Moon Seal); and Zhu Tianxin's 朱天心 (1958–) "Congqian congqian youge Pudao Tailang 從前從前有個浦島太郎 (Long Ago, There Was a Urashima Tarō). These well-crafted stories are not so much historical fiction as they are modernist fiction that does not pretend to be epic. Moreover, they are strongly lyrical and sometimes even melancholic. Obviously, these authors do not intend to document history. Rather than adhering to historical facts, they instead reflect on lived experience under specific historical circumstances or on the meaning of that history. Similar to this approach is the third type of MCP fiction, which keeps a distance from the history it examines.

In Taiwanese literature, accordingly, very few literary works take up the subject of failed revolution, primarily because the long-term martial law imposed by the KMT government and the resulting White Terror suppressed political dissent. (During the martial law period from the 1960s to the late 1980s, Chen Yingzhen was virtually the only author to explore the subject in question.)

"History"

Compared to Taiwan, the left-wing lineage of Mahua writers is more obvious. The nation's policy of racial segregation by language has perhaps inadvertently protected the existence of Mahua revolutionary literature, which barely rises above impoverishment. Another reason why this literature is permitted to exist is because, compared to armed resistance, revolutionary literature posed a minimal threat to the regime. For Mahua leftists, it does not take much for a work to qualify as literature, and although they had many writers, their actual literary accomplishments were relatively poor. After the Malayan Emergency was declared in 1948, the MCP went underground, and their works vanished from the Mahua realist canon. This disappearance is directly due to the political ban, which also pushed Mahua realism toward extinction because it could no longer fulfill the political promise of "reflecting the realities of the here and now." By the time the MCP reappeared in Mahua realism, the revolution had already ended, and the ban had been lifted. The specific "realities of the here and now" had already become "history."

Even for works written during the revolutionary journey (such as Jin Zhimang's *Hunger*) that were not widely circulated, by the time they were finally brought to light the revolution had already ended, and the revolution's failure became the works' interpretive context. Authors like He Jin who were lucky enough to outlive the end of the revolution could only sing another elegy for that generation of people who sacrificed their youth and offer a testimony with their own lived experience. For the generation of writers who were immersed in modernism—which is to say, authors of the third type of MCP fiction—both history and the failure of the revolution are possible objects for literary reflection. This is also how literature should position itself—retaining a critical distance from history while continuing to focus on fiction itself.

Coda

Why does a failed revolution need fiction? There are three possible answers to this question. First, fiction testifies to the will of the revolution, and it illustrates how, faced with great difficulties, revolutionaries do not lose heart or capitulate, nor do they ever regret expending their youth and making sacrifices. Although the revolution may not succeed, the will is not defeated. Second, fiction can document—or even stand in for—history and convey a "correct" version of revolutionary history, and the archnemesis of this type of fiction is probably the MCP members' memoirs. Third, history requires critical reflection, which applies not only to historical texts but also to history itself—especially the histories that have not been, or cannot be, written down. As part of this history, the MCP revolution should also become an object of literary reflection.

For Mahua realism, the MCP is a touchstone. In the three types of MCP fiction mentioned above, we can observe two types of Mahua realism—one of which has already accomplished its historical mission, while the other may have misunderstood its mission.

NG KIM CHEW is professor of Chinese literature at National Chi Nan University. He is an author and editor of numerous books, including short story and prose collections, and anthologies of scholarly articles such as *Mahua Literature and Chineseness* (1998, 2012), *Textuality, Soul, and Body: On Chinese Modernity* (2006), and *Minor Sinophone Literature: The Case of Malaysia* (2015).

PO-HSI CHEN is postdoctoral fellow in Taiwan studies at the University of Cambridge. His research interests include Taiwanese literature and cinema, modern and contemporary Chinese literature, and global leftism. He is the Chinese cotranslator of *Queer Modernity and Sexual Identity in Taiwan* (2012), *Black Earth: The Holocaust as History and Warning* (2018), and *The Cold War: A World History* (forthcoming).

///////////////////////////////////

Notes

1   For an overall discussion, see Phoon, "Wenxue yu lishi"; Ng, "Yi yi feng."
2   Tuo Ling, *Tuo Ling zixuanji*, v.
3   Liu Jun, *Zai senlin he yuanye*, 437.
4   Ibid.
5   Ibid.
6   Tuo Ling, "Guanyu," 124–25.
7   See Chin Peng, *Wofang de lishi*, 373–88.
8   Huang, *Geming, lishi, xiaoshuo*.
9   The relevant canonical texts include *Red Crag*, *Keep the Red Flag Flying*, *Chuangye shi* 創業史 [History of Entrepreneurship], *Qingchun zhi ge* 青春之歌 [Song of Youth], and so forth. For a discussion, see Hong, *Zhongguo dangdai wenxueshi*, chap. 8; Li, *50–70 niandai Zhongguo wenxue*; He, ed., "50–70 niandai wenxue."
10   Huang, *Geming, lishi, xiaoshuo*, 11.
11   Li, *50–70 niandai Zhongguo wenxue*, 1.
12   Coming from the opposite direction, in anticommunist literature stories either end with disillusionment (e.g., Jiang Gui's 姜貴 *Chong yang* 重陽 [Rival Suns] and *Xuanfeng* 旋風 [Whirlwind]), or they describe persecution under the PRC regime, especially during the land reform period (e.g., Eileen Chang's *Yangge* 秧歌 [The Rice Sprout Song]).
13   Li, *50–70 niandai Zhongguo wenxue*, 32.
14   Hong, *Zhongguo dangdai wenxueshi*, 123.
15   Ibid., 124–25.
16   For a detailed discussion, see Qian Zhenwen, *Hongyan*.
17   Huang, *Geming*, 2.
18   Zhu Chengfa, *Hongchao*. In an email (pers. comm., December 19, 2020), Liu Jun confirmed my reading of revolutionary historical fiction, noting that he read all those revolutionary novels, of which *Red Crag* left the deepest impression. He also confirmed that he intends to leave a historical record, and he suggested that, to understand the MCP, future generations will have to "read Liu Jun's fiction."
19   Jin Zhimang, *Ji'e*, iii.

20 Here, I am not implying that one influenced the other. The first edition of *Hunger* (1960) predates the first edition of *Red Crag* (1961).

21 For an alternative emphasis that emphasizes the plot of besiegement and sacrifice in *Hunger*, see Ng, "Zuihou de zhanyi."

22 Jin Zhimang, *Ji'e*, 368.

23 Luo and Yang, *Hongyan*, 565.

24 He Jin, *Ju Lang*, 431–33.

25 Phoon, "Zhengzhi buzhengque."

26 See Chen, "He Jin."

27 See my discussion on He Jin in Ng, "Zai huo buzai Nanfang."

28 Tuo Ling, "Guanyu."

29 Tuo Ling, *Tuo Ling zixuanji*, v.

30 Tuo Ling, "Guanyu."

31 Ibid., 125.

32 Liu Jun, *Linhai fengtao*, 440.

References

Cheah See Kian 謝詩堅. *Zhongguo geming wenxue yingxiang xia de Mahua zuoyi wenxue (1926–1976)* 中國革命文學影響下的馬華左翼文學 (1926–1976) [Malayan Chinese Left-Wing Literature under the Influence of Chinese Revolutionary Literature, 1926–1976]. Penang: Hanjiang xueyuan, 2009.

Chen Guoshou 陳國首. "He Jin tan chuangzuo yu rensheng" 賀巾談創作與人生 [He Jin on Creative Work and Life]. *Lianhe zaobao* 聯合早報, April 2 and 5 (2013).

Chin Peng 陳平. *Wofang de lishi* 我方的歷史 [My Side of History]. Singapore: Media Masters, 2004.

Fang Xiu 方修. *Mahua wenxue de xianshizhuyi chuantong* 馬華文學的現實主義傳統 [The Realist Tradition in Malayan Chinese Literature]. Singapore: Honglu qiye wenhua, 1976.

He Guimei 賀桂梅, ed. *"50–70 niandai wenxue" yanjiu duben* 「50–70年代文學」研究讀本 [Handbook of "1950s–1970s Literature"]. Shanghai: Shanghai shudian chubanshe, 2018.

He Jin 賀巾. *Julang* 巨浪 [The Mighty Wave]. Kuala Lumpur: Zhaohua, 2004.

He Jin 賀巾. *Liuwang: Liushi niandai Xinjiapo qingnian xuesheng liuwang Yinni de gushi* 流亡——六十年代新加坡青年學生流亡印尼的故事 [Exile: A Story about Young Singaporean Students Exiled in Indonesia in the 1960s]. Kuala Lumpur: Celue zixun yanjiu zhongxin, 2010.

Hong Zicheng 洪子誠. *Zhongguo dangdai wenxueshi* 中國當代文學史 [Contemporary Chinese Literary History]. Beijing: Beijing Daxue chubanshe, 2010.

Huang Ziping. *Geming, lishi, xiaoshuo* 革命.歷史.小說 [Revolution, History, Fiction]. 2nd ed. Hong Kong: Oxford University Press, 2018.

Jin Zhimang 金枝芒. *Ji'e: kang Ying minzu jiefang zhanzheng changpian xiaoshuo* 饑餓：抗英民族解放戰爭長篇小說 [Hunger: A Novel about the National Liberation War against Britain]. Kuala Lumpur: 21 shiji chubanshe bianjibu, 2008.

Li Yang 李揚. *50–70 niandai Zhongguo wenxue jingdian zaijiedu* 50–70年代中國文學經典再解讀 [A Reinterpretation of Chinese Literary Classics, 1950s–1970s]. Beijing: Beijing Daxue chubanshe, 2018.

Liu Jun 流軍. *Linhai fengtao* 林海風濤 [Blowing Wind in the Woods]. Singapore: Liu Jun xiezuoshi, 2015.

Liu Jun 流軍. *Zai senlin he yuanye* 在森林和原野 [In the Forest and Wilderness]. Taipei: Niang chuban, 2019.

Luo Guangbin 羅廣斌 and Yang Yiyan 楊益言. *Hong yan* 紅岩 [Red Crag]. Beijing: Zhongguo qingnian chubanshe, 1961.

Ng Kim Chew 黃錦樹. *Huawen xiaowenxue de Malaixiya ge'an* 華文小文學的馬來西亞個案 [Minor Sinophone Literature: The Case of Malaysia]. Taipei: Maitian, 2015.

Ng Kim Chew 黃錦樹. "Yi yi feng, yin yi yu—Mahua wenxue yu Magong xiaoshuo" 衣以風，飲以雨——馬華文學與馬共小說 [Clothed in Wind, Quenched by Rain—Malayan Chinese Literature and Malayan Communist Fiction]. In *Huawen xiaowenxue de Malaixiya ge'an* 華文小文學的馬來西亞個案 [Minor Sinophone Literature: The Case of Malaysia], 335–65. Taipei: Maitian, 2015.

Ng Kim Chew 黃錦樹. "Zai huo buzai Nanfang—Fansi zuoyi wenxue" 在或不在南方——反思左翼文學 [Present or Absent in the South—A Reflection on Left-Wing Literature]. In *Huawen xiaowenxue de Malaixiya ge'an* 華文小文學的馬來西亞個案 [Minor Sinophone Literature: The Case of Malaysia], 397–408. Taipei: Maitian, 2015.

Ng Kim Chew 黃錦樹. "Zuihou de zhanyi—Lun Jin Zhimang de *Ji E*" 最後的戰役——論金枝芒的《飢餓》 [The Last Battle: On Jin Zhimang's Novel *Hunger*]. In *Huawen xiaowenxue de Malaixiya ge'an* 華文小文學的馬來西亞個案 [Minor Sinophone Literature: The Case of Malaysia], 315–34. Taipei: Maitian, 2015.

Phoon Yuen Ming 潘婉明. "Wenxue yu lishi de xianghu shentou—'Magong shuxie' de leixing, wenben yu pinglun" 文學與歷史的相互滲透——「馬共書寫」的類型、文本與評論 [The Interpenetration between Literature and History—Genres, Texts, and Commentaries of the 'Malayan Communist Writings']. In *Cong jinxiandai dao hou Lengzhan—Yazhou de zhengzhi jiyi yu lishi xushi* 從近現代到後冷戰——亞洲的政治記憶與歷史敘事 [From Premodern to Post–Cold War—Political Memories and Historical Narratives in Asia], edited by Xu Xiuhui 徐秀慧 and Wu Xiue 吳秀娥, 439–76. Taipei: Liren, 2011.

Phoon Yuen Ming 潘婉明. "Zhengzhi buzhengque yu wenxuexing: Magong shuxie de 'Magong shuxie'" 政治不正確與文學性：馬共書寫的「馬共書寫」 [Political Incorrectness and Literariness: The 'Malayan Communist Writings' Penned by Malayan Communist Party Members]. *Suihuo pinglun* 燧火評論, February 28, 2015. http://www.pfirereview.com/20150228/.

Qian Zhenwen 錢振文. Hongyan *shi zenyang liancheng de—Guojia wenxue de shengchan he xiaofei* 《紅岩》是怎樣煉成的——國家文學的生產與和消費 [How Was *Red Crag* Tempered? The Production and Consumption of National Literature]. Beijing: Beijing Daxue chubanshe, 2011.

Tuo Ling 駝鈴. "Guanyu lishi xiaoshuo" 關於歷史小說 [About Historical Fiction]. In *Tuo Ling manbi* 駝鈴漫筆 [Random Writings by Tuo Ling], 124–25. Kuala Lumpur: Juehuo chubanshe, 2015.

Tuo Ling 駝鈴. *Shaya de hongshulin* 沙啞的紅樹林 [The Hoarse Mangrove Forest]. Perak: Pili wenyi yanjiuhui, 2000.

Tuo Ling 駝鈴. *Tuo Ling zixuanji* 駝鈴自選集 [Self-Selected Works by Tuo Ling]. Kampar: Manyan shufang, 2012.

Tuo Ling 駝鈴. *Xiaoyan sanjin shi* 硝煙散盡時 [When the Gunpowder Smoke Dissipated]. Perak: Pili wenyi yanjiuhui, 1995.

Zhu Chengfa 朱成發. *Hongchao: Xinhua zuoyi wenxue de Wenge chao* 紅潮：新华左翼文学的文革潮 [Red Tide: The Tide of the Cultural Revolution in Singapore Left-Wing Literature]. Singapore: Lingzi chuanmei, 2004.

BOON ENG KHOR

Counter-discourse
Strategies of Representing Ethnic Minorities in Sinophone Malaysian Literature

ABSTRACT Since independence, the ethnic Chinese community in Malaysia has lamented its marginalization by the Malay-Bumiputra elite, a theme that is often reflected in writings by ethnically Chinese Malaysian authors. This article, however, examines how ethnic Chinese authors depict *other* ethnic minorities, focusing on four approaches to forging counter-discourses used in the literary representation of minorities: binary opposition, rhetorical questions, paradoxical statements, and bystander narration. The discussion of each narrative strategy is supported by examples from works by writers from different eras, regions, genders, and generations. These modes of counter-discourse foreground minority voices and create a meaningful dialogue between the Sinophone community and other ethnic groups. Through these counter-discursive explorations, Mahua authors portray the Chinese in Malaysia in relation to other ethnic minorities. In some cases, we can also observe how Mahua authors employ this counter-discourse structure as a form of resistance against hegemonic state power.

KEYWORDS Sinophone Malaysian Literature, minority, representation, counter-discourse, power

Introduction

Since Malaysia was incorporated in 1963, the ethnic Chinese community in Malaysia has lamented its marginalization by the Malay-Bumiputra elite. They have faced widespread discrimination in areas including language, education, religion, the economy, society, and culture—including very practical issues such as government scholarships for college courses. As members of an ethnic minority group, Malaysian Chinese (Mahua 馬華) authors frequently encounter challenges that are reflected in the subject matter of their literary works; but which issues and concerns do these same authors highlight when they write about Malaysia's *other* minority ethnic groups?

According to Malaysia's Department of Statistics, in 2020 nearly 70 percent of the nation's population were Bumiputra (including both Malay-Bumiputra and the Indigenous-Bumiputra, who live primarily in the states of Sabah and Sarawak on the island of Borneo), nearly 23 percent were Chinese, less than 7 percent were

PRISM: THEORY AND MODERN CHINESE LITERATURE • 19:2 • SEPTEMBER 2022
DOI 10.1215/25783491-9966727 • © 2022 LINGNAN UNIVERSITY

Indians, and the remaining 1 percent were classified as "other."[1] The distribution of ethnic groups, however, varies considerably from region to region. For instance, while ethnic Malays make up a majority of the population in West Malaysia (the Malaysian peninsula), in Sarawak Ibans (a subgroup of the Dayak indigenous group) are the largest single ethnic group, accounting for approximately 28 percent of the population, while ethnic Chinese and Malays each make up roughly a quarter of the population.

The ethnic minorities featured in Mahua literature can be divided into three general categories. First, there are non-Malay ethnic groups that are officially recognized by the state, including non-Muslim indigenous ethnic groups. Second, there are a variety of unofficial categories of mixed-heritage Malaysians, including Eurasians, Chinese Peranakans (individuals with Chinese heritage), Jawi Peranakans (individuals with Indian and Malay heritage), and Chindians (individuals with Chinese and Indian heritage). Third, there are more recent immigrants, including illegal migrants from Sulu, Indonesia, and the Philippines. Moreover, although the term *minority* often carries connotations of economic, political, and sociocultural vulnerability, many Mahua literary works do not present minority figures as simply vulnerable figures, instead featuring complex dialogic engagements between Chinese and non-Chinese groups. Some of these works attempt to grant these minorities a virtual voice, whether via their language, their actions, or third-party representatives, and in this way they help avoid presenting these minorities as uniformly inferior and vulnerable.

Mahua literary representations of Malaysia's ethnic minorities may be viewed in relation to what Michel Foucault calls *discursive formations*, which Foucault argues have the potential to become accepted as "common sense" and to thereby shape the dominant ideology.[2] In "On the Genealogy of Ethics," Foucault specifies that "every new idea, every new political proposal, every new social movement even if explicitly 'progressive,' they are all 'dangerous' because they could all generate oppressive discourses."[3] At the same time, however, in a dialogue with Deleuze, Foucault proposes that "when those usually spoken for and about by others begin to speak for themselves, they produce a 'counter-discourse.' This counter-discourse is not another theory, but rather a practical engagement in political struggles."[4] He suggests that to resist the dominant discourse, marginalized groups must speak up for themselves, observing that "what had made power strong becomes used to attack it. Power after investing itself in the body, finds itself exposed to counter-attack in the same body."[5]

Some Mahua works, however, feature an interesting phenomenon wherein the ethnically Chinese authors propose counter-discourses by focusing not on ethnic Chinese characters, but rather on *other* ethnic minorities—thereby offering the possibility of a dialogue between Malaysia's ethnic Chinese and the nation's other ethnic minorities. Through readings of select fictional works, this article identifies several rhetorical strategies that Mahua authors deploy in writing about other ethnic minorities.

Narrative Strategies That Shape the Representation of Minorities

At first glance, some Mahua works appear to use a set of binary oppositions to reflect on ethnic tensions and power asymmetries. For instance, Chen Beimeng's 陳北萌 (1922–) "Gei ganniu de Jiningren" 給趕牛的吉寧人 (To an Indian Cowboy) is a colonial-era poem that describes how local Indians were exploited by capitalists.[6] The story presents a series of binary oppositions between owner and laborer, oppressor and victim, man and animal, which are complemented by a pair of images of whips and milk. The whip is used by a young Indian cowboy to control a cow, while the cow's owner uses the same whip on the cowboy if he makes any mistakes. Milk is extracted from the cow for profit, which in turn symbolizes the owner's exploitation of the laborers. The Chinese narrator's attempts to converse with the Indian cowboy suggests that Chinese subjects empathize with their Indian counterparts. The fate of the Indian boy resembles that of the Chinese narrator, as both were exploited during the colonial period and were treated like cows and horses in their workplaces (Indians mostly worked on rubber plantations, while Chinese worked in tin mines). The work suggests that the narrator uses an identification with the boy in order to protest the exploitative practices of the ruling elite.

Whereas some Mahua stories emphasize the gap between the ethnic Chinese narrator and other ethnic minority characters, other works present a more sympathetic relationship between the two. For instance, whereas in Shang Wanyun's 商晚筠 (1952–1995) 1976 short story "Mubanwu de Yinduren" 木板屋的印度人 (Indian in the Wooden House) the nine-year-old Chinese girl narrator describes her Indian neighbors as alcoholics, unhygienic, intolerant, cunning, and materialistic,[7] Li Zishu's 黎紫書 (1971–) more recent short story "Chuzou" 初走 (Runaway) instead presents an Indian student much more positively than it presents his Chinese classmates.[8] After being beaten by their parents for assaulting a teacher, two Chinese teenagers run away from home, not caring whether their actions make their parents anxious. The Indian boy, meanwhile, patiently cares for his bedridden mother while working part time to pay his tuition. He even carries his mother on his back to the railway station every day to beg, without complaining. At first glance, one might assume that the difference between Li's and Shang's works is due to the fact that the authors belong to different generations, given the widespread perception that younger authors like Li are more open-minded and tolerant, while older authors like Shang are more conservative. Nevertheless, one can easily find exceptions to these stereotypes. For instance, some older writers such as Pan Yutong 潘雨桐 (1937–), Li Yongping 李永平 (1947–2017), and Liang Fang 梁放 (1953–) often present minorities in a positive light, while a younger author such as Chen Zhihong 陳志鴻 (1976–) may offer a more negative perspective.

Another twist to this phenomenon of binary representations of minorities in Sinophone Malaysian literature can be found in works featuring Peranakan characters. Peranakans are Malaysians whose ancestry can be traced back to the earliest major waves of Chinese migration to the region in the sixteenth and seventeenth centuries. Over generations, the descendants of these early migrants interbred with locals and underwent a process of acculturation.[9] During the colonial period, the British often perceived Peranakans more favorably than more recent Chinese immigrants, since the former had developed close ties with the British over the years and were viewed as loyal subjects of the colonial administrators. In the contemporary period, meanwhile, Peranakans typically do not speak Chinese, identify neither as Chinese nor Malay, and are recognized as a distinctive ethnic group in their own right.

In Qiu Shizhen's 丘士珍 (1905–1993) story "Baba yu Niangre" 峇峇與娘惹 (Baba and Nyonya), for instance, Ah Mei is a new immigrant from China who is presented as being poor, old-fashioned, and conservative, in contrast to the story's two protagonists, Baba and Nyonya (which are terms of respect for Peranakan men and women, respectively), who are presented as being rich, modern, and liberal.[10] In the end, however, Ah Mei reveals Baba and Nyonya's incestuous affair and their complicity in murdering their father, remarking that "they behave like beasts, and I really can't bear it anymore" 卒因他們完全是禽獸般的行為，所以我實在是忍無可忍了.[11] Positioned on the side of the weak, Ah Mei challenges the relative superiority of the Peranakans. Nonetheless, the story's narrator does not explicitly critique Baba and Nyonya, and instead suggests that their incestuous affair and their act of parricide are attributable to their family environment. Their father, for instance, has several wives, one of whom not only has an affair with his driver but even seduces Baba—and the implication appears to be that this environment is responsible for Baba's and Nyonya's incestuous relationship. Moreover, the father is depicted as being selfish and heartless, and his decision to marry Nyonya off to a wealthy young man ultimately leads to her being pushed into sex work, which apparently contributed to her and her brother's later decision to murder their father. In this way, the story appears to use Baba and Nyonya's rebellion against their father as an allegory for the possibility that the oppressed ethnic minorities might challenge and even overthrow the colonial and capitalist ruling class.

A similar dynamic can be found in Mo Beiyang's 漠北羊 (1942–2020) short story "Hong shalong" 紅紗籠 (Red Sarong), which depicts the struggle of a Peranakan widow named Lucy.[12] After Lucy's husband dies in a workplace accident, the husband's Chinese boss recommends that she quit her job as a bargirl and also recommends that she not accede to a demanding foreigner, to which she responds, "This foreigner has lots of money, and I want his money. What's weird about being his mistress?" 洋丘八的鈔票多，我要他的鈔票，當他的情婦又有什麼奇怪?[13] Later, when the boss accuses Lucy of being depraved, she replies, "Don't we all have our own objectives? I want his money, and he wants my body. Fair enough. How can you say that I am depraved?" 我們各人都有一個目的，我要他的鈔票，他要我的身體，公平交易，你不該說我墮落? Given that Lucy's mother-in-law refuses to share her husband's insurance compensation with her, Lucy therefore needs to take on whatever job she can to ensure the family's survival, even if that means selling her body. When the boss advises her to marry a man who loves her, she retorts, "Oh! You're too naïve. I'm a bargirl. Do you think any man will be interested in me?" 哈哈，你說得很天真，兵營裡的阿媽，誰敢要? She then challenges him, "If I were to marry you, would you dare take me?" 我嫁給你，你敢要嗎?[14] Lucy's response suggests that she is practical, brave, and firm, and she dares to challenge the boss's moralistic views. "Would you dare take me?" is the most powerful question posed to the dominant persona, revealing the boss's hypocrisy with empty Chinese moral values that are of no practical help to Lucy.

In Pan Yutong's story "Xuejiama dutou" 雪嘉瑪渡頭 (Segamar Pier), the ethnically Dusun protagonist Nafushan is a woman from the state of Sabah who serves as a contract-wife for several ethnically Chinese men from West Malaysia.[15] Here, a contract-wife is usually an ethnic minority woman who is hired as a temporary wife by Chinese men from West Malaysia working in Sabah, but Nafushan is searching for Wang Han, her former contract-husband who owes her money. When Nafushan's current contract-husband Lim Ruixiang suggests that he is willing to release her so she may be reunited with her previous contract-husband, however, she replies sarcastically, "How can you Chinese from West Malaysia act like this?" 你們西馬的華人，可以這樣的嗎?[16]—suggesting that Pan Yutong is using the figure of Nafushan to critique the integrity of his fellow ethnic Chinese.

In Li Yongping's short story "Lazifu" 拉子婦 (The Dayak Woman), meanwhile, a Dayak woman named Aunt Lazi marries a Chinese man, which causes considerable consternation in her family. She is belittled, despised, and assaulted, and she is eventually sent back to her family's longhouse, where she dies. Her death highlights the tragedy of a mixed marriage in Sarawak in the 1960s. The main reason for her death is the Chinese family's mistreatment and exploitation of a vulnerable minority. However, it is worth noting that not all of the husband's relatives are opposed to Lazi. In particular, the narrator, his mother, and his younger sister are all clearly sympathetic to Lazi and attempt to defend her. For instance, the narrator explains why he has to continue using the derogatory term "Lazi": "If I don't call her Lazi and replace it with something that sounds nicer and more friendly, the Chinese would feel very awkward" 倘若我不喊拉子，而用另外一個

好聽點、友善點的名詞代替它，中國人會感到很彆扭的.[17] Similarly, when Second Sister reflects on the icy response of her family members upon receiving the news of Lazi's passing, she says: "Now I understand. There is no great and majestic reason. Just because Aunt Lazi is just a Lazi woman, a very insignificant Lazi! To express excessive sorrow upon her death would result in our losing our identity as noble Chinese!" 我現在明白了。沒有什麼莊嚴偉大的原因，只因為拉子嬸是一位拉子，一個微不足道的拉子！對一個死去的拉子婦表示過分的悲悼，有失高貴的中國人的身份啊![18] Both statements critique Chinese prejudice against other ethnicities, while at the same time using the figure of Aunt Lazi to critique prejudicial attitudes held against ethnic Chinese within Malaysian society.

"Longtuzhu" 龍吐珠 (Cledodendrum) was written in the 1980s by the Sarawak-based author Liang Fang (1953–). Like "The Dayak Woman," this story describes a marriage between a Chinese and a Dayak—in this case, a "Sea Dayak," the term for people from a subgroup also known as Iban.[19] The Dayak wife and her son, the narrator, are later abandoned by the husband, who returns to mainland China. Unfortunately, the son is influenced by his Chinese father and looks down on his Iban mother, and therefore tries to conceal his own Iban identity. While in middle and high school, he never welcomes his mother's visits to his dormitory, and after entering college he fails to stay in touch with her. Nevertheless, after the narrator later marries and has his own child, he realizes that his daughter bears an uncanny resemblance to her grandmother. Reminded of his Iban roots, the narrator regrets his past and arranges to return to his hometown to visit his mother. Unfortunately, it turns out that his mother had passed away the preceding year. The narrator finds that when his mother died she left behind a large box of his and his father's belongings, including toys, clothes, and photos, and when he finds these items, he weeps with regret and sorrow. The silence of this Iban mother is another example of a paradoxical mode of counter-discourse. Like the figure of Aunt Lazi in "The Lazi Woman," the mother in "Cledodendrum" never complains, and she demonstrates her love through her actions. In this way, she melts her son's pride and invites the reader's sympathy.

In other Mahua literary works, a counter-discourse is presented in the form of third-party narration. In these writings, the narrator identifies neither with the protagonist nor the antagonist, but rather highlights the position of a bystander figure, one who normally would play an insignificant role in the story. For instance, in Pan Yutong's "Ye Dian" 野店 (Outskirts Store), Susimah, an immigrant from Sulu, lives with her "husband" Lim Ah Seng, a Chinese seafood store owner from West Malaysia. Her only son with Lim, Ah Ka, is used as cheap labor to help run Lim's business and is not given a proper education. For their livelihood, the mother and son have no choice but to submit to Lim. Nevertheless, whenever Lim returns to West Malaysia for business reasons or to visit his legal wife and children, Susimah secretly meets up with her ex-lover Sasuman.

Hence, her son describes Sasuman as a rat that appears whenever his father is not around: "After Ah Pa left, Sasuman appeared out of nowhere" 阿爸一走，他就不知從哪裡閃了出來.[20] The text does not specify the precise nature of Susimah's and Sasuman's interactions, but instead highlights their conversations as a supplementary narrative.

The appearance of Sasuman underscores Susimah's resistance to Lim. At one point, the son's maternal grandfather recommends that he learn from Sasuman, implying that Sasuman was a respected figure in Susimah's home village. This remark, which appears as a digression, illustrates a counter-discourse strategy whereby the narrator uses Sasuman as a third-party bystander to strengthen Susimah's own resistance. At another point Sasuman remarks sarcastically, "Shall I say that both mother and son are stupid! Don't you know that he is devouring the two of you in one bite? Don't you know that he is a great shark from West Malaysia that has crossed the sea to come here" 我說你們母子倆笨啦，他一口吃了你們都不知道，他是從西馬渡海過來的大鯊魚![21] Sasuman also labels Lim as a West Malaysian, a term equivalent to an exploiter in the eyes of some East Malaysians. Hence, he adds, "As a Siputu man, I do not want you to cling to this West Malaysian man" 我是西布都的男人，所以我才不要你跟那個西馬人.[22] This statement reinforces the earlier point that whatever Sasuman has done, it is "actually all because of you." This expression draws these two Sulu immigrants into the common fate and community in which they are supposed to belong, except that Sasuman genuinely cares for Susiman, unlike Lim, who simply takes advantage of her. The conversation also reveals that Sasuman is fighting for their country under the Moro National Liberation Front to reclaim the land taken by others, and he is still "proud of the sultan of Sulu" 以蘇祿蘇丹為榮. This sentiment too emboldens Susimah against Lim's oppression.[23]

In another short story, "Redai yulin" 熱帶雨林 (The Tropical Rainforest), Pan Yutong employs a similar mode of counter-discourse.[24] The story depicts a female cook named Yily and how she deals with various men in her workplace. Yily is in a doubly vulnerable position as an undocumented immigrant from the Philippines among legitimate Chinese Malaysians, and as the sole woman at an all-male site. Interestingly, this female protagonist plays the dominant role in the story. First, although she is the senior boss's secret mistress, she does not seem to cling to one man. During her boss's absence, she seduces his son, Ye Yuntao (the junior boss), and takes complete control of their sexual relationship. In their conversation, she taunts Junior Ye with remarks such as, "Are you scared?" 你怕?, "Act like a man" 像個男人, "I do not solely belong to him" 我可不是只屬於他的女人, and "Aren't you always peeking at me?" 你不是天天在偷看我嗎?[25] In the end, Junior Ye apparently has no choice but to yield to her desire.

The more crucial part of the story, however, is the long conversation between Ye and his chief worker, Shan Gou, which portrays another side of Yily's character. According to Shan Gou, he is attracted to Yily, who is a competent woman and constantly keeps the kitchen spick-and-span. From Shan Gou's perspective, she is not an immoral woman, and his evidence is that she chased him away with a cleaver on one occasion when he tried to seduce her. Through Shan Gou's viewpoint, the reader also learns that Yily is a devout Catholic who is a regular churchgoer. Shan Gou longs to marry her and asks Junior Ye to be the matchmaker. The third-party figure expounds on this immigrant woman's good qualities, contrasting with the initial impression she conveys. From this third-party account, it becomes apparent that Yily's seduction of Junior Ye may be seen as a symbolic protest against Senior Ye for exploiting her body, suggesting a simultaneous challenge to both Chinese and male domination.

Conclusion

In *Problems of Dostoevsky's Poetics*, Russian literary theorist Mikhail Bakhtin pointed to the way in which a novel may feature an internal dialogic structure wherein multiple different voices and perspectives operate in tension with one another.[26] The Mahua works discussed above, which include poetry and works of short fiction, exhibit a similar heteroglossia, where multiple viewpoints associated with ethnic Chinese and other ethnic minorities intersect with one another in complex ways. In this way, these Mahua authors use a focus on other ethnic minorities as a foil allowing them to reflect on the discrimination that ethnic Chinese have endured, both during the colonial period as well as during the independence era.

BOON ENG KHOR obtained a doctor of literature (DLitt) degree from the Chinese Language and Literature Department of Nanjing University. He currently teaches in the Chinese Studies Department, Institute of Chinese Studies, Universiti Tunku Abdul Raman, and holds the post of associate professor. His main research interest is Malaysian Chinese literature and comparative literature. His most recent publications include *A Study of Malaysian Chinese Literary Types and Forms* (2014) and *Fourteen Lectures on Malaysian Chinese Literature* (2019), which he edited.

///////////////////////////////

Notes

1   "Current Population Estimates, Malaysia, 2020." Department of Statistics Malaysia, Official Portal, July 15, 2020. https://www.dosm.gov.my/v1/index.php?r=column/cthemeByCat&cat=155&bul_id=OVByWjg5YkQ3MWFZRTN5bDJiaEVhZz09&menu_id=L0pheU43NWJwRWVSZklWdzQ4TlhUUT09#:~:text=Malaysia's%20population%20in%202020%20is,rate%20of%200.4%20per%20cent.

2   Foucault, *Archaeology of Knowledge*, 31–39.

3   Foucault, "On the Genealogy of Ethics," 231–32.

4   Deleuze and Foucault, *Intellectuals and Politics*, 209.

5   Foucault, *Power/Knowledge*, 55–56.
6   Chen, "Gei ganniu de Jiningren."
7   Shang, *Chinü Ahlian*, 1–42.
8   Li Zishu, *Shan Wen*, 81–98.
9   For the most comprehensive study of Chinese Peranakans, see Tan, *Baba of Melaka*.
10 Qiu, "Baba yu Niangre."
11 Ibid., 62.
12 Mo, "Hong shalong," 27.
13 Ibid.
14 Ibid.
15 Pan, *Zuoye Xingchen*, 223–50.
16 Ibid., 225.
17 Li, "Lazi fu," 51.
18 Ibid.
19 Liang, "Longtuzhu," 575–82.
20 Pan, *Yedian*, 243.
21 Ibid., 251.
22 Ibid., 255.
23 Ibid., 254.
24 Pan, *Jingshui daxue*, 249–86.
25 Pan, *Zuoye xingchen*, 250.
26 Bakhtin, *Problems of Dostoevsky's Poetics*, 18.

References

Bakhtin, Mikhail. *Problems of Dostoevsky's Poetics*, edited and translated by Caryl Emerson. Minnesota: University of Minnesota Press, 1999.

Chen Beimeng 陳北萌. "Gei ganniu de Jiningren" 給趕牛的吉寧人 [To an Indian Cowboy]. *Chen Xing* 晨星 [Morning Star], literary supplement of *Xingzhou ribao* 星洲日報 [Sin Chew Jit Poh], February 26, 1948.

Deleuze, Gilles, and Michel Foucault. "Intellectuals and Politics." In *Language, Counter-Memory, and Practice*, edited by Donald F. Bouchard, 205–17. Ithaca, NY: Cornell University Press, 1977.

Foucault, Michel. *The Archaeology of Knowledge; and The Discourse on Language*, translated by Rupert Swyer. New York: Vintage Books, 2010.

Foucault, Michel. "On the Genealogy of Ethics." In *Michel Foucault: Beyond Structuralism and Hermeneutics*, edited by Hubert L. Dreyfus and Paul Rabinow, 229–52. Chicago: University of Chicago Press, 1982.

Foucault, Michel. *Power/Knowledge: Selected Interviews and Other Writings, 1972–1977*, translated by Colin Gordon et al., edited by Colin Gordon. New York: Pantheon Books, 1980.

Liang Fang 梁放. "Longtuzhu" 龍吐珠 [Cledodendrum]. In Boon Eng Khor 許文榮 and Yan Chuan Seng 孫彥莊, eds. *Mahuawenxue wenbenjiedu* 馬華文學文本解讀 [Interpretation of Mahua Texts], 575–89. Kuala Lumpur: PEJATI and Department of Chinese Studies, University of Malaya, 2012.

Li Yongping 李永平. "Lazi fu" 拉子婦 [Lazi Woman]. In *Li Yongping zixuanji 1968–2002* 李永平自選集 1968–2002 [Li Yongping's Selected Works 1968–2002], 51–62. Taipei: Maitian, 2003.

Li Zishu 黎紫書. *Shan Wen* 山瘟 [Mountain Plague]. Taipei: Maitian, 2001.

Mo Beiyang 漠北羊. "Hong shalong" 紅紗籠 [Red Sarong]. In *Mahua wenxue daxi* 馬華文學大系 [Compendium of Malaysian Chinese Literature], edited by Li Yijun, vol. 3, part 1, 19–29. Johor Bahru: Caihong chuban youxian gongsi, 2001.

Pan Yutong 潘雨桐. *Jingshui daxue* 静水大雪 [Still Water and Heavy Snow]. Johor Bahru: Pelangi, 1996.

Pan Yutong 潘雨桐. *Yedian* 野店 [Outskirts Store]. Johor Bahru: Pelangi, 1998.

Pan Yutong 潘雨桐. *Zuoye xingchen* 昨夜星辰 [Last Night's Stars]. Taipei: Lianhe wenxue, 1989.

Qiu Shizhen 丘士珍. "Baba yu Niangre" 峇峇與娘惹 [Baba and Nyonya]. In *Mahua wenxue daxi* 馬華文學大系 [Compendium of Malaysian Chinese Literature], edited by Li Yijun, vol. 4, part 2, 27–63. Johor Bahru: Caihong chuban youxian gongsi, 2001.

Shang Wanyun 商晚筠. *Chinü Alian* 痴女阿蓮 [The Idiot Ah Lian]. Taipei: Lianjing, 1977.

CARLOS ROJAS

Becoming Semi-wild

Colonial Legacies and Interspecies Intimacies in Zhang Guixing's Rainforest Novels

ABSTRACT This article borrows Juno Salazar Parreñas's concept of the "semi-wild" as an entry point into an analysis of Malaysian Chinese author Zhang Guixing's novels *Elephant Herd* (1998) and *Monkey Cup* (2000). Set in Sarawak, both works feature a relatively simple plotline interwoven with an intricate web of flashbacks. More specifically, each work's primary plotline features an ethnically Chinese protagonist searching for a relative who has disappeared into the rainforest, while also becoming romantically interested in a young Indigenous woman whom he meets during his quest. In each case, a fascination with the relationship between humans and Sarawak's various "semi-wild" flora and fauna is paralleled by an attention to the relationship between the region's ethnic Chinese and its various Indigenous peoples—and particularly two subgroups of Sarawak's Dayak ethnicity, the "Sea Dayaks" (also known as the Iban) and the "Land Dayaks" (who are often simply called "Dayaks"). Each work uses a set of quasi-anthropomorphized plants and animals (including silk-cotton trees, *Nepenthes* pitcher plants, elephants, crocodiles, rhinoceroses, and orangutans) to reflect on humans' relationship to the local ecosystem, while simultaneously using Indigenous peoples to reflect on the way in which overlapping colonial legacies have shaped the region's sociopolitical structures.

KEYWORDS Zhang Guixing, *Elephant Herd*, *Monkey Cup*, "semi-wild," Indigenous peoples

Zhang Guixing's 張貴興 2000 novel *Houbei* 猴杯 (Monkey Cup) begins with the protagonist, Yu Pengzhi ("Zhi"), on a flight home from Taiwan to the Malaysian state of Sarawak, in northern Borneo. As Zhi is eating his lunch, his seatmate—a middle-aged Taiwanese woman who is flying to Borneo with her daughter—begins chatting with him. The woman asks Zhi if he was born in Taiwan, to which he replies that he is from Borneo. She then asks him his nationality, and he replies that it is somewhat complicated: "I'm not exactly sure. I came to Taiwan for college when I was nineteen, and after graduating I used the dual citizenship system to acquire Taiwanese citizenship, after which I then relinquished my Malaysian citizenship. However, Taiwanese people still regard me as a Southeast Asian wild man ..." 也不清楚。十九歲來台灣念大學，畢業後用變重國籍入了台灣籍，隨後棄了馬國國籍。台灣人把我當作來自東南亞的野蠻人 .... The woman then interjects, "That's right. Just like an orangutan—after it is set free, it still wants to

PRISM: THEORY AND MODERN CHINESE LITERATURE • 19:2 • SEPTEMBER 2022
DOI 10.1215/25783491-9966737 • © 2022 LINGNAN UNIVERSITY

return to Borneo" 是啊。就像紅毛猩猩，放生時，還是要回到波羅洲. Ignoring his seatmate's remark, Zhi chews silently on a piece of cabbage, then continues: "Or a foreign worker. Actually, I'm all right, but some of my friends, be they college instructors or brickmasons, if they haven't already been naturalized, then they need to report on an annual basis to be tested for HIV, syphilis, and gonorrhea." 和外勞。我還好，我的一些朋友，只要沒有入籍，大學教書匠也罷，水泥匠也罷，一年規定篩檢一次愛滋、梅毒、淋病.[1]

Underlying the woman's garbled racist logic (which implies an equivalence between the "Southeast Asian wild man" slur and actual nonhuman primates), there is an allusion to the pressing question of the fate of previously captive Borneo orangutans that have subsequently been released. As Juno Salazar Parreñas describes in her monograph *Decolonizing Extinction: The Work of Care in Orangutan Rehabilitation*, even after theoretically having been "set free," most orangutans raised in captivity are unable to master the skills possessed by truly wild animals; therefore, conservationists attempting to rehabilitate them must settle for helping the primates become merely "semi-wild."

In her anthropological study on orangutan rehabilitation in Sarawak, Parreñas notes that the technical term typically used in the scientific literature for previously captive orangutans is *rehabilitant*, while the term *semi-wild* "is mostly used by workers and rarely appears in the primatological literature."[2] Parreñas, however, contends that this latter term is more accurate, given that very few of the primates in these rehabilitation centers will ever be "rehabilitated" to the point that they can truly return to the wild. As a term positioned at the outer margins of the professional discourses on the topic, moreover, *semi-wild* has a sort of "semi-wild" status of its own.

Beyond her focus on the process of orangutan rehabilitation itself, Parreñas positions her analysis against the backdrop of Sarawak's colonial history, suggesting not only that these colonial legacies directly inform the sociopolitical environment within which the state's orangutan rehabilitation efforts are being played out, but also that the political dynamics of the underlying processes of colonization and decolonization may be deployed to help better understand the relations between orangutans and humans. More generally, she argues that "decolonization is an ongoing process in Sarawak that simultaneously experiences an ongoing colonialism. The stakes of decolonization are not limited to issues of sovereignty, occupation, or knowledge production—all of which are contemporary struggles in decolonization and in continued colonialism more broadly. Instead, decolonization scratches at fundamental ways of understanding the world."[3] Parreñas's objective, in other words, is not simply to use colonialism as a model for understanding human-primate relations, nor is it simply to use orangutan rehabilitations as a model for rethinking decolonization. Instead, she attempts to use a consideration of interrelationship between these two processes to reflect more broadly on the relationship between power and knowledge production.

In the following discussion I take Parreñas's concept *semi-wild* as an entry point into an analysis of Zhang Guixing's *Monkey Cup* and his preceding novel, *Qunxiang* 群象 (Elephant Herd, 1998). Set in Sarawak, both works feature a relatively simple plotline interwoven with an intricate web of flashbacks. More specifically, each work's primary plotline features an ethnically Chinese protagonist searching for a relative who has disappeared into the rainforest, while also becoming romantically interested in a young Indigenous woman whom he meets during his quest. In each case, a fascination with the relationship between humans and Sarawak's various "semi-wild" flora and fauna is paralleled by an attention to the relationship between the region's ethnic Chinese and its various Indigenous peoples—and particularly two subgroups of Sarawak's Dayak ethnicity, the "Sea Dayaks" (also known as the Iban) and the "Land Dayaks" (who are often simply called "Dayaks"). Each work uses a set of quasi-anthropomorphized plants and animals (including silk-cotton trees, nepenthes pitcher plants, elephants, crocodiles, rhinoceroses, and, of course, orangutans) to reflect on humans' relationship to the local ecosystem, while simultaneously using Indigenous peoples to reflect on the way in which overlapping colonial legacies have shaped the region's sociopolitical structure.

Elephant Herd

Elephant Herd's primary diegesis begins in December 1973 and follows the protagonist, Shi Shicai, as he travels up the Rajang River with his ethnically Iban high school classmate, Zhu Dezhong. Shicai is searching for his uncle, Yu Jiatong, the leader of a local Communist guerilla unit known as the Yangtze River Brigade, which was part of Sarawak's Communist insurgency that began in 1963. All four of Shicai's elder brothers had previously joined the insurgency and were subsequently killed. Just a couple of months before Shicai embarks on his quest, a key Sarawak Communist leader by the name of Wang Dada has just surrendered to the Malaysian government, after which most of the remaining insurgents lay down their arms as well. Yu Jiatong and a handful of his followers, however, are among the holdouts and are hiding in a base camp deep in the rainforest.

On their way up the river, at one point Shicai and Dezhong stop at the home of Dezhong's clan, where Shicai meets and becomes romantically interested in Dezhong's sister, Fadiya (who doesn't speak Chinese, and instead communicates with Shicai primarily in broken English). After the young men leave Dezhong's home and continue their journey upriver, they encounter a group of Communist soldiers who agree to take Shicai to Yu Jiatong's base camp—but on the condition that Dezhong must remain behind, given that he has no personal connection to the elusive Communist leader. Shicai stays at the base camp for several months, until one night Dezhong unexpectedly appears at the camp and assassinates Yu Jiatong. The remainder of the novel then traces the denouement following the assassination.

Elephant Herd's intertwined themes of interethnic and interspecies relations are anchored by three sets of allusions to silk-cotton trees. These trees, with the botanical name *Cebra pentandra*, are known as emergents, meaning that their crowns rise significantly above the forest canopy, allowing them to access winds that carry their filament-covered seed pods to distant locations. The novel's most detailed discussion of a silk-cotton tree appears near the end of the work when, following Yu Jiatong's assassination, Shicai returns home and ensconces himself in his house for six months. On one of the few occasions when he leaves the house during this period, he ventures into the rainforest and climbs a silk-cotton tree, then spends the afternoon perched in its branches, watching the tree's fuzzy seeds blow through the air. The novel anthropomorphizes this botanical reproductive process, suggesting that the seeds appear unwilling to leave the "mother tree" 母 樹, even as the tree urges them to depart: "Quick, before the birds notice you—go find some fertile soil and grow!" 趁鳥類沒有發現你們以前，去吧，找一塊肥沃 濕潤土地，乖乖長大.[4]

While observing this scene, the boy suddenly experiences the urge to masturbate. He does so, and the narrative describes how "his semen spurted into the air and splattered onto the succulent leaves. The boy then hugged the tree trunk, feeling a thrill as though he had just copulated with the silk-cotton tree. His sperm spouted furry wings and soared off in all directions" 精液噴向空中灑在肥嫩密實 的葉子上。男孩緊抱樹身，有一種和絲棉樹交媾的快感. It turns out that there is a contingent of Japanese researchers nearby using video cameras to study the rainforest's ecology, but the narrative notes that, even with these advanced technologies, the Japanese "didn't even notice the modern human engaged in a love affair with a silk cotton tree overhead" 連頭上和絲棉樹繾綣的現代人類也沒有 發覺.[5] This description of an interspecies "love affair" 繾綣 between a "modern human" 現代人類 and a silk-cotton tree concisely captures the intertwined themes of interspecies relations and interethnic relations that run through the work as a whole.

Prior to this description of the interspecies love affair, the novel presents two other flashback sequences that feature allusions to silk-cotton trees. The first appears near the beginning of the work, as Shicai recalls a hunting expedition he joined when he was seven. The expedition was led by Yu Jiatong and included Shicai's four elder brothers and a dozen of Yu Jiatong's other followers. As the expedition makes its way through the dense rainforest, the landscape is described in highly eroticized terms:

> The forest's maternal qualities inspired the men to entertain many dreams
> and fantasies. Her breasts resembled overly ripe wild fruits, waiting for them

to pick and suck on them. Her private parts were like cherries, with smooth skin and tender flesh, and they resembled a nepenthes pitcher full of nectar. Her phallus was transformed into a hairless, eyeless, sausage-shaped mole rat, burrowing through soil that was full of rotting vegetation. At night, the boy saw dark shadows hiding in the vines outside his tent, ejaculating semen onto the dark, fertile soil.

雨林的母性使他們產生許多綺想、幻象。伊乳房像熟爛野果等他們去擷。去吮。私處如櫻桃，皮滑瓤嫩。如豬籠草裝滿蜜水。陰莖化成無眼無毛香腸狀的鼴鼠，在不滿腐植質的雨林土壤中扒穴覓巢。晚上男孩看見帳棚外一批黑影躲在蔓叢中將精液射入肥沃的黑土.[6]

In this passage, the entire forest is eroticized, and whereas the interspecies love affair passage culminates with a description of Shicai ejaculating onto the silk-cotton tree, in this earlier passage the prepubescent protagonist is only dimly aware of the older men in the expedition, who are perceived merely as "dark shadows hiding in vines outside his tent" and masturbating into the forest's "fertile soil."

This description of the rainforest's "maternal qualities," meanwhile, is immediately followed by an account of how the young Shicai suddenly falls ill:

One morning he missed the wake-up call, and therefore failed to go out with the rest of the expedition. Instead, he vomited onto a fig tree and then lay against an old silk-cotton tree. He was lying on the tree's purplish-brown root, which protruded from the ground like an elephant's trunk—as if the tree were about to use its roots to dig a hole in the ground where he was sitting and bury him.

趕不上起床號，趕不上隊伍,在一顆無花果樹上嘔吐，癱在一棵老絲棉樹下。男孩躺在絲棉樹凸起如象鼻的紫褐色根鬚上，彷彿老絲棉樹準備用根鬚將他刨入胯下埋葬.[7]

Here, the silk-cotton tree functions as a bridge to Shicai's parallel investment in the island's elephants. The connection to elephants is not only associative (in that the tree root resembles an elephant trunk) but also metonymic (in that the encounter with the tree occurs in the context of an elephant hunting expedition).

The novel explains that there are a variety of theories for how the elephants ended up on the island, but regardless of how they arrived, by the mid-twentieth century they had become exceedingly scarce. Despite—or perhaps precisely because of—the scarcity of actual elephants in the region, the animals enjoy a central position within the novel's cultural imaginary. In particular, the novel's elephants—which are repeatedly described as "appearing to be positioned at the interstices of reality and fantasy" 彷彿交錯於現實幻想中[8]—carry two sets of connotations. On one hand, the animals are coveted for their valuable tusks, but on the other hand they also come to acquire a much more personal significance for Shicai, who associates the mysterious beasts with an almost maternal tenderness.

Shicai's life is shadowed by these mysterious elephants, which leads him to develop a curious attachment to them. First, family lore describes how, on the day of Shicai's birth, a small herd of elephants broke into his family's vegetable garden and trampled all the vegetation. Next, at one point during the hunting expedition that Shicai joined when he was seven, he fell into a ditch as he was being carried by Jiatong, and he might have been left behind had not an elephant suddenly picked him up and placed him on Yu Jiatong's back. Although this incident occurs when Jiatong is in a feverish delirium, it nevertheless helps to cement his fond feelings for the majestic animals.

The island's elephants could be viewed as "semi-wild," but unlike Parreñas's orangutans, which have lost the ability to become fully wild as a result of having been born into captivity, the elephants are semi-wild as a result having spent generations learning to evade human predation:

> Experts believed that after having been hunted for several centuries, the elephants managed to develop techniques for protecting themselves and avoiding humans. They developed these techniques in response to their local conditions and passed them down from one generation to the next, such that they eventually came to resemble hermits in the rainforest, completely isolated from the outside world. Humans only heard about them, but rarely saw them. The elephants could only be found in some unknown location deep in the mountains, surrounded by clouds, where they enjoyed simple meals while reciting poems about the wind and moon.

> 歷經人類數百年追殺，象群早已習得各種保護家族和逃躲人類的智慧，耳濡目染代代相傳，使牠們在雨林中像隱士與世隔絕。人類只聞其名，不見其影。只在此山中，雲深不知處。粗茶淡飯，吟詩頌風月。[9]

This passage not only compares the elephants to poetry-writing hermits; it also implies that it was precisely as a result of the need to avoid human predation that the elephants came to acquire these humanlike qualities in the first place.[10]

The flashback to the elephant-hunting expedition concludes with another eroticized description of the rainforest that pivots around an evocative allusion to a silk-cotton tree. After an anthropomorphic description of the forest canopy ("the canopy also concealed many sensitive zones, and not even its features were visible—like a fox hiding in a fox hole or an elegant woman wearing luxurious clothing and a hazy veil" 林冠也隱匿著各種敏感地帶，連五官也不示人，如狡兔掩飾穴口，如端莊女子的贅衣喝朦朧面紗), there is a description of:

> a five-hundred-year-old silk-cotton tree completely covered in boils, holes, and odd angles, like the Great Wall of China. If you were to climb to the top, where would you end up? It was said that at the top of the tree there was a world that was completely different from the world on the ground. Up there, the air pressure was so low that people would secrete blood, sweat, and bloody urine. By the time the boy finished walking around the tree, areas previously hidden in shadows would be directly in the sunlight.
>
> 樹齡五百年以上的絲棉樹渾身癩瘤窟窿蜿蜒昇天像聳著的萬里長城，一路爬上去會通到什麼地方？據說上面有一個和地上截然不同的世界，氣壓會使人流血汗屙血尿。繞著絲棉樹走一遍，原來的陰處已陽光普照。[11]

This silk-cotton tree, like the island's elephant population, represents a link between past and present, reality and possibility. The tree's unusual height gives it a distinctive perspective over the rest of the forest, and the novel suggests that this height transcends even the limits of the human.

The novel's next silk-cotton tree allusion occurs after Shicai arrives at Yu Jiatong's Communist base camp. One of the first things Shicai observes at the camp is a suspension bridge positioned over a crocodile-filled section of the Rajang River. Every day, one of Yu Jiatong's soldiers goes to the middle of the bridge and tosses down some chickens and ducks. The novel notes that the base camp raises these birds solely for crocodile consumption, while the camp's human residents have to use whatever they are able to hunt in the rainforest to feed themselves. Yu Jiatong regards the crocodiles in the river as an extension of his camp, and he frequently jokes about wanting to feed his enemies to them.

In fact, one of the enemies who Yu Jiatong repeatedly claims "is only good for feeding to the crocodiles" 只配餵鱷魚[12] is his former rival Communist leader, Wang Dada. After Shicai returns home from the base camp, he visits Sarawak's first Crocodile Observation Park, which was founded by none other than Wang Dada, after he surrendered to the government. Paralleling the semi-wild crocodiles at Yu Jiatong's base camp (Yu Jiatong jokingly complains, "these little bastards are used to us feeding them, and therefore simply loiter here and refuse to leave" 這些小王八蛋被我餵習慣了，都賴在這條河上不肯走[13]), the crocodiles in Wang Dada's park are used for live performances; their hide is used to manufacture a variety of products, including boots and watch bands; and their meat is used for food. If Yu Jiatong's crocodiles are semi-wild because they have been quasi-domesticated while still residing in a natural setting, Wang Dada's crocodiles have instead been thoroughly integrated into a profit-driven enterprise that profits from their presence and their bodies.

While Shicai is at the base camp, his uncle often regales him with descriptions of his previous sexual relations. For instance, at one point Yu Jiatong tells Shicai how one day shortly after a young woman named Chen Yili joined the brigade, she and Jiatong were attacked by government soldiers and hid in a small burrow beneath a silk-cotton tree. While ensconced in the burrow, Yu Jiatong proceeds to assault his new recruit:

> The burrow was dark and humid, and was just barely large enough for two people. . . . Jiatong ripped open Yili's black shirt and pulled down her black pants. As Jiatong ejaculated, two Yangtze River Brigade troops were fleeing toward the silk-cotton tree, and beneath the tree they were hit by hand grenades and machine gun fire to the point that they couldn't even be recognized as human. Their blood saturated the mud like rain falling on drought-parched land, staining the tree's roots and the cave red, mixing with Yili's virgin blood.

> 洞中潮濕幽暗，勉強容納二人,. . . . 家同撕開宜莉的黑衣衫，褪下她的黑長褲。當家同射出精液時，兩位揚子江隊員正竄向絲棉樹，在絲棉樹下被機關槍和手榴彈轟得不成人形，血液像雨降旱地漫入泥土，染紅樹根和家同宜莉繾綣的整個穴，滲著宜莉的處女血.[14]

Although Yu Jiatong characterizes his subsequent relationship with Yili as romantic, this initial sexual encounter clearly unfolds under conditions of coercion and violence.

Moreover, this description of Yu Jiatong's initial sexual encounter with Yili intersects with two of the novel's key plotlines. First, immediately after telling Shicai about this encounter, Jiatong abruptly changes the subject and asks him, "Shicai, you came here to kill me, didn't you?" 仕才，你是來殺我的吧?[15] Startled by the question, Shicai neither confirms nor denies the charge, though we later learn that this was, in fact, his intention. But after asking Shicai if he plans to kill him, Jiatong continues telling Shicai about his relationship with Yili, leading up to another unexpected question:

> Making love to Yili in that cramped cave was like wrestling with a crocodile in a mud pit. . . . It was as though a giant python were squeezing us together, in order to devour us. . . . No matter how hard I tried, I couldn't move at all, and almost the instant I entered Yili, I immediately ejaculated. When the government troops departed, I once again crazily wanted her. Later, during countless expeditions, Yili and I would often temporarily leave the brigade. . . . Her

breasts were pale and translucent, and very ample, like a pair of jellyfish with their tentacles extended and floating on her soft and plump chest. . . .

在狹小的洞窟裡和宜莉做愛,彷彿在爛泥漿裡和鱷角力 . . . . 彷彿有一條大蟒蛇將我們纏在一起,將我們同時吃下 . . . . 我使盡力氣,做不出一點動作,幾乎進入宜莉那一霎,我就射精了。當政府隊員離去時,我又瘋狂的要了宜莉。以後在無數次行軍中,我和宜莉常短暫脫隊 . . . . 她的乳房蒼白透明,乳腺發達,彷彿觸手奮張的二隻水母,浮於柔軟豐潤的胸部 . . . .[16]

Jiatong then indicates that he knows about Shicai's interest in Dezhong's sister, Fadiya:

"I hear you got along quite well with the younger sister of that native, when you were staying with his family . . ." Jiatong rolled his empty bottle on the table as though he were kneading flour, and in the process making a sound like a pig snorting. "Chinese and aboriginal marriages are just one option. . . . You're the last descendent of the Shi family. You shouldn't let dirty native skin taint your pure yellow skin. . . ."

「聽說你在那個番人家中和那個番人妹妹關係不錯 . . . . 」家同在餐桌上像擀麵滾動空酒瓶,發出豬叫般的聲音。「華土通婚只是一種手段 . . . . 你是施家唯一的傳人了,別讓番人骯髒的膚色滲入你純種的黃色皮膚 . . . . 」[17]

The irony, however, is that Jiatong's dismissal of the possibility that Shicai might entertain a romantic union with Fadiya (Jiatong's remarks about Fadiya's "dirty aboriginal skin" are contrasted not only with his description of Shicai's "pure yellow skin" but also with Yu Jiatong's own obsession with Yili's "pale and translucent" breasts) is directly juxtaposed with Jiatong's practice of encouraging "Hua-native" 華土 unions between the ethnically Chinese men in his brigade and Indigenous women, "so that Communist thought might thereby permeate the entire [Iban] people" 讓共產思想滲透全民.[18]

At one point Yu Jiatong explains to Shicai that "our attempts to learn native language and encourage mixed Hua-native marriages are among the best means we have of helping the aborigines establish themselves. Therefore, I encouraged our troops to marry native women—not to mention the fact that there were very few female comrades in the brigade, and I didn't want to see our troops remain single their entire lives as they fought for revolution" 學習土著語言,華土通婚,是立足土著民族最好的方法。所以我鼓勵隊員娶土著為妻,何況隊中女同志極稀少,我不想看他們打光棍革命一輩子。[19]

In the end, however, Yu Jiatong's practice of encouraging male Communist soldiers to marry local Indigenous women turns out to be one of Dezhong's key sources of resentment and is one of the factors that led to Dezhong's determination to assassinate the Communist guerrilla leader. As Dezhong explains, "The Communist Party encouraged my people to join the insurrection, to serve as a human shield, but it provided us with very inferior equipment. . . . Party members married our women, in order to satisfy their ambition. . . ." 共產黨慫恿我們族人參加武裝鬥爭，做他們肉盾，給我們最差勁的裝備 . . . . 娶我們的女人，為了實現他們的野心 . . . .[20]

Although Dezhong is specifically criticizing Jiatong's use of interethnic marriage to advance the strategic interests of his guerilla brigade, it is unclear whether his critique extends to all interethnic unions, or merely those that are promoted by Communist leaders like Yu Jiatong.

These intersecting issues figuratively come to a head when Shicai and Dezhong stop at Dezhong's family home on their trip back down the Rajang River from the base camp after Yu Jiatong's death. The men are accompanied by a woman named Ling Qiao, who was one of Yu Jiatong's last comrades at the base camp when Shicai arrived (Yu Jiatong describes her as "my final lover in the Yangtze River Brigade" 我揚子部隊最後一個愛人).[21] That night, Shicai, Dezhong, and Ling Qiao sleep in separate rooms, but in the middle of the night a woman enters Dezhong's room and makes love to him in the dark. After they finish making love the woman leaves, and the next morning Shicai reflects that he has no idea whether his visitor was Fadiya or Ling Qiao.

Shicai's uncertainty about which woman visited him that night captures in miniature a larger indeterminacy that haunts the novel. While it is clear that the work is sympathetic to Dezhong's critique of Yu Jiatong's strategic exploitation of Indigenous Iban people (including Yu Jiatong's encouragement of Hua-native intermarriages), it is less clear what the work's attitude is with respect to Shicai's own romantic interest in Dezhong's sister. Although Dezhong himself appears to approve of this relationship, on the surface the romance resembles the interethnic unions that Dezhong condemns elsewhere.

Monkey Cup

Returning to *Monkey Cup*, it turns out that the reason why the protagonist, Zhi—who had been teaching high school English in Taiwan after finishing college—is flying back to Borneo at the beginning of the novel is because he has recently lost his job after having been caught having sex with an underage girl who was working as a prostitute (and who, as it turns out, was also his student). One of the first things Zhi does after arriving in Sarawak, meanwhile, is to go to the hospital to visit his adoptive sister, Limei, who has just given birth to a premature and severely deformed child. In the hospital, Zhi learns that Limei has not yet been updated on the condition of the infant, and even as her doctor is attempting to convince Zhi and his family to give the hospital permission to let the infant die (the doctor reveals that it was badly injured in utero), Limei unexpectedly takes the infant, leaves the hospital, and disappears into the rainforest. After Limei's disappearance, Zhi recruits a young Dayak woman named Yanini—who is the relative of another patient in the same hospital—to help him search for his sister. During the search, which leads them deep into the rainforest, Zhi falls in love with Yanini, although they are continually shadowed by another young man, Badu, who is from Yanini's clan and who resents Zhi's relationship with Yanini because he apparently wants her for himself. At one point, Zhi visits Yanini's family home, and four nights in a row she comes to his room to sleep with him. On the fifth night, however, Yanini makes a point of not coming to his room because her family has a custom that a couple must marry if they sleep together five nights in a row, and she doesn't want to pressure him to marry her. Nevertheless, although Yanini claims that she does not visit him that fifth night, a woman does visit him that night, though Zhi is ultimately unsure of who exactly it is.

This description of Zhi's search for Limei is interspersed with flashbacks to Zhi's family history. The flashbacks trace the family's history back to when, at the turn of the century, the British viceroy appointed Zhi's great-grandfather to manage a local plantation, on the logic that he would be able to communicate with the plantation workers since they were all ethnically Chinese. Later, a gambling partner trying to settle a gambling debt sells the great-grandfather his own daughter, a girl named Xiaohuayin, After Xiaohuayin enters the family, Zhi's grandfather, who at the time was still a young man, falls in love with her—but after Zhi's great-grandfather discovers this relationship and terminates it, the great-grandfather sexually assaults the girl before selling her to a brothel. Not only does the great-grandfather's rape of the young Xiaohuayin mirror Zhi's later sexual relationship with the girl student in Taiwan; that earlier assault also sets in motion a complex chain of events that culminates in one of the novel's key plot twists.

Just as the plot of *Elephant Herd* pivots around a set of silk-cotton trees and the paired figures of vegetarian elephants and carnivorous crocodiles, the crucial plot twist in *Monkey Cup* is similarly grounded on a silk-cotton tree and a different pair of vegetarian and carnivorous species. The silk-cotton tree in *Monkey Cup* is in front of the protagonist's family home, and it overlooks a pen containing a rhinoceros that the family has raised since it was a calf. When the family first found the rhino calf, Zhi's great-grandfather suggested that they should try to capture it alive so they could use it to guard their property. When Zhi's grandfather objected, noting that "it's a wild animal . . . it is already accustomed to being wild" 牠是隻野獸 . . . . 已經野慣了, Zhi's great-grandfather replied, "It's actually better if it is a bit wild. . . . It is still only a calf. It hasn't yet grown hair on its dick and therefore can't yet be considered a true man. Also, I have a way of subduing it" 野一點更好 .... 牠現在只是隻小毛頭。屌上沒毛,不算男子漢。我有辦法順服牠。[22]

The family named the rhino *Zongdu* 總督 (Viceroy), referring to the perception that rhinos rule over the rainforest with the same unrivaled authority with which the British ruled over their colonial territories. For this particular "semi-wild" animal, however, this British colonial name carries an ironic twist, given that the reason why the animal was captured in the first place is precisely because British colonial agents had slaughtered its parents. The fact that the rhino has a name at all, in other words, is a result of the animal's having been subjugated by what at that time was the region's preeminent colonial power. Moreover, the animal is deeply scarred by this earlier encounter; because the Englishman who shot the rhino's parents was disabled, throughout its life the rhino would always attack anyone walking with a limp.

The rhino's status as a symbol of colonial authority is ironic for another reason, because even as rhinos are presented as fearsome animals with no natural predators, they are actually vegetarian. However, even as the novel emphasizes the rhinos' vegetarianism, it simultaneously focuses on the carnivorism of nepenthes plants, also known as pitcher plants. Pitcher plants trap insects in a pitcher-shaped structure filled with digestive fluids, and their nickname, *monkey cup*, derives from the popular belief that monkeys would sometimes drink the liquid inside the pitchers. The novel not only includes numerous descriptions of actual pitcher plants; it also repeatedly references a tattoo of a pitcher plant that Limei has on her arm, though it is not until near the end of the novel that the tattoo's significance is finally revealed. It turns out that, decades earlier, many local women had been sold by their families to work in brothels. After the Japanese invaded and took over the plantation, around thirty of these women decided to escape, fearing that if the Japanese caught them they would force them to work as military sex slaves. The women then followed the Banang River deep into the rainforest and, forced to live off the land,

> they ate raw fruit discarded by bats, birds, and monkeys, as well as rotten fruit that had been masticated by long-haired boars and howling deer. They ate potentially poisonous mushrooms and drank water out of nepenthes pitchers. . . . When food was scarce or unreliable, they relied entirely on this water from nepenthes pitchers to slake their thirst. Eventually, they were taken in by some Dayak families, whereupon they accepted their fate of hard work, and they never again had tender, white skin. These women ultimately married Dayak men and gave birth to a passel of children. To commemorate the day of their mothers' escape, these children all had an image of a nepenthes pitcher tattooed on their arms.

他們採吃蝙蝠鳥猴啃過的生澀水果，撿食長鬚豬吼鹿嚼剩的爛果，冒險吞下可能有毒的蕈菇，喝豬籠草瓶子裡的涼水．．．．食物匱乏而不安全時，完全依賴豬籠草瓶子水解渴充饑。一百天後，她們被幾座長屋的達雅克人收留，結束驚心動魄的逃亡生涯。女人從此口吐達雅克語，言行表裡宛如達雅克，黑壯勤勞，認命幹活，不再細皮白肉。她們下嫁達雅克男人，生下一群子嗣，為了紀念那段逃亡日子，子嗣手臂上都紋著豬籠草瓶子。[23]

The novel explains that Xiaohuayin (the girl who had been sexually assaulted by Zhi's great-grandfather) joined these escaped sex workers, then married a Dayak man and had several children. One of Xiaohuayin's daughters later married an ethnically Chinese man who became one of Zhi's father's gambling partners, and who ultimately sold the child he had with Xiaohuayin's daughter to Zhi's father to settle a gambling debt. The girl in question was none other than Zhi's adoptive sister Limei, whom Zhi's grandfather later sexually assaulted the same way that, as a much younger man, he had previously assaulted Limei's own grandmother, Xiaohuayin. It is this matrilineal lineage of quasi-incestuous violence linking Limei to Xiaohuayin that explains the nepenthes pitcher tattoo on Limei's arm.

Just as *Monkey Cup* traces the region's colonial backdrop through interwoven threads of Zhi's family history, it also marks the degree to which Zhi's own romantic relationship with Yanini is inflected by the region's multiethnic and multilingual colonial legacies. For instance, in an exchange at the end of the novel, the narrative underscores the linguistically hybrid language that Zhi and Yanini use to communicate with one another: "Yanini used English, Chinese, Dayak, and sign language interchangeably, producing a linguistic arrangement that only Zhi could understand. This language contained glimmers of weirdness and a bright red beauty, like a mixed-race child with four different lineages" 亞妮妮英語、華語，達雅克語和手語交互應用，製造出一種只有雉才明白的語言情境，閃爍詭異，鮮紅美麗，彷彿一個有四種血統的混血兒。[24] Not only is the language used in this exchange described as hybrid; the topic under discussion is also one that speaks to issues of intergenerational, interethnic, and even interspecies hybridity.

In particular, it is precisely in this final exchange that Yanini reveals to Zhi more details about the fate of his sister, Limei, after she fled the hospital. Referring to Zhi as "Tai" and to Limei as "Ali," Yanini remarks:

Tai, maybe you didn't know, but Ali actually hated that infant. This is also why, while she was pregnant, she was constantly coming up with ways of tormenting the fetus. The fetus was your grandfather's offspring. Tai, it is not an exaggeration to say that when she took the infant from the hospital, her real intention wasn't to help the infant survive. Instead, she voluntarily nursed an orangutan. After she returned to the longhouse, we buried the infant according to our clan's customs—because, when all is said and done, this was still a child of our nepenthes pitcher clan.

泰，也許你不知道，啊麗其實痛恨嬰兒，這也是為甚麼她懷孕期間想盡辦法折磨嬰兒。嬰兒是你祖父下的種呀。泰，不誇張的說，她從醫院搶走嬰兒，真正的用意就是不想讓他活下去。她情願哺育一頭猩猩。她一回到長屋，我們就把孩子按照家族儀式葬了，再怎麼說，也是我們豬籠草家族的孩子呀。[25]

Here, Yanini not only confirms that Limei had repeatedly tried to kill the child that was the product of an intergenerational sexual assault, she also notes that Limei even took the breast milk that in theory was for her child and used it instead to nurse an infant orangutan she had found in the rainforest.

Limei's act of nursing an infant orangutan in place of her own child marks a moment of symbolic homecoming, not only for Limei—in that her decision to replace the bastard child that was forced upon her by the intergenerational rape with a nonhuman virtual "child" of her own choosing also coincides with her escape from her quasi-colonial position within the Yu household and her return to her original "decolonial" clan—but also for Zhi himself, in that this account of Limei's intimate relationship with the baby orangutan resonates with Zhi's conversation with the Taiwanese woman on the airplane at the beginning of the novel, in which the woman essentially compares Zhi to a "semi-wild" orangutan.

Monkey Cup concludes with two more substitutive inversions. First, after revealing Limei's fate after leaving the hospital, Yanini asks Zhi whether he would be willing to marry her. In response, he asks her if it was she that slept with him on what would have been the fifth night that he was staying at her home. Yanini figuratively shrugs and replies, "It must have been Limei. . . ." 是麗妹吧 . . . .[26] Sidestepping the perverse implications of this statement (in that it suggests that Zhi unwittingly committed virtual incest with the adoptive sister who had already been raped by his grandfather), Zhi replies, "I will marry you. Yanini, in my mind, you are already my wife" 我會娶妳的，亞妮妮。在我心目中，妳已經是我妻子了.[27] This is the final line of the novel.

Or rather, it was the final line of the novel until Zhang published a revised "twentieth-anniversary" edition of the work in 2019. In this new edition, the primary change is that the original "you are already my wife" line has been deleted, and in its place there are two new paragraphs (followed by a block of song lyrics). In the new concluding paragraphs, Badu unexpectedly appears and fatally shoots Zhi with poisoned arrows.[28] The result of this substitution is that, whereas in the novel's original ending Zhi appears to transcend his ancestors' (and his own) previous sexual transgressions, in the revised ending Zhi's murder points to a festering resentment of interethnic unions between Chinese like Zhi and Sarawak's Indigenous peoples.

Just as Shicai's uncertainty about whom he slept with on his final night at Fadiya's family's home—Fadiya or Ling Qiao—emblematizes a larger uncertainty over whether *Elephant Herd* ultimately views Shicai as marking a radical break from his uncle's exploitative practices or instead unwittingly following in his uncle's footsteps, and just as Zhi's uncertainty over whom he slept with on his final night at Yanini's family's home—Yanini or Li Mei—emblematizes a larger uncertainty over whether *Monkey Cup* views Zhi as breaking from his ancestors' pattern of quasi-incestuous abuse or instead unwittingly following in their footsteps, this change in the ending from the first edition of *Monkey Cup* to the second point to a key uncertainty at the heart of both novels: namely, whether the works view their respective protagonists' interethnic romance as a legitimate alternative to the exploitative practices detailed in the flashbacks (as implied by the original ending of *Monkey Cup*) or instead as simply an unwitting extension of the same (as implied by the second ending).

CARLOS ROJAS is professor of Chinese Cultural Studies, Gender, Sexuality, and Feminist Studies (GSF), and Cinematic Arts at Duke University. He is the author, editor, and translator of many volumes, including *Homesickness: Culture, Contagion, and National Transformation in Modern China*.

////////////////////////////////

Notes

1   Zhang, *Houbei*, 30.
2   Parreñas, *Decolonizing Extinction*, 189.
3   Ibid., 6–7.
4   Zhang, *Qunxiang*, 213.
5   Ibid., 214.
6   Ibid., 25.
7   Ibid., 26.
8   Ibid., 102. Similar variations on this formula also appear on pages 9, 95, and 135.
9   Ibid., 33.
10 Chia-ling Mei offers a similar discussion of this passage and of the status of elephants in the novel. See Mei, "Explaining 'Graphs' and Analyzing 'Characters.'"
11 Zhang, *Qunxiang*, 38.
12 Ibid., 127.
13 Ibid., 148.
14 Ibid., 170–71.
15 Ibid., 171.
16 Ibid., 172–73.
17 Ibid., 173.
18 Ibid., 73.
19 Ibid., 150–51.
20 Ibid., 205–6.
21 Ibid., 190.

22 Zhang, *Houbei*, 74.
23 Ibid., 277.
24 Ibid., 314–15.
25 Ibid., 315.
26 Ibid., 317.
27 Ibid.
28 Zhang, *Houbei* (2019), 304–5.

References

Mei, Chia-ling. "Explaining 'Graphs' and Analyzing 'Characters': Zhang Guixing's Novels and Sinophone Literature's Cultural Imaginings and Representational Strategies." In *Reading China against the Grain: Imagining Communities*, edited by Carlos Rojas and Mei-hwa Sung, translated by Carlos Rojas, 128–58. New York: Routledge, 2021.

Parreñas, Juno Salazar. *Decolonizing Extinction: The Work of Care in Orangutan Rehabilitation*. Durham, NC: Duke University Press, 2018.

Zhang Guixing 張貴興. *Houbei* 猴杯 [Monkey Cup]. Rev. ed. Taipei: Lianjing, 2019.

Zhang Guixing 張貴興. *Houbei* 猴杯 [Monkey Cup]. 2nd ed. Taipei: Lianhe wenxue, 2000.

Zhang Guixing 張貴興. *Qunxiang* 群象 [Elephant Herd]. Taipei: Shibao wenhua, 1998.

TOM G. HOOGERVORST

Urban Life in Two 1920s Sino-Malay Poems

ABSTRACT Batavia, the capital of the former Netherlands Indies, was home to a popular Chinese-run printing industry that published works in the Malay vernacular. Two 1920s Sino-Malay poems reveal firsthand accounts of the city's vibrant sociocultural landscape. *Sair park* (The Poem of the Park) narrates everyday life at the parks of the colonial metropole, including the opportunities these urban spaces provide for illicit encounters between men and women. *Pantoen tjapgome* (The Quatrain of the Lantern Festival) describes the festivities of an important holiday that increasingly drifted away from its religious origins and became a public spectacle attended by people from different ethnicities. Together, these poems provide intricate and otherwise unavailable details of everyday life in late-colonial Java. They also reveal some of the anxieties faced by its Chinese-descended population, including the specter of cultural loss and unwarranted interaction between young people from different genders and racial backgrounds. Yet despite this apparent rejection of an Indies-style hybrid modernity, an examination of the language of these poems—Batavia Malay with a substantial influence from Hokkien, the Sinitic variety historically spoken by many Chinese-Indonesian families—demonstrates that they are best approached as examples of Chinese-Indonesian acculturation.

KEYWORDS Netherlands Indies, Sino-Malay, Batavia, poetry, everyday life

Introduction

From the early twentieth century, Batavia, now Jakarta, offered an exciting world of entertainment and urban amenities.[1] It was home to a vibrant print culture in which Chinese entrepreneurs played an outsized role. This group was remarkably plurilingual. The ancestral language of most Indies Chinese families was Hokkien,[2] yet few could write in it. Literacy was primarily sought in Malay, Indonesia's lingua franca. Many Chinese also spoke the regional language of the town they inhabited. In addition, Mandarin-medium schools opened their doors for Chinese pupils from 1900, and Dutch-medium schools opened from 1908. In the printed domain, however, Malay remained the predominant language of choice. This so-called Sino-Malay tradition provides fascinating glimpses into the history of the everyday. Chinese-authored newspapers, novels, and poems were rife with societal dilemmas revolving around the perceived incompatibility of East and West, disagreements between China- and Indies-oriented groups, changing gender norms, and the bugbear of cultural attrition.[3] Linguistically, these sources

PRISM: THEORY AND MODERN CHINESE LITERATURE • 19:2 • SEPTEMBER 2022
DOI 10.1215/25783491-9966747 • © 2022 LINGNAN UNIVERSITY

FIGURE 1. Sirenepark. *Sin po wekelijksche editie* 1924, vol. 76, p. 390.

utilized the Batavian (Betawi) dialect rather than standard Malay as promoted by the colonial government. This Malay vernacular was saturated with influences from Hokkien. As neither Hokkien nor any of the Malay dialects spoken in Java enjoyed high prestige, they were able to produce a hybrid idiom, at a safe distance from the linguistic purism of colonial bureaucrats and elitist literati.[4]

This article unearths two Sino-Malay poems that grapple with the interplay of traditions, creolization, and urban modernity among Batavia's Chinese community. I will foreground their linguistic hybridity as a crucible to understand Sino-Batavian worldviews on a grassroots level. The first poem, *Sair park* (The Poem of the Park), was published in 1920. It captures and criticizes the cultural life of an unnamed park in Mangga Besar, which must have been Sirenepark—historically located near what is now the intersection of Jl. Hayam Wuruk and Jl. Raya Mangga Besar—on the basis of landmarks mentioned in the poem (fig. 1). The poet's flippant portrayal of the social ills of parks is echoed in the Netherlands Indies press. On Sirenepark specifically, Batavia's newspapers inform us that it served from 1917 as a place for performances, shows, and gatherings. Its closely packed food stalls repeatedly caused fires, while its large crowds attracted crime, sexual harassment, and street fights. The park was eventually transformed into residential housing in 1953.[5]

The second text, *Pantoen tjapgome* (The Quatrain of the Lantern Festival), written by Tjiong Soen Liang and published by the printing house Goan Hong 源豐, centers on a popular Sino-Southeast Asian holiday celebrated fifteen days after the Lunar New Year (*sinthjia* 新正, *imlek* 陰曆). In the Indies, as elsewhere in maritime Southeast Asia, this holiday was known as *tjapgome* 十五暝 or *goansiauw* 元宵. It was originally a religious celebration during which the deity Toapekong 大伯公 was paraded through Chinatown, accompanied by music and performances. In Batavia, however, these pious foundations soon gave way to large, multiethnic crowds attending the festivities chiefly to have a good time, dress up, eat, drink, spend, and dance through the city's main streets.[6] At the end of the day, then, attending the Lantern Festival in 1920s Batavia was not so different from visiting the city's notorious parks. Along with Malay theater (*bangsawan*), the cinema, and other locations where men and women could arrange illicit encounters, these sites were widely perceived as a threat to traditional notions of propriety.

In three sections, this article discusses the stylistic features of the two poems, their depiction of Batavia's urban culture, and the convergence of religious practices and popular entertainment. Combined, the sections provide insight into a late-colonial Southeast Asian world as experienced by two ethnic Chinese poets. Both authors are obsessed with cultural and linguistic markers of Chineseness, yet they simultaneously testify to a thoroughly hybridized, pluralistic metropole where different people encountered, befriended, and clashed with each other on a daily basis. The Sino-Batavian cultural landscape was firmly entrenched in the local, yet it was subtly oriented toward China through evocations of a glorious, if threatened, heritage.

Sino-Malay Poetry

Chinese authors who adopted Malay also typically embraced its literary aesthetics. Popular genres such as the *sair* and *pantoen* frequently show up in Sino-Malay newspapers and novels. They were also published separately or compiled with short stories or other poems. Narrative poetry could be read individually or performed with various musical instruments and vocal styles. To be successful, it had to be entertaining and funny. The genre offered considerably more freedom than literary fiction or journalism. As will be shown below, poets could switch to a different language to make controversial points. Our first author nevertheless felt the need to write under a pseudonym, even though the second one, who used his full name, arguably addressed more sensitive issues. Throughout his poem, Tjiong Soen Liang ridiculed existing and presumably easily identifiable people.

The rather unwieldy full title of the first text is *Poem of the Park, or the Behavior of Playboys and Hussies, Followed by the Poem of Tan Keng Siang: A Very Appealing Poem, Which Has Really Happened in Batavia*. It is followed by the clarification that "this poem can be read by men and women of all races, because in addition to being entertaining, it also contains advice for all people in the present time." This twenty-four-page publication narrates the circumstances of parks through a highly entertaining, rather moralistic diatribe replete with gender expectations and imagined ways these expectations are under attack by

FIGURE 2. *Tjapgome* in Batavia. *Sin po wekelijksche editie* 1941, vol. 933, p. 24.

parks, cinemas, and other locations frequented by people of different ethnicities. Sirenepark is described in detail, including its electric lights, ticket booths, guards, crowds, traffic, food, performances, music, contests, and especially its visitors—young and old—who loiter there in search of love. As was common in the late-colonial period, actors and actresses associated with Istanbul-style theater (*komedie stamboel*) are identified as a particular social ill. Visitors to parks, the poem concludes, risk losing their money and good name. *Sair park* ends by introducing a follow-up *sair* on Batavia's infamous criminal Tan Keng Siang, whose copious exploits deserve a separate study.

Tjiong Soen Liang's eighty-page *Pantoen tjapgome* is subtitled: "Very nice, funny, and entertaining, so that those who read it will certainly feel themselves part of the *goansiauw* celebrations in Batavia." The poem consists of six sections dealing with the nature of the holiday, the festivities leading up to it, various performances, the evening of *tjapgome*, the criminals operating during the event, and the thrills of dressing up, respectively. It relates how the festivities have changed from the 1910s (*tjapgwani* 十外年), especially due to the influence of Indigenous people. Reminiscent of Sirenepark, the festival was thronged with pleasure seekers from all classes, ages, and ethnicities (fig. 2). As the poem informs us in a half-Malay, half-Hokkien sentence, money was spent without calculating (*oewang dipake dengen bo-shoei-siauw* [無算數]). The author also mentions religiously motivated participants, such as people burning incense, only to add in jest that many of them secretly wished for luck in their gambling pursuits. The most eccentric partygoers are discussed last: people wearing masks and costumes. As we read, their boisterous dancing in the streets generated public disdain and annoyance.

The linguistic features of *Sair park* and *Pantoen tjapgome* illustrate the plurilingualism of Sino-Malay printing, colloquial speech, and popular performances. People conversant in Java's vernacular Malay often had trouble understanding the classical language used by performers from Sumatra and Malaya and promoted by the colonial government.[7] As the irony of history has it, the situation is now reversed; many lexical details in Sino-Malay publications are opaque for those schooled in standard Indonesian. While Betawi Malay can still be heard among Jakarta's original inhabitants, the specific slang of the 1920s and especially the code-mixing with Hokkien makes both poems rather inaccessible for today's readers. In *Sair park*, for example, well-groomed dandies were described in a fascinating type of Hokkien-saturated Malay:

The guests chatted while drinking tea	Sie tetamoe khongkoh [講古] bari minoem te [茶]
Their trim clothes made them more stylish	Berpakean netjis tamba perlente
Women and men dressed like teenagers	Prampoean lelaki seperti tjoete [子弟]
So that all observers found them attractive	Soepaia tjiong lang khoa oebakte [總人看有目地][8]

Somewhat further along, the poem introduces a Chinese lady who keeps returning to the park to watch *bangsawan* performances, squandering much of her money in the process. She confides to her friend that she has fallen in love with a female performer. The following passage, containing her friend's reply, is noteworthy for multiple reasons. Thematically it is a rare example of a lesbian relationship being discussed in an early Malay text, even though the elements giving it away as such are in Hokkien.[9] Stylistically it is an uncommon example of a satirical quatrain (*pantoen sindiran*) embedded within a *sair*. Linguistically, as mentioned, most of the words are from Hokkien, even though the stanzas fully adhere to the poetic conventions of Malay. The first two lines foreshadow the impossible love that is divulged in the last two lines:

A Suzhounese sash is made of woven silk	Angkin [紅巾] sotjioe [蘇州] boeatan pangsi [紡絲]
Dried bean curd is cut inside a tea cup	Potong tauwkhoa [豆乾] didalem tee-auw [茶甌]

| Your eyes are red, your heart is yearning | Baktjioe ang-ang simkhoa shiosi [目睭紅紅心肝惜死] |
| One day without seeing her feels unbearable[10] | Tje-djit bo-khoa simkhoa tong bee tiauw [一日無看心肝擋嘪牢][11] |

Pantoen tjapgome contains a single instance of Hakka influence. In a passage about young men sporting chic walking canes—which incidentally came in handy against attacking dogs or in street brawls—it is added that some rather unpolished individuals brought along homemade substitutes. The Hakka expression *mojoeng* 無用 (useless) epitomizes the relentless verdict of the local fashion police:

There was something else that raised laughter:	Ada lagi jang menerbitkan tertawa
Some canes were made from umbrella shafts	Sebab toengketnja dari gagang pajoeng
As these contraptions were found wanting	Kerna bawaän begitoe dianggap katjiwa
Many Hakka people uttered: "Useless"	Banjak orang-orang Khe [客] membilang mojoeng [無用][12]

Such gems of plurilingual richness would have certainly contributed to the popularity of Sino-Malay poetry when the community still had knowledge of Hokkien and in some cases Hakka. In present-day academia, these primary sources remain somewhat uncomfortably lodged between Malay and Chinese experts. It is clear, however, that the in-betweenness oozing from these texts provides some tangible instantiations of Sino-Southeast Asian lifeworlds from bygone times.

Metropolitan Life

Popular theater—including its music, its comedy, and even the tensions it introduced or exacerbated—has profoundly influenced Indonesia's urban life since the 1890s.[13] Sino-Malay poetry, too, was obsessed—not infrequently in a condescending way—with the impact of metropolitan and European(ized) lifestyles. Both poems describe Batavia's hectic traffic and vibrant street life. *Sair park* elaborates on the electric lights of Sirenepark, its firework shows, and the chaos of the cars and horse-drawn carriages, while *Pantoen tjapgome* recounts how the streets were closed off for vehicles, with policemen on guard to horsewhip drivers who flouted the rules. They were tasked to empty the streets in preparation for the holiday, which occasioned a parade of festively adorned people and decorated vehicles. The highlight was a spectacular replica of a ship, complete with a captain, crew, and flags.

As mentioned previously, Batavia's *tjapgome* celebrations had largely drifted away from the religious fundaments they still possessed elsewhere. Nevertheless, the poem does not neglect to mention the rituals leading up to the event. It describes women carrying incense across seven bridges to have their desires fulfilled. In the poet's imagination, most young women wished for a husband, older ones for their husbands to become successful, and the oldest ones simply to win at gambling.[14] In addition:

The eve of the ninth is even busier	Maleman Tjekauw [一九] terlebi rame
The large streets are filled with spectators	Djalanan besar penoeh penonton
So that even people who are almost blind	Hingga orang-orang jang tjeme [青瞑]
All come out and watch it	Pada kaloear aken menonton
The date mentioned above	Tanggal terseboet diatas ini
Is the evening to pray to God: Honor the Heavens	Maleman sembajang Allah, Khingthikong [敬天公]
Many of the devotees are husbands and wives	Banjak antaranja laki bini
Going out to burn incense in the Chinese temple	Pergi tiamhio [點香] karoema Toapekkong [大伯公][15]

Batavia's complex demographics constitute another central thread. Among the city's inhabitants, we read about the Chinese community (*tjina*, *tionghoa* 中華, *thunglang* 唐人), the local-born, acculturated Chinese (*pranakan*, *baba*), Indigenous people (*boemipoetra*, *hoana* 番仔), Batavian Muslims (*selam*), Javanese (*djawa*), Sundanese (*soenda*), Bantenese (*banten*), Malays (*melajoe*), Europeans (*olanda*, *blanda*, *holan* 荷蘭), and Arabs (*arab*). To enter Sirenepark, Indigenous people paid 6 cents, Chinese and Arabs 12 cents, and Europeans 36 cents.[16] The Lantern Festival attracted many Indigenous people from outside Batavia, who hoped to make some money by busking, selling food, or—for some women—dancing with male spectators (*najoeb*). Financial hardship made these people quite determined. Their ability to commute on foot and sleep on the streets without mats, all while bringing their families along, was rarely imitated by others.[17] At the same time, as the author points out with some astonishment, many people did not behave according to what might be expected from their ethnicity:

If that had been all, everything would still be fine	Tapi begitoe sadja, masi tra'mengapa
But some people forget which race they belong to	Ada djoega jang loepa kabangsaännja
They confidently dress like others, changing their appearance	Brani toeroet menjamar, menoekar roepa
That's the sort of party the Lantern Festival is	Seperti Tjapgome itoe ada pestanja[18]

The habit of adopting the attire of others will be discussed again later. It should also be noted that various items of dress were worn by all ethnicities, marking a contrast with earlier episodes of Dutch colonialism in which people were required to dress according to their ethnicity. For women, the transethnic fashion of the 1920s included an embroidered bodice (*koetang*), a lace blouse (*kabaja*), a batik cloth, a well-groomed chignon (*konde*) sometimes stuffed with fake hair (*tjemara*), and various types of jewelry.[19] Men made similar efforts to look stylish, donning a hat, glasses, shoes, an open jacket, necktie, shirt, and walking cane.[20]

Batavia's food culture was equally heterogenous. In the city's parks, one could enjoy low-priced traditional refreshments such as rice-flour cakes steamed in bamboo (*poetoe bamboe*), mutton satay (*sate kambing*), and fried rice crust (*kerak*) alongside fancy international fare like beefsteak and ice cream. At the center of Sirenepark stood a popular restaurant built in the form of a ship and aptly named the SS Sirene.[21] We encounter a similar culinary extravaganza at the Lantern Festival, with satay, noodles (*bahmi* 肉麵), fruit-and-vegetable salad (*roedjak*), jelly (*ogio* 薁蕘), and many other dishes on offer. The all-time favorite of *ketoepat*, rice cakes cooked in coconut leaves and often served with roasted chicken, could also be found in 1920s Batavia. Needless to say, restaurants, food booths, and street vendors optimally profited from the festivities. Beer was also served, and I assume this beverage was chiefly drunk by men, since the presence of intoxicated women would have certainly elicited a snide remark or two from the poem's author. The atmosphere is characterized matter-of-factly:

Most food booths are well set up	Kabanjakan waroeng bagoes diatoer
They wait for friends and servants to arrive	Menoenggoe datengnja kawan dan batoer
Beer is poured, glasses are collided	Bier die toeang glas kabentoer
People get giddy and wobble around	Soeda poesing djalan nelantoer[22]

The generous flow of alcohol, served at establishments employing attractive female staff and hosting theater performances, not infrequently led to controversial behavior. At this point it will no longer surprise us that the author of *Sair park* considered the locale of his poem a bastion of drunkenness, vice, and moral degeneracy. In his eyes, ladies of questionable reputation included the staff of food establishments, actresses, female dancers, clandestine prostitutes, and of course regular "modern girls." Even the most civilized men and women could purportedly lose their way amid such immorality, causing them to tarnish their good name, jeopardize their marriage, and throw away their life (or at least their life savings):

Because they are driven by lust	Lantaran ditoeroet hawanja napsoe
They start to behave dishonestly	Djadi berboeat hati jang palsoe
Husbands and wives end up in trouble	Soeamie dan istri mendjadi roesoe
As the Park causes them to mess up	Lantaran Park jang bikin gouwsoe [誤事][23]

The language of illicit sex was steeped in metaphors. Sundanese prostitutes, known as sisters from the Priangan region (*atjeuk Preangan*), flocked to Batavia's parks and plastered their faces with thick layers of powder, giving them a rather terrifying, pock-marked appearance. For this reason, people facetiously referred to them as speckled kingfishers (*tengkek boerik*).[24] Other creative allegories included "the park is like a net" and "there is a food booth with only women." At the latter place, patrons were considerably more interested in the female company than its limited culinary options. The excerpt below is fraught with innuendo, from the "chicken" on offer—which is a derogatory way of referring to sexually available women—to the way men walk home after encountering the suppliers of their gratification:

The food booth has rice cakes and roasted chicken	Kaloe die waroeng katoepat lah ajam panggang
Those who come there rarely remain isolated	Jang dateng djarang tempatnja renggang
If they grab hold of one of the random women	Prampoean sembarangan kaloe dipegang
The men end up walking with their legs slightly apart	Nistjaja sie lelaki djalan'nja ngegang[25]

During the Lantern Festival, too, otherwise respectable men were reportedly driven crazy by European dances, music, and women dousing themselves in perfume.[26] As the poet informs us, there was a specific method for approaching prostitutes, which required buying a so-called mistress flower (*kembang Njai-njai*) and presenting it to the lady in question. Insiders who knew this code would recognize women wearing such a flower as (hired) prostitutes. For this reason, prostitutes were designated in Batavian Malay as living flowers (*boenga-berdjiwa*). *Pantoen tjapgome* offers the following description:

If he brings a prostitute along	Dengen bawa si Boenga-berdjiwa
The pleasure becomes more appetizing	Plesiran itoe djadi bertamba kwipi [開脾]
While walking, chatting, and laughing	Sembari djalan mengomong dan tertawa
As well as attaching his nose to her cheeks	Dengen tempelin djoega idoeng kapipi[27]
. . .	
Those men, as the readers know	Lelaki itoe, seperti pembatja taoe
Intend only to accompany girls	Tida laen niatnja, membawa tjabo [查某]
Who go back and forth like boats	Jang moendar-mandir seperti praoe
Ready to be entered by vile men	Boeat toempangin lelaki jang tjerobo[28]

Another routine activity during Batavia's *tjapgome* celebrations was cross-dressing (*menjamar*), which took place across the divides of gender, ethnicity, and social class. Such a carnivalesque reprieve from colonial strictures—neatly confined to a specific occasion and location—is hardly surprising in view of Batavia's relentless social stratification. The Lantern Festival was not the only instance of this. Malay theater, for instance, has likewise been described as "a place for trying out what it felt like to walk around in the clothes of another person."[29] The *Pantoen tjapgome* describes in detail how people sought to achieve this. For children, glasses and fake moustaches were sold.[30] Some disguised themselves as the popular masked villain Zigomar, while others dressed up as hajjis, Javanese people, Dayaks, Europeans, Japanese, and Indian Muslims (*kodja*). In the latter case, they blackened their skin. Such minstrel performances were also popular among the Malays of Penang, who impersonated Africans, Chinese, Indians, and other ethnicities during the *boria* celebrations.[31]

I have not come across photographic evidence of the habit, but we find the following description in *Pantoen tjapgome*:

There are also people who daub their face	Ada djoega jang pérong moeka
With ink or the black residue from a pan	Dengen bak [墨] atawa pantat koeali
Such types of disguises are worn freely	Penjamaran begini dilakoekan dengen merdika
By Muslims and Chinese, neither one excepted	Selam dan Tjina, tida terkatjoeali[32]

In addition, able-bodied people walked around as though disabled or suffering from hernias, while rich people dressed like street vendors or servants. Some wore costumes that could partly be set on fire, horrifying those around them. The poem's longest treatise on people dressing in disguise was on men cross-dressing as women and vice versa. *Pantoen tjapgome* describes in great detail men wearing women's clothes, jewels, and make-up while stuffing their bodice with a pair of coconuts. In turn, their female counterparts donned jackets, Dutch trousers (*Holanko* 荷蘭褲), shoes, hats, and suits. In both cases, the transformation was surprisingly convincing, and sometimes only the shape of their buttocks or the way they walked gave them away.[33]

Such unruly affairs, filled with public singing, dancing, drinking, and shouting, often caused unrest. The vast sea of people washed up numerous sweaty, pushy, touchy men, whose conduct could lead to fights when the victim's family came to retaliate.[34] According to *Pantoen tjapgome*, some men exploited the anonymity of their costumes to grope women. Men dancing with other men was considered a lesser offense, as nobody ended up hurt:

Or men dancing with other men	Atawa menandak lelaki sama lelaki
Which should not be condemned	Itoe masi tida boleh ditjela
It's really what they wish to do	Sebagimana memang ada dikahendaki
So nobody can blame them for it	Siapa djoega tra'bisa kasi sala[35]

A greater threat were the brazen packs of thieves, pickpockets, jewel-snatchers, and brawlers attending the celebrations, many of whom were from out of town. Women showing off their wealth risked having their hairpins pulled out from behind or their diamond ear studs ripped from their ears, after which the culprits vanished into the darkness.[36] Similar malefactions were common in Batavia's parks. The visitors to Sirenepark, for instance, are warned about bike theft and groups of men looking for fights.[37]

Cultural Hybridity

Batavia's parks and *tjapgome* celebrations offered a platform for European, Chinese, Indigenous, and especially creolized forms of entertainment. People competed against each other in singing, stand-up comedy, playing the *gambang* (a xylophone-like instrument), and *krontjong* music.[38] The latter was a Portuguese-influenced type of music that had become extremely popular among Batavia's Eurasian lower classes from the 1880s. By the 1920s, the proliferation of *krontjong* competitions (*concourses*) heralded a professionalization of this once-marginalized genre.[39] Batavia's dazzling amalgam of Chinese, Indigenous, and European influences revealed itself in greatest detail during the *tjapgome* celebrations. Four days before the actual festival, groups of people performed lion dances (*barongsaij*),[40] dragon dances (*langliong* 弄龍), and a children's pageant about maritime creatures (*katjio*).[41] The origins of *katjio* or *katjio-katjioan*, which is no longer practiced or remembered, are obscure. Author Nio Joe Lan defines it as an enactment by children of sea life, including shells, shrimp, and lobsters made from cotton and wooden trusses, illuminated from within by a candle, with each creature carried by one person, and with the performance accompanied by a tambour and cymbals.[42]

Additional entertainment was provided by *tandjidor* for 4.5 (*sitoenphoa* 四盾半) or 5 guilders (*gotoen* 五盾) per evening. These open-air brass bands could be hired to march in rows while beating their drums.[43] Their music has remained popular in the Jakarta area, especially for Chinese or Islamic processions.[44] Another genre, known as *dangsoe*, enjoyed equal popularity during the Lantern Festival. Its creole Portuguese name reveals that it was originally a form of dance that later acquired acrobatic elements. Accompanied by percussion and punctuated by clowns, the show consisted of tightrope-walking with umbrellas, barrel-walking, roman ladders, Russian swings, jugglers, various balancing acts, and strongmen. The *dangsoe* performers derived their income from the fees they managed to collect,[45] which was undoubtedly the case for most other genres too.

A comparable spectacle was provided by troupes of illusionists, known in Batavia as *komedie hongyang*. The most popular ones hailed from Fengyang in Anhui, China. This county, known to Java's Hokkien speakers as Hong-Yang 鳳陽, apparently gave the genre its name. The performers were famed for their knowledge of magic tricks, medicinal plasters (*koyo* 膏藥) for curing injuries (*tio-siang* 著傷), and combat skills.[46] They started their show with various demonstrations of martial arts, including fighting with a staff (*toeia* 槌仔), a sword, and a trident (*shatje* 三叉), as well as empty-handed.[47] The following stanzas sing praise of their expertise:

People who understand the intri-cacies of fighting	Orang jang mengarti ilmoe poekoelan
Immediately know that these martial arts are "filled" [with inner power]	Lantas taoe: koentauwnja [拳頭 nja] ini berisi
Judging from their steps as well as their motions	Baek diliat tindakannja atawa djalan
Everything looks great, especially their horse stance	Semoea bagoes, teroetama mema-sangnja behsi [馬勢][48]

Other extraordinary skills performed by the *hongyang* artists included throwing balls and intercepting them with their heads, catching knives, and smashing their faces into a bench, seemingly without pain.[49] This, according to the author, was surely the result of Daoist magic (*hoatsoet* 法術). Next on the schedule were women performing a complicated series of fighting techniques, followed by balancing acts and feats of magic. Such public displays of strength and endurance were quite common in late-colonial Batavia. The Sino-Malay periodical *Sin po* 新報, for example, published a photo of a martial artist lying on a nail bed—the texts uses the Hokkien-Malay blend *djok* [褥] *pakoe*—with a heavy stone placed on his chest (fig. 3). In the background we see a selection of traditional Chinese blades, which would have undoubtedly been used for demonstrations in public parks and during festivals.

The enthusiasm Tjiong Soen Liang displayed for the above performances was anything but easily acquired. We discover his critical side when he describes the *chingay* procession (*tjeungge* 粧藝), which recreated scenes from Chinese theater through costumes and moving platforms. This tradition and its name originated from the Zhangzhou 漳州 area, where it was still practiced in the late nineteenth century.[50] In Batavia, it was said to have lost much of its glory by the 1930s.[51] It survived in Penang and Singapore, but it was stripped of its religious elements in the former city[52] and of its creolized elements in the latter.[53] As the author of *Pantoen tjapgome* explains, the quality of a *tjeungge* was assessed not only by the costumes, but also by the specific stories (*hiboen* 戲文) that were enacted. The first platform of the parade represented the fighting match (*piboe* 比武) between the general Xue Rengui (Sin Djin Koeij 薛仁貴) and the Korean warlord Yeon Gaesomun (Kaij Souw Boen 蓋蘇文), who kidnapped the Tang dynasty emperor Taizong (Lie Si Bin 李世民) in the popular story *Xue Rengui Clears the East* (Sie Djin Koei tjeng tang 薛仁貴徵東). The second contained a scene from another well-known tale, *Investiture of the Gods* (Hong sin 封神), in which a fisherman was summoned by a monarch. Aficionados of Chinese theater would have recognized the latter as King Wen of Zhou (Tjioe Boen Ong 周文王), enlisting the

FIGURE 3. A demonstration of Chinese martial arts. *Sin po wekelijksche editie* 1932, vol. 505, p. 563.

brilliant strategist Jiang Ziya (Kiang Tjoe Ge 姜子牙) in his army. The third platform depicted a battle from the *Five Tigers Conquering the South* (Ngo houw peng lam 五虎平南), in which the legendary general Di Qing (Tek Tjeng 狄青) was aided by the Princess of Eight Treasures (Pat Po Kiongtjioe 八寶公主). All three performances used carbide lamps for illumination. The military troops were played by children, and the platforms were flanked by flag soldiers (*tjaijkipeng* 彩旗兵) and people carrying lanterns (*teng* 燈).

The author was considerably less impressed by the dragon that followed, complaining that it was too short, since nobody manned its head and tail. Equally disappointing were the Eight Gods (Pat Sian 八仙), only three of whom had bothered to show up. The troupe from Weltevreden was reportedly the worst and consisted of only one person sitting on a platform. As the poet clarified, they only participated to "receive candles" (*sioe* [收] *lilin*). This remark becomes understandable when we realize that *tjeungge* performers could be paid with two red wax candles instead of money. For this reason, each group tasked one of its members to collect these valuable candles with a carrying stick.[54] The final troupes, too, were said to be atrocious. They lacked beautiful costumes, interesting stories, and proper illumination, other than some people carrying torches. The culprit behind this eyesore was a local big shot who sponsored a number of ugly *tjeungge* every year simply because nobody stopped him. Many spectators quickly closed their doors to avoid his abominations—and the payment expected for the dubious privilege of watching them—yet those who could not escape in time had to resign themselves to their fate:

Unless people are caught by surprise	Katjoeali kaloe jang soeda kapergokan
Then they're forced to put up with it	Apa boleh boeat, trima djoega
They think: a pair of candles is no big deal	Sebab pikir: lilin sapasang bosiangkan [無相干]
But next evening we have to watch out	Tapi lain malem moesti didjaga[55]

The next spectacle described in *Pantoen tjapgome* is introduced as a popular type of Chinese theater known as *tengwako* 唐話歌, which narrated the dalliance between a married lady and a juvenile playboy. Also spelled as *t'ang hua ko*, this performance type became obsolete in the 1930s. It reportedly featured children among its actors, a little painted drum among its instruments, and a boat made of bamboo and paper used for a stage.[56] According to the poet of *Pantoen tjapgome*, it was difficult for the producers of this genre to find Chinese women for the leading role, so they often recruited Chinese-looking Indigenous women. The latter incidentally accepted lower payment. The musical ensemble was also of a decidedly mixed nature:

The percussion chiefly consisted of the *gambang*	Tetaboehannja, teroetamanja adalah gambang
Followed by a flute, a standing drum, and a coconut fiddle	Berikoet soeling, keplek, dan teehian [提弦]
Their melodious sounds evoked anxious feelings	Soearanja merdoe, menerbitkan rasa bimbang
Enhanced by the three-stringed lute and two-stringed fiddle	Katambahan pengaroenja samhian [三弦] dan gihian [二弦][57]

The Malay *bangsawan* theater also embraced the tastes of its diverse Batavian audiences. By the 1920s, most of its actors were Indigenous men and women. While historically known for their beautiful costumes, the poet regretfully observed that many troupes had economized on their attire, wearing standard clothes also used for classical Javanese tales. The Chinese story *Five Rats Create Havoc in the Eastern Capital* [Ngo tji loan tang khia 五鼠鬧東京] remained an all-time favorite. The most popular Malay stories were *Hikajat toekang minjak* [The Tale of the Oil Vendor], *Nori dan bajan* [The Lorry and the Parakeet], *Si boeta* [The Blind Man], and *Tjerita ikan rawa* [The Story of the Fish in the Marsh], about which little can be found in the wider literature. A cautionary tale was that of Njonja Tjan Hoei, a Chinese lady who put too much trust in local witchcraft (*kongtauw* 降頭), guilelessly squandering her fortune and eventually assimilating into the Indigenous population (*djiphoana* 入番仔). Her fate revealed society's broader worries about the loss of Chinese values, in which convergence—either with Indonesians or Westerners—constituted a persistent concern for the Sino-Batavian community.

Pantoen tjapgome lists with some hesitation a proliferation of Indigenous genres that found their way into the celebrations, such as *wajang senggol*, *topeng*, and *oebroek*, whose performers travelled to Batavia from the countryside. According to the author, only a few types of entertainment could be considered fully Chinese:

Actually, the only true Chinese performances	Sabetoelnja permaenan Tionghoa [中華] jang sedjati
Are the *tjeungge*, the dragon dance, and the sea creatures	Tjoema Tjeungge [粧藝], Langliong [弄龍] dan Katjio-katjioan
Those are from the Tang dynasty, of emperor Li Zhi	Jaitoe di djaman Tong [唐], Hongtee [皇帝] Lie Ti [李治]
Who organized Lantern Festivals to create festivity	Jang adaken Goansiauw [元宵] boeat keramean
He also organized qilin ["unicorn"] and lion dances	Djoega diadaken Kilin [麒麟] dan Barongsaij
Tengwako, *Sinpeh*, and other such things	Tengwako [唐話歌], Sinpeh [新琵] dan laen-laen sebaginja
Including martial arts and Maitreya lion dances	Seperti Koentauw [拳頭] atawa Bilek Langsaij [彌勒弄獅]
So that Chang'an was filled with action	Hingga kota Tiangan [長安] teramat ramenja[58]

The author was probably unaware that many of the genres he traced to Tang China were in fact specific to the Indies and in some cases lacked counterparts outside Batavia. The genre called *sinpeh* 新琵, for example, was the invention of the Batavian organization Ngo Hong Lauw 伍鳳樓, which promoted traditional Chinese music but incorporated Javanese instruments like the *gambang* and recruited local-born boys and girls. These young artists memorized their lines in Mandarin, even though they chiefly spoke Malay at home.[59] Despite such examples of cross-pollination, the *Pantoen tjapgome* displays undertones of regret about the loss of Chinese traditions, the Westernization of social interaction, and the prominent role of Indigenous people in Chinatown's festivities.

Concluding Remarks

Sair park and *Pantoen tjapgome* are relevant to broader discussions on Sino-Southeast Asian experiences. Despite their indissoluble Hokkien veneer, these texts equally belong to the vernacular Malay tradition. Like Sino-Malay poetry in general, they chiefly followed the literary aesthetics of maritime Southeast Asia, albeit with strong predilections for popular entertainment rather than high art. At the same time, they touched upon classical Chinese tales, the way these tales were remembered and performed in late-colonial Batavia, and the way such performances entered the public realm. As such, the poems connected the written with the performed word and fused the Chinese cultural realm with that of Indonesia. This hybridity is substantiated by the very idiom in which the poems were written, which deliberately mixed the colloquial Malay of Batavia with Hokkien. In that sense, the authors were performing what they criticized: a hybrid, rather chaotic praxis in which languages, cultural traditions, and value systems intermixed. The exploratory, border-crossing nature of these poems belied society's widespread concerns about modernization and a perceived lack of order.

Both poems offer lively accounts of a creolized culture that flourished in 1920s Batavia. Of the city's Portuguese-inspired forms of entertainment, only *krontjong* has received sustained academic attention. Many, if not most, of the Chinese traditions described in the poems show far-ranging processes of localization. Lion dances, for example, were known under different names across Java and coexisted in some regions with Indigenous versions. The *chingay* (or *tjeungge*) procession, now restricted to some parts of the Malay Peninsula, was historically well-known in the Indies, and *Pantoen tjapgome* contains an important account of it. The *komedie hongyang* and the long forgotten children's game of *katjio* were presumably unique to the Indies. Other locally rooted genres, such as *sinpeh* and *tengwako*, relied on Indigenous or mixed-race performers. Such hybrid art forms have been somewhat shunned by the otherwise prolific academics from late-colonial times on whose shoulders much contemporary scholarship rests. Sino-Malay poetry, then, offers vistas into everyday life not otherwise acquired.

The poets indeed intended to give a realistic portrayal of Batavia's parks and its Lantern Festival. In doing so, they supplied the Indies Chinese with popular entertainment, which—due to its preponderance of Hokkienisms—must have been rather opaque to people from other backgrounds. Their deftly crafted vignettes also provide cultural-historical value for today's scholars. They complement textual sources of a more serious character on such issues as social tensions, entrance fares and societal expectations that differed from one race and/or gender to another, and the widespread fear of losing one's identity under colonialism. The inconspicuous niche of poetry and the arcane practice of language-mixing afforded scattered opportunities to address society's taboos, including cross-dressing and same-sex relations. Even though both authors approached Batavia's cultural hybridity with a degree of ambivalence, echoing broader sentiments within their community, their works deserve be treated as noteworthy instances of Sino-Indonesian acculturation. The echoes they encapsulate of a unique creolized culture merit academic attention and, arguably, cross-community pride.

TOM G. HOOGERVORST is senior researcher at the Royal Netherlands Institute of Southeast Asia and the Caribbean. His research focuses on historical linguistics and language contact in Southeast Asia and the wider Indian Ocean world. He is the author of *Southeast Asia in the Ancient Indian Ocean* (2013), *Language Ungoverned: Indonesia's Chinese Print Entrepreneurs, 1911–1949* (2021), and coeditor of *Sinophone Southeast Asia: Sinitic Voices across the Southern Seas* (2021).

////////////////////////////////

Notes

1   Keppy, "Keroncong, Concours and Crooners."
2   What is known as "Hokkien" in Southeast Asia corresponds to the Quanzhang 泉漳 dialect continuum of Southern Min. Hokkien words in Malay texts were invariably written in an Indies-style romanization. I have added their Chinese characters for the sake of recognizability.
3   Salmon, *Literature in Malay.*
4   Hoogervost, *Language Ungoverned.*
5   I have gleaned these insights from multiple Dutch newspapers uploaded to the Delpher database (www.delpher.nl).
6   The history of *tjapgome* in Batavia has been evocatively described by Kwee, *Nonton tjapgome*, 17–18. The "Sair tjap-go-me di Betawi" (Poem of the Lantern Festival in Batavia) offers another brief portrayal from the 1930s (Salmon, *Literature in Malay*, 462). A critical Islamic Chinese perspective on three Sino-Indonesian holidays—the Ghost Festival (*tjioko* 搶孤), the Boat Races Festival (*pitjoen* 扒船), and the Lantern Festival (*tjapgome* 十五暝)—is provided in the undated and incompletely preserved "Sair tjioko dan pitjoen" (Poem on the Ghost Festival and Boat Races Festival), cf. Lombard and Salmon, "Islam and Chineseness," 126.
7   Cohen, *The Komedie Stamboel*, 183–84; Keppy, *Tales of Southeast Asia's Jazz Age*, 219; Hoogervorst, *Language Ungoverned.*
8   Paradijs *Boekoe sair "park,"* 16.
9   In another Sino-Malay account on popular theater, same-sex attraction was described more covertly through an anecdote of a popular actress of male roles who captured the hearts and wallets of her female fanbase (cf. Nio, *Sastera Indonesia-Tionghoa*, 140).
10   I am grateful to Sim Tze Wei 沈志偉 for improving my translation.
11   Paradijs, *Boekoe sair "park,"* 23.
12   Tjiong, *Pantoen japgome*, 13.
13   Cohen, *Komedie Stamboel.*
14   Tjiong, *Pantoen tjapgome*, 53–54.
15   Tjiong, *Pantoen tjapgome*, 5.

16 Paradijs, *Boekoe sair "park,"* 7.

17 Tjiong, *Pantoen Tjapgome,* 17–18.

18 Ibid., 19.

19 Ibid., 14.

20 Ibid., 58.

21 Paradijs, *Boekoe sair "park,"* 9–10.

22 Ibid., 14.

23 Ibid.

24 Ibid., 19.

25 Ibid., 16.

26 Tjiong, *Pantoen Tjapgome,* 8.

27 Ibid., 20.

28 Ibid., 57.

29 Cohen, *Komedie Stamboel,* 15.

30 Tjiong, *Pantoen tjapgome,* 14.

31 van der Putten, "Burlesquing Muḥarram Processions," 213–14.

32 Tjiong, *Pantoen tjapgome,* 64.

33 Ibid., 72–79.

34 Ibid., 21, 65.

35 Ibid., 70.

36 Ibid., 14, 60–63.

37 Paradijs, *Boekoe sair "park,"* 7, 13.

38 Ibid., 20.

39 Keppy, *Tales of Southeast Asia's Jazz Age,* 143.

40 The word *barongsaij* is a mixture in itself, blending Javanese *barong* (mythological animal) and Hokkien *sai* 獅 (dance). Elsewhere in the archipelago, lion dances were known as *langsaij* 舞獅 or *samsie* 蟾蜍. The latter, also written as *samsoe,* originally denoted the three-legged "money toad" of Chinese mythology but became conflated with the lion dance in many parts of the Indies. The equivalent *bú-lāng-sai* 舞弄獅, seen in other Southeast Asian varieties of Hokkien, is unattested in the Sino-Malay literature.

41 Tjiong, *Pantoen tjapgome,* 5–6.

42 Nio, "Kunstenaars in bamboe en papier," 1016.

43 Tjiong, *Pantoen tjapgome,* 20.

44 Mangkudilaga, "Fungsi Tanjidor bagi Masyarakat Betawi."

45 Tjiong, *Pantoen tjapgome,* 28–33.

46 Liem, "Ilmoe soenglap Tionghoa," 14.

47 Tjiong, *Pantoen tjapgome,* 34.

48 Ibid.

49 Ibid., 35.

50 de Groot, *Jaarlijksche feesten en gebruiken,* 112; Salmon and Lombard, *Chinese of Jakarta,* lviii–lix.

51 Nio, "Kunstenaars in bamboe en papier," 1014–16.

52 DeBernardi, *Rites of Belonging,* 178.

53 Goh, "State carnivals," 120.

54 Nio, "Kunstenaars in bamboe en papier," 1015. From at least the early nineteenth century, devotees also offered a pair of large candles to the Chinese temple during Batavia's New Year celebrations (Medhurst, "Chinese Festival," 251; Salmon and Lombard, *Chinese of Jakarta,* lix).

55 Tjiong, *Pantoen tjapgome,* 27.

56 Nio, "Chinese Songs and Plays in Batavia," 200.
57 Tjiong, *Pantoen tjapgome*, 41.
58 Ibid., 49.
59 Nio, "Chinese Songs and Plays in Batavia."

References

Cohen, Matthew Isaac. *The Komedie Stamboel: Popular Theater in Colonial Indonesia, 1891–1903*. Athens: Ohio University Press, 2006.

DeBernardi, Jean. *Rites of Belonging: Memory, Modernity, and Identity in a Malaysian Chinese Community*. Palo Alto, CA: Stanford University Press, 2004.

De Groot, J. J. M. *Jaarlijksche feesten en gebruiken van de Emoy-Chineezen: Eerste deel* [Annual Celebrations and Customs of the Amoy-Chinese: Part 1]. Batavia: Verhandelingen van het Bataviaasch Genootschap van Kunsten en Wetenschappen 42, 1881.

Goh, Daniel P. S. "State Carnivals and the Subvention of Multiculturalism in Singapore." *British Journal of Sociology* 62, no. 1 (2011): 111–33.

Hoogervorst, Tom G. *Language Ungoverned: Indonesia's Chinese Print Entrepreneurs, 1911–1949*. Ithaca, NY: Cornell University Press, 2021.

Keppy, Peter. "Keroncong, Concours, and Crooners: Home-Grown Entertainment in Early Twentieth-Century Batavia." In *Linking Destinies: Trade, Towns, and Kin in Asian History*, edited by Peter Boomgaard, Dick Kooiman, and Henk Schulte Nordholt, 141–57. Leiden: KITLV, 2008.

Keppy, Peter. *Tales of Southeast Asia's Jazz Age: Filipinos, Indonesians, and Popular Culture, 1920–1936*. Singapore: NUS Press, 2019.

Kwee Tek Hoay. *Nonton tjapgome* [Watching the Lantern Festival]. Batavia: Panorama, 1930.

Liem Thian Joe. "Ilmoe soenglap Tionghoa" [Chinese Magic]. *Sin po wekelijksche editie* 934 (1941): 13–17.

Lombard, Denys, and Claudine Salmon. "Islam and Chineseness." *Indonesia* 57 (1993): 115–31.

Mangkudilaga, Sufwandi. "Fungsi tanjidor bagi masyarakat Betawi" [The Functions of Tanjidor for the Betawi Community]. *Jali-jali* 3 (1989): 21–28.

Medhurst, Walter Henry. "Chinese Festival of the New Year." *Asiatic Journal and Monthly Register for British India and Its Dependencies* 23 (1827): 251–52.

Nio Joe Lan. "Chinese Songs and Plays in Batavia." *China Journal* 23, no. 4 (1935): 198–200.

Nio Joe Lan. "Kunstenaars in bamboe en papier" [Artists in Bamboo and Paper]. *De Indische gids* 57, no. 1 (1935): 1008–17.

Nio Joe Lan. *Sastera Indonesia-Tionghoa* [Chinese-Indonesian Literature]. Jakarta: Gunung Agung, 1962.

Paradijs. *Boekoe sair "park"* [The Poem of the Park]. Batavia: Liauw Tjin Kwie, 1920.

Salmon, Claudine. *Literature in Malay by the Chinese of Indonesia: A Provisional Annotated Bibliography*. Paris: Éditions de la Maison des sciences de l'homme, 1981.

Salmon, Claudine, and Denys Lombard. *The Chinese of Jakarta: Temples and Communal Life*. Paris: Éditions de la Maison des sciences de l'homme, 1980.

Stenberg, Josh. *Minority Stages: Sino-Indonesian Performance and Public Display*. Honolulu: University of Hawai'i Press, 2019.

Tjiong Soen Liang. *Pantoen tjapgome* [The Quatrain of the Lantern Festival]. Batavia: Goan Hong, 1924.

van der Putten, Jan. "Burlesquing Muḥarram Processions into Carnivalesque *Boria*." In *Shi'ism in Southeast Asia: 'Alid Piety and Sectarian Constructions*, edited by Chiara Formichi and Michael Feener, 203–21. London: Hurst, 2015.

JOSH STENBERG

Ethnic Loyalty versus Spring Fancy
Gender and Southeast Asia in Hei Ying's Fiction

ABSTRACT Hei Ying 黑嬰 (1915–1992) wrote prolifically about the "southern isles," where he—a Hakka from Sumatra—was born. Written for a sophisticated urban readership in China that was curious about the exotic and erotic Nanyang, Hei Ying's 1930s fiction foregrounds questions of Chinese ethnicity and nation. Ethnicity interacts with gender against sultry and desultory backgrounds, with improper patriotic or sexual tendencies attracting narrative punishment. Drawing on three pieces of his short fiction from the 1930s, this article argues that Hei Ying's theme of sexual temptation in the tropics rehearses European colonial (or Han majority) views of the impulsive, sultry native, an image that is contrasted with Republican Chinese primness. The bourgeois woman awakening to Chinese ethnonationalism and rejecting sensuality in favor of patriotism makes her an ancestor to the sexless heroines of Chinese revolutionary culture, including some Hei Ying would write later. The sensuality of the tropics thus operates as a foil for passions correctly channeled—toward nation (and eventually also party-state).

KEYWORDS Hei Ying; Chinese Indonesian literature; Nanyang; Dutch East Indies; colonial literature

Introduction

Sumatra-born author Hei Ying 黑嬰 (1915–1992) is best remembered today for the short fiction he wrote and published in Shanghai in the 1930s before the age of twenty-five. On the basis of that work, literary historians have typically assigned his work to the New Perceptionist Movement 新感覺派,[1] a literary tendency that focused on cosmopolitan, urban life and made use of stream-of-consciousness techniques. Less well known and seldom reread are Hei Ying's Nanyang 南洋 (South Seas) works, though they arguably occupy the dominant place in his oeuvre. These stories are of increasing interest today as a way of rethinking the relationship between ethnicity and gender in pre–World War II writing in Chinese. Written for a sophisticated urban readership in China that was curious about the exotic and erotic Nanyang, Hei Ying's 1930s fiction foregrounds questions of the Chinese nation, worked through as gender politics against lush, sensual backgrounds. Drawing on three pieces of his short fiction from the 1930s, this article argues that Hei Ying's theme of sexual temptation in the tropics rehearses European colonial (or Han majority) views of the impulsive, languid native. This

PRISM: THEORY AND MODERN CHINESE LITERATURE • 19:2 • SEPTEMBER 2022
DOI 10.1215/25783491-9966757 • © 2022 LINGNAN UNIVERSITY

image is contrasted with a bourgeois image of Republican Chinese propriety and primness. The bourgeois woman awakening to Chinese ethnonationalism and rejecting sensuality in favor of patriotism makes her an ancestor to the sexless heroines of Chinese revolutionary culture, including some Hei Ying would write later. In such a reading, the sensuality of the tropics becomes a foil for the passions correctly directed toward nation (and eventually also party-state).

Hei Ying became a well-known literary figure at a very young age, thanks to his literary output that depicts a fragmented, cosmopolitan, cinematic vision of Shanghai.[2] In his body of work, numerous representations of his home in the colonial Dutch East Indies were contemporaneous with the Shanghai stories, including both conventionally progressive (i.e., explicitly left-wing) class-based tales of the sufferings of the proletarian Nanyang Chinese, and depictions of the Indies as a sultry, tropical natural environment inhabited by exotic, attractive, but also elusive and silent native women and girls. This article considers the Nanyang portion of his oeuvre, not merely to resituate him as a Sino-Southeast Asian or a Sinophone Indies author in a long-distance nationalist vein, but to consider the particular focus on the dynamics between patriotism and sexuality in three stories: "Nandao huailianqu" 南島懷戀曲 (Elegy for the Southern Isles, 1933), "Meiyou baba" 没有爸爸 (Got No Dad, 1933), and "Nandao zhi chun" 南島之春 (Spring in the Southern Isles, 1936), in which the redirection of libido to patriotism that will become explicit after 1949 already is becoming visible.

Born in 1915 to a shop employee in Medan, Hei Ying was of Hakka background, from the county of Meixian in eastern Guangdong, where he was sent for schooling between the ages of seven and thirteen.[3] Upon his return to Sumatra, he attended an English-language school and worked at Medan's *Xin Zhonghua bao* 新中華報 (New China News) until the age of seventeen. In 1932, he left for Shanghai, where he was at least in principle a student in the foreign languages department of National Chi Nan University, an institution specifically designed for overseas Chinese students—though academic study does not seem to have been foremost in his mind. Then, still in his teens, he began publishing the short stories and novellas that won him a place in the literary scene; his later work, which spanned half a century, is usually treated as a coda.

Hei Ying became loosely connected to the Shanghai-based writers associated with New Perceptionism, with whom he shared a focus on cosmopolitan, urban life and a proclivity for stream-of-consciousness techniques. The texts of his initial collection, *Diguo de nü'er* 帝國的女兒 (Daughter of the Empire, 1934), were all written in or near Shanghai. He quickly made friends with the well-known modernist Mu Shiying 穆時英, socializing with his circle in the cafés and dance halls of Shanghai.[4] The nightclubs and freewheeling morality, the foreign characters and flashing lights—an "international Babel of sounds and voices"[5]—who appear in Hei Ying's stories, including British sailors and Russian and

Japanese women, snugly fit the Jazz Age mold of Shanghai's Republican modern. In 1933, his short story "Wuyue de Zhina" 五月的支那 (China in May) attracted the attention of Mao Dun 茅盾 (1896–1981), who was already an influential arbiter of taste in Chinese literature. Between 1933 and 1937, Hei Ying would publish over sixty pieces of fiction in journals as well as two collections of short fiction in China, which were directed toward an urban readership that made Shanghai its focal point. Leaving Shanghai in the shadow of war in 1941, he returned to Medan and then went to Batavia (as Jakarta was called during the colonial period), where he was ultimately imprisoned for four years due to wartime resistance activities.

After his release from prison, Hei Ying's later fiction output was sporadic, though what he did produce tended to longer forms. In his works in the immediate postindependence period, including the novella *Hongbai qi xia* 紅白旗下 [Under the Red-White Flag] and the short story collection *Shidai de gandong* 時代的感動 [Poignancy of the Era], he subjected Chinese society in the emerging Indonesian republic to an orthodox Communist analysis: Chinese and Indonesians were engaged in the same struggle against imperialism. At the same time, he also stressed that "progressive" Indonesian Chinese in no way lagged behind mainlanders in patriotism and loyalty, so long as they were properly instructed.[6] He returned definitively to China in 1951, settling in Beijing and working as literary editor for *Guangming ribao* 光明日報 [Guangming Daily]. Sent away for reeducation and hard labor during the Cultural Revolution, he was nevertheless spared its worst excesses. He was an active member of the China Zhi Gong Party, a group that, despite early Kuomintang associations, would largely become an organ for the expression of overseas Chinese support for the Chinese Communist Party after the establishment of the People's Republic of China (PRC). Unlike many of his contemporaries, he lived to see a renewal of interest in his work in the 1980s, after decades during which the PRC canon focused on more overtly revolutionary authors and ignored the earlier strains of cosmopolitanism that especially Shanghai authors had produced.[7]

Hei Ying Constructs Nanyang

Republican Chinese audiences were fascinated by the way Nanyang Chinese were and were not Chinese. The region represented exotic milieus as well as ethnic differences, and the overseas Chinese were conceived of as "often rich but ill-mannered and poorly educated."[8] Whether it be Ling Jishi in Ding Ling's 丁玲 "Shafei nüshi de riji" 莎菲女士的日記 [Miss Sophie's Diary] or Fan Liuyuan in Eileen Chang's 張愛玲 "Qingcheng zhi lian" 傾城之戀 [Love in a Fallen City], Chinese men from or associated with Southeast Asia appear in Republican Chinese texts as alluring, sexually and linguistically transgressive, and—perhaps due to their complicity in colonial imperialism—fallen from social propriety into sheer materialism. Part of a wider romanticism about "returnee men," Nanyang men trouble dichotomies and trajectories by providing a third space where Chinese are as much implicated in colonialism as they are its victims, drawing some of the contempt and envy that the newly rich always do.[9] In the case of Fan Liuyuan, it also creates his hunger to find Chinese authenticity in romance, against which is plotted his own uncertain condition and identity.

In "Love in a Fallen City," Fan Liuyuan addresses Bai Liusu, the Shanghai woman he is courting:

> "I'll take you to Malaya," Liuyuan said.
> "What for?"
> "To go back to nature." He thought for a moment. "But there's just one problem—I can't imagine you running through the forest in a *cheongsam*. . . . But neither can I imagine you not wearing a *cheongsam*."[10]

> 柳原道："我陪你到馬來亞去。" 流蘇道:"做什麼？" 柳原道："回到自然。" 他轉念一想，又道："只是一件，我不能想像你穿著旗袍在森林裡跑。……不過我也不能想像你不穿著旗袍。"

The allegedly destabilizing effect of Nanyang's climate and economy on mores and identity was no less striking for women. The balance was tipped rather more against them, since manners and decorum are at a higher premium for women than for men, while the aphrodisiac effect of lucre is much lessened, since daughters might inherit little or nothing. This meant that the third space of Nanyang could be more damaging for women's reputations than for men's. As Bin Yang observes in a discussion of literature from this period, overseas Chinese girls "were said to be naïve and promiscuous, lacking as it were the polish of European etiquette and the refinement of traditional Chinese good manners."[11] As Yang Hui has pointed out, the descriptions of coconut palms and dark lasses in Hei Ying's fiction were directed to a particular taste of a Shanghai public and "injected the intellectual vibrancy of transnationalism" into the New Perceptionist circle,[12] but the stakes are much higher for the women, who must maintain propriety, than they are for the men, whose desires are permitted or at least countenanced and whose transgressions can be repaired.

"Elegy for the Southern Isles," appearing in 1933, is one of Hei Ying's first published stories, appearing in *Liangyou huabao* 良友畫報 [The Young Companion Pictorial], a popular magazine depicting the lifestyles and entertainments of the urban cosmopolites. The reader's eye is first drawn to an accompanying photograph of a clutch of palm trees.[13] The opening of "Elegy" leaves no doubt that the reader is being invited into an alluring, exotic world. The story has two subtitled sections: a brief lyrical "Prelude" is succeeded by "The Black Dream." The prelude, given here in full, sets the tone clearly enough:

How fondly I remember the blazing southern isles!

There, on the coast, stand the straight-backed coconut palms. There, in the markets, is the strange-tasting durian. There, beneath the palms, are the dark girls.

The sun blazes. The wind carries a tang of salt. In the quiet evening, a quiet moon; on the quiet riverfront, quiet singing. Oh, the island nation that once intoxicated my island youth's spirit.

In such a sultry land, such a sultry dream, how fondly I remember the southern isles! Blazing, blazing.

我是那麼地懷戀著炎熱的南島呵！

那兒的海邊有挺直了身子的椰樹的。那兒的市上有怪味的榴蓮的。那兒的棕櫚樹下有黑色的姑娘的。

太陽是炎熱的。風是帶著鹽味的。靜靜的晚上有靜靜的月亮；靜靜的河畔有靜靜的歌聲；曾經醉過我這島國少年的靈魂的島國哪。

那麼溫暖的國土裡，那麼溫暖的夢，我是那麼地懷戀著南島呵！炎熱的，炎熱的。[14]

In this encomium, and throughout the story, the narrator sketches a sultry, romantic tropical experience for his Shanghai readers, presenting himself simultaneously as an insider and an outsider. He is fatefully drawn to the darkness, though ultimately he will be saved by the very elusiveness of the "dark girl" 黑妮子, even though the prim Chinese girl he has brought with him has no comparable allure. The loose and dreamlike plot follows the narrator's pursuit of this "dark girl," whom he serenades:

I've run into you; today the dark girl is really beautiful!

A pair of black pearls, a row of white teeth. . . .

Before the song is over, she runs off! I set off in pursuit, pursuing her to that faraway place where the moon, poking its head out, lets its light fall underfoot, there she is exhausted and I can grab hold of her.

Panting, she struggles in vain; with my muscled arms I am able to subdue the dark girl. Without saying much she agrees to hear the end of my song, and so I start again from the beginning.

碰到你啦；今兒黑妮子真美麗！

有對黑珠子，有排白牙齒......

沒唱完她卻跑啦！便追著，一直追到遠遠地那邊兒：月亮伸出腦袋的腳下她沒氣力才給我捉住了。

喘著氣，掙扎可沒用的；我的胳膊那兒有栗子肉的，我能夠制服這黑妮子。
沒多嘴她答應聽完我的歌；便再從頭唱起。[15]

The entirety of the story, with its first-person intimacy, is concerned with the narrator's pursuit and his forceful, sometimes violent attempts to subjugate her. The dark girl allures and tempts the narrator, but she is constantly slipping out of sight. She never acquires a name and is barely individuated, and then only through the beauty of her teeth and eyes. In fact, she is perhaps only the representative of a group to begin with: at the very beginning of "Elegy" we are told: "There, beneath the palms, are the dark girls" 那兒的棕櫚樹下有黑色的姑娘的, with the Chinese text ambiguous about whether there is one girl or several. These girls appear as part of the scenery, natural, alluring, elusive, mysterious, ambivalent. Southeast Asia in "Elegy" is thus the abode of a tribe of dusky and noble girl savages, close to nature, instinctive, charming. The elusiveness is as crucial as the exoticism. Perhaps if the narrator ever achieved his mad pursuit, his separateness from the place (a prerequisite of his Chineseness) would be forfeit. Chineseness in such a story thus consists of "winning near the goal," of erotic pursuit never consummated for fear that actual union might spell the end of ethnic identity.[16] (Thus, later, it is only the independence of the Southeast Asian states, so deleterious for the Chinese in many individual cases, which opens up the possibility of cultural hybridity becoming expressed politically as local belonging.) Indeed, "Elegy" might be read as a story-length elaboration on the act of "running through the forest" in the undefined sensual pursuit that Fan Liuyuan's phrasing in "Love in a Fallen City" seems to suggest; the dark girls, however, have no *cheongsams* to disrupt the imagination. Male Sino-Southeast Asian characters like Fan or the "Elegy" narrator accrue some of the savagery and the nobility of the colonial sphere without too much damage to their virtue and therefore Chineseness. What translates into urbanity for men, however, becomes transgression for Chinese women.

This is the case of the protagonist of "Got No Dad," a story less oneiric and more concerned with the social problems of colonial life, also published in Shanghai in 1933. In that story, the young woman Weina is granted a little more identity—at least she has a name—and is given some room to make herself heard, even if ultimately her function is principally as beauty and victim. Like the narrator of "Elegy" she has been raised in "the southern lands" and "near the sea"; the fruits of the jungle are again invoked, for as Weina grows up "the sea breeze blows on her, the coconut and the durian nurture her: the hot pepper has raised her this far—the beautiful Weina" 海風吹著她，椰子和榴蓮培養著她；辣椒兒把她帶到這麼樣子大，一個美麗的維娜.[17] When she reaches the age when (like a tropical fruit herself) "virgins are overripe" 處女的爛熟期 (45), Weina is seduced by a sailor, Charlie, who seems to emerge from the sea itself and is "tall, high-nosed, long-faced, broad-shouldered, and his eyes are blue" 高個兒，高鼻子；長臉孔，闊膀子；那眼珠子是藍色的哪 (45), who is affected by the "tenderness of the southern lands" 南國的情調多溫柔啊 (46). He first addresses her in English with "Hallo, Baby" (46), but when she begins to run away it is revealed that he can also speak Malay (46), and she returns to converse with him. Addressing her as "a fairy of the southern lands" 南國的天仙 (46), he claims that "I sought you from America to Japan to China, four or five years I spent seeking, just to find you here" 從亞美利加我找到日本，支那，花費了四五年的辰光，如今在這兒我找到你了 (46). She is too sensible to believe him, but eventually succumbs to his seduction anyway, not least because he offers her an exciting evening wandering around the night market. Charlie departs after a single night, and Weina, who has been forced from home by her parents' cruel response to her transgression, raises her child—named "Little Charlie"—alone. The father, she tells the child, is dead.

Of course, neither the abandoned Asian woman nor the the mixed-blood fatherless child are unfamiliar figures, but the images of the southern lands and of the woman from those parts warrant a closer look. For one thing, is Weina Chinese or not? The story, of course, is written in Chinese, but we are told the characters are speaking Malay—although Malay would likely in any event have been the common language for a Chinese Sumatran and a (seemingly American) Charlie. We know she grew up on a coastal market garden, surrounded by coconuts and durian, and that she is charming and lovely. Like all the other young people in these stories, she is wondering when love will make its appearance. Market gardens were common Chinese migrant endeavors at this time, and her name is suggestive of the -na names popular since Republican times in names for Chinese women. But that is not entirely conclusive; nor is the fact that Weina's skin color is like a Philippine dancer's "slightly swarthy flesh" 微黑的肉 (48). Indeed, her anger at the dancer may suggest a recoil both from what she deems to be the performance's lewdness but also its dusky southernness. Moreover, for an author who gave himself a pen name meaning "Black Baby," a darker complexion can as easily suggest Chinese of the southern seas as it might Indigenous Southeast Asians.

Another fascinating clue to an unresolvable question: when Charlie has finished the list of places he has sought her (Japan, America, and China), Weina ignores the other options and says, "Looking for me? You went to China to look for me?" 找我？到支那去找我? (46)—which might suggest that Weina's true home (a place where he might have looked for and been surprised not to find her) is the mainland state or ancestral village, where she is not now, and to which she can never "return." The eclecticism of the night market—with its Indian, Javanese, Filipino, and Malay performances—operates as both a fulfilment of an exotic imaginary and an indication that Weina is external to them all. We notice that, despite the popularity of Chinese theater in Sumatra during the Republican period, no Chinese performances are referenced in this passage. Is the carnival of Southeast Asians to differentiate Weina, or to engage the Shanghai reader, or both? Is the sarong she wears a sign of her acculturation, or of Hei Ying lamenting the story of an Indigenous Sumatran?

Following up on a possibility that is perhaps deliberately never precluded or confirmed, we may read Weina as "displaced" ethnic Chinese. If so, the story's repeated associations of Weina with the sea, coconut trees, and sexual availability constitute an interesting example of a Chinese-language depiction of an indigenized, sultry, romantic, and exploited Chinese subject—a Chinese Butterfly whose indignity does not take place on Chinese soil—and perhaps takes place precisely *because* she is far from the political and moral protections of Chinese society, but whose cautionary tale can ring across the sea. Through such a reading, her abandonment by Charlie can be read as emblematic and symptomatic of the vulnerability of ethnic Chinese in the colonies, left without the security of society and state, and subjected to the depredations of the casual colonial. On such a reading, and despite any apparent animus against Charlie, we are already a step closer to the forcefully anti-imperialist Communist that Hei Ying would become a decade and a half later.

The Patriotic Imperative

In his incisive analysis of traveling Chinese writers' perceptions of Southeast Asia, Brian Bernards notes a "legacy of imperial Chinese perceptions of Southeast Asians as an exotic, primitive, feminized and hypersexualized Other."[18] Stories such as "Elegy" and "Got No Dad" show that not only travelers but Southeast Asia–born Chinese were capable of painting such scenes for an urban Chinese readership. Whereas the travelers' encounter with the Other was modeled as a transitory experience, for Hei Ying that liminal space represents the situation for a whole community, with concomitant political risks. As with the encounter with the erotically volatile and potentially destructive Other in "Got No Dad" or "Elegy," the political risk of tropical slothfulness is acted out by means of abortive romance in the third story, "Spring in the Southern Isles."

Gender relations, as expressed in a network of themes related to love, sex, and power, are a constant obsession of Hei Ying's early fiction, as they are for many young authors. The author's preoccupation with the fate of China, very natural in this period of Japanese aggression, is just as prominent but is a mark of the era: his best-known works are all written between the Mukden Incident (1931) and the Marco Polo Bridge Incident (1937). China's national existential crisis was the order of the day, the dominant concern of all but the most nihilist intellectuals.

Hei Ying's story "Spring in the Southern Isles" begins with the incontrovertible admission that spring in an equatorial country is a calendrical rather than a meteorological phenomenon:

These are the southern isles: the temperature shows over eighty degrees on the thermometer all year round, winter and summer. If you weren't oversensitive, how could you even tell what season it is now? It's gloomy weather today. Intermittent showers; the hazy rainscape outside the window offers a charm of its own. So Miss Hui says to herself: spring has come to the southern isles. Look at the calendar hanging on the wall: that's right, it really is springtime. It's been a year since Miss Hui has drawn a breath of spring air.

這兒是南島。——長年在寒暑表八十度以上的天氣，如果不是你的多心，怎能分出現在是什麼季節呢？這天的天氣是陰暗的。雨是斷續地下；霏霏的雨景從窗口望去另有一番景色。於是蕙小姐的心裡說：春到南島來了。
瞧瞧掛在壁上的日曆：不錯，季節的確是春天。蕙小姐不吸春的氣息足足已有一年。[19]

With the central metaphor in the title—the spring which is not a spring, the year which is not a year, the allegedly unchanging and perhaps unchangeable tropics—Hei Ying seems about to explore his common theme of youthful (i.e., "springtime") sexuality, and indeed, even the classical theme of girls blooming unnoticed in secluded gardens is a latent presence. The deceptiveness of names, however, also foreshadows the national question: just as there is no proper spring in a perpetually warm climate, the Chinese of this island are ethnically Chinese but fail to be patriotically Chinese.

The protagonist of the story is Miss Hui, an Indies-born woman about twenty years old who one year earlier had returned to "the southern islands" after having spent three exciting years in "southern China." Hei Ying, of course (who himself had once returned to Sumatra after several years in China), was probably evaluating the provinciality of Chinese society in Medan or Penang from his cosmopolitan but politically precarious vantage point in Shanghai. Miss Hui is deathly bored back home, for she lacks appropriate society. Her views are closer to hedonism than to vernal romance:

She has extracted a view of life from movies and literature; she would not love being the prisoner of love, nor does she believe that love is sacred or single-minded. In a movie, she has seen how a young girl, out of loyalty to her beloved, sacrifices her entire youth; she sneered at the girl's foolishness! Life is for youth to indulge itself, enjoy itself. Love? Love is the wellspring of life, love is the champagne of youth! So, why not love everything, one—or two— or three. . . . Why ever not?! Enjoy life while you love each other, and when it becomes necessary to split, then split; this is Miss Hui's view of life.

從電影和文學作品中她取到一種人生觀；她不愛做愛的囚徒，她不以為愛是神聖而專一的。她看到電影中一個少女為了忠於她的情人而犧牲了整個青春，她嘲譏

她的呆笨！人生應該抓住青春放情享樂的。愛嗎?愛是生命的源泉，愛是青春的
瓊漿 [漿]！所以，不顧一切去愛能，一個，兩個，三個，......這又何妨？！相
愛時好好地過生活，到分手不可時，也得分手；這是蕙小姐的人生觀。[20]

Miss Hui finds that, compared with China, the southern islands are "loveless, lifeless" 沒有愛，沒有生命,[21] perhaps due to the continual hot weather. But also, if southern China is the location of real life, it follows that ethnic Chinese outside the homeland are barely alive, nor do they have access to the dynamism of modernity promised in urban China, which Miss Hui experienced and has had to leave behind.

After the scene has been set, Miss Hui is coaxed out of her solitude to attend a ball, where she is appalled by the unpatriotic statements of the local affluent Chinese. They expect China to suffer at the hands of Japan but remain callously unconcerned for the welfare of the Chinese people:

A big-bellied foreman at a rubber plantation makes some remarks, followed by a long-faced lady with a long, wrinkled face; hearing these almost makes Miss Hui want to be sick, and then that fellow adds: "I wouldn't have thought it necessary for everybody to talk about affairs of state at a place and time like this; whether there is a nation or not, to tell the truth—what is it to us? . . . We gain nothing from China existing any longer; and if China perishes, we wouldn't necessarily be slaves, would we? Let's drink and dance, and make a night of it!"

"What kind of talk is that?" Miss Hui says angrily; she is about to warn him, but the band strikes up again, and they all return to the middle of the hall and take each other by the arm—they have forgotten the fatherland! Forgotten the danger the fatherland is facing!

說著，說著，大肚皮的什麼樹膠園大工頭一句，滿是皺紋的長面孔的什麼太太也
說一句；這些真教蕙小姐聽了要嘔出來了，而那男子也來說道：
　　——我以為，大家都不必在這麼一個地方，這麼一個時間談國事；國的有無，
老實說，與我們有什麼關係呢？中國存在，我們已不得到一些好處；中國亡了，我
想也不見得我們就要做奴隸吧！？我們飲酒，跳舞，我們好好地把今晚度過去吧！
　　這是什麼話？蕙小姐唱出火來了；她正欲起來給他一個警告，而音樂又奏
了，大家都起身走到中間去，一對一對地抱起來，他們忘了祖國！忘了祖國是在
危難之中！[22]

Miss Hui leaves in a huff, having discarded the entire milieu as being beneath reproach. A final scene finds her at home again, contemplating the grave deficiencies of local Chinese patriotism, her righteousness somewhat undermined by the comic presence of her dog Mimi. Since we are told that the spring is not a spring, perhaps we are to infer—given their inability to identify with or even care about the sufferings of the fatherland—that the southern isles Chinese are not real Chinese? The ending is irresolute, and little has been done to engage the South Seas Chinese in the defense or salvation of China. But perhaps it is enough that Miss Hui has struck a blow for Chinese patriotism in this parochial, deficient society? And youthful exuberance, the élan of luxurious, libertine experience in the dangerous and sensual urban life of China (presumably in her case also Shanghai) must give way before the patriotic imperative. Given the many contributions and sacrifices made by Southeast Asian Chinese to the Chinese war effort, perhaps the story is best understood as a warning that when real danger intrudes, only patriotic stances will be ethical. In historical perspective, Hei Ying was correct to point out that Nanyang Chinese could not afford to be unconcerned with Japanese aggression: before a decade had passed after the publication of "Spring in the Southern Isles," Sumatra was under brutal Japanese occupation.

It is these twin commitments to libido and the nation that frame the experiences of Hei Ying's Chinese Southeast Asian characters. Miss Hui in "Spring in the Southern Isles," like the male narrator of "Elegy," experiences a conflict between duty and eros. The *désoeuvrée* young woman in a lush false-springtime environment suggests the restlessness of sexual awakening. In principle, Miss Hui accepts the invitation to go to the ball not for any desire to be socially agreeable but because it seems possible that an erotic interest might appear (in this she is a modern woman in the Miss Sophie mold, who avows her desire and to whom it is permitted). The usual social possibilities occur, but any possibility of erotic development or advancement toward resolving the troubling question of Miss Hui's marriage is squelched by the other guests' unpatriotic statements. Miss Hui (and perhaps Hei Ying) does not yet have the political awareness that will make a revolutionary missionary of her, but she has enough "natural" patriotic feeling that unpatriotic men disgust her.

Conclusion

When Miss Hui accuses the Indies Chinese of being insufficiently patriotic, of failing to care for the tribulations of their Chinese brethren on the mainland, her analysis, perhaps unwittingly, opens the door to other possibilities of belonging, even if the vocabulary for any such shift would at the time—before decolonization—have been accessible to few. It also points the way forward to Hei Ying's later work. In his novels *Under the Red-White Flag* (1951) and, after a long departure from fiction, *Piaoliu yiguo de nüxing* 飄流異國的女性 (The Women Who Drifted Abroad, 1983), Hei Ying would be concerned with the ideological correctness of Chinese communities in the PRC period, leaving behind earlier modernist concerns, both thematic and formal, in order to adopt the strictly realist and politically embedded style of the PRC.[23]

The exotic femininity of his early stories—a feature of his Shanghai-set fiction, most famously in the Japanese prostitute protagonist of "Diguo de nü'er" 帝國的女兒 (Daughter of the Empire) but even more acutely visible in the "dark girls" of his 1930s Nanyang work—is replaced by the dutiful leftist patriot, first in *Under the Red-White Flag* and then most systematically rolled out in *The Women Who Drifted Abroad*, his last major work of fiction. Once China has "stood up" and is no longer prey to the ravages of Japanese and/or Western imperialism, eros and exoticism are subsumed in new state patriotism. The danger that libido will cross ethnic lines subsides, much as the sensual, experimental style of Hei Ying's youth is also replaced by the struggles of conventional narrative realism.

Despite their strangerhood and the outsider perspective they adopt in the stories about Huaqiao being "back" in China, Hei Ying's Chinese characters are not fully localized in the Southeast Asian locales of their birth. The local Chinese society appears as fully distinct from the ethnic majority (often silent or absent). On the other hand, the southern isles are defined in "Elegy" not only as island nations but also "my home." Moreover, the narrator is acclimatized to the south: he "can sing Malay songs, [has] a face like charcoal and sturdy arms—a typical island youth" 我會唱馬來的歌曲；我有副黑炭那麼的臉子，結實的肱膊。──一個典型的島國少年哪。[24] The dark complexion in particular contains autobiographical resonances, since the pen name Hei Ying means Black Baby, and it has been assumed from the outset that he chose the name as a reference to his dark skin tone.[25]

But Chinese characters throughout Hei Ying's work are also ethically judged according to the correctness of their political attachment to China—first out of concern and attachment to it as China struggles against Japan, and then hardening in Hei Ying's later works into more inflexible leftist attitudes. The license and eroticism attributed to (presumable) Southeast Asians stands in considerable contrast to the Huaqiao women whose patriotic (but sometimes also sexual) virtue is tested by the motherland's call in *The Women Who Drifted Abroad*. Weina, the protagonist in "Got No Dad" who is even more indigenized than the male narrator of "Elegy," loses her virtue as a function of having lost or marred her Chineseness.

This pseudocolonial aesthetic is channeled toward the way in which the protagonists in both "Elegy" and "Spring" avert a cardinal sin: the indulgence of eros. Miss Hui's own patriotic revulsion saves her. The man in "Elegy" avoids it through no merit of his own; when he goes to see the dark lass again, she has left her residence and gone away, retaining her mystery and winning a place in his nostalgic recollections. The text ends with the narrator's crestfallen song:

Where are you, where?
  Dark girl, I love you!
But . . .

你在那兒，那兒呵
  黑妮子，我愛你呢！
可是......[26]

In that hesitation with the ellipsis, a heavy line is drawn between the Chinese narrator (despite his sympathetic swarthiness) and the dark girl. Weina, on the other hand, succumbs to desire, in her weakness can no longer be meaningfully distinguished from Southeast Asians, and is punished for it by colonial exploitation and the bearing of a mixed child.

This tension between sexuality and duty recalls European colonial accounts of the impulsive and sultry native female, receptive but elusive, not named or individualized but featuring as a string of alluring attributes. The Chinese exoticism of the Southeast Asian woman, apparent also in the visual arts,[27] is not merely a secondhand product of European Orientalism (though this tendency was no doubt an inspiration and a reinforcement); it is also part of the same phenomenon that ultimately produces the transgressive PRC ethnic minority women of, for instance, Gao Xingjian's 高行健 *Lingshan* 靈山 (Soul Mountain). In the words of Dru C. Gladney: "The objectified portrayal of minorities as exoticized, and even eroticized, is essential to the construction of the Han Chinese majority, the very formulation of the Chinese 'nation' itself. In other words, the representation of the minorities in such colorful, romanticized fashion has more to do with constructing a majority discourse, than it does with the minorities themselves. This minority/majority discourse then becomes pervasive throughout Chinese culture, art, and media."[28] But while Gladney is interested primarily in this dynamic as it plays out in the PRC, it clearly has parallels and perhaps even origins in Republican-era Chinese writing, including the writings of late colonial encounters with Southeast Asia. Thus, while the role of exoticism of the West in the development of Chinese modernity is now widely recognized, it has not been fully acknowledged that when the same "struggle for aesthetic reinvigoration by initially employing new content in order to elicit new forms of expression"[29] is transferred to the ethnic dynamics of Southeast Asia, it creates a distinctly pseudocolonial aesthetic. Meanwhile, the prim Victorian colonial finds sisters among the proper Chinese girls such as Li-fen in "Elegy," who appears merely as a foil for the "dark lass." When patriotism later converts chastity to political purpose after the establishment of the PRC, this alchemy produces, one momentous generation later, what Rosemary Roberts describes as "beautiful yet sexless bodies abstractly representing revolution and a modern, strong China"[30] (even while these bodies remain objects of desire)—the austere heroines of Chinese revolutionary culture.

JOSH STENBERG is senior lecturer in Chinese studies at the University of Sydney. The author of *Minority Stages: Sino-Indonesian Performance and Public Display* (2019), his research interests include *xiqu* ("Chinese opera") in modern and contemporary periods, the culture of Sino-Southeast Asian communities, and Chinese translation studies.

////////////////////////////////

Acknowledgments
This research was funded by the Australian Research Council's Discovery Early Career Research Award. The author would like to thank the anonymous reviewers and the special issue editors, as well as the participants and audience at the "Between Mobility and Place-Making" symposium, for their valuable feedback on earlier drafts.

Notes

1. Also translated as "New Sensationists" and other similar names. For an overview, see Rosenmeier, "The New Sensationists," 168–80.
2. Hei Ying, meaning "Black Baby," was the principal pen name of Zhang Bingwen 張炳文, who also used the name Zhang Youjun 張又君 and at various points used numerous other pseudonyms.
3. Biographical information is largely drawn from Wu, "Hei Ying zhuanlüe," 179–85; and Qianren, "Hei Ying shengping jianjie," 196–98.
4. Zhang, *China in a Polycentric World*, 176.
5. Jones, "Black Internationale," 241.
6. In this respect, his work bears similarities to that of Baren 巴人. See Zhou, *Migration in the Time of Revolution*, 34–51, and Stenberg, *Minority Stages*, 76–95.
7. Field, *Mu Shiying*, xx.
8. Yang, "Under and beyond," 462.
9. Louie, "Romancing Returnee Men," 23–26.
10. Chang, *Love in a Fallen City*, 143; Zhang, *Zhang Ailing xiaoshuo*, 123.
11. Yang, "Under and beyond," 462.
12. Yang, "Chuanyue 'modeng' de jiaguo shuxie," 159.
13. Pang, *Distorting Mirror*, 110. This story was published a year before Hei Ying's better-known "Dang chuntian laidao de shihou" 當春天來到的時候 (When Spring Arrives) appeared in the same publication. Translation by May-lee Chai from Hei Ying, "When Spring Arrives," 31–38.
14. Hei Ying, "Nandao huailian qu," 14. Translation, in some instances lightly revised, by Josh Stenberg from Hei Ying, "Elegy for the Southern Isles," 79.
15. Hei Ying, "Nandao huailian qu," 14; Hei Ying, "Elegy for the Southern Isles," 79.
16. Hei Ying, like many *totok* (so-called pure, unacculturated Chinese, a term usually associated with Chinese migrants who retain cultural and linguistic proficiency, and/or were not locally born), tends to apply a deficiency model to culturally and genetically hybrid groups like the Peranakan, as can be seen in his later realist fiction.

17 Hei Ying, "Meiyou baba," 45. Hereafter, citations of this source will be given as parenthetical page numbers in the article text.

18 Bernards, *Writing the South Seas*, 38.

19 Hei Ying, "Nandao zhi chun," 32. Translation, in some instances lightly revised, by Josh Stenberg from Hei Ying, "Spring in the Southern Isles," 84. The author would like to acknowledge the contributions and corrections of the editors of *Renditions*, where the two translations used here were first published.

20 Hei Ying, "Nandao zhi chun," 32; Hei Ying, "Spring in the Southern Isles," 84.

21 Ibid.

22 Hei Ying, "Nandao zhi chun," 36; Hei Ying, "Spring in the Southern Isles," 90.

23 See Wu, "Hei Ying zhuanlüe," 182.

24 Hei Ying, "Nandao zhi chun," 32.

25 Qianzhe, "Yijiusansan de wentan xinren," 8.

26 Hei Ying, "Nandao huailian qu," 13; Hei Ying, "Elegy for the Southern Isles," 83.

27 For instance, it might be argued that the way that China-born artist Lee Man Fong 李曼峰, later Sukarno's palace painter, depicts Balinese dancers is similar to the depictions of European artists such as Adrien-Jean Le Mayeur de Merprès and Roland Strasser, as well as to PRC artists' depictions of minorities.

28 Gladney, "Representing Nationality in China," 94.

29 Fruehauf, "Urban Exoticism," 133.

30 Roberts, *Maoist Model Theatre*, 90.

References

Bernards, Brian. *Writing the South Seas: Imagining the Nanyang in Chinese and Southeast Asian Postcolonial Literature*. Seattle and London: University of Washington Press, 2015.

Bevan, Paul. *"Intoxicating Shanghai"—An Urban Montage: Art and Literature in Pictorial Magazines during Shanghai's Jazz Age*. Leiden: Brill, 2020.

Chang, Eileen. *Love in a Fallen City*, translated by Karen S. Kingsbury. New York: New York Review of Books, 2007.

Field, Andrew David. *Mu Shiying: China's Lost Modernist*. Hong Kong: Hong Kong University Press, 2014.

Fruehauf, Heinrich. "Urban Exoticism in Modern and Contemporary Chinese Literature." In *From May Fourth to June Fourth: Fiction and Film in Twentieth-Century China*, edited by Ellen Widmer and David Der-wei Wang, 133–64. Cambridge, MA: Harvard University Press, 1993.

Gladney, Dru C. "Representing Nationality in China: Refiguring Majority/Minority Identities." *Journal of Asian Studies* 53, no. 1 (1994): 92–123.

Hei Ying 黑嬰. "Dang chuntian laidao de shihou" 當春天來到的時候 [When Spring Arrives]. *Liangyou huabao* 良友畫報 [The Young Companion Pictorial], no. 87 (1934): 26–27.

Hei Ying 黑嬰. *Diguo de nü'er* 帝國的女兒 [Daughter of the Empire]. Shanghai: Shanghai kaihua shuju, 1934.

Hei Ying 黑嬰. "Elegy for the Southern Isles," translated by Josh Stenberg. *Renditions*, no. 95 (2021): 79–83.

Hei Ying 黑嬰. *Hongbai qi xia* 紅白旗下 [Under the Red-White Flag]. Hong Kong: Xianggang chidao chubanshe, 1951.

Hei Ying 黑嬰. "Huilixian 回力線 Hai Alai Scenes by Hei Ying," translated by Paul Bevan. In *Intoxicating Shanghai—An Urban Montage: Art and Literature in Pictorial Magazines during Shanghai's Jazz Age*, by Paul Bevan, 82–95. Leiden: Brill, 2020.

Hei Ying 黑嬰. "Meiyou baba" 没有爸爸 [Got No Dad]. *Wuming wenyi* 無名文藝 [Nameless Literary Arts] 1, no. 2 (1933): 49–55.

Hei Ying 黑嬰. "Nandao huailian qu" 南島懷戀曲 [Elegy for the Southern Isles]. *Liangyou huabao* 良友畫報 [The Young Companion Pictorial], no. 78 (1933): 14, 32.

Hei Ying 黑嬰. "Nandao zhi chun" 南島之春 [Spring in the Southern Isles]. *Neiwai zazhi* 內外雜誌 [In and Out Magazine] (1936): 32–37.

Hei Ying 黑嬰. *Piaoliu yiguo de nüxing* 飄流異國的女性 [The Women Who Drifted Abroad]. Harbin: Heilongjiang renmin chubanshe, 1983.

Hei Ying 黑嬰. *Shidai de gandong* 時代的感動 [Poignancy of the Era]. Jakarta: Yajiada Jiaoren chubanshe, 1947.

Hei Ying 黑嬰. "Spring in the Southern Isles," translated by Josh Stenberg. *Renditions*, no. 95 (2021): 84–92.

Hei Ying 黑嬰. "When Spring Arrives," translated by May-lee Chai. *Modern Chinese Literature* 9, no. 1 (1995): 31–38.

Hei Ying 黑嬰. "Wo de zuguo" 我的祖國 [My Homeland]. *Zhongguo wenxue* 中國文學 [Chinese Literature] 1, no. 1 (1934): 1–7.

Hei Ying 黑嬰. "Wuyue de Zhina" 五月的支那 [China in May]. *Wenxue* 文學 [Literature] 1, no. 1 (1933): 137–41.

Jones, Andrew F. "Black Internationale: Notes on the Chinese Jazz Age." In *Jazz Planet*, edited by E. Taylor Atkins, 225–44. Jackson: University Press of Mississippi, 2003.

Louie, Kam. "Romancing Returnee Men: Masculinity in 'Love in a Fallen City' and 'Red Rose, White Rose.'" In *Eileen Chang: Romancing Languages, Cultures, and Genres*, edited by Kam Louie, 15–32. Hong Kong: Hong Kong University Press, 2012.

Pang, Laikwan. *The Distorting Mirror: Visual Modernity in China*. Honolulu: University of Hawai'i Press, 2007.

Qianren 千仞. "Hei Ying shengping jianjie" 黑嬰生平簡介 [Brief Introduction to Hei Ying's Life]. In *Shenghuo bao de huiyi* 生活報的回憶 [Memories of *Shenghuo bao*], edited by a dedicated editorial committee, 196–98. Guangzhou: Guangdong World Books, 2013.

Qianzhe 前轍. "Yijiusansan de wentan xinren" 一九三三的文壇新人 [New Arrivals on the Literary Scene in 1933]. *Shiyue tan* 十月談, no. 17 (1934): 8.

Roberts, Rosemary A. *Maoist Model Theatre: The Semiotics of Gender and Sexuality in the Chinese Cultural Revolution (1966–1976)*. Leiden: Brill, 2010.

Rosenmeier, Christopher. "The New Sensationists: Shi Zhecun, Mu Shiying, Liu Na'ou." In *Routledge Handbook of Modern Chinese Literature*, edited by Ming Dong Gu, 168–80. London: Routledge, 2018.

Stenberg, Josh. *Minority Stages: Sino-Indonesian Performance and Public Display*. Honolulu: University of Hawai'i Press, 2019.

Wu Xiaoli 巫小黎. "Hei Ying zhuanlüe ji chuangzuo nianbiao" 黑嬰傳略及創作年表 [Brief Biography and Chronological Bibliography for Hei Ying]. *Xin wenxue shiliao* 新文學史料 [Materials for New Literary History], no. 4 (2001): 179–85.

Yang, Bin. "Under and beyond the Pen of Eileen Chang: Shanghai, Nanyang, Huaqiao, and Greater China." *Frontiers of History in China* 11, no. 3 (2016): 458–84.

Yang Hui 楊慧. "Chuanyue 'modeng' de jiaguo shuxie—Chongdu Hei Ying de Nanyang xushi (1932–1937)" 穿越"摩登"的家國書寫——重讀黑嬰的南洋敘事 (1932—1937) [Through the 'Modern' in Writing on Home and Country—Rereading the Nanyang

Narratives of Hei Ying]. *Zhongguo xiandai wenxue yanjiu congkan* 中國現代文學研究叢刊 [Modern Chinese Literature Studies], no. 5 (2016): 159–68.

Zhang Ailing 張愛玲. *Zhang Ailing xiaoshuo* 張愛玲小說 [Fiction by Eileen Chang]. Hangzhou: Zhejiang wenyi chubanshe, 2002.

Zhang, Yingjin. *China in a Polycentric World: Essays in Chinese Comparative Literature.* Stanford, CA: Stanford University Press, 1998.

Zhou, Taomo. *Migration in the Time of Revolution: China, Indonesia, and the Cold War.* Ithaca, NY: Cornell University Press, 2019.

SHIRLEY O. LUA

Recreating the World in Twenty-First-Century Philippine Chinese Speculative Fiction

ABSTRACT This article surveys contemporary Filipino Chinese authors' interest in speculative fiction. Many of the authors of this burgeoning movement were included in the anthology *Lauriat: A Filipino-Chinese Speculative Fiction Anthology* (2012), edited by Charles A. Tan. These authors find speculative fiction a fruitful genre for combining Western literary techniques and material gleaned from Philippine myth and folklore.

KEYWORDS Filipino Chinese, nonhuman, posthuman, speculative fiction

> David: The phrase *lan nang* really means . . .
>
> Eric: *We*, the people.
>
> David: No, that's the American Constitution. *Lan nang* means "we who are human." You see, the Chinese believe only the Chinese are human. Everyone else is some kind of a *gwei* or *kwi*.
>
> —Paul Stephen Lim, *Mother Tongue*

The Rise of Philippine Speculative Fiction

Philippine literary practices have continued to evolve in the twenty-first century, with writers engaging in the investigation and innovation of genres and styles. One of the rising forms covers what is known as speculative fiction. This umbrella category, encompassing genre types such as science fiction, fantasy, horror, dystopian, and superhero, projects an array of imagined worlds and alternate universes, pushing the boundaries of the real and transgressing the limits of the possible. In this sense, it interrogates and dismantles the traditional Western construct of realism and ponders the possibility of altering certain laws of reality, while simultaneously speculating on probable outcomes or consequences. The elements of "speculation" have their origin in conjectures or suppositions, raising the question of "what if." Nonetheless, speculative fiction is more concerned with human predicaments and responses, rather than the functions of science and technology. It can be deemed a product of the creative imagination in the age of globalization, multiculturalism, and digital technology. It accommodates

PRISM: THEORY AND MODERN CHINESE LITERATURE • 19:2 • SEPTEMBER 2022
DOI 10.1215/25783491-9966767 • © 2022 LINGNAN UNIVERSITY

tales and narratives informed by cultures outside the mainstream, such as those of minorities or Indigenous people.

The Philippine movement is spearheaded by an exciting brood of midcareer writers who have appropriated literary techniques and modes of Western (read: Anglo-American) origin.[1] Their subject matter, nevertheless, stems from native earth, and their materials are retrieved from the forgotten caves and hollows of Philippine mythology and folklore. Many of these writings have been published abroad or online, appearing in international anthologies or e-zines, and have their own specialized circles of readers and followers. By virtue of its position within a postmodern setting, speculative fiction deals with the interdimensional, the interstellar, and the multiversal. Inherent in the generic praxis is the criss-crossing of diverse modes and the effacement of borders between the real and the unreal. Therefore, speculative fiction necessarily engages with the virtual.

In light of these developments, many writers of Filipino Chinese descent are active members of the Philippine speculative fiction movement. They include Charles Tan, Kenneth Yu, Andrew Drilon, Budjette Tan, Caroline Hau, Yvette Tan, Douglas Candano, Gabriela Lee, Paolo Chikiamco, Dominique Cimafranca, Kristine Ong Muslim, and Crystal Koo, among others.[2]

By Filipino Chinese, I mean those who consider themselves *lan lang* 咱人/咱儂 (a Hokkien term that literally means "our people"). They include Chinese who have stayed for a considerable period in the Philippines, but also naturalized or native-born Filipinos of Chinese ancestry.[3] Geographically and historically deterritorialized, "Philippine Chinese literature" (*feihua wenxue* 菲華文學) refers to creative works composed in a variety of different languages and dialects by writers who identify as Filipino Chinese.

This essay examines how Filipino Chinese writers manipulate the genre to create their own brand of speculative fiction, and how the ethnicity factor works to localize the tradition. Of interest to this study are questions such as: What kind of world is being reconceived? What vital issues confronting the primary world are raised in these stories? How do the Filipino Chinese reimagine themselves? The main texts are selections from *Lauriat: A Filipino-Chinese Speculative Fiction Anthology* (2012), edited by Charles A. Tan, and they are examined within the context of Philippine colonial histories and neocolonial relations, ethnic Chinese narratives of mobility and displacement, Chinese cultural traditions, and the global phenomenon of genres.

The publication of *Lauriat*, overdetermined by complex and interrelated conditions that may possess ideological contradictions, raises issues concerning the hierarchical matrix of Philippine literature and the critical reception of speculative fiction in the globalscape. First, in order for a work to be identified as Filipino Chinese, it is necessary to view it as an articulation of the visions and experiences of a minority in contrast to the more hegemonic voices of the Philippine tradition. The Philippine canon—a hybridized cultural model mainly Western (and specifically Anglo-American and Hispanic) in orientation—includes works in both English and Tagalog. It adheres to the mode of social realism celebrated by literary historians and accepted by major literary award–giving bodies in the country. Furthermore, the Philippine publishing industry has, since its reformation during the US colonial period (1898–1946), been cautious about publishing works by authors deemed untried and experimental, particularly those who claim a minoritized identity. A greater problem is the perennial lack of readership for Philippine publications, meaning that an anthology like *Lauriat* would likely be perceived as a risky proposition.

Second, *Lauriat* is categorized as speculative fiction, and in the twenty-first century, this supergenre is a significant, escalating global sensation, attaining an invigorating position in the worlding of literature and attracting orbits of readers from the four corners of the earth. In an interview, *Lauriat*'s editor, Charles Tan, whose own stories have been nominated for the World Fantasy Award, spoke of the problems that plagued the Philippine publishing industry, and pointed out an irony: "In a certain way, I'm in a privileged position; [yet] if you mention my name in the Philippines, no one knows me. But in the science fiction or fantasy genre in the mainstream publishing industry, I'm usually known either as a blogger, reviewer, or interviewer."[4] Who, then, would want to invest in a publication of such a form by lesser-known and ethnic writers from a small archipelago across the seven seas? Only independent and alternative presses—such as Lethe Press, which specializes in speculative fiction and queer fiction—would be inclined to take the risk.

At first glance, the Filipino Chinese consciousness in *Lauriat* seems to be evinced by the Filipino Chinese personae in the stories, the sporadic use of ethnic historical events in the narrative (e.g., the seventeenth-century Sangley Massacre in the Philippines), and nuances culturally specific to Filipino Chinese (e.g., Hokkien words such as *ho-we*, *kai-shao*, and *Achi*).[5] The transformation and hybridization of this consciousness are manifested in the use of certain images that function as iconography of "Chineseness" but may not engage with the source tradition (e.g., the image of the Chinese papercuts in "Fold Up Boy" or the structural use of Chinese zodiac signs in "Zodiac").

The Nonhuman Presence in a Posthumanist Paradigm

One of *Lauriat*'s outstanding features is the striking presence of nonhuman characters, which invokes a biosphere where diverse kinds of beings, spirits, and other nonhumans cohabitate with humans, implying a complexity and multiplicity of relations. The genre, accordingly, invites a posthuman critique, seeking to interrogate and even negate the very notion of humanism and its anthropocentric worldviews—embarking on critical engagements to ruminate on evolving images of the human and seeking what lies beyond the concept of the human. Bruce Clarke and Manuela Rossini, editors of *The Cambridge Companion to Literature and the Posthuman*, define the posthuman in literature as "images and figurations in literary and cultural productions, in various genres and periods, of states that lie before, beyond, or after the human, or into which the human blurs when viewed in its essential hybridity. Instances of the posthuman present an image, extant or speculative, coupling the human to some nonhuman order of being."[6] The integration of the nonhuman, on the other hand, according to Richard Grusin, editor of *The Nonhuman Turn* (2015), is an act of "decentering the human in favor of a turn toward and concern for the nonhuman, understood variously in terms of animals, affectivity, bodies, organic and geophysical systems, materiality, or technologies."[7]

In these stories, how do Filipino Chinese writers speculate on themselves? How have they self-reconceptualized in response to the present times and in expectation of manifold possibilities of things to come? The human representations of the Filipino Chinese coexist, whether in congruence or in divergence, with a variety of nonhuman or posthuman subjects. The latter's imaginaries appear in the form of ghosts or dead figures in stories such as "Two Women Worth Watching," "Fold Up Boy," "The Stranger at My Grandmother's Wake," and "August Moon"; as animal metamorphs in "Dimsum" and "Cricket"; and in the form of mythical beings in "Ho-We" and "The Captain's Nephew."

For instance, the world of Erin Chupeco's "Ho-We" houses a range of beings from underworld mythology—including a vampire, a werewolf, a sasquatch, and a zombie—who play the boyfriends and suitors of Achi Marcie, the elder sister in the story.[8] The vampire boyfriend is 134 years old and is a former Katipunero who died in the Philippine revolution. The werewolf boyfriend is of Indian origin. The sasquatch is a Filipino music DJ. The zombie boyfriend is Filipino Chinese who stinks like raw sewage and has a dreadful decomposing nose. And Gilgamesh, the current secret boyfriend, is the epic hero resurrected from ancient Mesopotamia and is two-thirds deity. The second sister, Abigail, is married to a minotaur from mainland China who owns a textile firm, while third sister Leilani is married to a Taiwanese half dragon who owns a bottling business.

The story attempts to poke fun at traditional Filipino Chinese values and practices, particularly *kai-shao* 介紹 (a Hokkien term that literally means to introduce to a possible spouse). Father, the family patriarch and a businessman, insists that his eldest daughter must marry a "Chinese." Incorrigibly and ridiculously racist, he overlooks the unearthly and monstrous qualities of her boyfriends, complaining only that they are *hwana* 番仔 (a Hokkien term that literally means barbarian) and therefore not Chinese enough for her. For instance, Father's outrageously bigoted statements include: "I'm not going to let any daughter of mine date some *bombay* who sleeps all day because he likes to sneak around at night attacking people!" and "Being Chinese is still better than being just two-thirds god and *Arabo*!"[9] Ironically, he wants to set his daughter up with a zombie suitor, who is the son of his Filipino Chinese business colleague.

Stories like Chupeco's can be deemed a posthuman comedy, a form "willing to risk artistic ludicrousness in their representation of the inhumanly large and long."[10] Such a posthumanist worldview allows the story's deliberate, dynamic engagement in appropriating transnational tropes, intermixing cultures, and mismatching origins and figures, with utter disregard for any literary, historical, or cultural fidelity. "Ho-We" reinvents the world as a borderless, timeless realm, where the dramatis personae of human and nonhuman pedigrees cohabituate and join together in an almost romantic life-and-death continuum. With irony and humor, the story questions the rational and scientific ways of classifying all creatures great and small, even including the living and the nonliving. It inquires into the limits of social classifications such as race and ethnicity, and perhaps even renders them obsolete. It discredits monolithic constructs of "Chinese" origins, values, and attitudes. As a specimen of the speculative fiction genre, "Ho-We" recalls Martinican writer Patrick Chamoiseau's theories of creolization, where he underscores the significance of generic intermixtures in a globalized world and advocates for "a principle of literary intermixtures as appropriate for a world in which peoples, cultures, races, gods, traditions, languages, and explanations of the universe are increasingly interconnected, influencing and transforming one another."[11]

Another *Lauriat* story, Andrew Drilon's "Two Women Worth Watching," tells of two women friends. Faye is an international actress, and in the eyes of society, she has face, fame, and fortune. She works in Los Angeles, her schedule filled with commercials, endorsements, TV appearances, and film acting: "Her life has been dedicated to making others see what they want to see."[12] The narrator remarks, though, that the other woman, Mia, is a "celebrity too," with a "huge fan base." And in this place where they are having a cozy dinner and tête-à-tête, "their little room is overflowing with people"—followers and admirers of Mia (4–5). The story describes it this way: "The hairs [of the living] rise on their arms and they assume it's the air conditioning. The rest are invisible. Many stand in empty spaces. Their feet do not touch the ground. Some are pressed half-way through the walls while others suspend themselves from the ceiling. A few of them—children—are hanging from the chandeliers. Everyone is intent on Mia and Faye's table" (6). Mia's followers are all dead and unseen. They are everywhere, watching the living. From a young age, Mia has known she wants it all: money, love, recognition, success, and achievement. Her grandmother has counseled her, "Happiness is fickle and fleeting, but if you enjoy many blessings and look forward to many more, you can be happy all your life. But to attain that—well, you must first understand the nature of the dead" (8). Thus, Mia deliberately cultivates her life to become the greatest show on earth, and she builds an aura of a star persona for herself. Every day is a performance, and her audience consists of dead people. She makes certain that every month she has some thrilling activity or event that's worth watching—mountain climbing or another extreme sport, a singing contest, a rave party or a wild concert, a torrid love affair or a romantic breakup, a family quarrel, or even sex with a half-paralyzed fashion photographer. She knows how to connect to the dead and acknowledge their presence, even with a tiny gesture such as a wink or a sweet word.

At the end of the story, Faye is alone in her hotel room, watching a late-night rerun of her first film on TV. She then takes an antidepressant and scrutinizes herself in the mirror. The omniscient narrator remarks: "No one is watching. The dead are absent from her hotel suite. Something about her repels them. She is too obvious; too clichéd. Let the living enjoy her" (14).

In contrast, Mia goes home with a flock of followers on her heels. All their eyes are on her as she delivers a special treat to their devotees: she dances naked and with wild abandon in the darkness of her bedroom. She cries out, "You made me. All of you. You make me every day. . . . This one's for you" (16). The narrator comments, "She's not so real anymore. She's moving in and out of people, touching them as she goes" (16). As the audience bursts into silent applause, Mia lies exhausted on her bed and perceives that "she is so happy she could die" (16). Mia's strange connection to the dead rests on a liminal threshold; she herself becomes "not so real."

This story suggests that death is another form of existence—that people (not souls) continue to live on after their bodies have disintegrated and turned into dust. What kind of existence do the dead have? They roam the world, purpose-less, seeking anything that will mitigate the tediousness of their existence. Their only gratification is to watch the living. Of happiness, one character remarks, "Even the dead want it" (7).

The secondary world that Drilon envisions raises issues confronting our primary world today, such as our obsession with attention, the idea of happiness in a highly technological universe, and the perception of death. Social media, invented with good intentions, has unleashed within humanity a monstrous craving for public attention and renown. In this digital age, anyone can be a celebrity; anyone can invent and self-fashion a star persona. Facebook is the vital extension of our self, and we post selfies to elicit likes and red hearts, icons representing our simple happiness. YouTube videos create overnight sensations, rewarding those who post them and those who share them. And our day-to-day living consists of a lot of watching—watching screens, watching the virtual, watching ourselves, watching others. Drilon has ingeniously adopted this conceptual framing and transplanted it into his story's world. His dimension of the dead is the realm of social media and reality shows, with their inevitable effects of self-attention, the construction of a fan base, and the pleasure of watching. As one character ironically remarks, "They say attention is the global currency of the twenty-first century" (5).

As a posthumanist project, speculative fiction such as *Lauriat* has grown increasingly self-reflexive and self-conscious in this twenty-first century. As the characters enjoy a fusion cuisine of garlic *ma-chang* and *ming-ming laing*, so too the readers are treated to the fusion of contemporary reality, the hyperreal, and the supernatural.[13] As the physical world interrelates with the virtual, parallel dimensions coexist in speculative fiction. Its metafictional tendency seeks to efface the boundaries between genres, the real and the unreal, human and nonhuman, and life and death.

Lauriat's posthumanism also manifests as a radical faith in the plurality of Filipino Chinese identities and representations, a way to interrogate monolithic constructs of "Chineseness," with its disquieting historical baggage such as the Yellow Peril and the "weak man of Asia," and also, in a Philippine context, simplistic assumptions and historically constructed biases—including viewing Filipino Chinese as an affluent class *intsik*[14] or seeing them as identical with Chinese from mainland China. Another issue is the presumption that Filipino Chinese identity consists of a dual heritage—part Filipino and part Chinese. This is problematic, for what is considered Filipino, and what is Chinese? The term *Filipino* itself connotes a legacy, formed and conditioned by a complex set of histories (e.g., Spanish colonialism, US imperialism, and neocolonialism) that are varied and interrelated. *Chinese* is also a construct, recalling disquieting sociohistorical pressures of colonial subjugation and ethnic oppression (e.g., the Parian ghetto, the legal classification of Sangley, the three-gremio social structure of Binondo, the Chinese Exclusion Act, assorted immigration and naturalization restrictions, and the Filipino First Policy). Therefore, this hyphenated term cannot be reducible to a question of how many cultures an individual straddles. In depicting human affinity with the nonhuman or posthuman, *Lauriat* posits that the Filipino Chinese in the twenty-first century cannot be effortlessly defined nor easily fathomed apart from the nonhuman or the posthuman.

Toward a Globalgothic Style

Philippine history has been beset by violence and vicissitudes, from Spanish and US colonialisms to feudalistic tyranny and Japanese aggression, to revolts, social unrest, and natural catastrophes. The haunting legacy of this turbulent past has found its embodiments and renderings in Philippine literature and popular culture. The Philippine gothic is an evolving postcolonial quest to redefine and legitimize a national identity. It is a return to or a reclamation of the uncanny, of a wild and fearful precolonial past, of a "pure culture" believed to be "Filipino." This provokes varied acts of "writing back," such as the recuperation of folklore and

Indigenous practices, the integration of mythology in contemporary writing, and the propagation of regional cultural productions.

In embracing Philippine speculative fiction, *Lauriat* invokes the tropes and stylistic features of the Philippine gothic, such as the island space as the site of ethnocultural anxieties and postcolonial affliction, along with the spectacle of the uncanny.[15] The anthology also possesses the distinctiveness of a Philippine Chinese gothic, its singular perceptions of the gothic other, its culturally specific verbal codes of the uncanny, its nightmares of terror chained to Philippine colonial histories and neocolonial realities, and to the remote culture in *tengsua* (in Mandarin, *Tangshan* 唐山—this is a term *lan lang* use to refer to China) that troubles the memories and the lore of Filipino Chinese grandparents.

In *Lauriat*, I locate the specificity of the Philippine Chinese gothic in the nonhuman figures, peculiar tropes, and rhetorical techniques that potentially articulate a postcolonial affliction or an excruciating ethnocultural anxiety over, say, a historical crime or an impregnable obsession. Such shadows enshroud the Filipino Chinese individual and serve as metaphorical conduits to contemplate the blankness or complexity in a minority's history, and they extend to inquire into the entrenched mysteries of the Philippine psyche—and perhaps even of China's. As gothic scholar Eric Savoy observes: "Such an approach helps us to locate the territory of the Gothic not in history exactly, but rather in a particular historical sensibility and even more certainly in *historiography* (literally the study of the *writing* of history), the often convoluted and blatantly constructed discourse of narratives that circle around themes and events that are rarely susceptible to direct exposition."[16]

In Kenneth Yu's "Cricket," a year has passed since the death of the Chuang family's matriarch, Tai-mah, who lived to the grand old age of 108. The youngest son, Richard, and his family, who shouldered the burden of caring for the old lady through her senility, have inherited the house. A gathering of family and friends takes place over a sumptuous lunch to light joss sticks before the ancestral portrait as an act of obeisance to the dead. After the visitors have departed, a cricket suddenly appears, following the family around and speaking to them. In a fit of anger and fear, Richard kills it, to the shocked dismay of his wife and son.

What is the significance of the talking cricket? This is how the author describes the cricket's first appearance: "But now, the air hung still, as the joss sticks burned down, small, ember-red eyes glowing in the dark. Slowly, each one burned to a stub. When the last one winked out, dropping its ash-tip onto the pot's sand—when the last of the curls of incense smoke wafted up and vanished before the eyes on Tai-mah's portrait, a black cricket chirped and made its way forward from behind the pot."[17] The description of the atmosphere prior to the cricket's dramatic entrance uses a verbal device known as prosopopoeia, or personification, where objects such as joss sticks are given personal qualities. First the joss sticks are "small, ember-red eyes glowing," and then "the last one winked out." This signals a turn of events, a forewarning of something troubling and perhaps even terrifying. The cricket is a well-known symbol of good fortune, though its peculiar appropriation in the story marks the intrusion of the gothic, the advent of the uncanny. The chirp of the cricket echoes the shriek of Edgar Allan Poe's black cat, as the writer's adopted language resonates with that in the literature classrooms of the Philippines.[18]

On the individual level, the cricket's chirp represents Richard's terror:

> A darkness touched Richard's heart at that moment, a fear he thought he had escaped, or at the very least, could ignore.[19]
>
> The feeling of dread had magnified since the cricket's first appearance. He could not lay a finger on or say clearly what he feared, but he sensed some impending trepidation, a moment of reckoning that he had to face, and he knew he was not ready and would most certainly be found wanting. As to why, he could not say.[20]

What is this darkness, this fear, this something familiar that returns in the form of an unfamiliar nonhuman to torment Richard? With the passing of the matriarch, an intense burden in Richard's family has been eased. Familial strictures can now be bypassed or altered, perhaps the old house can be sold and a new house can be bought, or certain responsibilities have gone, as the next generation comes to another light.

However, the gothic cricket ironically halts this possible transformation as it heralds the return of the uncanny. The "words of wisdom" it offers Richard remind him that he has to deal with the "moment of reckoning," that what has been repressed will manifest, that familiar ancestral traditions—presumed gone with the matriarch's passing—have reemerged alive and kicking from the recesses of the individual's psyche; that ugly feelings such as pride, envy, and rancor burn recurrently in the dark attic of the mind. Poor Richard, the youngest son in a Filipino Chinese clan, is "anchored to a filial duty [he] resented, and infected [his wife] with."[21] He keeps his pride, as hatred for and bitterness about his sorry state of life assail him. The story describes Richard's bleak relations with his brothers, whose lives seem to be better off than his:

> He laughed and put up a front when he was before them, of course—nothing was wrong, everything was all right, I'm doing fine, I can handle this. All his worries he would never admit to anyone, but he blamed the secret unfairness of it all on his being the youngest in the family, neither for the first time, nor the last. Why must the burden of being left behind to care for the aging parents always fall on him? He let the self-pity wash over.[22]

The story speaks to the ethnocultural anxieties of the Filipino Chinese, encumbered with millennia of orthodox Confucian burdens they are obligated to uphold and filial accountabilities from a remote ancestral world they are expected to fulfill, even if they cannot comprehend their relevance in a different land, in a different era. Richard fears that he "would most certainly be found wanting," and "as to why, he could not say." Thus, Richard's pride or "putting up a front" is less of a humanistic failing than it is an ethnocultural value of having "face" (*mianzi* 面子), similar to self-respect or honor. This probably originated from the sense of "culturalism" during China's dynastic era—a strong feeling of pride that China's civilization was superior and without peer in the world. Chinese dynastic culture perceived itself as *tianxia* 天下, literally "all under heaven"—a self-contained, self-sufficient empire.[23] It possessed "the finest art, the noblest philosophy, the grandest poetry."[24] This specter of culturalism, passed on through migrations to the archipelago, haunts this generation of Filipino Chinese like Richard, placing the weight of history and culture on their shaking shoulders. Adding to this is the Filipino Chinese terror of being found wanting, of not measuring up to their imaginary superior ancestors. And this results in the monsters of pride, misery, and self-pity preying on his mind, giving him no rest.

At the story's end, as Richard numbly stumbles back to his home office, the narrator remarks, "The dread and fear inside him increased with each step, and even when he closed the door behind him, he knew that it would not be enough to keep his tragedy away."[25] Richard's tragedy is his ancestral burden, but there is more. Richard's chasing the cricket is described as "wild, violent," with furniture crashing to the floor, ceramics shattering to pieces, appliances toppling over, and Richard accidentally swinging a blow to his son David's forehead. The cricket's gothic chirp resounds with the boy's hysterical wail. The cricket is smashed to death, and the boy—his "face a mask of hatred and anger"[26]—throws his slipper at his father. The story suggests that these emotions of hatred and bitterness have become a family legacy, along with pride. And the greater tragedy is that David will inherit all these. The uncanny is an heirloom.

In Yvette Tan's "Fold Up Boy," young Kat Lim experiences a shock when a ragged, dirty, bloody boy falls out of her locker in school. In her mind, he is like a "badly made *zhezhi* 折纸, the ancient Chinese paper art that her grandmother liked to construct."[27] His appearance brims with touches of the gothic: "a ragged mess, clothes dirtied with mud and blood, smelling of soil and gore, hair matted and falling out of his braid, the exposed parts of his arms and legs covered with wounds and gashes, some scabbed, some still bleeding."[28] He is like "a walking wound. His head was bashed in, some of the wet, pulpy mass falling onto his face. His shirt was ragged, dirt rubbed in so much that she didn't know what color it had originally been."[29] This fold up boy is a ghost, a walking dead that only Kat can see. He informs her in Fookien (Hokkien), "I'm not from China. I was born here," and explains that he is on a quest to find his family.[30] He narrates his "memory," and they fall through an invisible portal to the past: the year 1603; the place, Parian; and the event, the Sangley Massacre.

The story uses prosopopoeia to provide a nonhuman body to a wound of history. "Fold Up Boy," in its restless, ghostly rendering, underscores a historical crime in Philippine chronicles—the horrifying massacres of the Sangleys during the Spanish colonial era. Coined by the Spanish rulers, the term *Sangley* refers to the traders and sojourners from the Ming and Qing dynasties. Also called *chinos*, they were segregated in a ghetto known as the Parian,[31] and cannons lining the stone walls of Intramuros (Walled City) were aimed at them. The Parian was subsequently destroyed, by fire and through massacres, and rebuilt on different locations.[32] This restricted quarter achieved the Spanish government's purposes to monitor the operations of the Sangleys and to suppress any possible riot. The limited mobility and dwelling restrictions were compounded by oppressive measures in the form of undue tax remittances, deportations and expulsions, and massacres. In this senseless ethnic cleansing, tens of thousands of Sangleys died, particularly in the years 1603, 1639, 1662, 1762, and 1820.[33]

"Fold Up Boy" is a recovery of the repressed minority past—a Filipino Chinese speculative narrative of incomprehensible ethnic violence and death, forgotten in the murky recesses of Philippine colonial annals, and twisted and trashed in the cobwebs of the Spanish archives. The representation of Filipino Chinese individual pain connects to the history of trauma experienced by the Sangley/Chinese community, and to a larger history of trauma, that of the Philippine nation under colonial control.

Similar to "Cricket," "Fold Up Boy" also speaks to another specific condition of the Filipino Chinese: the individual fear of being "uncivilized," of being culturally inferior to their forefathers, as suggested in young Kat's struggle to master Mandarin Chinese at school. This fear, in some way, extends to the Filipino Chinese communal guilt about their departure from (or abandonment of) their homeland, the loss of "civilized" traditions, and their anxieties about the threats and perils of exile, nonidentity, and nonbelonging.

Beyond repossessing the Philippine Chinese gothic distinction, the stories in *Lauriat* contend with contemporary anxieties against the forces of globalization, such concerns as transnational identities and the mobility of people, and the dominance of new media and technology. In positioning with the global trend of speculative fiction, *Lauriat* takes a turn toward the manifestation of the gothic and its reworking on a global scale—the globalgothic. On the renaissance of nonhuman gothic representations in twenty-first century literature, media, and cultural productions, Fred Botting and Justin D. Edwards in "Theorizing Global-gothic" remark:

> But these figures also adopt various guises: they are markers of otherness, artic-ulations of the threatening changes of economic and imperial power, signifi-ers of techno-scientific innovations, as well as representations of personal and communal losses and traumas. By enunciating these changes through creatures of collective dread, this fixation with the living dead signals more than a figura-tive or symbolic response to the impacts of globalisation. It constitutes a tangi-ble reaction to the distress and anxiety of a globalised system that erupts within or from public cultures across the world. Globalisation, then, has led to a new way of thinking about gothic production: globalgothic.[34]

As a globalgothic, *Lauriat* is, as scholar Justin Edwards underscores, "concerned not only with individual subjectivity (gender, ethnicity, religion, racial identity) but also with the relations between individuality and the spectral movements of global forces that are uncontrollable and unpredictable."[35] Stories such as "Fold Up Boy" address issues relevant to this age of social media, where fake news, histori-cal revisioning, and omission of truth abound. We recall our early meditation on Drilon's "Two Women Worth Watching," which speaks to our present-day appre-hensions about the power of social media and the virtualization of the human; our fascination with the unreal and the hyperreal; our intensified engagement with the nonhuman and the posthuman; and those dark, deep-seated yearnings in all of us for global attention and happiness, be they emoticonized, iconized, or pixelated. Stories such as "Fold Up Boy" and "Cricket" are not only testaments to the harrowing experiences of the Filipino Chinese; they also resonate with a larger history of trauma—including not only the Chinese diaspora in Southeast Asia, but also Chinese mobilities and dislocations in America, Europe, and else-where in the world.

Speculative fiction such as *Lauriat*, as a posthumanist project, performs a his-toriographic function, turning toward other histories, real or reimagined. This mode of reterritorializing, of reclaiming what has been lost or silenced by cycles of mobility, dislocation, and repression, seeks to secure multifarious possibilities for future revisioning. In the face of the uncanny, the past, with all its baggage of trauma and violence, must be repeated—in memories, in the realm of the imagi-nation; and in repetition, these stories manifest claims to survival and persistent resistance against extinction. *Lauriat*, with its globalgothic discourse on the dead, the ghostly, and the monstrosity, seeks to retrieve other narratives repressed in colonial histories and ignored by neocolonial disguises, and those tall tales or lore lost by displacement or forgotten under the supremacy of science and technology.

It ventures to articulate alternative and even oppositional narratives that connect with other narratives across the earth and form intertextual, paratextual relations. It meditates on the liminality of boundaries between the self and the world, the real and the unreal, life and death, the living and the nonliving, the human and the nonhuman, the local and the global, and the past, present, and future.

Thus, in this act of speculation, *Lauriat* recreates its own models of secondary worlds and forms "a theory for the world to come." As critic Matthew Wolf-Meyer declares:

> The theory for the world to come lies in these experiments, individual attempts to imagine, to model, to conceive of a future. It also lies in very real experiments with life after catastrophe, from rebuilding communities in the wake of natural disasters, to individual and family attempts to recover from disease, to societies reconstituting themselves in the wake of settler colonialism. These projects don't bring the future into being so much as make plain possible ways forward—and how they build upon the past.[36]

Postscript: Minority Report

In the twenty-first century, we cannot disregard the increasing visibility of China in the globalscape as an economic-political superpower, with astonishing advances in science and technology. The last two decades have seen the growing accessibility of Chinese speculative fiction. For instance, the *wuxia* 武侠 (martial arts) fantasy narratives in the form of TV and web dramas stream on various platforms with multilingual subtitles, and Hollywood action films appropriate Chinese martial arts techniques. Chinese science fiction has also begun to enjoy a worldwide circulation, with novels in translation such as *Santi* 三体 (The Three-Body Problem) by Liu Cixin 劉慈欣, the first Asian to win a Hugo Award; Chen Qiufan's 陳楸帆 *Huangchao* 荒潮 (Waste Tide) and Hao Jingfang's 郝景芳 *Liulang cangqiong* 流浪苍穹 (Vagabonds); and short-fiction collections such as *Invisible Planets: An Anthology of Contemporary Chinese SF in Translation*, and *Broken Stars: Contemporary Chinese Science Fiction in Translation*. These were all translated and curated by Ken Liu, himself an award-winning American SF writer of Chinese descent. Liu's intervention is a major influence in the repositioning of Chinese science fiction in the global realm. "Chinese" becomes a construct of novelty, a nova star—reflecting perhaps the West's Orientalist fascination. One blogger declares: "Chinese science fiction is fascinating for the exact same reason that Chinese literary fiction is fascinating: it comes from a place we have not yet imagined, and so to us, it is new and bold and beautiful. It's a revolution of the genre."[37]

This global circulation of Chinese speculative fiction has brought attention to Chinese-oriented works. The 2023 World Science Fiction Convention (Worldcon) will be held, for the first time, in China, in the city of Chengdu, a foremost industrial hub, including electronics and high-tech industries. At the 2007 Yokohama Worldcon, Derwin Mak, a Chinese Canadian author, met with SF writers from China and later published an article on Canadian Chinese SF writers in the Chinese magazine *Kehuan shijie* 科幻世界 (Science Fiction World). Mak then collaborated with Eric Choi, another Canadian Chinese SF writer, to curate *The Dragon and the Stars* (2010), published by DAW Books. This collection showcases the diversity of representations of the Chinese diaspora through stories of science fiction and fantasy.[38] It includes three Filipino writers of Chinese ancestry—Crystal Gail Koo, Gabriela Lee, and Charles Tan, who went on to curate *Lauriat*.

Tan's introduction to *Lauriat* suggests the anthology's intent to question stereotypical portraits of Chineseness, delineate the specificity of the Filipino Chinese experience grounded in minority history, and foreground ethnicity as a key player and vital component of speculative fiction in today's globalscape. *Lauriat* draws on the conventions of speculative fiction to localize Chineseness and to speculate on the significance of ethnicity in a culturally diverse, multiversal imaginary. The branding of "Filipino Chinese" calls for a rethinking of the supergenre. *Filipino Chinese* serves as a metaphorical vehicle, an implicit exploration of the transgressive possibilities of speculative fiction. In its modest approach, it attempts to disrupt the conventional cosmos of speculative fiction and undermine the history of its set practices that associate exclusively with the sociological, psychological, and cultural whiteness of the imaginary, which is to say, the master structures of American and European narrative traditions. Becoming Filipino Chinese reflects the ironic crossbreeding present in the stories and assumes a hybrid model of identities. Ethnicity is repeatedly constructed through the deployment of contrastive doubling, juxtaposing Filipino Chinese characters with figures of the nonhuman and even interchanging them, and integrating a posthumanist orientation to its speculative worlding. Such doubling serves as the imago of the repressed ego, a maneuver of survival against identitarian destruction, or the uncloaking of the ethnie's invisibility. As Sigmund Freud has pointed out, the creation of doubling is an act of "preservation against extinction [which] has its counterpart in the language of dreams, which is fond of representing castration by a doubling."[39]

We can say that *Lauriat*'s appearance in the twenty-first century is judicious, for it rides waves of interest in Chinese cultural production; the globalizing, circulating phenomenon of speculative fiction, especially with the onset of the internet and social media; and the breakers of discontent with Western literature's inadequacy in addressing issues of diversity and multiplicity in relation to race, gender, geopolitics, and other forms of representation. Conditioned by Philippine neocolonialist determinants, *Lauriat* cannot but speak in a reterritorialized Philippine English. This fortuitously boosts its circulation within the global readership of speculative fiction, gratifying the readers' appetite for freshness and difference in a supergenre where the potential for breaking boundaries and for the imagination to soar inhere within its form. Its mutability challenges the system of readers' expectations and incites the latter to a generic rediscovery. As scholar Wendy Knepper has observed, "This circulation of genres bears witness to a phenomenon that is increasingly characteristic of creative creolization in a world where genre's radiating and rhizomic web of mobilities involves local and global confluences."[40]

We may echo the global SF reader: Filipino Chinese speculative fiction comes from a place we have not yet imagined and moves toward a future yet to be imagined. It is a revolution of the genre.

SHIRLEY O. LUA is associate professor of literature at De La Salle University, Manila. She is a jury member of the Manila Critics Circle, which hands out the annual National Book Awards to the best books published in the Philippines; and of the Manunuri ng Pelikulang Pilipino, the film critics group that confers the annual Gawad Urian awards on outstanding Philippine movies. Her research interests include Chinese Philippine literature, Filipino poetics, film criticism, and genre studies. Her studies of Chinese Philippine literature include her doctoral dissertation, "Dragons Becoming Shrimps: Towards a Chinese-Philippine Poetics," and "The Repeating Parian: Tropic Positions of Chinese-Philippine Fiction in English," which appeared in *Writing Asia: The Literatures in Englishes* (2007). She coedited *Direk: Essays on Filipino Filmmakers* (2018).

////////////////////////////////

Notes

1 These writers include Dean Francis Alfar, Nikki Alfar, Charles Tan, Kate Osias, Kenneth Yu, and Angelo Lacuesta, among many others.

2 Charlson Ong is a generation ahead. His short stories have traces of magical realism, and whereas his novel *An Embarrassment of Riches* is a work of speculative fiction, his *Blue Angels and White Shadow* belongs to the genre of noir fiction.

3 Filipino Chinese hail primarily from Fujian and Guangdong Provinces. The later influx of Chinese to the Philippines (from roughly the 1990s onward), however, includes people from other regions of China.

4 See McCarry, "Diversity beyond Borders."

5 *Sangley* is a term that was used by the Spanish colonizers to refer to the traders, workers, and settlers from China. The Chinese binome 常來 (pronounced *changlai* in Mandarin and *shonglai* in Hokkien) appeared on the Boxer codex's sixteenth-century illustration of a Sangley man and woman, and it means "frequently visiting" or "constantly coming"—possibly pertaining to the regular influx of Chinese traders and sojourners. The association of Sangley with business and merchants, even by early Spanish historians like Fray Juan de Medina, OSA, in *Historia de La Orden de San Agustin de estas Islas Filipinas* (1630), shows how the term has evolved from its original meaning due to the visible and active involvement of the ethnic Chinese in the Philippine economy.

6 Clarke and Rossini, *Literature and the Posthuman*, xiii–xv.

7 Grusin, *Nonhuman*, vii.

8 *Ho-we* (possibly 相好) is a Hokkien term meaning boyfriend/girlfriend.

9 Chupeco, "Ho-We," 25–27.

10 Quoted in Clarke and Rossini, *Literature and the Posthuman*, xii.

11 Knepper, "Remapping the Crime Novel," 1433.

12 Drilon, "Two Women," 5. Further references to this work will be cited by page numbers in parentheses hereafter.

13 The story imagines a fusion cuisine, including those of Chinese and Filipino origins. *Ma-chang* (*zongzi* 粽子) refers to glutinous rice with meat, mushroom, and chestnut fillings, wrapped in flat bamboo leaves. *Laing* is a Filipino dish made of taro leaves in coconut milk broth, spiced with chilis.

14 *Intsik* is a Filipinized term referring to the "Chinese." It acquired a pejorative connotation and is used in phrases such as *intsik bejo tulo laway* ("old Chinese drooling with saliva").

15 The term *uncanny* is informed by the psychoanalytic rhetoric of Sigmund Freud. It refers to "that class of the frightening which leads back to what is known of old and long familiar" (Freud, "Uncanny," 60). This feeling ("feels an *unheimlich* horror") of dread, doubt, or terror is invoked by the reappearance of something that has hitherto been repressed or erased (Freud, "Uncanny," 63).

16 Savoy, "American Gothic," 168–69.

17 Yu, "Cricket," 191.

18 Through Philippine-US colonial and neocolonial relations, several English subjects in the country's basic curricula and undergraduate courses have a supremely Anglo-American Gothic orientation in literature. That is to say, the English canon includes fictional works such as those of Edgar Allan Poe and Nathaniel Hawthorne, and novels such as Charlotte Brontë's *Jane Eyre*, Emily Brontë's *Wuthering Heights*, Charles Dickens's *Great Expectations*, Wilkie Collins's *The Moonstone*, Mary Shelley's *Frankenstein*, Henry James's *Turn of the Screw*, and Robert Louis Stevenson's *The Strange Case of Dr. Jekyll and Mr. Hyde*. This has been (and is) the gothic presence that shadows our literature classrooms.

19 Yu, "Cricket," 192.

20 Ibid., 195.

21 Ibid., 194.

22 Ibid., 196.

23 A. Tan, *Chinese in the Philippines*, 74–75.

24 Ibid., 75.

25 Yu, "Cricket," 200.

26 Ibid.

27 Y. Tan, "Fold Up Boy," 141. *Zhezhi* means to fold paper.

28 Ibid.

29 Ibid., 142.

30 Ibid., 146.

31 See note 6 for a brief background on the term *Sangley*. The etymological origin of the term *Parian* is uncertain. Lorelei De Viana assumes that Parian is of local origin and could be from *pali*, meaning to argue or bargain, or *pali-an*, meaning a place for bargaining. Or it may stem from the word *diyan*, referring to place. The command "Go there" could be translated as *pariyan*. See De Viana, *Binondo Architecture*, 19. Historian Jose Victor Torres claims that *parian* is an old Tagalog term for "marketplace," citing the

1619 San Buenaventura's *Vocabulario de la Lengua Tagala. Magpaparian* means "to go to market." See Torres, *Ciudad Murada*, 7.

32 After the Sangley "mutiny" that resulted in the murder of Governor Gomez Perez de Dasmariñas in 1593, the Parian was moved outside the city walls of Manila. It was destroyed by fire seven times (1581, 1588, 1597, 1603, 1629, 1639, and 1642) and rebuilt each time on a different site. The Parian was finally abolished in 1860, with the flourishing of the Binondo district as the new commercial hub. Alip, *Chinese in Manila*, 16–18.

33 A. Tan, *Chinese in the Philippines*, 24–25.

34 Botting and Edwards, "Theorising Globalgothic," 11–12.

35 Edwards, "Locating the Globalgothic," 50.

36 Wolf-Meyer, *Theory for the World*, 4–5.

37 See Heath, "5 Groundbreaking Chinese Science Fiction Books."

38 Mak and Choi narrated this process in their afterword for *The Dragon and the Stars*.

39 Freud, "Uncanny," 70.

40 Knepper, "Remapping the Crime Novel," 1445.

References

Alip, Eufronio M. *The Chinese in Manila*. Manila: National Historical Institute, 1993.

Botting, Fred, and Justin D. Edwards. "Theorising Globalgothic." In Byron, *Globalgothic*, 11–24.

Byron, Glennis, ed. *Globalgothic*. Manchester, UK: Manchester University Press, 2013.

Chupeco, Erin. "Ho-We." In C. Tan, *Lauriat*, 18–30.

Clarke, Bruce, and Manuela Rossini, eds. *The Cambridge Companion to Literature and the Posthuman*. Cambridge: Cambridge University Press, 2017.

De Viana, Lorelei D. C. *Three Centuries of Binondo Architecture, 1594–1898: A Socio-Historical Perspective*. Manila: University of Santo Tomas Publishing House, 2001.

Drilon, Andrew. "Two Women Worth Watching." In C. Tan, *Lauriat*, 2–16.

Edwards, Justin D. "'She Saw a Soucouyant': Locating the Globalgothic." In Byron, *Globalgothic*, 50–64.

Freud, Sigmund. "The Uncanny." In *The Monster Theory Reader*, edited by Jeffrey Andrew Weinstock, 59–88. Minneapolis: University of Minnesota Press, 2020.

Grusin, Richard, ed. *The Nonhuman Turn*. Minneapolis: University of Minnesota Press, 2015.

Heath, Will. "5 Groundbreaking Chinese Science Fiction Books." *Books and Bao*, February 3, 2022. https://booksandbao.com/great-works-of-chinese-science-fiction/.

Hogle, Jerrold E., ed. *The Cambridge Companion to Gothic Fiction*. Cambridge: Cambridge University Press, 2002.

Knepper, Wendy. "Remapping the Crime Novel in the Francophone Caribbean: The Case of Patrick Chamoiseau's *Solibo Magnifique*." In "Remapping Genre," special topic, *PMLA* 122, no. 5 (October 2007): 1431–46.

McCarry, Sarah. "Diversity beyond Borders: A Conversation with Charles Tan." *TOR.com*, July 29, 2014. https://www.tor.com/2014/07/29/diversity-beyond-borders-a-conversation-with-charles-tan/.

Savoy, Eric. "The Rise of the American Gothic." In Hogle, *Cambridge Companion to Gothic Fiction*, 167–88.

Tan, Antonio S. *The Chinese in the Philippines, 1898–1935: A Study of Their National Awakening*. Quezon City, Philippines: Garcia, 1972.

Tan, Charles, ed. *Lauriat: A Filipino-Chinese Speculative Fiction Anthology*. Maple Shade, NJ: Lethe, 2012.

Tan, Yvette. "Fold Up Boy." In C. Tan, *Lauriat*, 140–54.

Torres, Jose Victor Z. *Ciudad Murada: A Walk through Historic Intramuros*. Manila: Intramuros Administration and Vibal, 2005.

Weinstock, Jeffrey Andrew, ed. *The Monster Theory Reader*. Minneapolis: University of Minnesota Press, 2020.

Wolf-Meyer, Matthew J. *Theory for the World to Come: Speculative Fiction and Apocalyptic Anthropology*. Minneapolis: University of Minnesota Press, 2019.

Yu, Kenneth. "Cricket." In C. Tan, *Lauriat*, 188–200.

Conclusion
States of Convergence

Exploring future research trajectories, this conclusion offers a methodological reflection by returning to the special issue's discursive point of departure, Singapore—the island-state that Wang Gungwu, historian of the Chinese overseas, has dubbed "the heart of Nanyang"— in order to contemplate its representational significance for wider Southeast Asia.[1]

In Singaporean director Yeo Siew Hua's award-winning film *A Land Imagined*, the character Wang Bicheng, a mainland Chinese migrant worker, takes Mindy, the attendant of the cybercafe he frequents, for a spin in his company truck. They end up going for a late-night swim in the sea. Afterward, while resting on the beach, Wang tells Mindy he has heard how the sand on which they lie comes from Malaysia, while other reclaimed areas of Singapore rely on sand from other Southeast Asian countries, including Vietnam, Indonesia, and Cambodia. Mindy then asks if they have left the island-state just by relaxing on the artificial beach, to which Wang responds, "Next time I can take you to other reclaimed areas . . . to see the world!" 改天帶你去別的填海地區看看 . . . 環游世界! The thought-provoking scene implies how Singapore embodies region- and world-making through the sand trade with its Southeast Asian neighbors. Located on Singapore's coastal peripheries, the land beneath the beaches—such as the one that the couple visited in the film—is both local and foreign. In this particular instance, when sand is displaced to a new locality, the identity of the resultant land becomes ambiguous and fungible.

Alongside the occurrence of spatial aggregation, Singapore's situatedness in a larger geographical region can be grasped from another perspective: its equatorial location means that the island-state overlaps with the Doldrums (also known as the Intertropical Convergence Zone), a low-pressure area in which the trade winds from the northern and southern hemispheres collide, yielding a state of stillness that becalms maritime vessels. This peculiar climate phenom-

PRISM: THEORY AND MODERN CHINESE LITERATURE • 19:2 • SEPTEMBER 2022
DOI 10.1215/25783491-9966777 • © 2022 LINGNAN UNIVERSITY

enon informs the making of *Zone of Convergence*, a series of artistic prints by Singaporean conceptual artist Charles Lim Yi Yong, whose work graces the cover of this special issue (figs. 1–3).

Rendered in different shades of white and blue, *Zone of Convergence* consists of twenty-eight collagraph prints that share a cloud motif cast in varied shapes. Because of the choice of colors and the motif's protean forms, the prints also evoke images of ocean waves. The series came about from Lim's sailing expeditions along the east coast of Singapore over six months, during which he applied a method of "staggered observations." The method involved taking note of the clouds and wave patterns at specific points and subsequently returning in time to register their changes. Out at sea, Lim's aim was to "see" the wind, the primary force of change in the weather system, whose invisibility requires him to draw upon senses beyond the visual—such as feeling and "tasting" the air—to fully experience its presence and "build a relationship" with it."[2]

Though the conceptual genesis of *Zone of Convergence* is tied to Singapore, the work, through its allusive links with the oceanic, conveys an expansive sense of Island Southeast Asia as well. Enacting Lim's idea and practice of spacing observations out over time, *Zone of Convergence* presents an intriguing tension between tranquility and turbulence that occasions a twofold interpretation. On the one hand, the clouds and waves in each print appear relatively static, reflective of their positionality in the windless Doldrums. On the other hand, when considered in seriality, they show sustained morphings due to the slow but invisible passage of time, which channel one's attention back to each print, enabling insights into how surface serenity can belie interior turmoil.

By indexing the steady but no less dynamic transformation of mutually interacting ecological elements, the movement of sand, water, and air that receives artistic engagement in the aforementioned works resonates with this special issue's thematic focus on the Chinese-related social and literary worlds of Southeast Asia that are inhabited and/or produced by authors and different ethnic and language communities. As Carlos Rojas mentions in the introduction to this special issue, ecological elements figure prominently in modern Chinese intellectual and cultural thought. Recall also that in the most broad-ranging contribution to this collection of articles, David Der-wei Wang's reframing of Sinophone Southeast Asian literature in terms of a *hua*華 - *yi*夷 fungibility pivots on the translation of "-phone" as *feng* 風, the Chinese character for wind, whose metaphorical meanings encompass "sound, trend, propensity, and above all, poetic sounding and cultural articulation," all of which connote a manifestation of and tendency toward change (*bian* 變). Building on how the seasonal monsoon that affects Southeast Asia "enacts maritime movements, bringing ethnicities, languages, beliefs, and customs into play with each other," he takes a mesological perspective

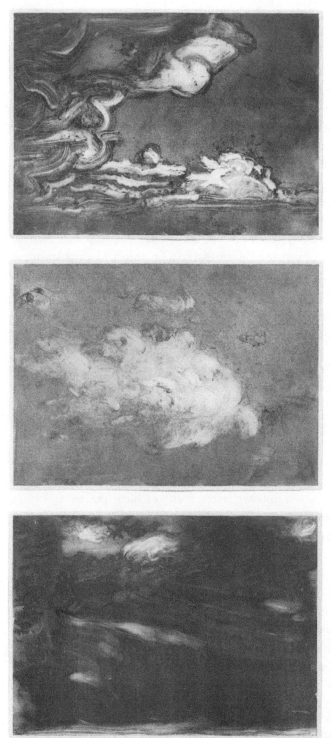

FIGURES 1–3. Charles Lim Yi Yong, *Zone of Convergence* series, 2021, exhibition installation images, *Staggered Observations of a Coast* (2021) at STPI Gallery, Singapore. Artwork © Charles Lim Yi Yong/STPI. Photo courtesy of the artist and STPI—Creative Workshop & Gallery.

to position the wind/earth/water triad as the "symbolic repository" of Sinophone Nanyang/Southeast Asian literary and cultural humanities.

Moving forward, just like its cinematic and art installation counterparts, Southeast Asian Chinese literature can be approached meaningfully as particular "zones of convergence." By "convergence," I refer to both the sense of coming from different directions to meet and mingle, as well as the sense of gradually changing to develop commonalities. Together, the two semantic layers open up Southeast Asian Chinese literary formations and related scholarship as discursive settings that host encounters, interfaces, and thresholds for generating novel perspectives on modern Chinese literary writings and studies.

This project arose from an intent to focus on Southeast Asian Chinese literary production that registers different states of contingent confluence between mobility and place-making. True to its original spirit, the special issue eschews making general pronouncements on the essential Southeast Asian character of Chinese literary practices. Rather, the emphasis is on juxtaposing the diversities of the porous region not just by mapping common literary traits and tracking sociocultural processes, but also by assembling consensus and dissensus on approaches to studying its Chinese-inflected sociotextual worlds. The result has been a Southeast Asia that embodies and emphasizes the fluidity and hybridity of people and ideas, a regional configuration that corresponds broadly to current geopolitical borders, but also traces areas of historical and conceptual influences and connections.

Echoing "a relational regional scholarship," the identified convergences that create the Southeast Asia in this volume are both geographical and ideational.[3] Besides surfacing less-noticed locational ties (Penang and Medan, East Malaysia and West Malaysia), a number of essays interpret the texts and contexts with an eye on styles of production in other places, such as China, Taiwan, and Hong Kong, locales not immediately associated with the geopolitical region today; nonetheless, they are familiar nodes in the creative and scholarly networks of modern Chinese literature. Obviously, the special issue does not include all the varied areal constituents of current-day Southeast Asia, but it recognizes the need for more expansive coverage for substantive theorizations across the various place-based bodies of work. Aligned with this geoconceptual thrust, it devotes considerable attention to Chinese literary texts and practices related to Indonesia and the Philippines, the two prominently multi-islandic states in Southeast Asia that have been relatively understudied despite ongoing scholarly interest in archipelagic cultural thought. Though Malaysia remains the most conspicuous object of critical scrutiny—and representative of Southeast Asian Chinese literature, given how Mahua literature has remapped global Chinese literary production—the case studies of Indonesia and the Philippines can help inspire the field to reassess the typicality of the Malaysian case by studying its literary corpora in greater detail.

Importantly, through analyses of scarcely acknowledged aspects of a writer (Stenberg), a forgotten literary tradition (Hoogervorst), and Anglophone creative expressions of ethnic Chinese (Lua), the historical and contemporary situations in Indonesia and the Philippines will inform future inquiries about how the internal diversities of nation-based literary polysystems in Southeast Asia are constituted differently. In addition, whereas some contributions evoke Chow Tse-Tsung's 周策縱 proposal to read Southeast Asian Chinese literature through his lens of "double tradition" (*shuangchong chuantong* 雙重傳統), which attends to influences from both China and the array of local cultural environments (Ng, Ko, Stenberg), others point toward alternative forms of "double traditions" that couple the local and the global (Lua, Bernards), while others call for examining lateral modalities of imbricated social and literary traditions that do not involve framing China as the fountainhead of Chinese cultural practices and phenomena (Hoogervorst, Chan).[4]

Methodologically speaking, the special issue parses "localization" through different optics by treating the process as either one of absorption of foreign influence, or one engaged in adaptation to new cultural contexts. The articles gather emergent analytical parameters (gender, social class, minority ethnic groups); fresh conceptual conjunctures (the Sinophone and the xenophone, the *huaxiaosheng* 華校生 and the *yimin* 遺民, archipelagic imaginaries and oceanic epistemologies, resource extraction politics and labor history, the condition of semiwild and posthumanism); and less examined literary genres (popular literature, classical Chinese and Sino-Malay poetry, flash fiction, Philippine-Chinese speculative fiction). Together, the contributions demonstrate the diverse ways in which adopting a multiscalar Southeast Asian perspective can reorient us, those who study the regional literary formation, toward new routes of examining cultural pasts with lingering effects on the present, which forge fresh prospects for creative writing and scholarship.

In assembling dispersed expertise on the subject, this special issue captures a precious Southeast Asian moment of modern Chinese literary studies. How can scholars in the field continue to harness the instructive potential of the open geographical region? Charles Lim's longitudinal practice of "staggered observations" inspires by drawing attention to the power of temporality. It would be ideal to develop, like Lim, an immersive, recursive, and accretive approach, engaging in what historian O. W. Wolters, in his discussion of literary inquiries in the context of Southeast Asia, describes as the process of "investigating the presence of connections, relationships, differences, disruptures, and instabilities mirrored in literature and also in the web of social and political happenings."[5] Mediated by the landscapes, seascapes, and windscapes, as well as the human and nonhuman environments, the texts and the milieus of their production constitute cultural zones in which the discernible and the not-yet-discernible changes intersect. In those zones of convergence, unexpected vectors of Chineseness or notions of interior alterity may flourish, attesting to the enduring conjugation of local self-understandings and extralocal perspectives of linguistic and ethnic relations to Southeast Asia.

CHEOW THIA CHAN is assistant professor of Chinese studies at National University of Singapore. His research interests include modern Chinese-Sinophone literature, Southeast Asian studies, and diaspora studies. He is the author of *Malaysian Crossings: Place and Language in the Worlding of Modern Chinese Literature* (forthcoming, 2022) and has edited "Transregional Singapore Chinese Literature," a special section in *Renditions: A Chinese-English Translation Magazine* (2021).

//////////////////////////////

Notes

1   Geographically speaking, this hub also includes Peninsular Malaysia, which is intimately linked to Singapore historically. See Chow, "Wang Gungwu."
2   See "Charles Lim Yi Yong: Staggered Observations of a Coast (17 December 2021 to 6 February 2022)," https://www.stpi.com.sg/exhibitions/charles-lim-yi-yong-staggered-observations-of-a-coast/, and "Charles Lim Yi Yong: Staggered Observations of a Coast," https://www.youtube.com/watch?v=eG_bjfp8QSA, 2:05–2:45.
3   Chua et al., "Area Studies," 8.
4   Chow, "Zongjieci," 359. Chow spoke at the 1988 Second International Conference on the Commonwealth of Chinese Literature, held in Singapore, which, according to Wong Yoon Wah, was the first international symposium that focused on Southeast Asian Chinese-language literature. See Wong, "Zouxiang shijie," 3.
5   Wolters, "Southeast Asia," 16.

References

Chow Tse-Tsung 周策縱. "Zongjieci" 總結辭 [Closing Remarks]. In *Dongnanya huawen wenxue* 東南亞華文文學 [Chinese Literature in Southeast Asia], edited by Wong Yoon Wah and Horst Pastoors, 359–62. Singapore: Goethe-Institut Singapore and Singapore Association of Writers, 1989.

Chow, Yian Ping. "Wang Gungwu: When 'Home' and 'Country' Are Not the Same," translated by Candice Chan. *ThinkChina*, September 24, 2019. https://www.thinkchina.sg/wang-gungwu-when-home-and-country-are-not-same.

Chua, Beng Huat, Ken Dean, Ho Engseng, Ho Kong Chong, Jonathan Rigg, and Brenda Yeoh. "Area Studies and the Crisis of Legitimacy: A View from South East Asia." *South East Asia Research* 27, no. 1 (2019): 1–18. https://doi.org/10.1080/0967828X.2019.1587931.

Wolters, O. W. "Southeast Asia as a Southeast Asian Field of Study." *Indonesia*, no. 58 (1994): 1–17.

Wong Yoon Wah 王潤華. "Zouxiang shijie de Dongnanya huawen wenxue" 走向世界的東南亞華文文學 [A Southeast Asian Chinese Language Literature Bound for the World]. In *Dongnanya huawen wenxue* 東南亞華文文學 [Southeast Asian Chinese Language Literature], edited by Wong Yoon Wah and Horst Pastoors, 2–4. Singapore: Goethe-Institut Singapore and Singapore Association of Writers, 1989.

Keep up to date on new scholarship

Issue alerts are a great way to stay current on all the cutting-edge scholarship from your favorite Duke University Press journals. This free service delivers tables of contents directly to your inbox, informing you of the latest groundbreaking work as soon as it is published.

To sign up for issue alerts:

1. Visit **dukeu.press/register** and register for an account. You do not need to provide a customer number.

2. After registering, visit **dukeu.press/alerts**.

3. Go to "Latest Issue Alerts" and click on "Add Alerts."

4. Select as many publications as you would like from the pop-up window and click "Add Alerts."

read.dukeupress.edu/journals